The Roman Empire and the Silk Routes

The Roman Empire and the Silk Routes

The Ancient World Economy and the Empires of Parthia, Central Asia and Han China

Raoul McLaughlin

PEN & SWORD
HISTORY

First published in Great Britain in 2016 by
PEN & SWORD HISTORY
an imprint of
Pen & Sword Books Ltd
47 Church Street
Barnsley
South Yorkshire
S70 2AS

ISBN 978-1-47383-374-6

A CIP catalogue record for this book is available from the British Library.

Typeset by Concept, Huddersfield, West Yorkshire, HD4 5JL.
Printed and bound in England by CPI Group (UK) Ltd, Croydon CR0 4YY.

Pen & Sword Books Ltd incorporates the imprints of Pen & Sword Archaeology, Atlas, Aviation, Battleground, Discovery, Family History, History, Maritime, Military, Naval, Politics, Railways, Select, Social History, Transport, True Crime, and Claymore Press, Frontline Books, Leo Cooper, Praetorian Press, Remember When, Seaforth Publishing and Wharncliffe.

For a complete list of Pen & Sword titles please contact
PEN & SWORD BOOKS LIMITED
47 Church Street, Barnsley, South Yorkshire, S70 2AS, England
E-mail: enquiries@pen-and-sword.co.uk
Website: www.pen-and-sword.co.uk

Contents

List of Plates

Acknowledgements

I was educated at Lagan College in Belfast, the first cross-community integrated school to be established in Northern Ireland, founded to offer young people of all cultural and economic backgrounds an education free from the divisions of race, religion or social class.

My undergraduate degree in Archaeology and Ancient History was completed in Belfast and the early stage of my doctoral research was financed by the Northern Ireland Department of Education and Learning (between 2002 and 2005). In the absence of further funding, I used my spare time and limited earnings to continue this research and in 2010 I completed my monograph, *Rome and the Distant East*. This was followed by the publication of *The Roman Empire and the Indian Ocean* by Pen & Sword Press in 2014.

Publishing my research in a series of books without the support of an academic position or regular income has created personal hardship and would not have been possible without the generosity of my parents. This book is therefore dedicated to my immediate family, my parents, my brother Leon and my sister Thayna.

Raoul McLaughlin
Belfast
September 2015

Abbreviations

C.I.L. = *Corpus Inscriptionum Latinarum.*
I.L.S. = *Inscriptiones Latinae Selectae.*
Periplus = *The Periplus of the Erythraean Sea.*
The 'Muziris Papyrus' = *P. Vindob. G.* 40822 (*Papyri Vindobonensis Graecus*).

Chronology

Early period

550–330 BC: The Persian Achaemenid Empire rules western Asia.
334–323 BC: Alexander of Macedon conquers the Persian Empire and the Indus kingdoms.
323–303 BC: The Macedonian Empire splits into rival Hellenic kingdoms.
250 BC: Greek commanders establish a separatist kingdom in Bactria.
238 BC: A steppe warlord named Arsaces forms the Parthian Kingdom (Iran).
230–221 BC: The Six Chinese States are conquered by Qin.
221 BC: Qin regime unifies China. Qin Shi Huang becomes the First Emperor.
210 BC: Death of the First Emperor Qin Shi Huang.
209 BC: Formation of the Xiongnu Empire under the rule of Chanyu Modu.
209 BC: The Seleucid King Antiochus III campaigns in Bactria.
206 BC: Liu Bang becomes the King of Han.
202 BC: Liu Bang becomes the first Han Emperor of China.
200 BC: The Chinese are unable to defeat the Xiongnu and agree peace terms.

Second century BC

192–188 BC: Roman armies defeat the Seleucid King Antiochus III.
180 BC: Demetrius I of Bactria begins a conquest of the Indus Kingdoms.
176–174 BC: The Xiongnu expel the Yuezhi nation from their homelands.
155 BC: The Sakas are forced westward by the Yuezhi as they occupy Transoxiana.
150 BC: The Parthians inflict severe losses on the Greco-Bactrian Kingdom.
148–138 BC: Parthians conquer Iran and Iraq from the Seleucid Kingdom.
145 BC: The Greco-Bactrian Kingdom is overrun by Saka war-bands.
141 BC: The Han Emperor Wu comes to power.
139–124 BC: The Han envoy Zhang Qian explores Central Asia.
133 BC: China begins renewed offensives against the Xiongnu.
123 BC: China campaigns to control the Hexi Corridor and reach the Tarim States.
124 BC: The Yuezhi defeat a Parthian army.
120 BC: The Yuezhi move from Transoxiana into Bactria.
120–63 BC: Reign of Mithridates IV of Pontus in Asia Minor.
118 BC: Greek ships begin voyages from Egypt to India.
104–101 BC: Chinese armies attack Ferghana to acquire superior horses.
100 BC: China gains control over the Tarim States.
100 BC: Parthia sends envoys to China.

First century BC
66–63 BC: Pompey brings Asia Minor and Syria under Roman control.
60–51 BC: The Xiongnu are split by civil war and become subject to China.
53 BC: Parthians massacre an invading Roman army led by Crassus.
50 BC: Sakas establish royal regimes in the Upper Indus region.
50 BC: The Sarmatians invade and occupy the Pontic Steppe.
36 BC: Mark Antony leads a failed Roman invasion of Parthia.
36 BC: Chinese-led Tarim troops defeat Chanyu Zhizhi near Lake Balkhash.
31 BC: The Roman general Octavian defeats Mark Antony and annexes Egypt.
27 BC: Octavian becomes the first Roman Emperor Augustus.
20 BC: Political agreement securing peace between Rome and Parthia.
10 BC: Parthian Princes conquer the Indus Kingdoms from the Sakas.
1 BC: Renewed peace agreement between Rome and Parthia.

First century AD
AD 9–23: Wang Mang gains power and the Tarim kingdoms cede from China.
AD 25: Restoration of the Han Dynasty at the new imperial capital Louyang.
AD 35: Caucasus Kingdoms recruit Sarmatian war-bands to attack Armenia.
AD 44: The Greek philosopher Apollonius visits northwest India.
AD 49: Revolt in the Chersonesos Kingdom and Roman-Aorsi alliance.
AD 50: *Periplus of the Erythraean Sea* describes Roman voyages to India.
AD 50: Kujula Kadphises unites the Yuezhi nation and forms the Kushan Empire.
AD 55: Kujula Kadphises attacks the Parthian Empire.
AD 60: Iazyges occupy the Hungarian plain forcing refugees across the Danube.
AD 69: Roxolani raid Roman territory across the Lower Danube frontier.
AD 75: Alani raid Armenia and attack Parthia.
AD 74–97: General Ban Chao re-establishes Han control over the Tarim kingdoms.
AD 80–100: Vima Takto conquers the Indus Kingdoms and northern India.
AD 87: The Parthians send envoys to Han China.
AD 89: The Han decisively defeat the Northern Xiongnu.
AD 90: A Kushan army attacks Han forces in the western Tarim territories.
AD 92: Iazyges raid Roman territory and destroy a Roman Legion.
AD 97: Chinese envoy Gan Ying sent to make contact with the Roman Empire.

Second Century AD
AD 101: Syrian merchant Maes Titianus sends his agents to Han China.
AD 105–106: Trajan completes the conquest of Dacia.
AD 106: Indian/Kushan envoys attend Trajan's victory celebrations in Rome.
AD 114–116: Trajan invades the Parthian Empire.
AD 127: War between the Parthian and the Kushan Empires.
AD 132–137: Arrian is Roman governor of Cappadocia.
AD 161: Marcus Aurelius Antoninus becomes Roman Emperor.
AD 161–166: War between the Parthian Empire and Rome.
AD 162: Pandemic kills or debilitates one third of Han frontier troops.
AD 165: Outbreak of the Antonine Pandemic in Babylonia.

AD 166: Roman envoys sent by 'Antun' sail around Malaysia to reach Han China.
AD 169: Invading Iazyges defeat a Roman army.
AD 173–175: Roman forces defeat the Iazyges and conclude peace terms.
AD 184–205: Yellow Scarves Rebellion destabilises the Han Empire.
AD 192–197: Civil war in the Roman Empire.
AD 214–218: Indian/Kushan missionaries reach Roman Syria.
AD 220: End of the Han Empire: China is divided into three successor kingdoms.
AD 220–280: Three Kingdoms Era in China.
AD 226: A Roman merchant named 'Lun' reaches China via the sea route.
AD 235–284: Period of warfare and severe political upheaval in the Roman Empire.
AD 230–276: Germanic Goths settle the Pontic Steppe and raid Black Sea territories.
AD 255–257: Goths conquer the Crimean Kingdom of Chersonesos.
AD 304: The Sixteen Kingdom Era begins as China fragments into numerous warring states.

Late Antiquity
AD 311-316: The Han Zhao (Southern Xiongnu – 'Hun-nu') sack the Chinese capitals Louyang and Chang'an, capturing two Emperors.
AD 313: Date of the *Sogdian Letters.*
AD 351–376: The Former Qin unifies northern China and the surrounding steppe.
AD 322–336: Emperor Constantine subdues the Goths and Sarmatians.
AD 330: Constantinople (Byzantium) becomes the eastern Roman capital.
AD 356–368: 'Huna' migrate into Transoxiana and attack Persian territories.
AD 370: Huns cross the Volga to attack Goths and Alani on the Pontic Steppe.
AD 376–378: Armed Gothic refugees settle in Roman territory.
AD 370–395: Huns merge with defeated Alani on the Pontic-Caspian Steppe.
AD 399: A Chinese monk named Faxian travels to India to recover Buddhist texts.
AD 395: Hunnic army crosses the Caucasus Mountains to attack Roman Syria.
AD 400: Huns occupy Hungarian grasslands close to the Roman frontier.
AD 405: Germanic and Alani refugees fleeing Hunnic conquest breach Rhine frontier.
AD 409: Hunnic forces paid to fight Goths.
AD 410: Rome is sacked by the Visigoths.
AD 425: Large Hunnic army asked to participate in Roman succession dispute.
AD 429: Germanic Vandals cross from southern Spain to conquer North Africa.
AD 434: Attila unites the Hunnic territories in Western Europe.
AD 441–443: Hunnic armies attack and plunder the Balkans.
AD 449: A Roman envoy named Priscus visits the Hunnic court.
AD 451: A Hunnic army invades Gaul.
AD 452: A Hunnic army devastates Northern Italy.
AD 453: Death of Attila and disintegration of the Hunnic Empire.
AD 476: The last Western Roman Emperor is deposed by a Germanic king.

Ancient Chinese Authors

145–86 BC: Lifetime of the Chinese scholar Sima Qian, author of the *Shiji* (*The Historical Records*).

81 BC: Records are produced from an imperial court debate on state monopolies known as the *Discourses on Salt and Iron*.

AD 3–54: Lifetime of a Han court official named Ban Biao who began writing the *Hanshu* (*History of the Former Han Empire:* 210 BC–AD 9).

AD 32–92: Lifetime of Ban Gu, son of Ban Biao, who contributed to the *Hanshu*.

AD 45–116: Lifetime of Ban Zhao, daughter of Ban Biao, who completed the *Hanshu*.

AD 239–265: Lifetime of a Chinese official named Yu Huan who compiled the *Weilue* (*Brief Account of the Wei Dynasty*: AD 220–265) including a chapter called 'Peoples of the West'.

AD 398–445: Lifetime of the Chinese historian Fan Ye who used court records to compile the *Hou Hanshu* (*History of the Later Han Empire*: AD 23–220).

Kushan Kings and Emperors

King Heraios (AD 0–30): 'Ruler of the Kushans'.

Emperor Kujula Kadphises (AD 30–80): unified the Yuezhi nation in Bactria. Conquered Kabul Valley, Swat, Gandhara, Taxila, Kashmir and Arachosia.

Vima Takto (AD 80–102): Conquered Indus kingdoms and northern India.

Vima Kadphises (AD 102–127): Empire extended to cities in the Upper Ganges.

Kanishka (AD 127–151): Further Ganges conquests and war against the eastern Parthian king Vologases III (AD 105–147).

Huvishka (151–187): Roman and Greco-Egyptian deities depicted on Kushan coinage.

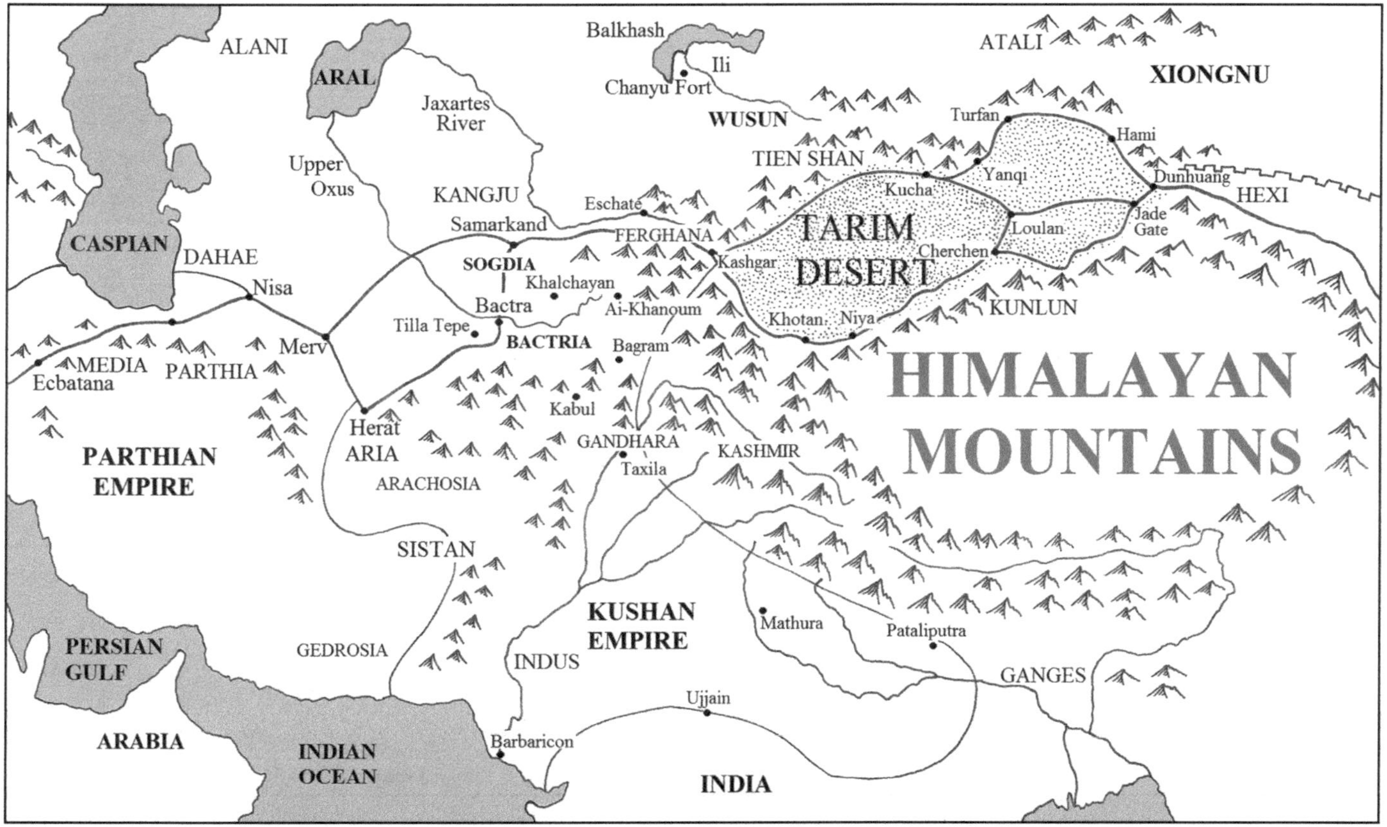

Ancient Asia.

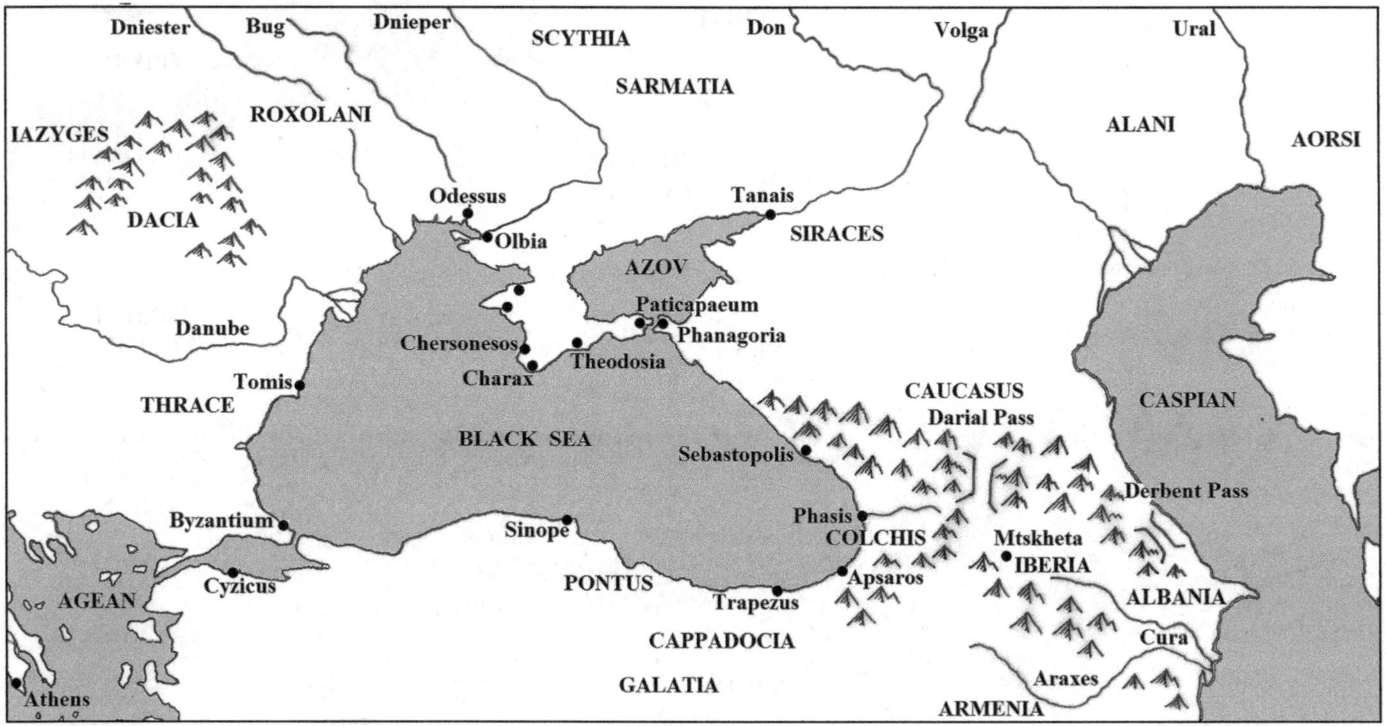

Central Asia.

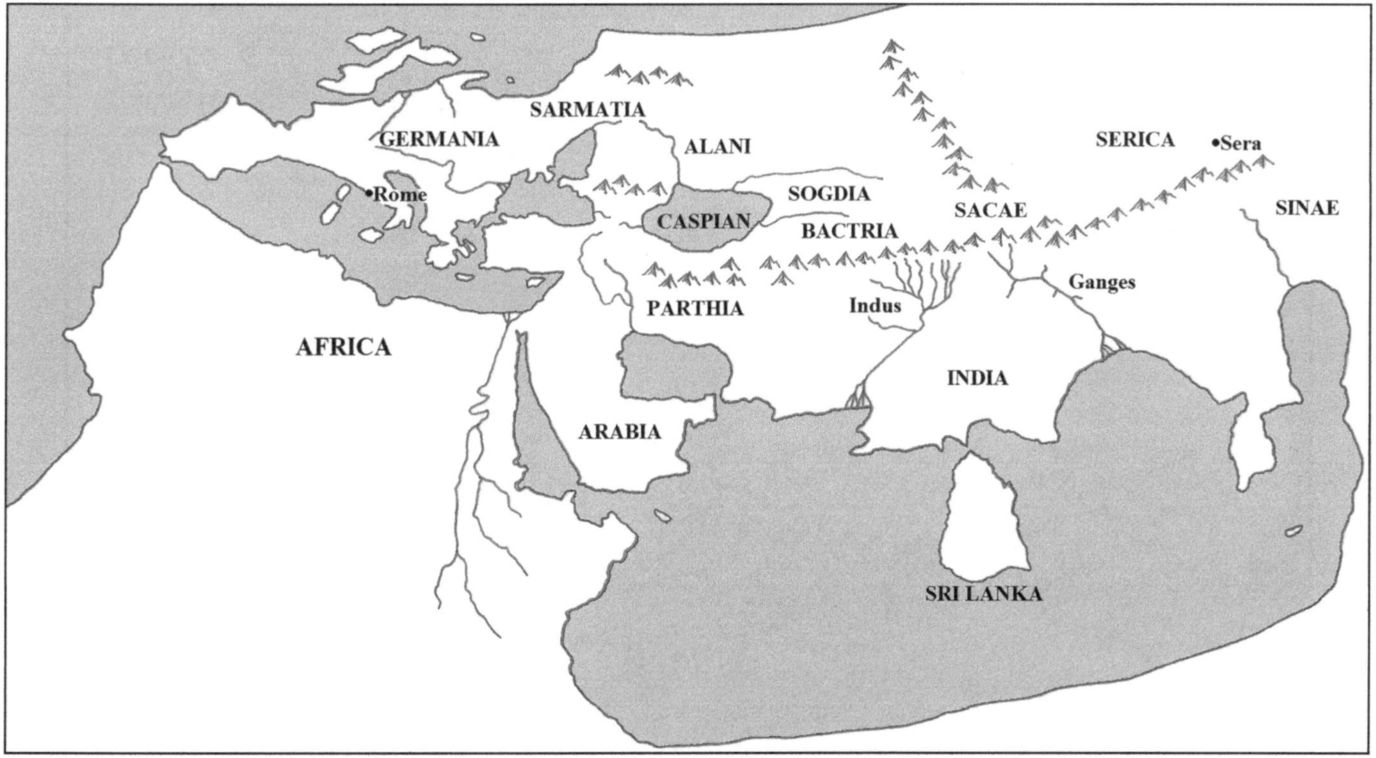

Claudius Ptolemy world map (Ad 150)

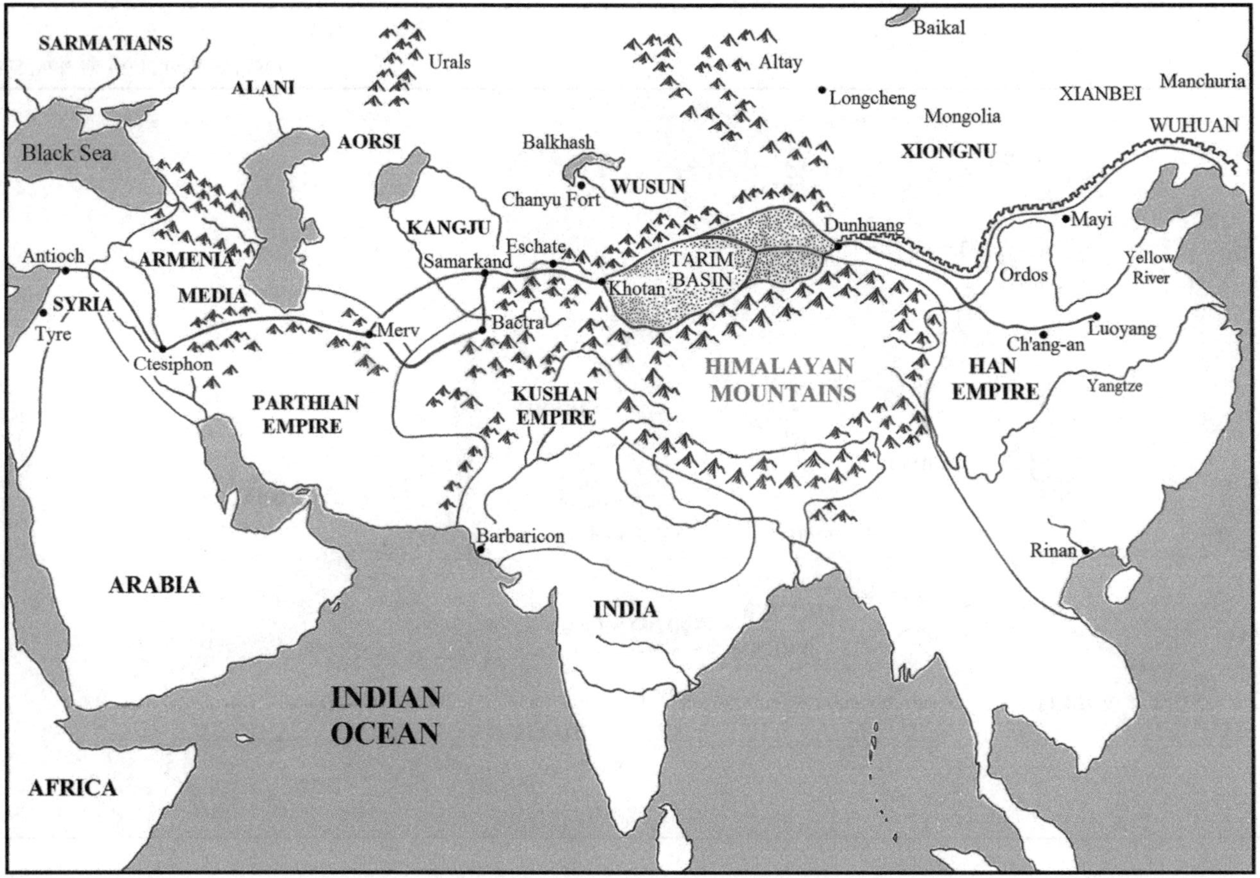

The Black Sea.

Introduction: The Ancient World Economy

The subject of this book is long distance trade in the ancient world. It studies how ancient commerce transferred valuable resources over great distances to enhance the prospects and prosperity of far-off regimes. It considers how Han China created the silk routes through Central Asia and how imperial Rome profited from these commercial exchanges.

This study of the silk routes examines ancient steppe-based regimes that rivalled Rome and contains the research for a monograph and taught university course entitled *The Roman Empire and the Steppe Nations: Parthians, Sakas, Kushans, Sarmatians and Huns*. There are five appendices at the back of the book which provide a context for assessing ancient economic evidence, including revenue figures and military capacities. The book is limited to four non-colour maps, but the reader can copy and enlarge these images to add additional labels and incorporate further detail including political boundaries, population movements, trade routes, campaign courses and military capabilities. The successor volume in this series contains detailed maps of Parthia, Syria and Arabia.

There is a lack of academic attention given to this subject because leading Classical Scholars and Ancient Historians are reluctant to engage in the detailed study of archaeological remains, or consider texts from eastern civilizations. This book examines the ancient evidence without the agendas or limitations of on-going academic disputes.

There is currently only one other scholarly work that examines Sino-Roman connections in detail and that is John Hill's *Through the Jade Gate to Rome* (2009). The work presents passages of ancient Chinese text in translation alongside extensive notes and modern analysis. Consideration of the classical texts relating to the Far East can also be found in John Sheldon's *Commentary on George Coedes' Texts of Greek and Latin Authors on the Far East* (2012).

The term '*Seidenstrassen*' or 'Silk Routes' was first used by the nineteenth century German geographer and explorer Baron Ferdinand von Richthofen, uncle of the First World War aviator Manfred von Richthofen, known as the Red Baron. In the early 1870s Ferdinand Richthofen surveyed the land routes that crossed Central Asia from Afghanistan to China. He studied itineraries contained in ancient Chinese and Roman texts and considered the practicality of these routes for the construction of a proposed railway line across Central Asia that would have linked the German economy to Chinese markets.

The term 'Silk Routes' was appropriate since mountains, desert environments and scarce resources meant that pre-modern travellers were limited in the paths they could use to cross Central Asia. Ancient texts recovered from the region reveal that Chinese authorities recognized permitted routes that restricted travellers under their control to fixed itineraries. A Chinese text called the *Weilue* outlines these routes and confirms that the concept of planned courses is legitimate.[1] The adjective was justified, as silk was the most internationally important commodity conveyed along these overland routes. This is confirmed by contemporary Greek and Roman texts which refer to the Chinese as the 'Seres' or the 'Silk People'. The first Greek account to mention China (*Thinae*) by name records that from this country 'silk floss, yarn, and cloth are conveyed by land via Bactria to Barygaza [Afghanistan to the Indus ports].'[2] When the sixth century Byzantine scholar Cosmas Indicopleustes described the world he asked his readers to imagine a cord 'stretched from China (*Tzinitza*) that passes through Persia until it reaches Roman territory'.[3]

The Qin Dynasty united China in 220 BC, two centuries before Rome fully conquered the Mediterranean and Augustus was acclaimed Emperor. For almost four hundred years from 202 BC to AD 220, China was governed by the Han Empire which ruled as many people as the Roman regime at the height of its power. Rome was confined to western Europe and the Mediterranean, while China extended its Empire deep into Central Asia. The Han acquired resources and developed technologies to overcome the mounted warrior populations that occupied the vast Eurasian steppes. Chinese workshops mass-produced high quality steel to equip their armies with powerful multi-shot precision crossbows. Han armies returned from Ferghana (Uzbekistan) with a breeding-stock of superior horses for use in steppe warfare and imperial envoys brought alfalfa seeds back from Bactria (Afghanistan) so that Chinese fields could produce abundant forage for new cavalry regiments. Between 121 and 100 BC the Han Empire conquered the Tarim kingdoms that led west into Transoxiana and the main land routes into Afghanistan, India and Iran. Under Chinese protection a system of overland trails around the Tarim deserts developed into a network of commercial highways known to modern scholars as the silk routes.

The world changed when China secured the Tarim territories and established contacts with India through Bactria. India had a very large population and produced many unique commodities from high-altitude mountain ranges, tropical monsoon forests and warm ocean shores. In Bactria and other intermediary markets, Indian spices, pearls, ivory and cottons were exchanged for highly sought-after bales of unique Chinese silk. These commercial contacts changed the fortunes, prospects and ambitions of the populations that occupied southern Asia. In 118 BC, only seven years after the first Chinese envoy returned from Transoxiana, an Indian ship sailed around the Arabian Peninsula and entered the Red Sea. The ship was wrecked in the process, but a Greek patrol ship from the Ptolemaic Kingdom of Egypt managed to rescue a single survivor. This Indian mariner was brought to the court of King Ptolemy VIII Physcon at Alexandria and, after learning Greek, revealed how sailings could be made to northern India using the seasonal monsoon winds. Physcon funded the first Greek voyage to the Indus kingdoms and the precedent was set for Mediterranean merchants to begin commercial ventures across the Indian Ocean.[4]

The Romans knew about India, but were unaware of the Far East until the first century BC when silk began to reach the Mediterranean through the Parthian Empire which ruled in ancient Iran. The Parthians sent their first envoys to the Han Empire in 100 BC and it was from these early contacts that they learned of the profits to be made by controlling the overland trade in Chinese goods, including silk and steel. Parthian subjects blocked Roman access to the caravan courses that crossed Iran and for security and profit they restricted the flow of information that reached the Mediterranean concerning the distant Han Empire.[5]

A second advance in the ancient world economy occurred in 31 BC, when the Roman general Octavian defeated the Ptolemaic Queen Cleopatra VIII and her consort Mark Antony. This conflict was the final civil war of the Roman Republic and after his victory Octavian took control over the eastern legions and annexed Egypt. The economic prospects of the Roman regime were transformed when Octavian seized the accumulated wealth of the Ptolemaic Kingdom and distributed the funds amongst the citizen population of Rome.[6] The resultant commercial boom occurred at the same time as the Empire gained direct control over the Red Sea shipping lanes that led into the Indian Ocean. Within five years, there were over a hundred Roman ships sailing to India, and Mediterranean markets were inundated with eastern products.[7] By the first century AD Indian imports into Egypt were worth over a billion sesterces per annum and the Roman Empire was receiving more than 250 million sesterces from the quarter-rate custom tax it imposed on its Red Sea frontiers.[8]

The Empire received further high-level income from taxing eastern goods entering Roman Syria by way of the Persian Gulf and the Parthian caravan routes that crossed Iran. An inscription from the frontier city of Palmyra confirms that Rome must have received revenues of a least 90 million sesterces from this caravan traffic.[9] To place this figure in context, Caesar imposed tribute worth 40 million sesterces on his Gallic conquests and by the first century AD the Rhineland frontier was defended by eight legions (80,000 soldiers) at a cost of 88 million sesterces.[10] This meant that the taxes that Rome collected from international trade surpassed the revenues of entire subject countries and were sufficient to pay the costs of large permanent armies. Every year Rome required up to a billion sesterces to finance its Empire and the ancient evidence suggests that a third of this amount came from taxing eastern commerce conducted through the Indian Ocean and Iran.[11]

In 27 BC, Octavian took the name Augustus and received formal recognition as the first Emperor of Rome. The new revenues derived from international commerce enabled Augustus to reform the Roman military, transforming an ad hoc system of short-term citizen service into the first full-time professional army devised by any ancient regime. Augustus calculated that almost thirty legions including 300,000 career soldiers were needed to protect the Roman Empire from external threat and maintain control over its subject nations (the *Pax Romana*).

This military force was maintained at a cost of over 330 million sesterces per annum, the single largest expense in Roman government spending.[12]

The revenues raised by eastern commerce helped the Roman regime meet its military costs, but this prosperity was generated by the export of gold and silver to pay for exotic commodities in foreign markets. Pliny the Elder, an advisor to the Emperor Vespasian, estimated that more than 100 million sesterces of bullion left the Empire every year as a consequence of international commerce.[13] This bullion was exported to acquire expensive stocks of Arabian incense, Indian spices and Chinese silks. The problem for Rome was that its gold and silver reserves were finite; while the products that the Romans sought in eastern markets were renewable resources for the regimes that controlled production. Consequently, the Roman Empire's long-term prospects were determined by its economic position in the ancient world economy and the interests of China and other powerful regimes in Central Asia affected the fortunes of western civilization.

CHAPTER ONE

Steel and Silk

The ancient evidence suggests that by the first century AD almost 50 million people out of a total world population of perhaps 250 million were under Roman rule.[1] During this era, the city of Rome was the largest urban centre in the ancient world with over a million inhabitants.[2] But Rome did not exist in isolation; there were large-scale economic connections between the leading Mediterranean cities and the commercial centres of Asia.

In ancient times many regions of the world produced unique products that were considered valuable commodities in distant markets. During the reign of the first Emperor Augustus (27 BC–AD 14) large quantities of foreign imports from Arabia, India and China became widely obtainable in Mediterranean markets as popular consumer goods.[3] Amongst these eastern imports were incense from the southern Arabian kingdoms of the Saba-Himyarites in Yemen and the Hadramaut in Dhofar. These valuable fragrant resins were used in perfumes and burnt as religious offerings in Greek, Roman and Persian cultures. Indian Kingdoms provided spices that were much sought after and valued across the ancient world as flavourings for foods and ingredients in remedies. Other Indian products included precious stones, ivory, pearls, crystals and cotton. Most eastern ports adjoining the Indian Ocean also offered turtle shells that were carved into decorative objects by Roman craftsmen. Merchants, traffickers and consumers were prepared to pay large sums for these unique goods, and the regimes that controlled the production, or conveyance, of valuable commodities acquired long-term advantages in the ancient world economy.

In the Roman Empire eastern imports became synonymous with social prosperity, perceptions of male status and concepts of feminine beauty. Foremost amongst the unique products transported through eastern trade routes were oriental steel and durable Chinese silks spun from the thin protein strands of insect cocoons. Western civilizations did not yet possess the knowledge or skill required to manufacture these commodities, so the Romans had to rely on foreign supplies to fulfil their consumer demands. Silks and steel from China entered Roman Syria from Iranian caravan routes that crossed the Parthian Empire from Transoxiana (Uzbekistan) to Mesopotamia (Iraq).[4] Oriental goods were also shipped from India through the Persian Gulf to reach Parthian markets in Babylonia (southern Iraq).[5] This consumer demand encouraged international commerce and provided the finance for Roman trade ventures to distant lands beyond the previous limits of classical knowledge.

The Manufacture of Iron and Steel

Oriental steel had a significant value in distant markets since Roman workshops could not mass-produce metals with comparable strength and sharpness. Steel is a metal alloy manufactured by heating iron ore to high temperatures, then combining the molten metal with carbon or other strengthening elements. The grade of steel produced by these techniques depends on the sustained temperature of the furnace and the quantity and condition of the added compounds. Good quality steel is harder than iron and has much greater flexibility and tensile strength. Blades made from steel therefore maintain a sharper edge for a longer time and have a greater resistance to rust than their equivalent in iron.

Widespread steel technology would have improved the long-term prospects of Roman civilization by permitting the manufacture of more effective agricultural blades, construction tools, armour and weaponry. But imperial Rome lacked the expertise to mass-produce reliable steel as western civilizations did not have sufficient knowledge of the required carbon compounds that were added to the molten iron. Instead, the Romans produced wrought iron by first heating iron ore in a furnace to separate metal from waste slag in a process known as 'smelting'. This technique was used throughout the Roman Empire to make tools and bladed weapons. The resultant iron also acquired a trace of strengthening carbon from the charcoal fuel. The cooling lump of soft white-hot metal was then 'forged' by being beaten and drawn into the required shape using hammer and tongs. During this process the iron was repeatedly reheated in a furnace to keep it malleable and 'quenched' in cold water to fix and harden the blade. Hence the name 'wrought' or 'worked' iron. Iron quenched in oil produced a more malleable metal that was suitable for hobnailing military sandals or providing metal rims for vehicle wheels.[6] Roman military bases stored both hard and malleable iron along with charcoal to fuel the open hearth furnaces used by their armourers.[7]

A more costly and advanced method of iron manufacture was the production of 'cast' iron. In this process the ore was smelted in an enclosed furnace, but the temperature was increased until it melted into a semi-liquid state. The molten metal would then be poured into a mould to take the shape of the finished object. During the heating process the melting iron rapidly absorbed large amounts of carbon, so the finished 'cast iron' piece was hard, but relatively brittle. This meant that it was liable to crack or shatter under a heavy blow and could not be forged by reheating, or using hammer-strikes to modify its shape. The production of cast iron was rare in the Roman Empire due to the design of furnaces which could not easily produce and sustain the high temperatures required to convert the metal into the required molten state.

Wrought iron has a carbon content of about 0.5 per cent, while cast iron contains about 4 per cent carbon. Fine quality steel has a carbon value close to 1 per cent, which produces a metal that is sharper and harder than wrought iron. With this percentage of carbon content steel does not have the brittle structure of cast iron and can withstand heavy impact shocks. The problem for ancient metallurgists was therefore how to control carbon levels in the furnace so that the resultant iron had the qualities of steel. Sometimes Roman smiths would create a batch of iron with steel properties, but these were chance occurrences that were not easily replicated. Roman authorities recognised that ore from certain territories created better quality iron due to natural compounds in the slag material, but Roman metallurgists never learnt how to replicate this process and produce consistent steel from ordinary iron deposits.

The use of better metal components might have engendered important technological advances in classical society. For example, during the imperial era Greek engineers in Alexandria experimented with small steam-powered devices. In the first century AD, Heron of Alexandria designed a primitive steam-engine called an *aeolipile* that consisted of a brass sphere that could rotate on an axis and was fitted with outward pointing bent nozzles. Water was heated inside the sphere or fed into the device, so that pressurised steam rushed from the nozzles and forced the orb to rotate at speed.[8] However, one reason why these contraptions could not be developed into more practical machines was the lack of suitable metal components.

The best quality iron produced in the Roman Empire was extracted from mountains near Noricum on the north side of the Alps. Elements of manganese contained in Noricum ore produced iron that had steel-like properties and consequently was in high demand across the Empire. Ovid refers to the famous strength of this metal when he describes desires: 'harder than iron tempered by Noric fire'.[9] Horace also mentions strong emotions such as pain and anger, 'undefeated by Noricum swords'.[10] He describes certain death as, 'a leap from the highest tower, or your chest pierced by an Alpine blade'.[11] The Emperors recognised the value of these iron resources and Hadrian had the text 'met[alla] nor[ica]' placed on his coins. This was perhaps to celebrate an imperial visit to Norica, or the discovery of new ore reserves in the region (AD 134–138).

Noricum iron was used for axes, agricultural tools, chisels and stonecutting equipment while Roman doctors recognised that the sharp cutting edges of Noricum blades made superior tools for fine surgery. Galen devised a special instrument for dissecting spinal cord which was made from Noricum steel so it would not easily blunt, bend or break. He recommended these instruments for abortions, or removing a foetus that had died in the womb. The surgery required, 'a straight one-sided cutting blade: blunt-pointed. Novacula or razor: blunt-pointed *bistoury*, ring-knife for dismembering the foetus'.[12]

Noricum iron ore was quarried at two ancient sites that were nearly 40 miles apart (Erzberg and Eisenerz in modern Austria). During the first century AD, metal production was concentrated at the nearby town of Virunum which was established as a *municipium* by the Emperor Claudius. The site of Virunum was near modern Magdalensberg and resembled a small Italian town with elongated *tabernae* (workshop-residences) facing the forum (central town square). Two smithies on the northern side of the forum had cellar storerooms which have been subject to excavation.[13] Both cellars had business notices scratched into their plaster walls recording how bulk orders were assembled and collected by contractors from distant regions. Steel rings, iron disks and hooks were sold wholesale to visiting businessmen in batches of over 500 items. Some of these batches weighed over a ton when they were collected and transported from the site. One order included 115 anvils while another records the sale of 225 anvils to a single contractor.[14] Many of these consignments were transported across the Alps into Italy where the nearest port was Aquileia on the Adriatic coast more than 120 miles distant from Virunum. Some consignments were destined for workshops in Northwest Africa and one of the buyers who visited Virunum several times was a man named Orosius, a citizen of Volubilis in Mauretania.[15] The town of Volubilis (near Meknes in Morocco) was more than 1,200 miles from Virunum and 100 miles inland from the Mediterranean coast.

Other towns founded by the Romans were famous for their iron production, including Bilbilis in northeast Spain (near Calatayud). Bilbilis was 100 miles from the Mediterranean coast, but it produced and exported iron to other provinces. Martial was born in Bilbilis and he describes his hometown as 'renowned for its mines of cruel iron' and a place well-known for 'resounding with the noise of metal-work'.[16]

The situation was different in the Han Empire where Chinese metalworkers using more advanced furnaces had identified the natural compounds that created better quality iron during the smelting process. Through continual practice they had refined the measurements needed to ensure that the compounds added to iron ore introduced sufficient carbon to create a reliable quality of steel. The Chinese had developed large enclosed furnaces and double-action piston bellows that used bamboo nozzles to produce steady streams of air. This made it easier to keep the fire at a steady heat and control reactions within the furnace. Chinese furnaces also burned coal cakes which further increased temperatures and reduced fuel costs. This was significant because mass-produced cast iron could be transformed into steel by applying blasts of oxidizing cool air to the molten metal (the 'Hundred Refinings Method'). The Chinese also knew how to turn wrought iron into steel. Blades were wrapped in fruit skins rich in carbon containing a small amount of slag, charred rice husks and specialist powdered minerals. These packages were then sealed in clay crucibles and heated at high temperatures over a sustained period (up to twenty-four hours) until the metal absorbed the necessary carbon and strengthening elements. In China these techniques were used to mass-manufacture knives, hatchets, chisels, adzes, drill bits, hammers, ploughshares, hoes, spades, shovels, rakes, sickles, wheelbarrow axles, cooking pots, pans and kettles.

This important development allowed the Han regime to mass-manufacture high-quality metal including armour-piercing crossbow bolts. The Han understood that steel manufacturing techniques provided Chinese troops with superior armour and weaponry. Consequently, the regime tried to restrict the spread of this technology to foreign peoples and prevent the export of Chinese steel supplies to the Steppe nations.[17] However, there were strong incentives for Chinese merchants to break the embargoes and offer steel at high prices to foreign traders. Smuggling became a problem and the warlike Xiongnu ('Hun-nu') people of Mongolia were able to capture Han metalworkers when they raided Chinese territory. From these prisoners the Xiongnu learnt how to produce supplies of their own steel weaponry which they offered for exchange with other Steppe peoples.[18] In this way supplies of superior oriental steel reached the Parthian Empire in Iran.

The superiority of this steel weaponry was demonstrated on the battlefield of Carrhae in 53 BC when a legionary army encountered a Parthian battle-host from eastern Iran. The steel-tipped arrows carried by the Parthians easily punched through Roman shields and armour, and their steel lances were able to pierce through the entire bodies of the legionaries. On the battlefield, mounted Parthian *cataphracts* were protected by layers of steel-enhanced armour and they seemed to be impenetrable to javelin strikes and stabs from the short *gladius* swords carried by Roman infantry.[19]

The early Roman Empire possessed no weapons or armour comparable to that of the Parthians. Consequently, Roman authorities did not fully understand the significance of the metal used by their Iranian rivals. It was assumed that Parthian steel was the product of unique iron ores that could only be found in the distant east and no initiative was taken to try and determine how these metals could be produced. Pliny describes 'Parthian iron' as superior to all other ferrous alloys with the exception of the steel produced by the Seres or 'Silk People' (the Chinese). He explains that 'of all the different types of iron, the Seres produce the most excellent variety and they send it to us along with their delicate fabrics and animal furs.'[20] This 'natural resource' explanation seemed reasonable when the Romans considered how geography and climate provided the distant east with better fabrics, greater stocks of precious stones and more potent flavourings in the form of spices and incense. The Romans never realised that with commonplace compounds and the correct techniques, their workshops could have manufactured large amounts of steel for their legions.

The Parthians restricted Roman access to the caravan routes across Iran in order to control the overland traffic in oriental products, including steel.[21] But some steel reached Roman markets via India and the maritime trade routes that crossed the Indian Ocean. A Greek merchant handbook dated to AD 50, known as the *Periplus of the Erythraean Sea*, records that Chinese goods were available at city-ports near the Indus and Ganges.[22] India also possessed sophisticated iron-working technologies and by adding phosphorous to wrought iron they could create rust-resistant alloys. Ctesias claims that the Persian king Artaxerxes II (404–358 BC) possessed a pair of royal Indian swords that had a supernatural resistance to monsoon weather.[23] Curtius also reports that when Alexander defeated the Indian king Porus he was presented with 5,700 pounds of prized Indian steel (326 BC).[24] Macedonian engineers likely used this weather-resistant metal to construct a permanent bridge across the Upper Euphrates. Pliny records that centuries later Roman engineers had to replace the rusted iron chains that secured the bridge at Zeugma, but the original links remained miraculously uncorroded.[25] A six-ton iron pillar erected by the Indian Emperor Chandragupta Vikramaditya (AD 375–413) still stands in modern Delhi. This monument is

23 feet high and remains uncorroded by centuries of exposure to a climate that brings both drenching monsoon rains and prolonged dry seasons.

Apuleius mentions the quality of eastern iron when he lists the various products that typified the power and wealth of ancient India. He describes how 'there are marvellous stories told about India, with its vast stores of ivory, abundant pepper harvests, cinnamon exports, finely-tempered steel and the streams of gold and silver within its mines.'[26] A Roman customs list known as the *Alexandrian Tariff* records that imports of 'Indian iron' were taxed as they entered Egypt and this probably included batches of oriental steel, as well as rust-resistant Indian alloys.[27]

Quarter-rate import taxes were imposed on the imperial frontiers and goods could be offered instead of cash. This meant that the Roman government might have received significant quantities of eastern steel. However, Roman consumer demand probably ensured that most steel imports found use as costly display items, rather than as materials to arm the legions. Evidence is limited, but incoming supplies seem to have been used for small and expensive domestic items such as cutlery. Clement of Alexandria refers to this fashion when he complains, 'does the table-knife not cut unless it has an ivory handle studded with silver and do we have to use metal forged in India to carve our meat?' But knives fashioned from bright eastern steel were treasured objects and Clement describes a host who 'calls for this cutlery like a soldier calls for a weapon before battle'.[28]

Silk in the Roman Empire

It was said that the first Romans to see Chinese silk and steel were the legionaries that the Republican general Crassus led into northern Iraq in 53 BC. When the mounted Parthian army began their cavalry advance across the desert plain, they unfurled silken banners and discarded their drab coverings to reveal gleaming armour. Crassus and his legions watched in dismay as the Parthians rode forward with coloured silk pendants billowing dramatically above the heads of mounted archers and heavily-armoured lancers. According to Florus the Parthians appeared 'with their standards fluttering with gold and silk pennants; then without delay the cavalry, closing in on all sides, showered their weapons as thick as hail or rain upon the Romans. Thus the Roman army was destroyed in a terrible slaughter.'[29]

Wild silks were produced in certain parts of the ancient world including the Greek island of Cos. Aristotle describes how these silks were produced from a particular form of large grub that had a six-month cycle from caterpillar to moth. He explains that it was the work of certain women to 'unwind and reel off the cocoons of these creatures, and afterwards weave a fabric with the threads'.[30] Pliny describes how the islanders searched through undergrowth for the insect cocoons and collected them in earthenware vessels. The containers were stored in a warm environment until the tiny moths emerged several months later. Only then were the empty chrysalises soaked and stretched apart into weak, fractured filaments. The threads from these cocoons were woven into rare semi-translucent fabrics known to the Greeks and Romans as 'Coan silk'. Pliny refers to these thin fabrics as having 'a web-like weave' and confirms the fabric possessed the status of a 'luxury material suited for female garments'.[31]

Wild-silk fabrics produced on Cos were coarser than oriental silk and did not have the same translucent sheen. There was therefore confusion about the true origin of eastern silks and when Propertius and Tibullus describe certain types of 'Coan' silk as 'smooth and glossy', they are probably describing Chinese, rather than Mediterranean fabrics.[32] Arab merchants received their oriental silk from India and this explains why Propertius describes the appearance of his mistress, 'shimmering in her Arabian silks'.[33] Classical references to Coan silk disappear by about AD 20 when an increase in Chinese silk imports probably forced the coarser Coan fabrics from the Roman luxury market.[34]

Before the reign of the Roman Emperors, eastern silks were so rare and costly that they were perceived as the preserve of Hellenic royalty. But during the imperial period, oriental silk became popular in Roman society for status-defining garments and the fabric became synonymous with the best fashions. In the first century BC, small amounts of thickly woven Chinese silk were passed through ancient Persia until they reached Phoenician cities on the Mediterranean coast, including Sidon and Tyre. In these Syrian ports the material was carefully unravelled by skilful textile workers and rewoven into lighter cloth.[35]

Silk Workshops

The oriental silks that reached the Roman Empire in their original condition had a bland patina and pale colorations. These heavy Chinese weaves were bleached white, unpicked and respun into lightweight and opaque fabrics with a delicate transparency. Silk cloth could then be coloured with vivid textile dyes that significantly increased the price of processed fabric.[36] The most expensive dyes in Mediterranean society were the red, blue and purple colours extracted from the glands of sea-snails harvested on the Phoenician coast near Tyre.[37] Silk clothing was also coloured with crimson kermes dyes made from the crushed extract of insects gathered from the bark of trees in Spain and Asia Minor.[38] Retail prices for silk clothing remained high because the buyer was paying for the material, the cost of processing and dying the fabric and the skill of the tailor to create the garments.

Inscriptions found near Rome reveal the existence of fabric merchants in the city who specialized in silk materials. In the first or second century AD, a man named M. Nummius Proculus erected a monument to his 'excellent and deserving wife' Valeria Chrysis at the town of Tivoli, 19 miles north of Rome. Proculus describes his profession as a *sericarius* meaning 'silk manufacturer'.[39] Two further inscriptions record the presence of a *negotiator sericarius* or 'silk dealer' at the town of Gabbi which was 10 miles east of Rome.[40] An inscription from Rome honouring Thymele Marcella as a *sericaria* confirms that women could have been prominent in these businesses.[41] Some of these household industries might have employed a significant workforce and graffiti from Pompeii lists thirteen female slaves who worked in a wool-weaving shed. The text records the weight of yarn they had spun and the length of cloth they were producing.[42]

Many weavers were paid for their work and Diocletian's *Price Edict* lists the maximum prices that workers could demand for their services. A woolworker making light-weight cloaks could expect the same daily wage as a rural labourer (25 debased denarii).[43] Silk workers making part-silk and unpatterned silk clothing could expect to match this income and also receive 'maintenance' from their employer. Silk workers who produced fabrics 'in the diamond weave' were paid 40 debased denarii per day. Skilled silk workers could earn higher wages and an embroiderer working on part-silk tunics would earn eight times the wage of an ordinary woolworker (200 debased denarii). A worker making pure silk tunics might be paid twelve times the basic wage (300 debased denarii).[44]

There is evidence that urban workshops in Egypt still manufactured silk clothing in late antiquity. A papyrus dated AD 325 records how the Roman governor of Egypt ordered councillors from the Nile city of Oxyrhynchus to buy silk for the imperial stores. The councillors purchased 150 gold-embroidered silk chitons called *paragaudia* that were valued at 65,000 debased denarii per garment.[45]

The Emperor Aurelian claimed that the finest reworked coloured silks were worth more than their weight in gold and confirmation of this comes from the empire-wide price regulations published by the Emperor Diocletian in AD 301.[46] The *Price Edict* suggests that a labourer could buy a tunic with the money earned from twelve days of work.[47] A pound of white silk fabric cost the same as forty army tunics, or more than the labourer could earn in an entire year. The *Price Edict* records that purple-dyed silk was worth more than twelve times the price of white silk and a single pound of coloured fabric cost more than the labourer would earn in a decade.[48] These figures suggest that during the early imperial period, plain white silk was probably priced at up to 2,000 sesterces per pound, while the same weight of purple-dyed silk cost nearly 24,000 sesterces.[49] But because Roman society was obsessed with displaying affluence, wealthy people were prepared to pay large sums for costly imported fabrics.

The 'Secret' of Sericulture

The rare cloth produced from wild insect cocoons was always inferior to mass produced Chinese silk. In wild silk production the larvae chew through the cocoon and sever the thread into uneven lengths with many weak strands. This meant that the finished fabric had low lustre, poor elasticity and frayed easily. Clothing made from wild silk therefore coarsened over time and quickly lost its shape. Wild caterpillars also ate a mixed diet that stained the thread filament and created uneven beige tones that were difficult to bleach or dye. By contrast Chinese silk was made from intact threads that were unravelled as a continuous skein free from discolouration. This allowed the Chinese to produce uniquely smooth and durable silk garments in pale tones that could easily be bleached white, then dyed a range of vibrant colours to produce alluring fabrics with a prismatic sheen.

In ancient times, the Chinese were the only nation that could mass-produce high-quality silk. This process, known as 'sericulture', was practised in China thousands of years before the time of the Han Dynasty or the Roman Empire.

Ancient Chinese legend accredits the discovery of silk to a princess who was preparing a bowl of hot tea when an insect cocoon accidently dropped from the branch of a mulberry tree into the scalding liquid. She watched as the delicate filaments unravelled to produce a thin thread and discovered this could be woven into lightweight and alluring garments.[50]

The true origins of sericulture are unknown, but ancient inscriptions on oracle bones and tortoiseshell artefacts dating to the third and second millennium BC contain the characters for silkworm, mulberry tree and silk (*si*).[51] From these early origins the Chinese were able to increase the productivity of domesticated silk worms (*bombyx mori*) by selective breeding, and over thousands of years they created a pupa that could produce up to ten times the volume of filaments spun by its wild counterpart.

Rural Chinese homesteads could pay their land and property taxes by producing silk floss or fabric bundles for state officials.[52] As a result the government accumulated large stores of silk to be used as political gifts to secure the compliance of foreign regimes. By the first century BC, sericulture was a common household industry in China and the superior silk fibres it produced were highly sought after by foreign cultures. But the Chinese kept strict control over this important industry and limited the spread of sericulture beyond their frontiers. The Han used their monopoly to dominate external markets and managed their silk exports to bring valuable goods into their empire.[53]

Most silk produced in ancient China was woven into thick, durable fabrics designed for use as practical clothing and other functional everyday necessities. Silk also came from imperial-run workshops that mass-produced the fabric to supplement supplies received from regional markets.[54] The material was taken to central government warehouses to be distributed to state-employees and gifted as government aid to vulnerable individuals including refugees, widows and orphans. Any surplus was sold in urban districts where the fabric was purchased by working people. Chinese troops on the frontiers also received parcels of silk as part-payment for their military service.[55] The state understood that merchants would supply the border troops with local supplies in exchange for valuable silk rolls that would fetch a premium price in foreign markets.[56]

By the Han era many farms and estate gardens had an area set aside for the cultivation of stunted, but fast-growing, white mulberry trees (*morus alba*) which produced leaves for feeding silk grubs. Sericulture was traditionally practised by the womenfolk within a Chinese family, working mostly indoors while the men tended crops and managed animals in the fields. Silk production was considered a valuable task that granted females the opportunity to contribute to the prosperity of their families and help pay the state taxes imposed on their households.

The cycle of silk production begins with a small number of cocoons that are not processed so that adult moths can emerge. These domesticated insects cannot fly and die soon after mating to produce a new batch of eggs. Each female moth produces about 400 tiny eggs and these remain in a dormant state until a sharp rise in temperate triggers hatching. The new generation of silk worms must be kept at the egg stage until spring when the fresh leaf-growth of the mulberry crop allows the cultivation of a new batch of larvae. For five months the eggs are allowed to develop in a warm environment (24 degrees), then, to suspend their lifecycle, they are transferred to a cool storeroom (5 degrees) for a further five months. The entire life-cycle is a delicate process and temperate fluctuations, or even strong odours, can interrupt the incubation period or affect the appetite of the pupa. Complete batches of silk worms can die if they hatch too early when their required food is not in season.

In spring, under the care and supervision of Chinese grandmothers, wives and daughters, the silk worms were hatched from minute grey eggs that were the size of a pinhead. The eggs were encouraged to hatch by being placed in a humid environment while the temperature was gradually increased back to 24 degrees. The miniscule hatchlings weighed half a milligram, but five weeks of constant feeding increased their weight 10,000 times. During the pupa stage the grubs needed a warm environment, so they were kept indoors in trays and baskets well-stocked with fresh leaves cut from mulberry trees several times a day. Each pupa could potentially eat its entire body-weight of leaves in one day.

The silk 'worm' or caterpillar has sixteen legs formed in pairs along the length of its body. The six appendices along its thorax are functioning legs while the remaining ten limbs are abdominal pseudopods used for grasping leaves. The grub has prominent mandibles and its rear end is split into two appendices that allow the insect to grip onto twigs. This complex anatomy, along with the idea of producing a 'thread', explains why some classical authorities thought that oriental 'silk insects' might be a species of spider.[57]

Five to six weeks after hatching, the caterpillars are up to 3 inches long and ready to enter the larval stage of their development. Each caterpillar unravels a single strand of delicate raw silk from its salivary glands and wraps the minute thread thousands of times around its body in a figure of eight pattern. It takes four days for the insect to wind the soft elastic thread around its form. As this is occurring the silkworms are attached to racks or false tree branches so that the cocoon is suspended and forms into a perfect cylindrical shape. The thread then hardens into a large protective cocoon. Each cocoon is formed from a single thread several thousand feet long, but over 2,000 of these cocoons are required to make a single pound of silk.

To process the cocoons, they are immersed in scalding water to kill the pupae. This must be done before the pupa can destroy the silk strands by secreting a fluid called 'coconase' that will degrade the fibre permitting the emerging moth to chew through the chrysalis. The cocoons are floated and stirred in steaming hot water to dissolve a gummy protein known as 'sericin' that holds the silk strands together. Dexterity is required to pull apart the chrysalis, locate the end of a strand and unravel the cocoon into a fine, lustrous filament of strong, light-weight thread.

This was a skillful and time-consuming process with each cocoon yielding a single filament that was half a mile (800 metres) long. After reeling, the delicate filaments were twisted, spun and spliced together into a thread containing up to fourteen strands. These threads could be woven into cloth or gathered into yarn that was 'thrown' into loops and coiled into skeins. Waste filaments and damaged cocoons were combed and spun to create yarn with less transparency and sheen than the woven thread. Silk floss was created by placing the pupae on a flat surface to spin thick clusters of silk matting, rather than cylindrical cocoons. These matted cocoons were teased out into fluffy wads that made an ideal soft and lightweight material for bedding quilts and insulating winter jackets.

Eventually the techniques involved in true sericulture spread to the Tarim kingdoms on the western edge of the Chinese Empire. The method of transmission is unknown, but in later centuries a semi-legendary story was circulated to explain how this came about. A Chinese Buddhist monk named Xuanzang travelled the silk routes in the seventh century AD and in the oasis kingdom of Khotan he heard a story of how the secret of sericulture was finally smuggled out of China. Xuanzang was told that the people of Khotan sent a delegation to the Chinese Emperor asking for the secret of silk. The Emperor laughed at them and replied, 'It is forbidden to let outsiders find out how silk is made.' Then the Emperor had all border stations watched to ensure that nothing was smuggled out of China that could establish sericulture in Khotan. But the King of Khotan had another plan. He asked the Emperor if he could marry a Chinese princess. When the Emperor agreed, the King sent an envoy to the princess to tell her that the people of Khotan wore only rough clothing. The envoy explained that if the princess 'wanted to wear silk, she would have to bring some seeds and eggs, so that the people of Khotan could fashion beautiful dresses for her'. On hearing this, the princess acquired mulberry seeds and silk worm eggs and hid them in her elaborate head-dress. At the border gates, the guards searched her clothes and possessions thoroughly, but they did not dare touch her person, or her carefully arranged hair. The princess was received with great ceremony at the Khotan royal palace where she handed over the concealed items. However, the princess was still mindful of the womenfolk of her homeland and gave the instruction, 'It is prohibited to kill the silkworm.' Consequently, the silks produced by Khotan had the rough texture of broken threads as the larvae chewed through their cocoons. But perhaps it was Buddhist prohibitions against killing living creatures that caused the people of Khotan to spare the silk worms. Xuanzang was told, 'Only when the butterfly has gone can the silk be twined from the cocoon and whoever offends against this rule may be deprived of divine protection.' Even so, 'The secret of making silk was taken from China, and the people of Khotan began to wear fine silk clothes along with their furs.'[58]

CHAPTER TWO

Silk in Roman Society

Chinese silk reached the Roman Empire as fabric rolls, or bundles of thread to be rewoven into thin cloth and reworked into styles for popular male and female clothing. Roman silk garments were often dyed in vibrant colours to produce some of the most expensive and esteemed outfits available in the ancient world. During the height of the Roman Empire valuable silk garments were one of the most publicly visible and controversial of all eastern imports as silk was brighter, stronger, more durable, lighter and more comfortable than any western material made from animal products or plant fibres.

Silk Drapes

From an early period, Roman commanders were able to acquire large amounts of oriental silks to promote their own interests. In 46 BC, Julius Caesar organized a series of monumental triumphs in the city of Rome that he hoped would upstage the dramatic victory displays enacted by his predecessor Pompey. On the day of the celebrations, the linen awnings in the Roman Forum were replaced with canopies made from delicate silks. Dio Cassius describes how 'Julius Caesar had silk curtains stretched over the spectators, so they would not be irritated by the glare of the sun.' The ordinary people of Rome had never seen so much expensive silk fabric on public display and were amazed by the extraordinary colours and translucent sheen. Pliny reveals that the awnings continued along a large part of the parade route as Caesar had 'stretched awnings over the whole of the Roman Forum and the Sacred Way leading from his mansion, right up to the Capitol'. A bolt of Chinese silk contained about 20 square feet of fabric, so the equivalent of 800 rolls might have been used per half-mile. This display was so successful that it became more of a talking point than the victory parade, or the magnificent gladiatorial combats that formed the finale of the celebrations. Pliny reports that 'this exhibition of silk was thought to be even more wondrous than the show of gladiators that Caesar offered.'[1] But many soldiers considered the display to be 'a reckless squandering of money' that might have been added to their military bonuses.[2]

The display staged by Julius Caesar established silk as an appropriate material for public events connected with imperial authority. This practice was continued by later Emperors and in AD 39, when Caligula formally granted new territories to eastern client princes, the public ceremony was conducted in the Roman Forum under the shade of silk awnings. During the ceremony Caligula sat between the consuls on a rostrum decorated with a bright canopy of delicate silk drapery. From this ornate platform the Emperor received the client kings as they ascended the dais to offer their public pledge to Roman authority.[3]

This pageant further encouraged silk fabrics to be displayed in private households in the form of upholstery or drapes. Pliny the Elder describes a fashion for red awnings within the inner courtyards of private homes and it is possible that the wealthiest patrons had these canopies fashioned from silk.[4] Further classical accounts indicate the popularity of silk amongst the Romans. In his tragic play *Phaedra*, Seneca describes the night sky as 'a gauzy web-like cloak dyed in Tyrian purple'.[5]

By the time Nero came to power in AD 54, Roman ships were bringing large quantities of silk back from the main ports of India.[6] Consequently, when Nero stretched star-spangled blue awnings over his amphitheatres, these were probably made from superior Chinese silks.[7] Nero also commissioned a theatre awning dyed purple and embroidered with a giant image of himself driving a chariot 'with golden stars gleaming all about him'.[8] It has been suggested that some of the Colosseum awnings shading Roman crowds from the glare of the sun were made from imported oriental fabric.[9] The effect of silken fabrics in Roman theatres added to the drama and Lucretius describes how 'yellow, scarlet or maroon awnings are stretched flapping and billowing on poles and rafters over our spacious theatres.' Both the crowd seated below and the stage scenery was 'made to glow and flow with the colours of the canopy'. Lucretius explains that on sunny days, 'the more completely a theatre is enclosed by surrounding walls, the more it is lit up by this flood of colour.'[10]

Sacred Silks

In the imperial era, reworked Chinese silks became a popular fabric for decorating Roman military standards, including the *signa* carried by cohorts. Silk was lightweight and its strong protein fibres could be easily worked into tassels, fringes and decorative embroidery threads. Silk panels could also be painted and these properties made it the ideal fabric to adorn army standards which were viewed as prestigious symbols of martial identity and loyalty to the imperial order. On parade, or in conflict, these standards functioned both as military focal points and devotional icons for the Roman army. For these reasons they required reverential treatment and were consequently made from the best of materials.

A funeral inscription found at the Roman frontier in northern Britain confirms that oriental silk was used in imperial banners throughout the Empire. The inscription is from the Roman fort of Coria (Corborage) on the River Tyne and records how a Syrian silk merchant named Barates supplied fabric and decorative trimmings to nearby garrisons on Hadrian's Wall. The inscription reads: 'To the spirits of the departed Barathes the Palmyrene, a *vexillarius*, who lived 68 years.' The term *vexillarius* would indicate that Barates was a supplier of *vexilla:* flags, standards, and ensigns. He probably also offered silk to private buyers, but the proudest claim on his memorial was that he supplied fabric to the local legions for their military standards.[11]

In wider Roman society silk became associated with piety. Coloured silks were cut into strips and sown into devotional garlands. These wreaths were presented to images of the classical gods and offered to the protective household deities. Women oversaw the fabrication of garlands and there was public status to be gained by incorporating the most exotic and costly items into displays. Expensive wreaths were also displayed at family tombs and placed on graves to honour the dead. Pliny reveals the influence of eastern imports in this practice when he writes that 'no garland is fashionable unless it is stitched together with genuine petals and now flower petals are fetched from India and the lands beyond.' He reports that 'the most acclaimed garlands are made from nard leaves or multi-coloured silks steeped in perfumes – for this is the latest extravagance devised by our women.'[12]

Some Romans imagined their pagan gods wearing silk fabrics woven by female attendants, 'who make tunics to suit the season'.[13] Apuleius describes an encounter with the Egyptian goddess Isis who appeared 'in fine silk vestments of combined hues, sometimes yellow, sometimes pink, sometimes flame-like, and sometimes a troublesome dark and obscure tone'.[14]

Naked statues of the Greco-Roman gods were sometimes dressed in silk garments for special occasions including ceremonial processions when the statue was paraded through the streets. Apuleius describes how a statue of Isis was robed in purple fabric and covered by 'a small silken veil'. Her religious attendants were outfitted in 'ribbons and saffron-coloured clothes made from cotton and loosely-fitted silk'.[15] Avienus describes how female attendants who joined the Ionian procession to celebrate Bacchus wore silk shawls and, according to Prudentius, the lead pagan priest who conducted bull sacrifices in Rome wore a gold crown and a tightly wound toga secured with a silk girdle.[16] The binding was probably for practical reasons, but the choice of material is significant.[17]

Apuleius describes a ritual procession where participants were dressed in the distinctive costumes of particular occupations such as soldier or hunter. One of the followers 'was dressed in gilded slippers and a silk gown, wearing expensive ornaments and a wig, he swung his hips as he walked in imitation of a woman'.[18] It was believed that Vertumnus, the god of seasons, could alter his physical form, and consequently his androgynous cult statues were dressed in male or female clothes. Propertius imagines the words of Vertumnus: 'my nature is adaptable to every form and subject to your wish – dress me in Coan silk and I will be a noble and good woman, but when I wear the toga, who will say I am not a man?'[19]

Imperial Silks

During his reign, the Emperor Caligula dressed in expensive silk garments, including ethereal costumes tailored in Persian styles that some authorities considered effeminate (AD 37–41). On one occasion he had the breastplate of Alexander the Great exhumed and he wore it over 'a purple silk *chlamys* (short military cloak), embroidered with much gold and many precious stones from India'. Caligula also began to carry symbols of 'divinity', exhibiting himself with emblems of the gods. Sometimes he attached a golden beard to his chin and held a thunderbolt so that he resembled Jupiter, or he would brandish a trident to represent the sea god Neptune. Caligula also appeared before the people carrying the emblem of the messenger god Hermes, a staff with the image of two entwined snakes beneath a winged motif (the *caduceus*). On one occasion Caligula went to the extreme of dressing up in female clothes to represent the goddess Venus. Dio reports, 'he pretended to be a god while supplications, prayers, and sacrifices would be offered to him. At other times he appeared in public in silk or in triumphal dress.'[20] Suetonius sums up the confusion that these displays provoked when he writes that 'Caligula did not follow the clothing styles of his country, the appearance of masculinity, or even the fashions of ordinary mortals.'[21] But for the Roman public there was no greater endorsement for silk than to see the Emperor wearing this fabric tailored in the supposed fashions of the gods.

Even Emperors with a reputation for austerity chose silk garments for important state occasions. For example, senior Roman commanders wore purple and crimson costumes during celebrations to mark the end of the Jewish War in AD 71. Josephus describes the scene in Rome when 'at daybreak Vespasian and Titus emerged dressed in traditional robes of crimson-purple and wearing laurel wreaths.' The generals proceeded to the Portico of Octavia where the Senate and the senior magistrates awaited. At the climax of the ceremony the ranks of soldiers shouted acclamations to bear witness to the military prowess of their commanders. The central figures in this spectacle were arranged in tableau, each without his weapons, seated on ivory chairs, wearing silken robes and crowned with victory laurels.[22] The actions of the Emperor and his commanders would have further encouraged the fashion for silk fabric.

Other Roman Emperors who were thought of as decadent or tyrannical were often criticised for wearing silk apparel. The overindulgent Emperor Commodus (AD 180–192) was seen wearing delicate silk robes in the theatre and at gladiatorial displays. His dress was considered vulgar and inappropriate because he had a tumour on his groin and the public could see the swelling through the drapery of his robes.[23] Commodus spent lavish sums on public entertainments and re-equipped the imperial court with expensive costumes fashioned from silk.

After Commodus was killed by conspirators, the new Emperor Pertinax was forced to auction the palace treasures to meet the cost of payoffs and rewards expected by his military backers. According to the *Historia Augusta*, 'among the sale of items belonging to Commodus, the following articles were especially noteworthy: silk-woven robes with remarkable gold embroidery; tunics, mantles and coats; Dalmatian-style long-sleeve tunics and fringed military cloaks.'[24]

During his brief reign, the Syrian-born Emperor Elagabalus tried to replace traditional Roman religion with an esoteric foreign cult based on solar worship, embodied in a black stone (AD 218–222). The *Historia Augusta* accuses the young emperor of performing the eastern rituals of eunuch priests and engaging in promiscuous conduct with other men. Elagabalus rejected linen fabrics and appeared in public dressed in a Syrian priestly silk gown that 'displayed influences from the sacred robes of the Phoenicians and the luxurious garb of the Medes'.[25] It was said that Elagabalus 'only approved of silk fabrics' and 'loathed Greek and

Roman garments because they were made from wool which he thought was an inferior material'.[26] He introduced silk into the imperial court and presented guests to his banquets with 'silk garments that he regarded as a rarity and a mark of honour'.[27] It was rumoured that when Elagabalus feared an uprising, he 'prepared cords entwined with purple and scarlet silk so he could end to his own life by using a noose.'[28] Elagabalus was ultimately assassinated by his own Praetorian Guard.

By contrast an 'honourable' emperor was seen as someone who could resist the trappings of indulgence as signified by silk. In AD 168 Marcus Aurelius sold the heirloom collection of gold-embroidered silk dresses that his wife had inherited from the consorts of previous emperors. This auction gave Marcus Aurelius the funds he needed to finance a war against the Germanic tribes who were overrunning the northern frontiers.[29]

The reformist Emperor Severus Alexander restricted the display of silk in imperial costume (AD 222–235). Alexander refused the title 'Lord' and generally appeared in public wearing a simple red military cloak or the plain white toga of a Roman citizen.[30] The *Historia Augusta* reports that he 'had very few silk garments and he never wore entirely silk fabrics or gave away clothing that was partly silk.'[31] Third century Emperors were expected to dress in silk-fashioned uniforms while overseeing military parades in Rome, but on these occasions Alexander 'never spent large sums on the standards of those on parade or on the royal outfit of gold and silk. He declared that imperial power was not based on display, but on valour.'[32]

During the military crisis of the mid-third century AD, the pragmatic Emperor Aurelian also refused to wear silk and 'would keep no clothing made of pure silk in the imperial wardrobe and would not present these garments to anyone at court' (AD 270–275). When his wife begged him to keep a single robe of expensive purple-dyed silk, he replied that 'no fabric should be worth its weight in gold.'[33]

The last emperor appointed by the Senate was Marcus Claudius Tacitus who was elected to this supreme office in AD 275. During his command Tacitus continued to wear the same togas and tunics that he had worn as a wealthy Roman citizen and he 'forbade any man to wear a garment made entirely from silk'.[34]

Silk in Male Fashion

Early Roman sources confirm silk fabric as a durable, lightweight and reflective material. When Martial received a thin metal cup as a gift from his friend Paulus, he described it as thinner 'than a spider-web and slighter than the work of a silk insect'.[35] Silk was known to be water-resistant which must have added to its appeal. Plutarch reports an ancient discussion about air density and atmospheric pressure in which an intellectual named Theon asks 'What if the same material can be both tenuous and dense like silk cloth.' He explains, 'oil does not remain on the cloth, but will run off the surface if the weave is exact and fine.'[36]

Conservative Romans thought that lightweight and sensuous fabrics such as silk were effeminate and therefore inappropriate material for male fashion. The main item in traditional male clothing was the toga, a long woollen or linen garment wrapped and draped around the entire length of the body. The traditional toga was heavy and impractical, but the costume signalled that the wearer was a legitimate Roman citizen with all the status and legal rights that this privileged position granted. Roman dignitaries and imperial office holders displayed fixed symbols of rank and authority on their togas through the use of certain coloured strips. For everyday activities a Roman citizen would have worn a practical short linen tunic similar to the clothing worn by most other people in the Empire.

The correct display of status mattered to the early emperors and Augustus insisted that Roman citizens wore togas at state events. On one occasion in 20 BC, he instructed the *aediles* (senior public officials) to prevent entry to the Forum or its neighbouring precincts to any citizen who was not correctly attired in a toga without a cloak.[37] Likewise the Emperor Hadrian ordered that all senators and *equites* were to wear the toga whenever they appeared in public.[38]

When the Roman government issued Sumptuary Laws in the Republican era, strict controls were placed on the decorative appearance of the toga. The laws were designed to preserve the recognised symbols of social rank and state authority granted by imperial office. However, because oriental silks were not available when these laws were formulated, the legislation said little about the toga fabric. The legislation prevented non-citizens from wearing the toga and the colour and decoration on the garments was strictly controlled. Most ordinary togas were off-white as this was the natural colour of the thick woollen fabric from which they were traditionally made, but Roman men also wore black woollen togas to indicate private mourning.[39] It was common practice that candidates running for office would add chalk powder to their costumes to make their togas appear whiter and more visible in a crowd.[40] Members of the nobility, including senators and *equites*, were permitted to display a purple stripe on the border of their togas to signify their higher social rank. Distinctive purple bands were displayed on the togas of magistrates and priests as a mark of office.[41] One of the highest status togas was the *toga picta* which was purple-dyed and embroidered with gold. This costume was reserved for triumphant generals and the clothing that adorned statues of the gods.[42] During the imperial period the *toga picta* was also worn by Emperors and senior magistrates to perform unique duties on special occasions.[43]

The appearance of silk in the Empire disturbed this status quo because the heavy wool used for togas was replaced with oriental materials. In particular, silk fibres were woven into the matrix of wool and linen fabric to create radiant togas in a more attractive and lightweight cloth. Oriental silk therefore offered wealthy Romans an opportunity to display status and affluence in a way that was not connected with traditional honours. A wealthy freedman wearing a white part-silk toga could visually upstage a conservative aristocrat wearing the same costume fashioned in wool or linen.

This situation was acceptable as long as silk was readily available to the upper classes who had the privilege of displaying the additional marks of status on their own togas. However, in AD 9 the Han Dynasty that ruled ancient China was temporarily usurped in a palace conspiracy and the Tarim kingdoms broke off communications with the new Xin Emperor Wang Mang. The tributary systems that sent silk into Central Asia ceased and long-distance caravans had to operate without Chinese protection. This meant that less silk reached Roman markets and supplies of the fabric became increasingly scarce and expensive. Wealthy citizens with the best trade connections could still acquire silk cloth, but this caused resentment amongst many conservative Romans who had obtained their fortunes from landed estates and publically disdained commercial activity.[44]

In AD 16, the conservative elite took action and called upon the Senate to introduce new anti-luxury legislation. Advocates of the new measures were probably concerned that wealthy citizens with business contacts might gain greater prestige than individuals with recognised nobility and traditional honours. They therefore demanded that new laws were enacted to impose restrictions as to how citizens and members of the political classes could spend their fortunes. One of these limitations involved the wearing of silk, and an ex-consul named Fronto made a strong case for banning the use of the fabric in togas and other male garments. Fronto expressed his argument in terms of morality and demanded that 'oriental silks should no longer be used by the male sex because it is degrading.'[45]

The arguments of the reformists were unsuccessful, but they made a strong case by appealing to traditional values. The matter was reconsidered in AD 22 when the Emperor Tiberius approved legislation to forbid Roman men from appearing at public events dressed in silk garments.[46] During this period oriental fabrics were disappearing from Roman markets and as silk stocks dwindled, the new law was easily enforced. But in AD 23 the Han Dynasty regained power and restored stability to the Chinese Empire. Meanwhile in Central Asia a powerful Tarim kingdom named Yarkand subdued its political rivals and secured a southern route for merchant caravans around the Tarim Basin. Within a decade the silk routes had been restored and large amounts of silk were once again reaching the Roman Empire.

The Roman ban on the use of silk in male attire was still in force in AD 37 when Caligula became Emperor. Caligula ignored previous legislation and appeared before Roman crowds wearing Persian-style silk garments. Suetonius reports that the Emperor 'wore a long-sleeved tunic and sometimes appeared in silks which men were forbidden to wear by law'.[47] This imperial endorsement made it impossible for traditionalists to prosecute any colleagues who reintroduced silk into their male attire. Soon Roman men were able to indulge in whatever silk fashions they chose, as the only impediment was conservative opinion.

The first stage of the return of silk for popular male fashion was when silk fibres were woven into the woollen fabric of togas to make the costume lighter and smoother. The incorporation of silk filaments made a cumbersome garment more comfortable and light-reflective in the summer heat. Another way to enhance the toga was for the coloured strips that denoted rank to be made from bright, opaque silk.

According to Pliny togas made from smooth cloth first became widespread and fashionable late in the reign of Augustus.[48] Quintilian refers to these garments in a metaphor to explain how traditional Roman rhetoric was being embellished by charm and emotional appeal. He writes, 'I agree with current styles and think that a toga ought to be made from smooth material. But I would not insist that silk should be woven into the fabric.'[49] In a letter promoting Stoic values Seneca asserts that nature had provided sufficient materials for each region and argues 'surely we can be clothed without trade with the Seres'.[50] But this practice continued into late antiquity and Claudian describes how in AD 395 two brothers from an influential family both held consulships. For the inauguration ceremony their mother prepared gold-embroidered togas to enhance their official rank. The folds of the togas were secured by silk cincture girdles interwoven with gold and 'gleaming with the thread which the Seres (Chinese) comb out from their delicate plants'.[51]

Most Roman citizens who could afford the cost probably opted for part-silk fabrics, especially as this material defined their public status more than anything else they owned. The scale of consumption cannot be calculated, but there were over 200,000 citizen males in the city of Rome who registered for the grain dole as a state privilege.[52] Early in his reign the Emperor Augustus calculated from census reports that between 4 and 5 million men held citizen status within the Empire.[53] Even if only a small percentage of the male population possessed silk-augmented clothing, this usage would have been significant for ancient world commerce.

During the early empire silks were worn at private events. Martial describes an overindulgent Roman named Zoilus who clothed himself in luxurious attire at his banquets. At these events the overweight Zoilus lounged on a couch wearing an 'effeminate kind of robe' effusing the scent of rich perfumes. When food was served, he sat propped up on purple silk cushions, nudging his elbows into his guests and drinking wine from crystal vases imported from Parthia. Then, before his guests had left the table, Zoilus ordered silence and fell asleep on his rich upholstery snoring loudly.[54] Apuleius also describes a Roman feast where even the table attendants were dressed in silk robes to pour wine into the crystal goblets of the wealthy guests.[55]

In time, many affluent Roman men wore tunics fabricated entirely from silk in the summer months. There was some justification for this practice, since the summer heat made other fabrics seem heavy and uncomfortable.[56] Wealthy men in Alexandria took the trend a stage further and wore silk robes dyed in bright colours and embroidered with intricate images. The Jewish philosopher Philo challenged this fashion when he asked 'Who desires thin and transparent summer robes? Who wishes for a garment as delicate as a spider's web? I tell you it is a wealthy man overly concerned with the vain opinion of others.'[57] Ausonius describes a wealthy Roman from an undistinguished family who had 'the names of Mars, Remus and our founder Romulus, woven into his silken gowns to promote his supposed ancestry'.[58]

Many Roman teachers wore a heavy woollen robe while engaged in their professional duties. This outfit was called a *pallium* and was adapted from the *himation* worn by early Greek philosophers. During one particularly hot summer in the 460s AD, Sidonius urged a friend in Rome to leave his teaching position in the overcrowded city and spend some time in the cooler climate offered at the countryside estate of a friend. He writes, 'At this time of year some men sweat in linen and others in silk, but you are wearing a heavy woollen gown over your other coverings.' He urged, 'if you have any thought of your health, promptly withdraw from the panting oppression of the town.'[59]

Silk was also awarded as a valuable prize to charioteers and this would have further endorsed the fabric as a suitable choice for male attire. Consuls in the late Empire who sponsored spectacular chariot races awarded expensive silk costumes to winning teams. The *Historia Augusta* claims that during the consulship of Furius Placidus, racing prizes had almost reached the value of patrimonies with the presentation of 'part-silk tunics, embroidered tunics made of fine linen, and even horses'.[60] Apollinaris reports that the fifth century Emperor Anthemius ordered silken ribbons to be added to the palm leaves and crowns awarded to victorious charioteers.[61] Diocletian's *Price Edict* reveals the variety of silk-based clothing available to Roman society by the start of the fourth century AD. The edict records part-silk tunics, part-silk dalmatic (long) tunics with or without hoods and plain all-silk tunics hooded or unadorned.[62] Tailors also charged for attaching smooth silk neckbands to the collars of ordinary clothing.[63]

During the imperial period Rome developed from a culture that was geared towards martial exploits to a society where many wealthy and influential people dedicated their lives to personal pleasures and the acquisition of prized possessions. Pliny reports that 'now men wear silk clothing in the summer because of its lightness and they do not feel ashamed.' He explains, 'At one time we used to wear leather military breastplates, but fashions have become so bizarre that even the toga is considered to be unnecessarily heavy.' Perhaps Pliny considered robust tunics cut in silk and styled in the Roman fashion to be just about acceptable, but long silken robes were associated with decadent eastern courts and the attire of Persian eunuchs. Pliny concludes his remarks about Roman fashion with the observation, 'at least we have left Assyrian silk dresses to the women – for the time being.'[64]

Silk in Female Fashion

Silk had a special appeal to Roman women because the fabric was uniquely alluring and attractive. Affluent Roman women enjoyed silk dresses and appreciated using silk accessories such as ribbons and parasols. Silk was expensive enough to be exclusive, yet could be woven into thin, revealing, gauze-like clothing in the style of traditional garments. Pliny claimed to know the name of the woman who originally invented the process of weaving translucent fabrics from wild Coan silks and according to tradition she was called Pamphile. Pliny comments, 'She has the undeniable distinction of having devised a way to reduce women's clothing to the appearance of near nakedness.'[65]

During the Republican period reputable Roman women dressed in a *stola*, a cumbersome ankle-length linen dress that fell in heavy folds. Horace provides a description of a respectable Roman matron surrounded by costume-dressers and attendants with her torso 'covered by an upper garment and her long robe down to her ankles'. Therefore, 'a multiplicity of obstacles hinders you from having a decent view of the lady.'[66] By contrast, affluent courtesans wore a different sort of fashion to display their sexuality. Courtesans and divorcees who had committed adultery frequently wore a shorter *tunica*, a shift dress that was usually an undergarment worn beneath the *stola*. But this shorter outfit was not thought respectable when worn without any further outer covering.

In the first century BC Ptolemaic Egypt received silks from its maritime trade with India and these fabrics were rewoven to suit the royal preference for delicate, diaphanous garments. Lucian depicts the 'fatal beauty' of Queen Cleopatra who dressed in silk in order to seduce Roman generals, appearing before them suffused in unguents and decorated with pearl jewellery. Lucian describes how 'faint beneath the weight of gems and gold, her pale breasts were visible beneath her Sidonian fabric.' He explains that her translucent garment was once a 'close-textured weave made by the skill of the Seres, but it has been separated and loosened by the needle of a Nile worker, who has stretched the fabric into a light web'.[67]

In the Augustan era, as greater amounts of oriental fabrics reached Roman markets, the use of silk was adopted by women who were not constrained by conservative opinion. This included affluent courtesans who wore delicate silk garments to reveal their figures. Propertius describes how girls were encouraged into expensive prostitution by the promise of wearing 'the pleasing weave of silk from Cos'.[68] Referring to female dress, Horace describes how a Roman man could inspect the figure of an expensive prostitute without any hindrance, because 'you can see through her Coan silk gown as if she were naked.' He compares this process to the inspection of horses sold as livestock and explains that beneath the gauze-like silks of the courtesan 'you can see if she has a poor leg or an unsightly foot and you can appreciate her whole body with your eye.' He asks why any man would risk a courtship with a respectable Roman lady and have his money extorted before he could fully inspect the 'product' on offer.[69] Alciphron describes Greek courtesans wearing silken shift dresses that were so transparent they revealed the colour of the woman's unblemished skin. He describes how one courtesan invited men to admire her as 'through her silk dress her hips swayed and she glanced over her shoulder at the movements of her buttocks'.[70]

Tibullus was infatuated by a Roman courtesan who was attended by an entourage of exotic Indian slaves. She dressed in 'a filmy web of gleaming Coan weaves with golden embroidery'. This lady dressed her attendants in contrasting purples and blues, 'to make her dress appear even fairer'.[71] Propertius also had a love affair with a girl named Cynthia who was probably a courtesan. He confronted her with the verse, 'why do you walk around that way with your hair done up and those Coan silk dresses covering your delicate breasts?'[72] According to Apuleius, 'When women wish to prove their true loveliness they should remove their dresses, slip off their garments and show their naked forms, knowing they will be better liked for the blushing glow of their skin than the gilded tissue of their silks.'[73]

Juvenal describes the appearance of the *Gladiatrix* – slave women trained to fight semi-naked in the arena. He invites his reader to 'watch her breathing heavy as she goes through her prescribed exercises' and suggests that women such as these would find even the thinnest robes restrictively uncomfortable. According to Juvenal, 'their delicate flesh would be chafed by even the finest silk gauze.'[74]

The connection between the perceived sensuality of silk fabric and overt feminine beauty became a popular theme in Augustan literature. Propertius asked, 'what comfort is found beneath coloured silk?'[75] He described his lover as the inspiration and passion behind his poetry, and because 'she moves with the gleam of Cos, my whole book will resemble Coan silk'.[76]

Some Roman authorities objected to the new silk fashions because they contravened conservative Roman ideas concerning female chastity and modesty in public. Seneca represents this view when he writes, 'I see silk dresses – but how can they be called clothing when they offer nothing that could give protection to the body or provide any modesty? A woman who wears these silks can hardly say with a clear conscience that she is not stark naked.'[77] In his tragedy, *Phaedra*, the heroine, renounces eastern fashions with the words, 'No necklace at my throat, no snowy-pearls, no gift of the Indian Ocean to weigh down my ears. Let my hair hang loose unscented by Assyrian nard.'[78]

But the disapproval shown towards silk garments had another aspect. Silks were imported at great cost from distant nations and this was possibly a greater source of concern for the Empire than any moral criticisms. Seneca explains, 'These fabrics are imported at a vast expense from nations that are unknown to our merchants, so that our matrons may show as much of their persons in public as they do to their lovers in private.'[79]

Over time silk gained respectability as a material for female fashion, especially when the wives and mistresses of the Roman Emperors began dressing in fine silk garments for public occasions. These durable and exquisitely fashioned gowns were generally worn a few times at public ceremonies and then placed in storage. This meant that the imperial household gradually accumulated a large collection of beautiful and exclusive garments. But the link between silk and sensuality remained and Martial describes a kiss from his beloved as 'more precious than the silken robes of the Empress from her Palatine wardrobes'.[80]

Eventually all classes of women began to dress in silk fabric. Moderately translucent silks allowed women to wear lightweight garments that maintained the shape of traditional dress. Chinese silk or wool-silk blends also provided a more comfortable material than standard linen. Another option was to enhance an ordinary outfit with a coloured silk shawl worn over the head to protect the wearer from the bright Mediterranean sunshine. Martial compares wine-filled crystal glasses to 'the female beauty that shines through silk folds like pebbles visible in clear waters'.[81]

The widespread fashion for silk gowns probably began amongst younger Roman women. Writing in the Augustan era, Propertius advises young women, 'While springtime is in your blood and you have no wrinkles, make use of your beauty, adorn your hair and drift about in thin silk Coan dresses.'[82] But the trend was soon followed by more mature females and Horace accused Lyce, one of his former lovers, of dressing too young for her age. He describes how she was striving to look attractive in 'Coan purple silks and bright jewels', but 'these will never bring back her former glamorous self'.[83] In a poem addressed to an ageing prostitute Horace describes how 'the little works of the Stoics might prefer to rest between silken pillows.'[84] Martial writes of a woman named Galla who may have been a courtesan in her youth. She had false teeth made of ivory, applied heavy make-up and wore an elaborate wig. Martial remarks, 'Your ringlets of hair are prepared far away from your head and when you remove your silk garments at night, you remove your teeth with them.'[85] Popular Roman hair-dyes could cause long-term damage and Ovid warned Roman women to 'stop dyeing your hair or you will have no hair left.' He advised women to release their luxuriant hair from high coiffeurs and let it fall down their sides, 'like a coloured veil of silk or the strands spun from a spider'.[86]

By the mid first century AD, many affluent Roman women expected to be dressed in silk and paid high prices for this luxury. The amount of fabric required to make a single silk *stola* cost up to 2,000 sesterces and after it was tailored, embellished and embroidered, a finished gown could easily have been sold for more than 10,000 sesterces.[87] Retail prices were further increased by the cost of expensive dyes, or styles of embroidery that used thin threads of gold wire to add further value to the item. A fine quality silk dress could therefore cost more than a Roman soldier earned in a year. But for a Roman matron in a wealthy household supported by landed estates, this would not be considered an excessive expense.

Silk in Courtship

From the Augustan era, gifts were important in courtships undertaken by affluent Roman men and expensive silk garments were considered one of the most prestigious items that a suitor could offer. Propertius advised young women to give their attention to men who offered them expensive gifts but advised, 'Anyone who brings verses, rather than gifts of silken gowns, ignore him, because those recitals cost him nothing.'[88] Tibullus confirms that Roman girls asked for dresses from affluent suitors. He condemns female avarice and blames eastern merchants for bringing expensive and exotic goods back from distant lands. Tibullus cursed them 'for making girls greedy and desirous of Coan silks and lustrous pearls from the Indian Ocean'.[89] Ovid advised Roman suitors to 'favour and compliment' their mistresses and 'if she is dressed in Tyrian robes, praise Tyrian; if she is wearing Coan silk, consider Coan fashionable. If the dress has gold thread then she is more precious than gold.'[90]

Roman men who could not afford to give their lovers expensive silk dresses could opt for gifts of gold pins or colourful silk ribbons to fix elaborate hairstyles into position. During the Saturnalia festival, Martial suggests that a gold hairpin be given to a girl with the verse, 'Insert this hairpin, so that your perfume-oiled hair will not stain your splendid silk dresses.'[91] Roman women sought other silk accessories including delicate parasols to shade them from the glare of the sun. These portable canopies were carried by attendants and the fabrics were often dyed vivid colours. In a fantasy written by Apuleius, the goddess Venus appears shaded with a silk parasol held by an attendant Triton.[92] Juvenal refers to green parasols in his satires and Marital suggests these would be suitable gifts to women acquaintances during the Saturnalia.[93] Some wealthy women also had the open frames of their small private coaches fitted with silk veils and Propertius describes 'that silk-panelled coach' of Cynthia that 'drives in triumph with its wheels skimming over the cobbles'.[94]

By the late first century AD there was a silk market in Tuscan Street near the centre of Rome. When Martial complains about the cost of seducing his mistress he writes, 'She will have no dress except the very best silks from Tuscan Street and will casually ask me for 100 gold coins as though they were brass,' adding, 'if only my mistress were worthy of such presents.'[95] This suggests the cost of the garment was 100 gold coins, equivalent to 10,000 sesterces or more than six years pay for a legionary soldier.

Eventually silk items also become an integral part of traditional Roman rituals with silk established as the most sought-after material for wedding garments. Wedding ceremonies gave the bride's family an opportunity to demonstrate the affluence of their estate and this could be achieved through the display of costly garments and furnishings. During Roman marriage ceremonies a model bed was sometimes displayed in the entrance hallway of the wedded couple. The husband carried his bride over the threshold and led her to a marriage chamber decorated with symbols of fertility, including flowers and fruit. Silk drapes were often included in this display and Apuleius describes a 'bed finely and boastfully prepared, covered with silk and those other things required'.[96] When the fourth century Emperor Honorius married the daughter of a senior military commander, the nuptial chamber was decorated with 'yellow-dyed silks from China and tapestries from Sidon spread on the ground'.[97]

A Roman bride usually dressed in a simple white gown gathered at the waist by a girdle tied in a symbolic 'bridal knot' that was undone by the groom after the main marriage rites. Before the ritual, the girl's hair would be parted with a ceremonial spear point, then braided and tied up with flowers before a yellow veil called a *flammeum* was placed over her head.[98] For the affluent family, all of these items were fabricated in expensive silks.

Wealthy fathers seem to have spent fortunes on wedding attire for their daughters. Petronius had to remind parents that 'honour and virtue are the truest gems' and question 'Is it right that our brides should wear dresses like the woven wind and stand there exposed in garments as thin as air?'[99] Plutarch offers advice to a young woman named Eurydice on what was really important in a marriage. He tells her to give 'joy' to her husband and suggests that other women will admire her for this, just 'as much as they will admire your rare and precious jewels'. Plutarch confirms the costs involved in many wedding ceremonies when he addresses the bride, 'Your good character during marriage is as precious as the expensive pearls and foreign silks that have been are bought for you at such a high price.'[100] In an adventure story written by Heliodorus the lead characters are visited on their wedding day by eastern ambassadors. These 'Seres' (Chinese) bring with them 'the fabric webs of their insects, one garment dyed purple and the other white,' confirming 'the yarn was spun by the insects that are bred in their country'.[101]

Despite the cost, most Roman fathers were willing to bear the expense of silk and jewels, especially as these items were considered an addition to the dowry. When Pliny the Younger heard the tragic news that the teenage daughter of his friend Fundanus had died shortly before her intended wedding day, he wrote 'No words can express my grief when I heard that Fundanus had given the order that the money he had intended for clothing, pearls and jewels was to be spent on his daughter's funeral incense, ointment and spices.'[102] His actions probably followed traditional Roman funeral practices which also came to incorporate silk. Statius describes the elaborate funeral staged by Flavius Abascantus for his wife Priscilla. Expensive liquid myrrh, balsam and Indian incense were burned around her funeral pyre and at the centre of this display the deceased Priscilla was laid out 'on a high couch of silk beneath the shade of a Tyrian awning'.[103]

Silk in Common Usage

Paradoxically, some of the most vivid accounts of expensive Roman fashions are provided in the second century AD by a Christian theologian named Clement of Alexandria in order to condemn this extravagance. One of his main objections was that affluent women in Christian congregations were competing with each other to wear the most expensive and eye-catching costumes. He describes how this competition for status was making some Christian gatherings resemble a colourful pageant instead of a reverential congregation of equals coming together to worship God.[104]

Clement confronted these affluent women by asking, 'Why must they pursue what is rare and costly in preference to what is cheap and readily available?' He claimed that if these ladies were stripped and sold as slaves, the price of their naked bodies would be less than the value of their apparel. In terms of their own consumer-driven value system, 'the women themselves are less valuable than the cloth that covers them.' He suggested that silk fashions were indecent and harmful to society and denounced transparent dresses, arguing that these 'see-through materials barely cover the shame of the body with more than a slender veil.' He believed that tightly-fitting opaque silk garments were as objectionable because these heavier and more luxurious dresses would cling to the female figure. Although the woman's nakedness was hidden from view, 'these dresses fit close to the body and easily take its form, following the curves of the woman to reveal her distinctive female shape.' Therefore 'her whole form is still visible to onlookers, even though they do not see her actual flesh beneath.'[105]

Listing the fashions of his time Clement advises respectable Christian women to avoid 'silk shawls that flare with colour in the sunlight, luxury garments variegated with gold, fabrics stained purple, dresses decorated with animal motifs, saffron-dyed apparel, robes dipped in ointment and expensive outfits made from many-coloured layers of silk-gauze'. He also refers to the Roman practice of weaving delicate gold threads into expensive fabrics and confirms that the colour ranges for female fashion were almost limitless with every hue available from olive-green to rose-pink. He did not consider any of this clothing to be functional, but dismissed it as 'fabrics worn purely for decoration'.[106]

This Christian criticism of silk continued into the late Roman period. In the fifth century, Jerome advised Christian women to avoid relatives who took them to social gatherings held in 'the pleasant gardens of suburban villas'. He warns that any woman who wore practical clothes and a 'sober garb, might find herself put to stand among the slave youths' and 'it will only do you harm to see other women attired in silk dresses and gold brocades.'[107] Gerontius describes how a girl named Melania from a Senatorial family tried to keep her adherence to these strict Christian principles secret from her relatives. The girl was expected to honour and obey her parents who demanded that she wear silk gowns as a symbol of her social status. To meet her obligations both to ascetic Christianity and her parent's wishes, 'Melania began to wear a coarse woollen garment under her silken attire.' After Melania announced her faith to her family, her first son was born prematurely and died soon after baptism. Gerontius explains that the grief-stricken Melania 'took the occasion of her child's death to renounce all her silk garments'.[108]

But silk had also a practical functional use because it combined tensile strength with great elasticity. Apuleius describes how a domestic cook for a Roman household wore a silk binding as she went about her work dicing innards for stuffing, mincing meat and preparing soup from offal. She was 'dressed in a white tunic girdled beneath her breasts with a red silk band and as she rotated the cooking pot, she stirred it with a circular motion so that her body flexed and her hips wriggled'.[109] Writing in the fourth century, Ammianus claims, 'the use of silk was once confined to the nobility, but it has now spread to all classes without distinction, even to the lowest people.'[110]

Other professions found a use for oriental silk including Roman surgeons asked to perform amputations. The Greek doctor Galen recommended tying ligatures around arteries, 'if the exposed vessel is large or pulsates strongly'. These ligatures had to be made from a material that did not rot within the wound and Galen advised, 'If you are practising in a city outside Rome, use suture material spun from silk. Rich women in the Roman Empire often have silk thread, especially in large cities, where there are many of these ladies. If silk is not available, choose the material most resistant to decay.'[111] Modern medical research confirms that sutures made from braided silk will lose tensile strength slowly and the protein fibres will be absorbed into the surrounding tissue within two years of implantation.

For many Roman subjects oriental silk must have seemed a ubiquitous and indispensable commodity. In the Christian *New Testament* the wealth of Rome was connected to foreign imports including the traffic and sale of oriental silk. When the prophet of *Revelations* foresees the destruction of Rome, 'the merchants of the earth weep and mourn over her, for no man buys her merchandise any-more; merchandise of gold, silver, jewels, pearls and fine linen, purple, silk and scarlet.'[112]

An event towards the end of the Roman Empire indicates how oriental silk remained popular throughout the imperial era. In AD 408, a German warlord named Aleric from the Visigoth nation invaded Italy and threatened to sack Rome unless he was granted a large ransom by the western Senate. The ransom included 5,000 pounds of gold, 30,000 pounds of silver and 4,000 silk tunics. The Senate sent agents to seize garments from wealthy citizens, but people hid their precious clothing from the government bailiffs so that the full ransom could not be raised.[113] It seems that many people in Rome risked the destruction of their city, rather than hand over their prized silk garments to save the state.

Silk Route Supplies

During the Roman imperial period, silk was one of the most expensive and desirable of consumer goods available to western society, but most people in the Roman Empire had little idea about the true origin of this unique fabric. The Romans knew that there were major population groups living in the Far East and their existence was confirmed by the large quantities of silk reaching India and Parthia from a range of distant intermediaries. But great distances lay between their respective frontiers and this restricted direct contact between China and Rome.

Ancient records suggest that from the Euphrates frontier in Syria a merchant caravan would have taken at least 100 days to travel across Parthian Iran with a further 50 days to traverse Bactria (Afghanistan) in the Kushan Empire.[114] From there, it was a 25-day journey to a trade outpost called Tashkurgan which was midway between Bactria and the oasis kingdom of Kashgar on the western edge of the Tarim Basin.[115] It would therefore have taken commercial travellers at least 150 days, or nearly five months, to cross just the western section of the silk routes that led to the Tarim kingdoms.[116]

Chinese sources confirm that during periods of intense political activity more than ten state-authorised caravans left China every year for destinations along the Tarim Silk Routes.[117] This figure suggests the scale of the trade that could be conducted between China, the Tarim kingdoms and Transoxiana. Chinese accounts suggest that an Iranian caravan leaving China could consist of 600 camels loaded with 10,000 silk rolls (4 tons of fabric).[118] Ten caravans this size could export 100,000 rolls or 40 tons of silk. There were over 50 million people in Han China, so exports weighing 40 tons would represent under 1 ton of silk per million people. This is not a large figure compared with the regular tribute that the Han Empire gave to the Xiongnu nation to maintain peace on its northern frontiers. By 1 BC the Xiongnu were receiving as much as 27 tons of silk per annum from the Han government.[119] These figures may seem large, but they represent only a small percentage of ancient Chinese production. The *Chin Shu* records how in AD 204 Chinese authorities imposed a levy that required every household to supply more than a pound of silk. Records from AD 301 reveal that the imperial treasury had stockpiled 4 million *pi* (40,000 tons) of silk in its stores.[120]

Only a fraction of the silk exported from China reached the Roman Empire, but this international trade was still an important phenomenon – 10 tons of plain Chinese silk would be worth 16 million sesterces in Roman markets and provide enough fabric to make 8,000 tunics or 16,000 dresses. This is a moderate figure given that the Roman Empire may have had a population of about 50 million people by the first century AD. It suggests that perhaps only the top 1 per cent of Roman society might have enjoyed new silk materials. But a larger share of the Roman population would have received silk attire that had been pre-used or refashioned from other articles.

Roman Knowledge of China

The Romans called the Far Eastern suppliers of silk the 'Seres' meaning the 'Silk People'. The name Seres derives from the Chinese word for silk, '*si*' which the Romans probably heard from Indian or Iranian merchants. Greek-speaking Roman traders changed *si* to *ser* and derived further words from this root. The word *sericos* meant 'made of silk' and *Serica* 'the land where silk comes from'.

Roman authorities had very little idea how silk was produced in the Far East and thought it might be a vegetable fibre harvested like cotton or linen. Strabo speculated that eastern silk was 'wool dried out from certain barks' while Virgil imagined that the 'Seres comb their fine fleeces from leaves.'[121] This could be a reference to cocoons plucked directly from the leaves of mulberry trees and Pliny repeats the opinion that Seric silk was 'wool found in their woods'.[122] Writing in the second century AD, Pausanias was able to correct some of these claims when he reports that 'the Seres make their clothes from threads which are not produced from a tree, but are made by an insect that the Greeks call *ser*.' Pausanias describes this creature as 'a large beetle, like a spider, that can spin webs in trees' and offers an impression of Chinese sericulture when he reports 'the insect is reared by the Seres who build shelters for them in winter and summer, while the creatures produce fine thread which they roll around their feet.'[123] These reports probably came from Indian merchants who reached China through the overland Silk Routes.

During the early first century AD, Roman knowledge of Central Asia did not extend far beyond Ferghana on the western edge of the Tarim territories. Most educated Greeks and Romans thought that the Asian continent ended somewhere north of the Ganges and the central Himalayas.[124] In this worldview there was no place for a distant oriental empire as large as its Roman counterpart. The Romans therefore assumed that the Tarim populations who trafficked silk were the main producers of this material.

Silius imagined that the Seres experienced the effects of the Vesusius eruption near Pompeii as 'their silk-producing groves were illuminated and affected by Italian ash'.[125] In the third century AD, Heliodorus of Emesa also mentions the Seres as foreign visitors in a fictional adventure story set in Ethiopia.[126] The fourth century Latin poet Ausonius supposed that the Seres were involved in ocean voyages and writes, 'see the loose-robed Seres prepare their woodland fleeces and now over the sea, darts the merchant.'[127] But this verse comes from a poet who invented exotic themes and introduced evocative motifs as part of his genre. The reality was very different.

CHAPTER THREE

The Chinese Empire and the Xiongnu

Written accounts from early China offer an important insight into the Han Empire and its significance in the ancient world economy. Many political and religious studies survive from the Han period (202 BC–AD 220) but the most significant texts for the consideration of world events are three main Chinese histories. These are the *Shiji* (*The Historical Records*), the *Hanshu* (*History of the Former Han*) and the *Hou Hanshu* (*The Later Han Histories*).[1]

The *Shiji* written by Sima Qian describes the early history of China until about 86 BC when the author died. The *Hanshu* was based on official archives and covers the period between 210 BC and AD 9 (the Former Han Empire). This official history was begun in the mid-first century AD by a Han court official named Ban Biao. When he died, work on the text was continued by his children, his son Ban Biao and then his daughter Ban Zhao. The *Hou Hanshu* deals with the later history of the Han regime from AD 23 to 220. It was compiled in the fifth century AD by an author named Fan Ye who accessed original sources, including authentic Han court records.[2]

Another history, called the *Weilue* (*Brief Account of the Wei Dynasty*), describes a regime that emerged in northern China after the collapse of the Han Empire in AD 220. The *Weilue* does not survive, but it contained a chapter called 'Peoples of the West' which was copied by later scholars and is preserved in a larger work called the *San Kuo Chih* (*Account of the Three Kingdoms*) (AD 220–280).[3]

The Chinese called Greek civilization *Li-Jian* since its presence in western Asia originated from the conquests of Alexander of Macedon (*A-Li-Jian-der*) and his Greek successors. According to Chinese naming systems, *Li-Jian* was therefore a dynasty that gave its name to a people, just as Han China took its name from the founding Qin Empire (pronounced '*Chin*') and the succeeding Han Dynasty. When the Chinese became aware of the Roman Empire they called it *Da Qin*, meaning 'Great China' because they recognised that Rome ruled over a territory that equalled their own regime in size and political power.[4]

The Foundation of the Chinese Empire

In the third century BC, China was divided into seven powerful agricultural kingdoms, including the Qin regime that ruled lands to the west of the North China Plain. The armies of the old kingdoms traditionally went into battle with infantry and chariots, but the Qin achieved military superiority by organizing equestrian units that used the equipment and tactics of foreign mounted warriors from the Asian steppe.[5]

Between 230 and 225 BC the Qin conquered their main rivals and brought the core territories of ancient China under a single imperial regime. The Qin ruler Zhao Zheng declared himself the first Emperor of a unified China and took the name Qin Shi Huang (First Emperor Qin). The Qin Dynasty ruled for fourteen years as a strict and cruel regime, exhausting the Chinese population with burdensome requisitions that included labour services. But during this period the Qin were able to create a nation-wide, standardised system of administration and military order that successfully unified the country. In 215 BC the First Emperor Qin ordered his general Meng Tian to enlarge Chinese territory by expelling a steppe-based population of nomadic Xiongnu horsemen from the extensive bend of the Yellow River which encloses the Ordos Desert. Meng Tian commanded 100,000 troops and a further 200,000 men were brought into service as soldiers, labourers or colonists.[6] This force conquered all lands south of the Yellow River and extended the Chinese frontier north to the foothills of the Yin Mountains which stretch almost 1,000 miles along the edge of the Gobi Desert.

After this conquest, Meng Tian began to consolidate and expand the northern border defences of ancient China to create a more unified system known to the ancient Chinese as *The Wall of Ten Thousand Li*, or the 'Great Wall' to modern scholars. The Great Wall included components from previous kingdom-defences that had guarded passage between semi-wilderness steppe lands and the agricultural territories settled by Chinese populations. This discontinuous line of fortifications stretched more than 3,100 miles (10,000 li) across the northern borders of the Chinese Empire from the Korean Peninsula to the western edge of the Ordos Desert. The defences used natural topography including woodlands and mountains that blocked or impeded the passage of horse-riders from the steppe. Sima Qian explains that Meng Tian 'utilized the natural mountain barriers to establish the border defences, gouging out the valleys and constructing ramparts and building installations at other points where they were needed.'[7] In the winding passes of the Yan Mountains, lookout posts and rubble drystone walls were constructed across gullies and ravines. Along the western frontier longer sections of the wall stretched across low hills, blocked river floodplains or extended in a continuous line across rolling grasslands and desert margins.

During its two-year construction period, tens of thousands of civilian conscripts were transported to the frontiers and organized into work teams to cut timber, quarry stone, dig trenches and build ramparts. Stretches of wall built along the steppe lands were made from compacted earth excavated from deep trenches. One work team would erect a high timber frame to support two parallel screens made from bamboo or poplar poles. Rubble, gravel, branches and soil excavated from the external ditch were packed into the space between these screens and pounded down to create a solid earthen barrier. Then the wooden frame was removed and the exposed earthen wall was coated with a rough clay mix that was allowed to dry in the sun. Meanwhile the wooden frame was carried further down the construction line for the next section of the wall. The composition of the wall depended on local resources and in some regions the clay-like earth made a firmer barricade, while in other areas the fine dusty loess added calcium carbonate to create a cement-like hardness to the structure. Some of these rammed-earth barriers were up to 18 feet high and 6 feet wide. These long-running ramparts and ditches permanently disfigured the Chinese landscape and it was said that after completing the wall Meng Tian was filled with remorse for having 'cut through the veins of the earth'.[8]

The Great Wall included an integrated network of garrison forts and outposts with watchtowers and signalling stations. The forts had stables and a courier system to deliver dispatches between garrisons, while 'all-clear' signals were conveyed between outposts using flags. The towers were fitted with signalling beacons consisting of a fuel bucket attached to a long pivoted beam that could be swung 40 feet into the air if mounted steppe raiders were sighted. In total more than 10,000 soldiers were required to garrison the frontier forts and watchtowers along the wall. In addition, up to 60,000 colonists were settled along the frontier in farms and irrigation works designed to provide food, equipment and infrastructure for the border garrisons. Sima Qian records that Meng Tien 'built forty-four walled county towns and populated them with people sentenced to guard the borders'. These figures suggest that some of these new frontier towns might have been assigned more than 10,000 people as occupants or field workers. Meng Tien also established an important new transport and communication route along the frontier called the 'Direct Road'.[9]

The Emperor Qin Shi Huang extended the scope of Chinese civilization, but he was also remembered as a cruel and despotic ruler who gave orders for historical scrolls to be systematically burned and had dissident scholars put to death by being buried alive.[10] Qin Shi Huang died in 210 BC leaving his empire to his inexperienced son Qin Er Shi, who was less than 20 years old. Within a year the Qin Empire was subject to a series of regional uprisings that led to fighting between rival Chinese warlords. One of these warlords was a popular leader named Liu Bang who began his rise to power as a minor provincial official. At the start of the civil unrest, Liu Bang was tasked with delivering a large convict workforce to the enormous mausoleum and burial mound of the first Emperor Qin at Mount Li (Shaanxi Province). But when severe weather delayed his arrival, Liu Bang decided not to face the strict punishment imposed on those who failed to meet the imperial schedule. So he released his captives and went into hiding as their leader. The fugitives formed the basis of Liu Bang's rebel army which grew to include peasant militia and dissident regiments from the Chinese military. During the ensuing power struggles Liu Bang acquired the title 'Regent of the Han' and after defeating his military rivals he seized supreme power in the capital city. Liu Bang reunified China, changed his name to Gaozu and established the Han Dynasty that ensured centuries of security and prosperity. But as a tribute to the Qin, the land became known as 'China' or 'the Middle Kingdom', since the Chinese nation seemed to be positioned at the centre of the known universe.[11]

By the second century BC the Han Empire was the largest regime in the ancient world with a population revealed by census records to be greater than 50 million people.[12] But the Han had powerful rivals on the Asian steppe lands that lay to the north and west of central China, including a confederation of mounted nomads known as the Xiongnu ('Hun-nu' or Huns). Faced with these opponents, the Han government used silk to devise commercial strategies that would guarantee the long-term supremacy of their empire. In particular, Han policymakers believed they could use trade exports to cause foreign powers to be economically reliant on Chinese products and manufactured items. Then, if the foreign regime did not comply with Chinese authority, the Han could impose trade sanctions that would cause economic damage.[13]

The Chinese Army

The Han Empire was capable of conducting war on a massive scale. The early Han regime used conscripts in their armies and most of the active combatants were young peasants. These conscripts were required to undergo a year's training and a year's service, before returning to civilian life with the benefit of military experience. All Chinese soldiers were supplied by the state with military equipment produced in government workshops and rations obtained as tax revenue. They had their wages paid in base-metal coins, or sometimes with standardised rolls of silk fabric that could be sold or exchanged in frontier markets. The conscription process meant that a large section of the Chinese population was experienced at bearing arms and could be easily recruited for local militia duty. This system also meant that in times of military crisis or other emergency, hundreds of thousands of ex-soldiers could be rapidly drafted into service.

In times of war the Han Empire could quickly train and field up to 300,000 recruits, but few of these men would be professional soldiers. During the later Han period the Empire probably had less than 40,000 troops permanently employed as career soldiers and these veteran units were usually posted near the capital Louyang and several key frontier stations in northern China.[14] The Later Han Empire also incorporated large numbers of mounted steppe warriors into its professional army as part of political agreements with allied powers.[15] This enabled the Chinese Empire to protect its frontiers with comparatively few troops.

The ancient Chinese developed sophisticated hand-held crossbows that could stack, then fire, racks of armour-piercing, steel-tipped bolts.[16] Chinese bowmen also attached an adjustable arrow loop to their bowstring which allowed them to shoot safety and more accurately from a wider range of angles.[17] Ancient documents recovered from the frontier region of Yinwan describe the military equipment that was stored in the western Han capital Chang'an in 13 BC. This weaponry was stockpiled for use by the existing military force and to prepare for any future campaigns on the Asian steppe. In this period the central state armoury contained more than 23 million items of equipment, including 500,000 crossbows and over 11 million crossbow bolts.[18]

The best evidence for the arms and appearance of early Chinese soldiers comes from an extraordinary archaeological site excavated near the mausoleum of the First Emperor, Qin Shi Huang, who died in 210 BC. The tomb of the First Emperor is marked by a 300-foot high burial mound known as Mount Li. The Han historian Sima Qian describes the internal tomb as a subterranean 'replica of palaces, viewing towers and a hundred officials' with 'chambers containing treasures and rare artefacts'. The centre of the complex was said to contain a vast model of the known world with a celestial chart painted on the ceiling and a map of the earth sculpted onto the floor. Pools of liquid mercury filled the depressions in this representation of the earth, creating the effect of flowing rivers and ocean expanses which shimmered in the light of long-burning whale-oil lamps. It was considered unfitting for members of the imperial harem to bear children by another man, so when the Emperor died the entire female company was put to death and entombed. Sima Qian reports that before the inner chambers were sealed, 'craftsmen were instructed to make automatic crossbows primed to shoot at intruders.' It was said that when the emperor was interred in this underground palace, his architects and leading craftsmen were also sealed inside the outer complex. Sima Qian describes how 'the inner passages and doorways were blocked and the exits were sealed to trap the workers and craftsmen inside. No one could escape the tomb and vegetation was planted on the mound so that it resembled an ordinary hill.'[19] Today, the mausoleum is covered by a giant pyramid-shaped earthen mound of reddish soil which, although it remains unexcavated, probably contains chambers resembling the halls and compounds of an imperial palace. A modern analysis of soil samples extracted from the mound reveals high levels of mercury pollution, which suggests that parts of these ancient descriptive accounts could be reliable.[20]

In 1974 Chinese farmers digging irrigation wells about a mile from the burial mound unearthed an underground chamber containing life-size figures of Qin soldiers. This 'army' was probably intended to be a 'spiritual guard' for the Emperor in the afterlife. Subsequent excavations at the site have revealed three chambers containing uniformed ranks of terracotta soldiers in a smashed or fragmentary condition. Current estimates suggest that the chambers contain over 8,000 infantry, 130 four-horse chariots and 150 cavalry horses with attendant riders. These figures were originally sealed inside three large wooden halls submerged beneath the earth. The halls resembled palace galleries joined by broad connecting passageways. The first hall contained more than 6,000 infantry in a chamber 750 feet long and 200 feet wide. The second hall was filled with cavalry, chariots and further infantry ranks, while a third hall housed officers and command staff. The complex also contained a fourth hall that appeared to be empty, but might have held provisions or other perishable offerings. The remains of burnt rafters among the smashed terracotta figures suggest that the barracks was looted and burned, probably during the uprisings that occurred after the death of the First Qin Emperor.[21]

At the time of the first emperor, government workshops already had experience in manufacturing terracotta drainage pipes for imperial building projects and this provided the skills basis for creating the replica army.[22] Different government-owned workshops were tasked with creating components which were marked with small factory stamps and then assembled near the site. The terracotta figures were cast in parts using clay moulds to manufacture the head, torso, arms and legs of each warrior.

The hollow tube-shaped legs of the replicas resemble segments of drainage pipes which confirm their design origins.[23] Around eight different moulds were used for the heads, but for each figure, distinct facial features and expressions were shaped directly onto the casts. The uniform and hairstyles of the terracotta figures vary according to duty and rank. They were originally painted in pallid hues applied to the clay, but most of the pigment has now flaked and faded. The bulk of the infantry were painted with dark red and black uniforms, while the officers were depicted in purples and blues.[24]

Over half of the infantry soldiers are depicted wearing some form of body-armour including the black-lacquered lamellar armour that soldiers wore over their torsos like a jacket. These suits were created from dozens of small leather or metal plates fastened together in a scale-like arrangement that overlapped at the shoulders. Further evidence for lamellar equipment is provided by sets of ceremonial stone armour found buried a short distance from Mount Li. The armour was made from numerous stone platelets held together by metal cords and the set included a large open-faced helmet made from skilfully fashioned stone plates. This armour was not a practical item, but its design and manufacture indicates the likely appearance of Chinese equipment made from materials which generally leave little archaeological trace, including leather, iron and steel.[25]

Each figure in the Terracotta Army was equipped with real battlefield weapons, including swords, shields, halberds and crossbows, but most of this equipment was probably looted soon after the Emperor was interred and the uprisings began. Additional terracotta figures have been found in small pits near the barracks and they have intact weaponry including straight double-edged swords preserved by a rust-resistant layer of chromium oxide. Some of the manufacture marks on these weapons date their production to between 245 and 228 BC, confirming that actual battlefield equipment had been entombed with the terracotta spirit-soldiers.[26]

The front rank soldiers armed with crossbows are depicted kneeling with their fingers poised at the trigger of weapons that were either looted in ancient times or rotted into fragments during the centuries of entombment. But in some instances the imprints of the long-decayed crossbows are preserved on the hardened loam that filled the collapsing chambers. The terracotta cavalry are depicted leading small stout horses that are barely larger than modern ponies. The cavalry possess a harness and saddle, but the riders have no stirrups, as this equipment was not developed in either China or Rome until late antiquity.

Further excavations near Mount Li have confirmed that the burial mound was at the centre of a larger complex. This complex was laid out in the plan of an imperial estate with two rammed-earth walls delineating a rectangular inner and outer quadrant. According to this design, the chambers under Mount Li formed the central palace while the terracotta army occupied the main barracks. Two fragmentary bronze carriages were found buried within the inner compound. One of these models was a half life-size replica of a military chariot and the other was a domed sleeping carriage pulled by a team of four horses. Further excavation pits dug within the inner quadrant just south of Mount Li have uncovered life-size terracotta models of court scholars and legal officials dressed in *Hanfu* (court robes). They are depicted with cords on their waistbands that held the seals used to mark their dispatches. Their equipment includes small grinding stones for powdering the minerals used to prepare inks. They carry bladed scrapers to sharpen writing tools or clean the surface of the thin wooden strips that were used to record state business. Excavations in the outer quadrant uncovered a chamber containing terracotta models of kitchen staff, and further test pits unearthed figures depicting court entertainers including strongmen, acrobats and story-tellers. Burials beyond the outer wall contained life-size bronze replicas of decorative park animals including the cranes and ducks that would have roamed the Emperor's ornamental gardens.[27]

According to Sima Qian, several hundred thousand conscripts and prisoners were transported to the site to construct the imperial mausoleum.[28] Confirmation comes from the mass burial plots uncovered nearby that include thousands of graves. Some of these graves contained pottery tiles scratched with the name of the labourer, their home district and their crime against the state. The crimes included debts to the government incurred by households when state taxes were not paid. Those who owed money to the state were expected to work off their debt in the labour camp at the rate of eight coins per day, or six coins if they could provide their own food and clothing.[29]

Additional evidence for the appearance of Chinese soldiers comes from the tombs of Han dignitaries who were sometimes buried in chambers with painted ceramic figurines representing their attendants. These included soldiers equipped with miniature weapons and depicted in non-battlefield dress. A tomb from Yangjiawan in Shaanxi Province contained a miniature army comprised of 1,800 infantry and 580 cavalry.[30] The soldiers wear white, red or black uniforms and carry tiny bronze weapons. Some of the models are depicted wearing padded felt caps and sleeveless chest armour made from lamellar plates. These finds suggest that the preferred weaponry of Han troops included crossbows, halberds or 3-foot long swords.

The Xiongnu Threat

As China was brought under the rule of the first Han Emperor, a powerful confederation of mounted nomads called the Xiongnu (Huns) achieved dominance on the Mongolian steppe. These events occurred during a period of world climate change about 200 BC; pollen particles preserved in ancient lake sediments suggest that Eurasia entered a warmer period at this time.[31] During this era grasslands and field systems become more abundant and this natural process encouraged the population growth that assisted the development of complex political systems in both China and Mongolia.

Unlike the Chinese, the Xiongnu were not a settled population and their steppe nation was formed from tribes of nomadic pastoralists who held jurisdiction over vast tracts of grassland. The Xiongnu occupied just one section of the Eurasian steppe which formed a continuous expanse of grassland stretching over 8,000 miles from Manchuria in northeast China to the plains of Hungary on the edge of Europe. The homelands of the Xiongnu were on the arid high-altitude Mongolian plateau which lay to the north of the Chinese Empire. But the Xiongnu nation also extended westwards across a broad belt of grassland known as the East Asian Steppe. This portion of the steppe extended over 1,500 miles from the prairies of Manchuria in northern China to the rugged Altai Mountains which lie deep in central Asia. The East Asian Steppe is about 500 miles broad from north to south, meaning that the ancient Xiongnu occupied a homeland larger than the combined territories of modern Western Europe. Between China and the Mongolian steppe was a wide expanse of desert known as the Gobi which formed a natural barrier between the two cultures.

The Gobi is an inland desert swept clear of soil and sand by eroding winds. It consists of low hills, bare-rock plateaus, shallow gravelly basins and wide stony plains. The desert stretches over 1,000 miles from east to west and covers an area almost 500 miles across at its broadest extent. At its western edge the Gobi merges into the broad expanse of the bleak Ordos desert which is filled with solid dunes formed from heavy clay-like sand. The northern frontiers of the East Asian steppe were subject to extreme cold and extended into Siberia where the landscape was covered by a dense belt of coniferous snow forest known as the Taiga. This forest zone continued into the Arctic Circle in a region far from the reach of urban civilization.

The climate of the Xiongnu homelands was severe with harsh winter temperatures and frequent strong winds blowing directly across the exposed plains. Precipitation was limited on the broad arid grasslands and the frost-free grazing season was short. Settled agriculture was impractical and the main livelihood of the people came from large herds of horses and horned cattle that could graze on sparse open grasslands. This livestock had to be moved regularly between territorial pasturelands to prevent overgrazing. Some of these pastures were hundreds of miles apart and this mobility made any attack on the steppe nations a difficult undertaking.

The Xiongnu people dressed in woollen textiles and lived in large domed tent-like structures known as yurts, made from animal skins and felt. Their primary diet consisted of dairy products and meat which was provided by their herds and they used dried animal dung as fuel for their fires. Their traditional alcoholic beverage was made from fermented mare's milk and when food was scarce they would drink the blood of their livestock. The Xiongnu reliance on livestock made them vulnerable to adverse climatic conditions such as severe winters or prolonged droughts. But the Xiongnu also traded with neighbouring cultures to supplement their material needs. They received gold nuggets, amber and animal furs, including sable and bear pelts, from remote northern populations living near the Taiga forests. They also valued Chinese silk which they used to line fur clothing and silk floss which they used as warm padding for quilted winter outfits.

The early Xiongnu had no cities that could be captured and no crop fields that could be seized or destroyed by invaders. Even the Xiongnu royal sites were temporary camp-like structures that could be dismantled and relocated at short notice. The *Hanshu* explains: 'They live on the northern frontier, wandering from place to place following the grass to herd their animals' and 'they have no walled cities where they stay and cultivate the fields, but each has his own land.'[32] According to the *Discourse on Salt and Iron*, 'the entire wilderness is their habitation and their homes are tents. They wear animal skins, eat uncooked meat and drink blood. They wander far to exchange goods and they remain in place only to graze cattle.'[33]

The Xiongnu menfolk were skilled warriors. Due to their livelihood as drovers they were accomplished horsemen who could shoot small prey using archery. The *Hanshu* describes how Xiongnu boys were taught to ride from a young age and learned how to shoot small birds and animals from horseback with the bow. Then, 'when they are strong and can pull a warrior's bow, they all become armoured cavalrymen.'[34] The Xiongnu continually practised for war; their tribal leaders could rapidly mobilize a large part of the male population and summon several hundred thousand warriors to fight. They fought as highly mobile mounted archers who could move quickly to encircle and attack columns of invading infantry, or cut-off crucial enemy supply lines. Iron resources were limited on the steppe which meant that most Xiongnu probably wore light armour fashioned from hardened leather. Steppe armies had a mobile infrastructure that could support campaigns hundreds of miles from their homelands, but their population could also withdraw deep into the steppe beyond the reach of an attacking force. The Xiongnu were therefore an exceptionally dangerous and elusive enemy for the early Chinese Empire.

The steppe peoples used powerful light-weight bows, known as 'composite bows' because the manufacturing process combined specialist materials that significantly increased the tensile strength of the weapon. These weapons are also described as 'reflex bows' because the bent limbs of the bow curved away from the archer until the tension of the string hooked into position. Steppe bows had a core made of sapwood with a belly (side facing the archer) layered with pliable plates of cattle horn steamed or boiled before being shaped to fit the weapon. After the bovine plates were glued in position, multiple layers of a collagen-rich preparation made from boiled sinew would be applied to the bow to increase its tensile strength. The powerful hind leg tendons of horses produced the strongest glues and coatings. This was a slow process as each layer was allowed to dry and set in a non-humid environment before a further coat was applied. But the effect was significant as this collagen coating maximized the power, range and penetration force of a relatively small and lightweight weapon. The result was a compact, but powerful bow that could be fired from horseback. Shots could be fired in quick succession with the rider drawing arrows from an open quiver. A trained rider in a wood-framed saddle could control his horse with his knees and fire on the gallop. He could turn in the saddle and, with the advantage of an elevated position, send multiple arrows into his target.[35]

The Xiongnu nomads were unified around 209 BC by a Chanyu (Khan or Chief) called Modu. The Chinese historian Sima Qian describes how Modu was the son of a tribal leader named Touman, but he was not favoured for succession and was therefore sent as a political hostage to the ruling household of a rival steppe people called the Yuezhi. When Touman ordered an assault on the main

Yuezhi camp, he expected Modu to be killed in retaliation. But Modu had been warned about the raid and stole a horse to escape, returning home to the widespread acclaim of his people. His father was forced to honour Modu's actions and gave him command of a *tumen* (a force of 10,000 steppe horsemen). Modu began to train and organize these men using new, unfamiliar methods. He used special arrows that whistled loudly in flight and trained his bodyguard to shoot as a disciplined group at a selected target. He devised training exercises and tests to guarantee the personal loyalty of his followers and ensure that his orders were followed without question or hesitation. To confirm the absolute compliance of his warriors, he shot a whistling arrow into the flank of his favourite horse. He then executed every member of his bodyguard who had not immediately followed by shooting their arrows into the wounded animal. Modu repeated the same drill with his wife as the next target and then his father's favourite horse. This was the final test and when Modu was hunting with the royal household, he suddenly fired a whistling arrow into his father Touman. Horrified onlookers saw their chief killed by a hail of arrows and Modu, with the support of his disciplined and devoted guard, had himself proclaimed as the new Chanyu.[36]

Under the leadership of Modu, the Xiongnu began to rapidly expand their territory. They subdued neighbouring nations and either absorbed their manpower as new allies or expelled the defeated tribes from newly seized land. The Chanyu commanded a ruling council from a hierarchy of commanders and administrators who were granted specific titles. Official posts were designated as either Left or Right (East or West) and the army was divided into decimal units ranging from 10 to 10,000 men. The lowest commander in this system was the Chief of Tens who could lead several decimal units. At its height the Xiongnu Empire was a confederation of twenty-four steppe divisions who were each designated a territory and governed by an appointee known as a 'Great Officer'. Each Great Officer could assemble a force of up to 10,000 fighting men under the overall command of the Chanyu. The Chanyu ruled with the assistance of two senior subordinates known as the 'Wise King of the Right' and the 'Wise King of the Left'.[37] The government was mobile, but the regime had a recognised royal settlement at Longcheng ('Dragon Site') on a spur of the Khangai Mountains in central Mongolia. The Xiongnu aknowledged territorial boundaries and conducted an annual census of subject steppe populations and their cattle herds at designated seasonal meeting sites.[38]

As the Xiongnu grew more powerful, their mounted war-bands began to launch more ambitious raids across the Chinese frontiers to plunder farm produce and loot urban products from the settled communities of northern China. In response to this threat, the First Han Emperor Gaozu launched a large-scale war against the Xiongnu to protect his frontier subjects. In 200 BC Emperor Gaozu mobilized a Chinese force of 320,000 soldiers and led a large army into the frontier zone to locate and engage the mounted warriors of the Xiongnu.[39] But in this period Chinese regiments were mostly infantry-based and they required extensive supply lines to support prolonged campaigns over long distances. The Chinese had problems with their equipment and provisions during these operations. For example, one fifth of the Chinese soldiers in the force commanded by Gaozu lost fingers due to frostbite. The main Chinese army was outmanoeuvred, ambushed and surrounded in the hills near Pingcheng (Datong, Shanxi) by a Xiongnu force that included several hundred thousand mounted warriors. After seven days blockaded by the enemy, the Emperor Gaozu was forced to concede to Xiongnu terms and promise costly gifts and bribes to Modu. In return, Modu gave his assurance that the Xiongnu would end their raids into Chinese territory. To maintain this 'Peace and Alliance' settlement, Emperor Gaozu agreed to give regular tribute to the Xiongnu in the form of food stocks and large quantities of silk. Modu approved of the terms and demanded that the Chinese Emperor present a Han princess to join his wives. This was an acknowledgement that the two regimes had become political equals or 'Brother States'.[40] Evidence from a later period suggests that the silk payments alone may have included up to 10,000 *pi* of silk per annum (4 tons).[41]

Enriched by regular supplies of Chinese products, the Xiongnu confederation increased in size and prosperity to become an even more powerful presence on the East Asian steppe. Many of the items that the Xiongnu had previously gained through raids on Chinese communities their leaders now received as political ransom. Modu distributed this food and fabric amongst his subjects and used the Han payments to reward his political allies on the wider steppe. This situation was acceptable to the Chinese because they realized that payment of tribute was less expensive than the cost of large-scale military mobilization and the risk involved in conflict with the Xiongnu. By purchasing a relative peace, Chinese authorities avoided the destructive raids along their northern frontiers that diminished agricultural production, reduced tax gains and caused disruptive movements of refugees.

Steppe Invasions: the Yuezhi, Sakas and Parthians

A nomadic steppe nation called the Yuezhi inhabited lands to the west of China, including a strategically important region called the Hexi (Gansu) Corridor. This arid territory lay at the base of the Tibetan Plateau where a series of oasis sites allowed passage from Central China through a broad corridor of land leading northwest onto the Asian steppe. The Yuezhi maintained generally peaceful relations with the Han Empire and obtained Chinese goods through large-scale trade exchanges. In return for silk and other Han produce, the Yuezhi offered the Chinese a valuable green ornamental stone called jade which they acquired from their contacts in inner Asia. As the crops, land and climate of central China were not good for horse rearing, Yuezhi traders also offered the Chinese army prized horses bred from their own large herds. These animals were an important resource for the Han military which faced the prospect of future war against the mounted Xiongnu.

Shortly before 176 BC, the Xiongnu attacked the Yuezhi and forced them from their traditional grazing lands in the Hexi Corridor. The Yuezhi fled west into Central Asia and escaped to somewhere so remote that it was beyond the knowledge of the Chinese regime. The Xiongnu then moved south to occupy the

Hexi Corridor themselves and in 174 BC the Chanyu sent a letter to the Han Emperor informing him that 'because of the excellence of his warriors and the strength of his horses, the Xiongnu has exterminated the Yuezhi. Every member of that nation has been slaughtered or forced into submission.'[42] The Chinese learned from foreign informants that Laoshang, the son of Modu, had ordered the skull of the Yuezhi Chief to be made into a ceremonial drinking goblet.[43]

Later Chinese records indicate that the surviving Yuezhi migrated thousands of miles westward along the foothills of the Tien Shan mountain range which forms the southern limit of the Central Asian Steppe. Over several decades they migrated almost 2,000 miles west of their Hexi homelands to arrive on steppe territories near the northern reaches of the Oxus River. The Oxus (Amu Darya) is one of the longest rivers in Inner Asia, flowing over 1,500 miles in a south-north direction from glacial sources in the Pamir Mountains (Tajikistan) through northern Bactria (Afghanistan) to discharge into the inland Aral Sea. As the Yuezhi moved west they defeated and expelled a nomadic steppe nation called the Sakas who fled south into Bactria.

Bactria was part of the ancient world already known to classical Greco-Roman civilization as the region that had been conquered by the Macedonian King Alexander the Great (334–323 BC). Alexander and his successors settled thousands of Greek and Macedonian colonists in Afghanistan to guarantee their control over this distant region. After the death of Alexander and the division of his empire, Bactria came under the control of the successor Seleucid regime which ruled territories stretching from Syria across Iraq to northern Afghanistan. But the Greek governors of Bactria revolted in 250 BC and established an autonomous kingdom in the region. By 200 BC Bactria had become a well-urbanized and wealthy Greek kingdom ruled by fully autonomous kings.

In this same period a territory called Parthia in northeast Iran also gained independence from the Seleucid Empire. Parthia was ruled by a steppe nation called the Parni who had invaded and occupied this part of northern Iran in 238 BC. The Parni assimilated the indigenous Parthian population and despite ruling over an urbanized region, they maintained their traditional fighting style as mounted steppe archers. By 140 BC the Seleucid Kingdom was in serious decline and was losing its political and military authority in western Asia. The Parthian King Phraates II therefore planned conquests to claim Iran and Iraq from the Seleucid regime.

King Phraates II took advantage of population movements on the steppe and offered the displaced Saka war-bands a position in his armies. However, the Saka were slow to send assistance and their horsemen arrived to fight in Iraq after the main Parthian army had already captured Babylonia from the Seleucids. By that time Phraates II was preparing to attack Syria and because he no longer required or trusted his new allies, he ordered them to return to Transoxiana (the Oxus territories). The Saka were insulted by their dismissal and disappointed by the loss of plunder promised from the Seleucid wars. Consequently on their return journey through Iran they renounced the treaty terms and began to rampage through the rich homelands of the Parthian realm.

Phraates II was forced to call an immediate halt to his planned Syrian campaign to deal with this unforeseen threat. He reasoned that Greek mercenaries captured during his battles against the Seleucids could be induced to fight for the Parthian cause and he ordered thousands of these infantry troops to march east to wage war against the Sakas. But the Greek soldiers were opportunists who despised their Parthian masters and when they were assembled on the battlefield to engage the Saka, they turned to attack the Parthians instead. Phraates II was killed in the fighting and the mounted Parthian army fled the battlefield in disarray. The Greek mercenaries then marched back to Syria, while the Sakas returned to Bactria.

In 124 BC, the Yuezhi also decided to test the strength of the Parthian realm by launching an invasion from the east. This conflict is described by Roman historians who refer to the Yuezhi as the Tocharians. Justin reports that the Parthian King Artabanus was mortally wounded in a battle against the Yuezhi and the regime seems to have lost their outlying eastern territories to these new steppe invaders.[44] By 100 BC, an isolated oasis called Antiochia Margiana (Merv) had become the main eastern outpost of the Parthian Empire.

The Xiongnu Threat

By occupying the Hexi Corridor the Xiongnu gained greater access to the resources of Central Asia and became an increased threat to the Chinese Empire. During the 170s BC the Xiongnu began to breach the terms of their 'Peace and Alliance' treaty with China by crossing the Great Wall and raiding Han territory with greater displays of force. In 177 BC a Xiongnu force moved south to occupy Peiti Commandery located near the Great Bend of the Yellow River and entered the nearby Shang Commandery (Shaanxi Province). The Xiongnu only withdrew when the Han government mobilized 85,000 cavalry and sent a large army north to expel the occupying force.[45]

In 169 BC the Emperor Wen convened a council of ministers to explain to him what advantages the Xiongnu possessed in warfare. The Emperor was informed 'the Xiongnu horses are better at ascending and descending hillsides, crossing river torrents and streams. Their warriors can shoot arrows while riding along difficult roads and sloping narrow passages. Mounted Chinese soldiers cannot match this skill.' It was also explained that the typical Xiongnu warrior had a greater capacity for enduring 'wind, rain, fatigue, hunger and thirst' than his Chinese counterpart. The Chinese had the advantage on level terrain where they could deploy ordered ranks of soldiers armed with halberds and long-ranged multi-shot crossbows. The Emperor was advised, 'if the ranks are well armoured and advance together with sharp weapons and repetition crossbows, they will overcome the Xiongnu. Specially trained troops must fire rapidly so that their arrows hit their targets together in a single stream. If this is achieved, the leather armour and wooden shields of the Xiongnu will not be able to protect them.' If the enemy horsemen dismounted to fight on foot they would be easily defeated in close quarter combat since 'the Xiongnu lack infantry training'.[46] During this debate the Emperor received proposals to formally accept units of refugee and surrendered steppe warriors, including dissident Xiongnu, into the Chinese army. These soldiers were to be equipped in their native fighting styles and placed under the direct command of Han officers.[47]

Xiongnu raids continued throughout the 160s BC with tens of thousands of horsemen moving into the frontier Han territories to graze their livestock and seize resources from the Chinese agricultural population. These occupations would last for months and result in crop-fields being trampled and tax resources lost. In 158 BC a force of 30,000 Xiongnu moved into Shang Commandery on the northeast frontier while another 30,000 occupied the Commandery of Yun-chung.[48] But when the army of the Han mobilized and moved north to repel the invaders, the Xiongnu would avoid a decisive battle by retreating back into the steppe taking with them thousands of Chinese captives including skilled craft-workers. Sima Qian explains, 'the Xiongnu are skilled in the use of troops that lure the enemy into an ambush. When they see the enemy they look for booty and descend like a flock of birds. When they meet with hardship and defeat, they disintegrate and scatter like clouds.'[49]

Economic Strategies

Rather than risk direct warfare the Chinese developed economic strategies to control their foreign enemies. One of these policies involved the establishment of border markets that could supply Chinese goods to foreign populations who might otherwise resort to raiding to acquire what they wanted. The Han realised that they could use these exchange centres to bring valuable steppe resources under Chinese possession. Chinese accounts confirm that 'the Xiongnu were greedy, delighting in the border markets. They longed for Chinese goods and the Han allowed them to trade in the markets in order to diminish their resources.'[50]

Significant border markets first appeared in the reign of the Han Emperor Wen (180–157 BC) when some Chinese commanders began to establish camp markets near their military outposts on the frontier.[51] Steppe dwellers and other frontier peoples could visit these military-managed sites to acquire silk fabrics and other state-issued materials. In return the soldiers received useful products that were not part of their regular supplies. The success of these initiatives encouraged the Han government to devise larger purpose-built commercial establishments on the frontier.

Under the Emperor Ching (157–141 BC) the Han regime founded a series of large border markets near well-guarded gateways in the Great Wall.[52] A Chinese study called the *Hsin Shu* explains the operation of this policy which was designed to make the Xiongnu economically dependent on Chinese products. The Chinese recognised that 'the Xiongnu badly need the border markets and have sought desperately to obtain them from us, even resorting to force.' Therefore the government 'should immediately establish many border markets in locations of strategic importance'. The scheme required that 'each of these market sites must have sufficient military forces for self-protection. Every large border market should include shops which specialise in selling raw meat, wine, cooked rice, and delicious barbeques. All the shops must be large enough to serve 100 or

200 people.' This would ensure that 'the markets beneath the Great Wall will surely swarm with the Xiongnu'. Once this economic dependency was established then the Chinese could exert political pressure on the Xiongnu by threatening to withhold or limit their access to Han products. The *Hsin Shu* explains, 'if the Xiongnu kings and generals try to lead their people away, they will be defied by their followers. When the Xiongnu have developed a craving for our rice, stew, barbeques, and wine, they will have a fatal weakness.'[53]

At the border markets the Xiongnu could acquire Chinese materials by exchange, rather than invasion. The Xiongnu traded wool, leather, jade, horses and donkeys for Chinese silks and grain stocks including wheat and millet. The *Discourse on Salt and Iron* describes 'unbroken lines of mules, donkeys and camels entering the frontier'. The steppe people offered horses, 'furs of sables, marmots, foxes and badgers, coloured rugs and decorated carpets, jade and auspicious stones, corals and crystals'.[54] Sima Qian confirms that the policy was successful and although the 'Xiongnu became bolder, they did not carry out any major invasions during the reign of Ching'.[55]

Chinese texts from the first century BC explain the economic policy that promoted Chinese interests in maintaining these markets. The *Discourse on Salt and Iron* explains that 'a piece of plain Chinese silk can be exchanged with the Xiongnu for articles worth several pieces of gold and we can thereby reduce the resources of our enemy.' Silk was a renewable product for the Chinese economy and therefore 'new goods are received while the government retains abundant supplies. National wealth is not being dispersed into foreign countries and the people enjoy abundance.'[56]

Within a few decades of their establishment the border markets were an important strategic interest and a focus for negotiation. When the Emperor Wu (141–87 BC) wanted to launch surprise retaliatory attacks on the Xiongnu he sent four generals, each in command of 10,000 cavalry, to the crowded border markets.[57] When the Xiongnu made peace proposals in 98 BC they requested that the Chinese reopen the largest border markets and allow the Xiongnu admittance.[58] The scale of this frontier commerce is demonstrated by an event in AD 135 when steppe raiders from the Wuhuan nation crossed the northeast frontier and robbed a Chinese caravan that included over 1,000 ox-drawn wagons (500 tons).[59]

During the second century BC, the Xiongnu court received senior defectors from the Han regime. These men warned the Xiongnu leadership that the Han were devising economic strategies to bring the steppe nations into compliance by making them dependent on Chinese goods. Once this dependence was established, the Han hoped to coerce the Xiongnu into submission by restricting access to their market goods. A Chinese traitor advised the Xiongnu, 'the strength of the Xiongnu comes from the fact that their food and clothing are different from those of the Chinese and they are not dependent upon the Han for anything. But now the Chanyu has fondness for Chinese things and this is changing Xiongnu customs.' He warned, 'although the Han sends no more than a fifth of its goods here, it will eventually succeed in dominating the whole Xiongnu nation.'[60]

CHAPTER FOUR

The Discovery of the West

When the Emperor Wu came to power in 141 BC he was determined that the growth of the Xiongnu nation should be checked by military action. He therefore planned large-scale campaigns to break the power of the Xiongnu in the grasslands of Mongolia and the unknown regions of Central Asia. These initiatives established the first direct contacts between Chinese civilization and the urbanized kingdoms of ancient Transoxiana, Afghanistan, India and Iran. This was the origin of the Central Asian Silk Routes which created an unprecedented growth in international commerce that enhanced and enriched distant regimes, including Rome.

The Han Offensive

The first stage in the Han offensive against the Xiongnu was to gain allies on the Asian steppe who would agree to fight alongside Chinese infantry regiments, or provide the Han military with good stocks of effective cavalry horses. At this stage the Chinese did not know where the Yuezhi had settled after their escape into the west, so the Emperor Wu sent an envoy named Zhang Qian to find a route through Central Asia and make contact with their old allies. Zhang Qian was given command of a party of 100 Chinese soldiers, scouts and advisors, including Xiongnu defectors and former prisoners who had sworn allegiance to the Han.

In 139 BC, Zhang Qian left the western frontiers of the Han Empire and set out across the steppe into dangerous unknown territories. The expedition headed north-west through the Hexi Corridor to the alpine-like ridges of the Tien Shan Mountains. North of the Tien Shan Mountains was open steppe where foreign interlopers could be easily captured by the Xiongnu and their mounted allies. South of the Tien Shan Mountains the inland core of Central Asia was a vast arid expanse and the Han party were last reported heading west towards the formidable sand-filled Taklamakan Desert. When all contact ceased, the Han government assumed that Zhang Qian and his followers had succumbed to the extreme environment, or had been captured and killed by steppe raiders.[1]

Emperor Wu therefore accepted that China could not expect foreign assistance against the Xiongnu enemy and prepared the Han population for full-scale war. Large numbers of Chinese peasants were conscripted, trained, armed and readied for the planned conflict. But war against the Xiongnu was a difficult prospect as Chinese armies would need to make long-distance expeditions into the steppe to seek out mobile hordes of Xiongnu horsemen. These campaigns involved over-extended and vulnerable supply lines and Chinese battle-groups could expect setbacks and defeat far away from rescue or reinforcement. The Emperor Wu therefore decided to engage the Xiongnu within Chinese territory.

It was well known that trade was important to the Xiongnu and that they frequently visited the Chinese frontiers to offer valuable animal furs in exchange for silks and other manufactured goods. They sought Han metalwork and were supplied with iron and steel by Chinese smugglers who were prepared to risk the death penalty to offer these contraband goods. This suggested a way for the Chinese to lure the Xiongnu into a military trap that would devastate their fighting forces in advance of an offensive.

In 133 BC, a leading smuggler named Nie Yi offered to betray the Chinese frontier city of Mayi to the Xiongnu. Nie Yi and his band of men promised to open the city gates to admit the Xiongnu, who could then plunder the city and capture the Chinese workers engaged in various urban trades, including the production of steel. The Chanyu was enthusiastic about this prospect and assembled 100,000 of his best horsemen to ride against the city. But this opportunity was a carefully orchestrated trap and Nie Yi was actually an agent working for the Han government. Ahead of the Xiongnu attack the Chinese deployed 300,000 soldiers in the Shanxi region, concealing them in the district around Mayi (modern Shuozhou). The highway to Mayi was cleared so that the Xiongnu would have an unobstructed approach towards the fortifications of the city. At a given signal, the Chinese army planned to encircle the Xiongnu and block their retreat back into the steppe lands. They hoped to kill and capture the bulk of the enemy fighting force. But this plan involved removing the peasant population from the conflict zone and when the Xiongnu rode towards Mayi, they realised that the surrounding fields were empty of people and livestock. Sensing that something was wrong, the Chanyu called an immediate halt to the raid and fled before the Chinese could fully launch their assault.[2]

The Chinese then attempted to defeat the Xiongnu by destroying the livestock the steppe population depended upon for their core economic wealth. In 129 BC, Emperor Wu sent two large armies into the Mongolian steppe to attack the Xiongnu at one of their main sacred sites. This military action began a decade of campaigns to drive the Xiongnu from the outer fringes of the Gobi Desert and the southern part of their steppe homelands. During the conflict the Han settled thousands of Chinese colonists in Inner Mongolia and established a new frontier city named Shuofang at the northern limit of grasslands suitable for agriculture. Shuofang was created at the centre of a militarized buffer-zone and the city became a staging post from which Chinese forces could conduct further campaigns into the Mongolian steppe.[3]

In 123 BC the Han army launched several major campaigns into the steppe that resulted in 19,000 Xiongnu warriors being killed. But Chinese losses during the course of this war were severe and over 100,000 soldiers and horses were killed or incapacitated during the fighting. To maintain morale the Emperor took large reserves of gold from the treasury and distributed this wealth as ingots to his successful troops to reward their services.[4]

Han Battlefield Tactics

Several incidents during this period reveal the effectiveness of Chinese tactics, equipment and leadership. In 120 BC a Han general named Li Guang commanded a supporting battlegroup of 4,000 Chinese cavalry in combat against a large mounted horde of Xiongnu warriors. Li Guang was sent into the steppe to reinforce the main Han army who were operating deep within enemy territory. However, after several hundred miles the column led by Li Guang was intercepted by more than 40,000 Xiongnu horsemen. At first the Xiongnu concealed their full numbers and sent forward a small advance guard to engage the Chinese force. The Xiongnu planned a fake retreat to lure part of the Han column into an ambush prepared some distance from the main battle site.

But General Li Guang was familiar with this common tactic and sent a token force forward to trigger the feigned retreat. The historian Sima Qian explains: 'When the Xiongnu appeared the Chinese troops were all terrified, but Li Guang ordered his son Li Gan to gallop directly at the enemy with only twenty or thirty riders. He knew that this would send them into feigned retreat.' When the enemy fled, Li Gan did not pursue them, but abruptly turned and rode back to his father. Li Guang announced to his battlegroup that the Xiongnu were cowards and reassured his troops that the enemy were unprepared for battle.

The main Xiongnu hoard waited at the planned ambush site, but as the feigned retreat had failed, they regrouped to ride directly against the Chinese column. Li Guang suspected that a large-scale attack was imminent and used the delay to move his battlegroup into better defensive positions. He ordered his cavalry to dismount and arranged his forces into a circular formation to withstand an enemy force that was almost ten times their size. The Chinese soldiers waited for the coming onslaught with their bows and crossbows loaded and ready. Sima Qian describes how 'the Xiongnu charged furiously down on the soldiers and their arrows fell like rain. Over half the Han soldiers were killed and the arrows of the remaining troops were almost entirely gone.' As the Xiongnu encircled their position, General Li Guang ordered a sudden halt to the Chinese missile fire. He calculated that the unexpected ceasefire would cause the distinctively clad enemy commanders to expose themselves to view. Sima Qian reports, 'Li Guang readied his large, long-range, yellow crossbow and he shot the sub-commander of the enemy force and killed several other leading Xiongnu.' With their front-line commanders suddenly dead or injured, the enemy riders began to fall back from the battlefield.

As night fell the Chinese soldiers began to despair at the size of the Xiongnu army surrounding their position. Sima Qian reports that 'every one of the officers and troops turned pale with fear, but Li Guang was calm, confident and appeared unaffected. He worked to get the Chinese ranks into better formation until his soldiers realised that no one could match him for his bravery.' On the third day of combat a relief force from the main Han army reached their position and the Xiongnu fled the battle site. General Li Guang's force had suffered heavy losses, but this was a war of attrition and they had managed to inflict large-scale casualties on their attackers. Consequently this engagement was judged to be a military success.[5]

The following year, 119 BC, the Chinese launched another major offensive against the Xiongnu. Two large Chinese armies, each consisting of 100,000 infantry and 50,000 cavalry, were tasked with crossing the Gobi Desert to enter the homelands of the Xiongnu nation. As the Xiongnu retreated into northern Mongolia, they hurled dead animals into the streams to pollute the water courses used by the pursuing Chinese armies. The contaminated water caused an outbreak of disease amongst the Chinese who were forced to withdraw when their overstretched supply lines proved insufficient to meet their increased needs. It seemed that the Han generals had reached their operational limits on the northern steppe and conflict on this scale was exhausting the Chinese capacity for war. The Chinese army had lost four-fifths of its cavalry corps during the fighting, but the campaign was considered to be a success because an estimated 90,000 Xiongnu warriors were killed during the conflict.[6]

For the next two decades the Chinese continued to launch punitive expeditions into the Mongolian steppe to challenge the Xiongnu and damage their capacity for war. One of the best recorded expeditions involved an infantry force consisting of 5,000 veteran soldiers led by an experienced Han general named Li Ling. In 101 BC Li Ling led his regiment north into the Mongolian steppe in an attempt to provoke an engagement with the Xiongnu. His regiment was barely the size of a single Roman legion, but each man was trained and equipped for steppe warfare. They wore jacket-like coats of lamellar armour fashioned from rawhide leather or steel platelets and carried bows for trajectory missile-fire and crossbows for long-range marksmanship. They travelled with a defensive line of reinforced supply wagons carrying a store of half a million steel-tipped arrows and crossbow bolts. Li Ling marched his regiment several hundred miles into Xiongnu territory and then waited for the enemy to attack.

On the chosen battlefield, the Chinese supply wagons were drawn up into a defensive ring with the soldiers arranged in ranks around this protective position. The front-line troops were equipped with long steel pikes to deter oncoming cavalry charges, while the inner ranks were placed in dense order and stood ready to fire bows and crossbows at any approaching targets. Above the noise and confusion of battle, drums and gongs were used as signals to issue attack orders and control the rate of missile fire. Small hand-pushed wheelbarrow carts brought forward new missiles and removed any wounded soldiers from the front ranks. Only when the enemy cavalry broke their formation in disorder was a signal to be given to advance. When this occurred, the infantry rushed forward and engaged the Xiongnu riders in close-quarter combat using their long steel-bladed swords to stab and hack at the enemy. Each man defended himself with a small ridged shield raised above his head to deflect the downward blows from their mounted opponents.

The first engagement was a victory for the Han, but the Chanyu himself was leading the Xiongnu attack and his reputation rested on annihilating this small Chinese regiment. For eight days General Li Ling withdrew his battlegroup towards the safety of the Han frontier, a distance of more than 250 miles. Throughout this period he maintained a well-ordered retreat with the wounded being wheeled along on hand-drawn carts as his regiment was relentlessly pursued and harassed by the enemy. Meanwhile the Chanyu sent riders to summon a Xiongnu force of 80,000 mounted archers to ensure the eradication of the Chinese. They surrounded and ambushed Li Ling in a valley, but his crossbow-armed troops were able to drive the Xiongnu archers from the surrounding hillsides and resume their trek towards the Chinese border fortifications.

By the time Li Ling had reached a mountain pass close to the Han frontier, his regiment had almost entirely exhausted its supply of missiles. Li Ling waited for the cover of darkness and then smashed and buried his regimental battle-standards rather than risk their seizure by the enemy. Then, with what remained of his mounted guards, he rode out of his camp creating a loud distraction that gave many of his surviving troops an opportunity to escape into the surrounding hillsides. Scarcely 400 of his soldiers made it safely back to the Chinese frontier and Li Ling himself was overtaken and captured by the Chanyu. His regiment had killed almost 10,000 enemy warriors, but the Emperor Wu considered the military expedition a defeat. A court scholar named Sima Qian tried to defend the general by arguing that Li Ling had performed a heroic endeavour against impossible odds. The Emperor was provoked by this objection and he ordered that Sima Qian be condemned for committing a 'grand insult' against imperial authority. Sima Qian was removed from his imperial position and subjected to the humiliating penalty of castration. However he did not commit honourable suicide as expected. Because Sima Qian had promised his father that he would complete a historical record of the Han era, his duty was to finish the task. His record survives as the *Shiji* (*The Historical Records*) which has become the central text for the study of Chinese Ancient History.

The Emperor Wu soon regretted his angry dismissal of Li Ling and sent an expedition force to find and rescue the general from Xiongnu custody. The mission failed, but the Chinese learnt from enemy captives that a senior Han defector was helping to train and prepare the Xiongnu to counter Han battlefield strategies. The Emperor wrongly believed that the traitor was Li Ling and in retaliation had his entire family put to death. When Li Ling learned of this, he accepted a military position in the Xiongnu regime and by marrying the daughter of the Chanyu he abandoned any prospect of ever returning to his homeland.[7]

The Chinese Discovery of the West

In 139 BC, the Emperor Wu had sent an envoy named Zhang Qian to lead an expedition into Central Asia to find their former allies, the Yuezhi. It was assumed that Zhang Qian had died in distant lands, but in 124 BC, over a decade after his departure, he returned to China with a single survivor from his original expeditionary force. Zhang Qian brought the extraordinary news that there were sophisticated urban civilizations in the distant west and this would change Chinese prospects in their war against the Xiongnu.

Zhang Qian offered the Han court a dramatic account of his mission to previously unknown regions in the distant west. He began by describing how he had been taken prisoner by the Xiongnu shortly after leaving China. He was held captive in their nomad camps for ten years, during which time he married a Xiongnu woman and had children who he raised according to steppe traditions. But Zhang Qian was waiting for an opportunity to escape and when the chance came, he fled with his remaining followers. The group evaded the Xiongnu by following the southern foothills of a vast mountain range that the Chinese came to know as the Tien Shan or 'Celestial Mountains'.

The Tien Shan range stretches almost 1,700 miles from steppe lands near the Hexi Corridor to the Pamir Mountains on the eastern edge of Afghanistan. Some of the lower slopes of the Tien Shan range are forested, but the higher peaks are covered in permafrost. This mountain range consequently forms a vast linear barrier between the Central Asian steppe to the north and to the south, a desert-filled arid wasteland known as the Tarim Basin. When Zhang Qian followed a trail along the southern base of the Tien Shan Mountains, he discovered a series of large oasis communities that had developed sophisticated urbanised cultures. Near the edge of the Tien Shan Mountains the Chinese group passed through a fertile valley known as *Dayuan* (Ferghana) which led west to the Oxus River and the new homelands of the Yuezhi. The Ferghana Valley was 180 miles long and it was almost 1,000 miles between the Tarim Basin and the Upper Oxus River.

Zhang Qian was welcomed by the leaders of the Yuezhi who still respected their past associations with the Chinese. They told Zhang Qian how they had fled from the Xiongnu and after decades of conflict and thousands of miles of travel across the steppe, they had been able to claim new territories near the upper reaches of the Oxus River. But the Yuezhi had no interest in resuming their conflict with the Xiongnu, so after a year in their company, Zhang Qian headed south into Bactria to learn more about the peoples of the distant west and perhaps secure alternative allies for the planned Han offensive.

The Greek kingdom in Bactria had been severely weakened by continual wars against neighbouring peoples and sometime about 150 BC the Parthians had inflicted a decisive defeat on the regime.[8] Saka war-bands from the neighbouring steppe territories exploited this opportunity to overrun large parts of the region and permanently end Greek rule in Bactria. Consequently, when Zhang Qian reached Afghanistan in 127 BC, he witnessed the immediate aftermath of the Greek downfall. The urban population was still recognisably Greek, but there was no overall ruling authority to unite the cities and coordinate any further defence of the territory. The Hellenic cities of Bactria were still prosperous and well-connected by commercial ties, but they could no longer field an effective military force. Zhang Qian observed that '*Daxia* (Bactria) has no great king, but only minor leaders ruling the various cities.' But the region still had a recognised capital described as a city, 'where all sorts of goods are bought and sold'. Compared with the crossbow-equipped Chinese troops, these remnants of Greek civilization were judged to be 'weak in the use of weapons and afraid of battle, but the people are clever at commerce'. Ancient Bactria covered an area about half the size of modern France and Zhang Qian estimated that its population included more than a million people.

Zhang Qian spent almost a year in Transoxiana gathering information about the nearby Parthian Empire and the distant commerce conducted by the kingdoms of northern India. He also learned about southern routes around the desert-filled Tarim Basin that could be used to evade the Xiongnu. When Zhang Qian decided to return to China, he chose to follow a trail along the base of the Kunlun Mountain range which forms the southern limit of the Tarim Basin. These mountains stretch in a low arc almost 1,900 miles from the Pamirs to the Hexi Corridor and form the outer ranges of the vast Tibetan Plateau. As Zhang Qian trekked along the base of the mountains he discovered further urban centres on the frontiers of the desert. These oasis sites were distant from neighbouring communities, but they were irrigated by melted snow from the high mountain ranges and were rich in agricultural products.

Zhang Qian survived this second journey around the Tarim Basin, but he was captured again by the Xiongnu as he approached the Chinese frontiers. He was kept prisoner for another two years until the death of the Chanyu created disorder in the nomad camps. Zhang Qian seized this new opportunity to escape and finally returned home in 124 BC, fourteen years after he had left the Han Empire. Only one member of his original expedition survived these adventures, a loyal Xiongnu scout who had remained with Zhang Qian throughout his explorations and captivity.[9]

The discoveries made by Zhang Qian were a revelation to the Han government. The west offered important prospects for advancing Chinese civilization with the opportunity for distant political alliances and the exploitation of significant new resources. Sima Qian explains: 'Thus the Emperor learned of Dayuan, Daxia, Anxi [Ferghana, Bactria, Parthia] and the other countries which were all great states, rich in unusual products and engaging in settled agriculture, like the Chinese. He was informed that these states were militarily weak and prized Chinese products and wealth. He also learned that to the north of them lived the Yuezhi and Kangju nations who are militarily very strong, but who might be persuaded by gifts and the prospect of gain to acknowledge allegiance to the Han Empire.' Success in these schemes would extend Han influence 10,000 *li* (over 3,100 miles) into the distant west.[10]

Chinese interests in the Western Regions included the acquisition of foreign crops and livestock that could transform the Han war effort against the Xiongnu. Zhang Qian described how the settled population in Ferghana cultivated grapes and produced superior wines that could be stored for decades without spoiling. The Chinese were also unfamiliar with alfalfa, a fast growing crop that provided excellent fodder for horses without the need to secure large tracks of pastureland. Han envoys were immediately sent west to bring back cuttings, seeds and the knowledge required to introduce these new crops into China. Within decades, the imperial estates around the Emperor's Summer Palace were entirely covered with foreign vegetation and observers on the multi-storey watchtowers described seeing fields of the new crops stretching far beyond the horizons.[11] Foreign vegetables introduced into China during this period included carrots, sesame and garlic, along with different forms of coriander, onions, cucumbers and beans. The new trees that were grown for the first time in China included walnut and pomegranate, orange and fig. Linen was introduced into China, along with decorative scented flowers including roses, azaleas, chrysanthemums and saffron.

The Han envoys reported that the steppe people who occupied the Ferghana Valley had access to a superior breed of horse that was said to possess unmatched speed and stamina. Emperor Wu was anxious to acquire these animals in order to rebuild the cavalry forces that China had lost in its ongoing wars against the Xiongnu. With improved fodder and superior horses, the Chinese knew they could increase their dominance and create armies that would be unmatched in steppe warfare. But first they had to secure routes of contact between China and the resource-rich territories that Zhang Qian had discovered in the distant west.

War in the West

To access the distant west the Han Empire had to gain reliable routes into Central Asia and this meant controlling the Hexi Corridor. The Hexi Corridor was a broad belt of relatively flat arid grassland almost 600 miles long that contained a chain of oasis sites along its length. The southern part of this land passage was hemmed in by the snow-capped Qilian Mountain range that extends to the high-altitude Tibetan Plateau and the vast Himalayas. The northern reaches of the Hexi Corridor were exposed to the bleak Ordos Desert, a barren tract of land with a surface swept by frequent fierce windstorms. The Ordos stretched into Mongolia and merged with the surrounding Gobi Desert.

The surface of the Hexi corridor was covered with sandy soil that supported patches of short wiry grass, camel sage and low thorny bushes. The region was subject to extremely cold winter temperatures, but in spring the limited seasonal rainfall produced tinges of green vegetation growth across the bleak terrain. The Xiongnu had claimed the Hexi Corridor, but with their new knowledge of western civilization, the Chinese had their own plans for the region.

The Han military seized control of the Corridor between 123 and 119 BC by defeating, expelling, or accepting the surrender of the occupying Xiongnu communities. The Chinese then began to garrison the region to prevent Xiongnu counter-attacks from the surrounding steppe. Thousands of Han settlers, including peasant volunteers, conscripted labourers, dissidents, convicts and refugees from famine-struck districts in China, were sent to colonize the region. They prepared the land for agriculture and populated the newly-built fortified towns and cities that were established to control the main oasis sites. Trackways were laid down between these cities and supply caravans travelled along a system of watchtowers and fortresses which enabled Chinese troops to guard the new settlers. The Great Wall was extended several hundred miles west to an outpost called Dunhuang and more than 570 watchtowers were built to monitor traffic and keep a lookout for mounted steppe raiders.

Sima Qian suggests that frontier food supply was a problem during this period and when 'the grain produced on the border was not sufficient to feed the troops, the government granted honorary titles to those who could supply grain and transport it to the border garrisons.'[12] The scale of the supply system is indicated by events in 121 BC when tens of thousands of Xiongnu from the Hexi frontier surrendered to the Chinese Empire and agreed to become Han subjects. The government sent 20,000 carriages to provide these new associates with provisions and rewards, before conveying their leaders to the Han capital. The cost was high and Sima Qian records that the combined value of diplomatic gifts and rewards to the soldiers increased state spending in that year to more than ten billion cash. Consequently, the following year, 'the government treasuries were so depleted that the fighting men received hardly any of their pay.'[13]

Within a decade the Hexi Corridor was secure and the Han Empire controlled a 600 mile conduit connecting China to the outer Tarim territories. The fortified frontier city of Dunhuang, 'Blazing Beacon', was established on the western edge of the newly settled region, receiving its name from signal fires lit to communicate with Chinese outposts positioned along the Hexi Corridor. West of Dunhuang was the Yumen Pass, known as the 'Jade Gate' because it controlled the main route into the Tarim territories that produced this prized ornamental stone. In the Yumen Pass the Han army established a military outpost and a customs station at the newly established western limit of their enlarged empire.

Beyond Dunhuang there was a parched desert region known as the 'Flaming Sands' where agriculture was impossible and sustenance could only be obtained from isolated waterholes. To cross this area, wheeled vehicles were left behind and travellers had to journey on foot across shifting sandy surfaces with lines of camels, donkeys or horses burdened with supplies. Three routes led west from Dunhuang into the Tarim territories. The northern route stretched 400 miles across the pale sands and desiccated salt fields of the 'White Dragon Desert' which lay between Dunhuang and the oasis outposts of Hami and Turfan. Turfan was a major agricultural centre positioned close to passes in the Tien Shan Mountains which led into the northern steppe. The site was therefore strategically important for trade and for the defence of the Tarim territories and the outer Chinese frontier.

The central route headed 300 miles due west from Dunhuang and Yumen Quan, the 'Jade Gate', to the oasis outpost of Loulan, 'City of the Dead'. This route followed the marshy northern fringes of a vast lifeless wasteland known as Lop Nor, the 'Salt Desert'. The centre of the Lop Nor desert was formed by the desiccated and encrusted remains of an ancient seabed with mineral residues that contaminated the surrounding watercourses. The third route headed south of Lop Nor from Dunhuang through Yang Quan, the 'Sun Gate' on a 500 mile path to the oasis settlement at Cherchen. Travellers using these routes had to carry water and food supplies along courses marked by the droppings of camels and the bones of dead animals. People avoided travel during midday, carrying bedrolls and light tents for shelter in temporary camps.

The three routes leading west from Dunhuang allowed passage into the Tarim Basin, a vast hollow in the centre of Asia encircled by some of the highest mountain ranges in the world. The Taklamakan Desert fills the interior of the

Basin with a wasteland of shifting sand that stretches over 600 miles from east to west and is 250 miles across at its geographical centre. According to these measurements the Taklamakan Desert covers an oval-shaped area larger than modern France. The greater part of the Taklamakan Desert is composed of fine red-gold coloured rock particles piled by the wind into dunes that can rise to more than 40 feet high. The desert is more than 1,000 miles from the nearest ocean and due to its extreme inland position there is virtually no cloud cover. Daytime temperature can soar above 100 degrees Fahrenheit (38°C), only to plummet below freezing during the hours of darkness (down to −20°F or −29°C).

Travellers tried to remain on the fringes of this desert by following the path of old watercourses formed by glacial streams flowing down from the surrounding mountains. Much of the journey was made at night, but some hazards could not be avoided. There were swirling sandstorms that could suffocate ancient travellers and the airflow across the desert created illusionary sounds and mirages that lured people away from the relative safety of recognised desert tracks. Sharp temperature changes caused sudden avalanches of sand from the towering dunes and these seemingly inexplicable phenomena were believed to be the actions of malevolent supernatural entities. Modern explorers using traditional caravan equipment have been able to travel the northern route around the Tarim Basin in about two months (Loulan to Kashgar in 59 days). This is a distance of about 780 miles at an average pace of 13 miles per day.[14]

In ancient times no living creature could journey through the centre of the Taklamakan Desert, but shaggy-coated Bactrian camels could travel along its outer fringes. Bactrian camels had evolved as migratory herd animals and were consequently well adapted to the extreme contrasting environments found in Central Asia. From an early period Chinese prospects in Central Asia depended on the exceptional attributes of these animals. As domesticated livestock, Bactrian camels are excellent pack animals and their unique abilities make them invaluable for long-distance journeys through difficult terrain with few natural resources.

The breed stands between 6 and 7 feet at shoulder height and has two large humps on its back that store vital reserves of body fat. Bactrian camels are covered with a dense woolly coat of thick hair that provides superb insulation when exposed to sub-zero conditions. During the warmer summer months they rapidly shed this coat to withstand the high desert temperatures encountered along their ancient migration routes. They have evolved tough flat footpads with two broad toes on each foot. This allows them to traverse a variety of landscapes including slopes covered in icy snow, rocky plains with sharp stones, or shifting desert sand dunes. Long lashes protect their eyes and sealable nostrils keep out dust and sand, allowing them to withstand the abrasive sandstorms which are frequent occurrences in their desert habitats. Bactrian camels also have well-developed vision and an acute sense of smell that can locate water and vegetation from a considerable distance. The toughened mouths of Bactrian camels can crush thorns and their digestive systems can consume vegetation that is too prickly, dry or salty to be eaten by other livestock. They can drink brackish water and are one of the few animals that regularly eat snow without their body temperature lowering to dangerous levels. They can trek up to five days without water and if they have access to vegetation they can endure weeks of travel without drinking. Their humps become limp and flabby as their fat is depleted, but recovery is rapid and a thirsty camel will drink up to thirty gallons of water in fifteen minutes.

The usual practice for Central Asian caravans was for the camels to carry supplies, cargo and water, while the travellers walked alongside. Bactrian camels can carry loads of up to 1,000 pounds, which is double the weight borne by Arabian camels with their more slender and less robust frames. As pack animals, they can walk long distances at a relentless pace, normally covering about 15 miles in a day. Bactrian camels are also highly sensitive to environmental changes and they will try to cluster together when they perceive the approach of fierce suffocating sandstorms. This gives advance warning to the caravaneers to halt the caravan, secure their possessions and instruct the travellers to cover their faces with thick felt wrappings.[15]

Chinese expeditions crossed the Tarim territories by following a series of oasis settlements watered by seasonal streams of melted snow that flowed down from the surrounding mountain ranges. The oasis kingdom of Loulan was on the eastern edge of the Tarim Basin and from this outpost it was a 600 mile circuit around the Taklamakan Desert with travellers either following the northern or southern route. One trail led north along the upper fringes of the Taklamakan Desert and the foothills of the Celestial Mountains (the Tien Shan mountain range) that extend over 1,100 miles across central Asia and contain peaks up to 20,000 feet high. The other route headed south along the lower reaches of the desert where the Kunlun mountain range rises up to the edge of the Himalayas. The Himalayas are breached by mountain passes that are at least 18,000 feet above sea level. The western end of the Tarim Basin was enclosed by the Pamir Mountains which merge into the Karakoram and Himalaya ranges. These routes around the Tarim Basin were restricted by geography and climate, access to water supplies and the compliance of intervening communities. Consequently, during this period, the journey was extremely difficult and dangerous with travellers facing the risk of dehydration, starvation, exhaustion or attack by local raiders.

There were more than thirty oasis kingdoms scattered along the outer fringes of the Tarim Basin and as each controlled a different stretch of the route, they could either facilitate, or hinder, foreign travellers planning to cross the region. Some of these kingdoms had an urban nucleus with orchards and large field systems supporting a walled capital city with thousands of inhabitants. Caravan treks around the Tarim Basin were strenuous forced marches and these outposts provided places of rest where travellers could repair their gear and replace lost animals before beginning the next stage of their journey. The northern route around the Tarim Basin was an easier course for caravans as shorter distances separated the oasis sites that existed along the foothills of the Tien Shan Mountains. The glacial rivers that fed these oasis sites also watered peripheral grazing land that could be used by caravans or steppe nomads who entered the Tarim territories from the Ordos region. By contrast the oasis settlements on the southern Tarim route were widely spaced. This made the southern journey more challenging, but caravans using this route were less likely to be intercepted by steppe raiders.

The Kunlun Mountains formed an almost impenetrable barrier along the southern edge of the Taklamakan Desert. A broad belt of gravel extended from the desert to the barren mountain slopes and the glacial waters that flowed from these peaks rushed through inaccessible deep-cut gorges. The only major route through the mountains was close to the oasis city of Khotan near the south-west edge of the Tarim Basin. Travellers choosing this route followed a steep path through the Karakoram mountain range leading south into Kashmir and crossings on the Upper Indus that allowed passage into northern India.

The two caravan routes around the Taklamakan Desert converged at the large oasis settlement of Kashgar on the western edge of the Tarim Basin. From Kashgar travellers could follow relatively short routes through the closely-clustered Pamir Mountains. The towering boulder-strewn peaks of the Pamirs rise to a height greater than 24,000 feet and are covered with glacial ice. The steep mountain passes that wind through the Pamirs are littered with stones and are virtually treeless. Travellers on this route experienced bitter cold and nauseating altitude sickness and for this reason the ancient Chinese called the Pamirs the 'Headache' or 'Onion Mountains'.[16]

Caravans leaving the Pamirs descended into the clement atmosphere and landscape of the fertile Ferghana Valley. Ferghana occupied an oval-shaped depression about 180 miles long and 40 miles wide. The territory was flanked by mountain spurs which shielded Ferghana from the Central Asian Steppe and neighbouring Bactria (Afghanistan). Rivers flowing down from the snow-capped heights irrigated the land with streams that were rich with soil particles. These rivers created a landscape of well-watered plains that were extensively cultivated with field systems, orchards and gardens. Many of these streams united in the broad central valley to form the wide Jaxartes River (Syr Darya). The Jaxartes flowed northward out of the open valley onto the surrounding steppe to form a frontier between Sogdia and the steppe lands. The river flowed more than 1,000 miles westward until it emptied into the landlocked Aral Sea. Ferghana was urbanised by Iranian and Greek civilizations, but in the second century BC it was overrun and conquered by a steppe nation called the Kangju. Ferghana provided the Kangju with excellent breeding grounds for their herds which were fed on fodder made from crops of alfalfa that grew waist-high in this fertile valley.

From the eastern steppe, the Xiongnu were able to send mounted war-bands through passes in the Tien Shan Mountains to demand regular tribute from the small oasis cities on the northern Tarim territories. This tribute included agricultural produce, urban goods and valuable commercial resources such as jade. Tarim wealth therefore went to enrich the Xiongnu and bolster their influence on the East Asian Steppe.

The Emperor Wu realized that the Xiongnu would be severely weakened if the oasis states of the Tarim territories could be brought under Han control. Chinese court officials believed that this achievement would be like 'cutting the right arm off the Xiongnu nation'.[17] The Han tribute system offered a model for foreign relations that could form long-term alliances between China and the Tarim kingdoms. The Han government therefore sent state-organized caravans through the Jade Gate to establish contact with Tarim rulers and offer them valuable goods in return for long-term assistance and political guarantees. Rather than surrender their wealth as tribute to the Xiongnu, the Tarim rulers were offered the opportunity to receive gifts and protection from Han China. The goods presented by Han envoys were diplomatic gifts, but they were offered in such large quantities that they persuaded many Tarim rulers to renounce their support for the Xiongnu and declare their allegiance to China. These gifts included bales of the finest Chinese silk, a material softer and more durable than any of the rough fabrics produced in the Tarim territories. Han envoys promised regular deliveries of these diplomatic 'rewards' to any Tarim rulers who could provide support for their empire. They also offered to protect certain Tarim allies with small Chinese garrisons to help deter and resist Xiongnu raids. Some rulers accepted, but many of the more distant kingdoms remained wary and decided not to commit themselves to the seemingly remote Chinese Empire. The *Hanshu* explains that 'the Han envoys had to use money or silks to procure food and visit markets to obtain mounts for riding. This was because people considered China to be wealthy and remote.'[18]

The importance of Cavalry

The raising and maintenance of horses was a labour-intensive activity and required extensive pasturelands for grazing. This created problems for China as the core agricultural territories of the Han Empire were composed of crop fields and vegetable plots. Donkeys and oxen were the preferred agricultural animal for load-bearing activities and it was not profitable for small farms to keep horses. Furthermore, traditional Chinese horses were small pony-like breeds with hooves that wore down quickly on roads or hard surfaces. They could not carry heavy riders and had to be rested for long periods between campaigns to allow the protective horn of their unshod hooves to regrow.

The cavalry mounts of the Xiongnu were short, stout, powerful horses that were bred for strength and endurance. They could withstand prolonged cold weather, root through thin coverings of snow for meagre vegetation and survive on a frugal diet of wiry steppe grass supplemented by bark and twigs. Each Xiongnu warrior engaged in a long-range foray would bring several spare horses so that he could change his mount at frequent intervals to prevent fatigue and damage to unshod horses. Even these robust animals would wear down their hooves riding across the hard and uneven surface of the deserts that bordered on the steppe.

To become the dominant military power the Han Empire had to acquire a reliable stock of superior horses. This opportunity came in 117 BC when the envoy Zhang Qian led a Chinese expedition to the homelands of a steppe people called the Wusun. The Wusun had ceded from the Xiongnu Empire and after subduing a people called the Sae (Sakas), occupied territories lying to the north of the Tien Shan Mountains. Zhang Qian offered the Wusun people Chinese gold and silks worth more than 100 million in Han currency in exchange for a breeding stock of several thousand steppe horses.[19] This particular breed was reported to be sure-footed on mountain slopes and could easily jump across low rock falls or small ravines. The Emperor received a large delivery of Wusun horses in 109 BC and personally tested their riding abilities on the imperial estates.

When the Emperor Wu learned that the Kangju of Ferghana had larger and stronger horses than the other steppe nations he was determined to acquire a breeding stock of these animals. The Kangju mounts were taller, sleeker and faster than Xiongnu or Wusun horses. They had tough hooves that were resistant to long-term wear and well-defined muscles lined their broad backs. These Ferghana horses were raised on highly nutritious alfalfa fodder and secreted a peculiar reddish substance in their sweat. For this reason the Chinese called the breed 'Heavenly Horses' or 'Blood-Sweating Horses'.

In 107 BC, a Han envoy arrived in Ferghana after crossing the Tarim territories and the Pamir Mountains. He met with a steppe warlord named Kokand to request a breeding stock of the prized mounts known as the 'Heavenly Horses'. When he was refused, the envoy warned that China might use force to obtain the breed. Kokand was insulted and had the man killed for issuing such a threat. He reassured his followers that they had nothing to fear from the Chinese Empire as the intervening Tarim kingdoms could not provide sufficient food and fodder for more than a hundred Han troops. Kokand calculated that the Tarim routes could not support the passage of an army large enough to exact meaningful retaliation.

In 104 BC the Emperor Wu responded by dispatching a large force of Chinese soldiers to attack Ferghana. This army included many convicts and outcasts who wore the distinctive red jackets and iron neck-collars of penal troops and had their heads shaved to indicate their status as criminals. This army set out on a 1,000 mile march from Dunhuang that took them around the northern rim of the Tarim Basin. To secure their communication and supply lines, the expedition had to capture and garrison every oasis site that would not submit to Chinese authority. Consequently, when the commanding General Li Guangli reached Ferghana, he found that he did not have enough troops left to successfully engage the enemy. Li Guangli had to abandon the expedition and return with his army to China.

The Emperor Wu would not accept this failure, because 'an unsuccessful expedition against a small country, such as Ferghana, would cause Bactria and other neighbouring states to feel contempt for China. The Han would never receive its pedigree horses.' Therefore, when Li Guangli reached the Jade Gate he found his passage blocked by Chinese guards who had been issued orders to kill any solider attempting to re-enter the Empire. Emperor Wu offered Li Guangli the command of 60,000 soldiers to complete his objective. This second mission involved greater planning and the infantry regiments were divided into smaller divisions to pass successfully through the Tarim kingdoms without exhausting available supplies. The expedition included 100,000 oxen and 30,000 horses, while numerous donkeys and camels were assembled to supply the Chinese army by carrying food and military equipment in relays across the fringes of the Taklamakan Desert. It was said that all parts of the Empire had to make contributions which included enormous stocks of rice and dried food.

When the Chinese army reassembled in formation at the edge of Ferghana, the steppe chief Kokand took refuge in a fortified city that the Chinese called Ershi (Alexandria Eschate or 'Alexandria the Furthest'). This city was at the western entrance to the Ferghana valley and had been established next to the Jaxartes River in 329 BC by the Macedonian King Alexander.[20] The city had originally been settled by Greek and Macedonian soldiers, but their descendants had become subject to steppe rulers after the Sakas invaded Bactria in about 150 BC. General Li Guangli surrounded Ershi and after a forty-day siege, Han forces breached the city walls. In desperation, the steppe nobles murdered Kokand and promised to provide the Chinese with 3,000 of the Heavenly Horses in return for their lives.

Despite the extensive preparations, over half of the Chinese campaign force had died on the arduous journey or in combat with the enemy. Only 1,000 of the prized Heavenly Horses survived the return journey to China where they were placed in imperial stables to begin a selective breeding programme. But the victory was celebrated in court literature and popular imperial iconography.[21] Sculptures from this era depict the Heavenly Horses as tall muscular animals that seem to fly through the air in a gallop with three legs lifted from the ground. The animals could carry heavily equipped cavalrymen and this permitted the development of steel-clad armour for mounted Han solders. To celebrate his new military supremacy the Emperor issued a new form of gold ingot cast in the shape of a miniature horse hoof called a *madijin*. Bullion payments made to vassal rulers were issued in these new units of *madijin*.[22]

Some Asiatic Greeks may have fought alongside the steppe warriors who defended the city of Alexandria Eschate from the Chinese assault. It was Chinese policy for surrendered foreign fighters to be reconciled within Han rule and settled as military colonists in new frontier districts. Consequently, some of these captives might have been transferred from Ferghana to the Hexi Corridor to guard the main approaches into China. Ancient Chinese records refer to a garrison town in Hexi called Li-Jian. The name suggests that the population were Greco-Macedonians, a remnant of the 'Alexander Dynasty' (*Li-Jian*). A Chinese cadastral register from AD 5 includes Li-Jian in a list of over 1,500 Chinese cities and urban districts. Li-Jian is listed in the Hexi corridor along with other outposts bearing the names of foreign territories. These include the towns of Kucha and Wen-siu (Turfan) which were settled by people captured in Chinese wars against kingdoms in the northern Tarim territories. Confucian practice required that places had names that conveyed their origin and in AD 9 Li-Jian was briefly renamed 'Jie-lu' meaning 'Captives Promoted'.[23] Its original inhabitants were therefore officially recognised as a foreign community that had been captured during an earlier conflict. The Chinese town of Li-Jian possibly took its name directly from Alexandria Eschate (*Li-Jian Ershi*). If so, then this particular community of Asiatic Greeks ended their adventures 1,000 miles from Alexandria Eschate and 5,000 miles from the Mediterranean homelands of their Hellenic ancestors.

CHAPTER FIVE

Securing the Silk Routes

The Han victory in Ferghana demonstrated that the Chinese could launch large-scale wars across the entire expanse of the Tarim Basin. After this conflict, dozens of Tarim kingdoms submitted to Chinese protection and renounced their obligations to the Xiongnu. Embassies also came from Sogdia and Bactria in search of political alliances that would grant them an opportunity to access the remarkable goods produced in the Orient. The *Hou Hanshu* explains that the Western Regions were 'overawed by the military strength and wealth of China. All their rulers presented strange local products as tribute and their beloved sons as political hostages. They bared their heads and kneeled down toward the east to pay homage to the Son of Heaven [the Han Emperor].'[1]

With the support of the Tarim kingdoms, Han envoys in charge of state expeditions travelled even further west until they reached the frontiers of the Parthian Empire in 100 BC and were taken to the Iranian capital Hecatompylos.[2] From these contacts the Chinese learned that the most western parts of the known world were still subject to *Li-Jian* rule under the Greek successors of Alexander, the Seleucids of Syria and the Ptolemaic Dynasty in Egypt.

After their victory in Ferghana, the Chinese established permanent military garrisons in some of the main oasis settlements that surrounded the Tarim Basin. These garrisons were farming colonies tasked with producing surplus food as provisions to state-authorized travellers, official caravans and campaign forces dispatched by the Han Empire. The soldiers were accompanied by their families and given costly agricultural equipment that was paid for by the Han government and transported over long distances to the destination site.[3] The garrisons worked at reclamation and irrigation projects, bringing marginal land under cultivation with new farming technologies and water management strategies. They helped to construct underground water reserves and sub-surface channels to convey glacial streams further into the desert fringes. The first farming installations included about 500 soldiers, but later garrisons were larger, such as the outpost at Korla which included 1,500 men.[4] The initiative also came from the Tarim kingdoms and in 77 BC the king of Loulan asked the Han Emperor to establish a military colony in his territory to strengthen his rule and regional security.[5] The *Hou Hanshu* describes the effect of this policy: 'military agricultural colonies were established in fertile fields and post stations built along the main highways. Messengers and interpreters travelled without cessation and foreign merchants and dealers came to the border frequently.'[6]

This Chinese political and economic expansion was achieved with great effort and expense. The enormous cost included the outlay on mass military mobilization, manpower deployment on labour projects, equipment costs, animal requisition and breeding programmes, provisions and supply lines, troop salaries, fortification building, construction works, the management of distant expeditions and large payments to foreign states. Over five decades the aggressive strategies pursued by the Emperor Wu (141–87 BC) created severe pressures on the Chinese Empire. Therefore, to raise further revenues, the regime imposed new taxes on travel, trade and domestic animals. The government also issued temporary currencies fashioned from a silver-tin alloy and created state monopolies on salt extraction, iron manufacture and liquor production within the Empire. The *Hanshu* explains that 'gifts were sent up to 10,000 *li* [3,100 miles] to states in the Western Regions and the costs involved in the military expeditions against the Xiongnu were beyond calculation. When expenditure became deficient, the government had to cast white-metal money and establish a monopoly on liquor, salt and iron.'[7] *The Discourse on Salt and Iron* confirms that 'a system of equable marketing had to be introduced; the production of goods was increased and wealth multiplied to furnish the frontier expenses.'[8]

Enriched by incoming Chinese tribute and with increased caravan traffic, the Tarim kingdoms entered a new phase of urban expansion and economic growth. The first caravan expeditions to cross the Tarim territories were state-managed operations, with travellers engaged in transporting diplomatic gifts and tribute between distant kingdoms. In any year, up to ten official caravans would depart from China, each comprising several hundred travellers. Sima Qian reports, 'depending on their importance, these missions were attended by a hundred or several hundred men. At least five or six expeditions were dispatched each year, with more than ten missions sent to the distant countries.' Many envoys would spend a long time in foreign courts and return to China several years after beginning their missions.[9]

From an early stage these state-missions involved trade exchanges and profit-making deals as some of the envoys offered unique and valuable merchandise to traders in faraway markets. Sima Qian explains: 'The envoys were from poor families and they handled the government gifts and goods that were entrusted to them as though they were private property. They looked for opportunities to buy goods at a cheap price in the foreign countries and make a profit on their return to China.'[10]

Soon private merchants began to join the state caravans, offering bribes to the Chinese envoys in charge of making regular caravan deliveries to the Western Regions. The main oasis kingdoms began operating as route stations to provide large groups of travellers with supplies and protection for long-range ventures around the Tarim Basin. Subsequently, merchant-run caravans were officially permitted to travel along the routes and this brought traders from all parts of Inner Asia together for the widespread conveyance and interchange of merchandise.

The scale and value of this commerce is demonstrated by events in the first century AD. In AD 94 a Han general named Ban Chao attacked the small Tarim state of Yanqi (Karasahr) which lay on the northern silk route between Turfan and Kucha. He was able to mobilize 1,400 extra combatants by arming Han administrative staff and bringing numerous caravan guards into temporary military service.[11] While on campaign in the Tarim territories, Ban Chao received letters from his brother Ban Gu who described commercial opportunities in China and made requests for various trade items. Ban Gu had heard that a Chinese nobleman named Tao had spent 800,000 cash on ten expensive rugs imported from the Western Regions. Ban Gu therefore sent his brother 700 pieces of coloured silk fabric and 300 bolts of plain white silk with instructions to procure similar profit-making foreign goods on his behalf. These items included Yuezhi horses, *su-ho* incense and prized woollen fabrics.[12]

Operations beyond Ferghana

The most ambitious Chinese venture against the Xiongnu occurred during the mid-first century BC at a time when the Tarim kingdoms had been under Han protection for almost two generations. In 56 BC, a Xiongnu warlord named Zhizhi seized the royal title from his brother Huhanye. Huhanye appealed to the Han Empire for assistance and after pledging loyalty to China, he received large amounts of gold, silk and grain. He used this to obtain support from the steppe peoples and reclaim his authority in Mongolia. Faced with defeat, Zhizhi fled into the distant west with a large number of his followers. They planned to occupy lands far from the reach of his brother Huhanye and the influence of the Han Empire.

By 40 BC, the renegade Xiongnu had settled on steppe grasslands several hundred miles to the north of Sogdia. Their new homelands bordered on a long landlocked expanse of brackish water known as Lake Balkhash (modern Kazakhstan). In ancient times Lake Balkhash extended more than 400 miles from east to west and was filled by long rivers which flowed from glacial sources in distant mountains. One of these watercourses was the Ili River which came from the northern Tien Shan Mountains and crossed over 1,000 miles of steppe to discharge through a broad delta into Lake Balkash. These rivers facilitated the mass movement of livestock and cavalry across the Central Asian Steppe and at Lake Balkhash, Zhizhi and his exiled Xiongnu controlled the nexus of these migratory routes.

The Xiongnu rebels who occupied the southern shores of Lake Balkhash formed an alliance with the Kangju steppe nation who occupied Sogdia. Han reports suggested that the Kangju were able to field over 80,000 skilled archers, so their involvement with the rebels was a serious threat to Chinese interests in Central Asia.[13] Zhizhi consolidated his control over his new territories by building a combined fortress and palace at a strategic site to the west of the Ili River (near modern Taraz). This complex, known to the Chinese as the Chanyu Fortress, consisted of a powerful citadel surrounded by a compound of outer walls made from heavy timber beams embedded into compacted sun-baked earth. From this new capital the Xiongnu began to extend their authority into Ferghana and endanger Chinese contacts with Transoxiana.

In this era the senior Han commander in the Tarim Territories was a military governor known as the Protector General. The Protector General managed relations between China and the thirty-six Tarim kingdoms that were subject to the Han Empire. He was responsible for maintaining diplomatic links, overseeing political obligations, ensuring tribute payments, and guaranteeing travel and trade connections across Central Asia. The Protector General also managed agreements with western powers such as the steppe-based Wusun beyond the Tien Shan Mountains, the Kangju of Sogdia, and the rulers of Bactria and Iran. The political headquarters of the Protector General was at Wu-li near the centrally placed oasis kingdom of Kucha on the northern Tarim Basin. Wu-li was over 400 miles from the Chinese frontiers at the Jade Gate and consequently the Protector General had considerable scope for autonomous action. The Chinese headquarters at Wu-li was garrisoned by only a few hundred Han troops, but the Protector General could summon thousands of soldiers from the subject Tarim kingdoms.

The Protector General Gan Yen-shou was unwilling to act against Zhizhi since any campaign against the rebel Xiongnu involved entering remote territory far beyond the limits of any previous military operations. But when the Protector General became ill, his deputy Chen Tang seized the opportunity to launch a military expedition against the rebels. In 36 BC he issued an edict and mobilized an army that included nearly 40,000 troops from the Tarim kingdoms subject to Han authority. The target for the campaign was the centre of dissident Xiongnu rule on the Central Asian steppe, the walled palace-complex known as the Chanyu Fortress.

By the time Gan Yen-shou learned about this mobilization, the necessary forces were already converging near the oasis settlement of Kashgar and moving into position to march against Zhizhi. This act of war had not been authorised by the Emperor and the Protector General realised that he faced the death penalty for exceeding his authority. He therefore had no choice but to proceed with the expedition in the hope that a victory might excuse his obvious failure to control his subordinates.

From Kashgar it was a 500 mile trek to the enemy stronghold and the Chinese-led army had to march for thirty days across the steppe. As they travelled along the route their column was attacked by a large force of Kangju raiders fighting in alliance with the rebel Xiongnu. When the Chinese reached the Chanyu Fortress, Zhizhi paraded his army in front of the outer timber defences. Maybe he reasoned that the Chinese expedition would exhaust their supplies during a prolonged siege, or he required more time to summon mounted reinforcements from the surrounding steppe.

The Han government were offered a vivid account of the subsequent battle from eye-witness reports and a set of specially painted scenes were commissioned to illustrate the conflict.[14] Both the Xiongnu and Kangju fought as mounted archers, so the Chinese lookouts were surprised to see disciplined infantry forces within the enemy battle-line. Sima Qian reports that about 100 infantry performed a manoeuvre at the fortress gate displaying 'a fish-scale battle formation with their shields'. These unusual units carried their shields in an overlapping arrangement that to the Han observers resembled the interlocking scales of a

Chinese carp. In 1957 an Oxford professor named Homer Dubs suggested that this unit could have been formed by a group of Roman soldiers who had escaped from their Parthian captors and found service with the steppe warlords who occupied Transoxiana. Dubs noted that in 53 BC the Parthians settled thousands of Roman prisoners at the oasis settlement of Merv, which was only a few hundred miles from the Oxus River. He argued that groups of Roman runaways could have joined foreign armies as paid mercenaries and the 'fish-scale' drill might be a distinctive Roman shield formation known as the *testudo* or 'tortoise'. The testudo was an infantry drill whereby the front rank of a legionary line locked their shields together to form a wall-like barrier while troops behind raised their shields above their heads to create a roof-like shelter to protect the unit from missile fire.[15] But there is another explanation for the foreign infantry that served Zhizhi at Chanyu Fortress. Asiatic Greek soldiers from Sogdia would also have fought with their shields held in 'fish-scale' formation – the Macedonian phalanx.[16]

The foreign 'fish-scale' infantry unit was too small to affect the course of the ensuing battle and they retreated with the rest of the defenders as the Chinese fired a barrage of arrows and crossbow bolts at the fortress. Xiongnu bowmen on the battlements were pinned down with missile fire while the Chinese soldiers advanced behind a line of troops carrying large oversized shields. Tinder and logs were dragged into position beneath the palisade and by nightfall the blazing edifice was in danger of collapse. A force of Xiongnu horsemen attempted to breakout, but they were caught by a cordon of Chinese troops and killed with a salvo of crossbow fire. As the Chinese breached the outer walls, the remaining Xiongnu defenders retreated into the inner citadel where Zhizhi issued weapons to his queen, his concubines and their courtiers.

Just before dawn a relief force of 10,000 Kangju cavalry reached the fortress. They raised a battle-cry to give hope to the defenders, but the Han commanders had erected a series of high palisade barriers to guard their flanks and the mounted attackers were driven back by a dense volley of missile fire. Meanwhile in the citadel, Zhizhi was wounded in the face by a Chinese arrow. Drenched in his own blood he was no longer able to shout commands to his followers. Within hours the Chinese had raised earthen ramps tall enough for assault troops to clamber over the citadel walls and gain access to the inner palace. Zhizhi died from his wounds, but many Xiongnu nobles were taken alive, including the queen and the crown prince.

After this victory the Chinese-led army withdrew from the region and returned to the Tarim kingdoms. Over 1,000 Xiongnu had surrendered and 145 captives were taken back to China under military custody.[17] Some of these prisoners could have been members of the 'fish-scale' infantry, but if so, they were too few in number to form a full garrison settlement on the Chinese frontier.[18] However, if consideration was given to their origin culture, then perhaps they were deployed in the frontier post of Li-Jian, along with the other descendants of classical civilization who had found themselves in the distant east on the boundaries of ancient China.

Settlement with the Xiongnu

After 60 BC the Xiongnu nation split into two separate political divisions. In Inner Mongolia the rulers of the Southern Xiongnu sought Chinese protection and made a request to become a tributary state of the Han Empire. They offered military service in return for access to Chinese goods and the opportunity to settle in the fortified northern frontier territories of the Han Empire. The Han Emperor Xuan (91–49 BC) agreed to their demands and offered enormous quantities of Chinese gifts and subsidies to guarantee their loyalty.[19]

In 53 BC hostage princes from the Southern Xiongnu were accepted into the Han court and when the leader of the Southern Xiongnu visited the Han capital in 51 BC, to pay homage to the Emperor, he was rewarded with over 2 tons of gold, 200,000 Chinese coins, 77 Han suits, 8,000 bolts of silk, 6,000 catties of silk floss and 34,000 *hu* of rice.[20] The following year the rewards were increased and the visiting Xiongnu envoys were granted 110 suits, 9,000 silk bolts and 8,000 catties of silk floss. This subsidy became an annual payment to the Southern Xiongnu to ensure their loyalty as frontier guards and allies of the Empire. The payments were not fixed, but graded according to the level of commitment and submission the Southern Xiongnu displayed towards China. By 33 BC the annual award had doubled to 18,000 silk bolts and 18,000 catties of silk floss.[21] By 1 BC the Chinese government were delivering 30,000 silk bolts and 30,000 catties of silk floss to the Southern Xiongnu.[22] The result was a continual outflow of silk products from the Chinese Empire that the Xiongnu used and traded across the steppe frontiers and Central Asia.[23]

With the support of Han subsidies and access to prized grazing land on the Chinese frontier, the Southern Xiongnu population increased almost fourfold as they were joined by other incomers from the steppe. Between 50 BC and AD 90 they grew from a population of perhaps 60,000 people to a nation numbering more than 230,000 individuals.[24] By AD 90 the Southern Xiongnu were receiving Chinese provisions worth thousands of millions in cash.[25] The *Hou Hanshu* explains: 'They have been growing on Han soil, depending entirely on China for food. But each year the tribute and occasional gifts they present are worth only a few hundred million cash.'[26] This discrepancy was the price that China paid for security on its northern frontiers. During this period the Northern Xiongnu, the ancestors of the Huns, were displaced further north into unknown lands in Outer Mongolia.

Parthia and the Overland Impediment

The Han historian Sima Qian describes how in 100 BC Chinese envoys were greeted by a force of 20,000 mounted Parthian warriors at the oasis site of Merv. In this era Merv formed the eastern frontier of the Parthian Empire and from this border outpost the Han envoys where escorted west to the Iranian capital Hecatompylos on the plains beneath the Caspian Sea. Sima Qian reports that 'the king of *Anxi* (Parthia) sent his own ambassadors to go with the envoys back to China, so that they could understand the extent and power of the Han Empire.'[27] This meeting between ancient world powers did not involve Rome and the

Chinese dismissed the classical world of *Li-Jian* (Alexander of Macedon) as a declining influence in international affairs.

The Chinese called the Parthians 'Anxi' since their political system was established by a King Arsaces who founded the regime's ruling dynasty between 250 and 211 BC.[28] By the first century BC the main routes across the mountains and deserts of ancient Iran operated through a network of caravanserai that the Greeks called *stathmoi*.[29] The Parthians allowed merchants from the Roman Empire to visit Babylonia (Iraq), but these travellers were barred from joining the caravans that crossed Iran to reach Transoxiana and the silk routes that led to China. A Han text called *Hou Hanshu* explains that '*Anxi* (Parthia) wishes to control the trade in multi-coloured Chinese silks and so blocks the route to prevent [the Romans] getting through.'[30]

Some of the silk exported from China was offered to markets in the Tarim kingdoms, but large quantities were also trafficked further west into Sogdia and Bactria. In the first century AD a Greek businessman wrote a guidebook for Roman merchants involved in trade ventures across the Indian Ocean. This *Periplus of the Erythraean Sea* explains that 'great quantities of silk are transported from Thina (China) to Bactria.'[31] Some of these silk bales were trafficked down the Indus and Ganges Rivers to Indian ports where they were loaded aboard visiting Roman vessels.[32] Other silk bundles that reached Bactria would have been collected by Parthian caravans that carried merchandise overland across Iran to Ctesiphon and the main commercial cities of ancient Babylonia. Syrian caravans then transported silk and other oriental goods from Babylonia to seaports in the eastern Mediterranean.

Contacts between China and Rome

In AD 9 there was a power struggle in the Chinese government and the supporters of an official named Wang Mang sized control of the Empire from advocates of the Han Dynasty. But when Wang Mang asked the Tarim kingdoms to acknowledge his rule as Emperor, they refused and ceded from Chinese control. The Han Dynasty was able to reclaim power in AD 23, but it was several decades before they could successfully restore Chinese interests in the Western Regions (the Tarim territories).

When the Tarim kingdoms were brought back under Chinese control (AD 74–97), the Han government received information about the Roman Empire. During this period Chinese-led armies commanded by a Protector General named Ban Chao had campaigned as far as the Pamir Mountains which separated the Tarim territories from ancient Afghanistan. On these operations Chinese officers received reports from foreign merchants and envoys suggesting that a significant new empire had emerged in the far west. This new regime was reported to be as large and powerful as the Han, therefore the Chinese commanders called the Empire *Da Qin* meaning 'Great China'.[33]

Chinese information about the Roman Empire is preserved in the *Hou Hanshu* which records that '*Da Qin* [the Roman Empire] is also called *Li-Jian* [the Hellenic territories]. It is located west of the sea [the Indian Ocean] and is also called the *Kingdom of Haixi* [Egypt].' The Chinese possibly received their information about Rome via the Indus Kingdoms, so this explains why the *Hou Hanshu* records that '*Da Qin* trades with *Anxi* (Parthia) and *Tianzhu* (northern India) by sea.'[34]

The *Hou Hanshu* reports that '*Da Qin* extends for several thousands of *li*. It has more than 400 walled cities and several tens of smaller dependent kingdoms.' Unlike the steppe nations, the Romans 'cropped their hair and wore embroidered clothes'. The *Hou Hanshu* adds, 'The people of this country are all tall and honest. They resemble the people of the Middle Kingdom [China] and that is why this state is called *Da Qin* ['Great China'].' According to the *Hou Hanshu*, 'the people of *Da Qin* are honest in business; they don't have two prices. The grain and foodstuffs are always in good supply and the resources of the State are abundant.' The Chinese were informed that the Romans had an effective postal relay system (the *cursus publicus*) to convey dispatches quickly across their domains. Roman government was also said to be receptive to diplomatic contact with foreign regimes and 'when envoys from a neighbouring kingdom arrive at their border, they are presented with gold coins.' The Chinese reports confirmed that the Romans 'use courier stations to get to the royal capital'. Roman lands were said to be wooded with pines and cypress trees and the common people are described as 'mostly farmers cultivating grain crops'.

In this era workshops in Syria rewove oriental silk into thin fabrics that were stained vibrant colours using unique Mediterranean dyes and some of this material was sent back to Parthian markets for Iranian caravans to transport into Afghanistan. The presence of these silks in Central Asia suggested to the Chinese that the Roman Empire also had a silk industry similar to the Han system. It was therefore assumed that the Romans reared their own silkworms and grew mulberry trees. When the Chinese inquired about transport in the Roman Empire, they were told, 'the women travel in screened couches and small white-roofed one-horse carts.'[35] This is probably a description of Roman litters which consisted of a fabric-screened box-chair carried by footmen and Propertius confirms that upper-class Roman women rode in small carriages that were fitted with thin silk drapes.[36]

The Chinese were well informed about certain Roman commodities and they received many of these items through the Tarim Silk Routes. The *Hou Hanshu* therefore devotes an entire section to the valuable products traded by the merchants of *Da Qin*. The Chinese were told 'this country produces plenty of gold, silver, and precious jewels, luminous jade, bright-moon pearls, fighting cocks, rhino horn, coral, yellow amber, opaque glass, whitish chalcedony, red cinnabar, green gemstones, drawn gold-threaded and multi-coloured embroideries, woven gold-threaded net, delicate polychrome silks painted with gold, and asbestos cloth.' The *Hou Hanshu* also mentions Roman fabrics made from wild silkworm cocoons and a silky product known as 'byssus' that was produced by marine molluscs. Byssus was derived from the filaments that a large species of Mediterranean clam (*pinna nobilis*) secreted to anchor its shell to rocks on the seabed. Rare byssus fabrics could be spun into delicate golden-coloured gauze that was lighter and finer than silk.[37] The Chinese were also informed that the Romans 'blend all sorts of perfumes by boiling fragrant juices' (*storax*) and possess 'all the precious and rare things that come from various foreign kingdoms'.[38]

The Indian and Parthian merchants who received Roman coinage did not transfer this money into Central Asia. Instead, they reinvested their profits in trade goods and selected valuable commodities, such as incense and spices, for transport along the silk routes to China. As a consequence, Chinese agents in the Tarim protectorates were not familiar with Roman currency. The Han where informed that the Empire of *Da Qin* 'produce gold and silver coins with ten silver coins worth one gold coin'. In reality twenty-five silver denarii were worth one gold aureus in the Roman currency system, but in India the actual value of silver to gold was 10:1, which explains the discrepancy.

Chinese accounts of the *Da Qin* capital included information about Rome mixed with details about Antioch and Alexandria, as these cities were each leading centres of imperial rule. The capital of *Da Qin* is described as a vast city with five palaces fitted with prominent pillars and equipped with crystal tableware. The *Hou Hanshu* reports that 'each day the ruler of *Da Qin* goes to one of the palaces to deal with matters of State.' These 'palaces' could refer to the imperial court, senate building, citizen assemblies, law courts or temples, all of which were used as venues by the Roman Emperor to conduct important political and judicial business. The Chinese heard that the ruler of Rome was directly petitioned by his people and 'a porter with a sack will always follow the royal carriage, so when somebody wants to discuss something with the ruler, he throws a note in the sack.' The Chinese understood that the Roman ruler had direct judicial authority and 'when he arrives at the palace, he opens the bag, examines the contents, and judges if the plaintiff is right or wrong.'

The Han were informed that *Da Qin* 'has a government department of archives' and 'a group of thirty-six leaders who meet together to deliberate on affairs of State.' This political organization was perhaps an advisory group formed from ex-consuls, or perhaps the Chinese account refers to the thirty-six Roman governors who administered the provinces. The Han were also told that the Roman rulers were 'not permanent' because 'they select and appoint the most worthy man and if there are unexpected calamities in the domain, such as frequent extraordinary winds or rains, he is unceremoniously rejected and replaced.'[39] This is possibly a reference to the Roman position of 'Emperor' being allocated as a supreme office, rather than an honour inherited through direct dynastic links. The elderly Emperor Nerva was ruling Rome in AD 97, but he was unpopular with the military and since he had no familial heir, he came under intense political pressure to adopt a suitable successor from his senior commanders. In AD 98 Nerva granted the supreme position of Emperor to Trajan. Dio explains that 'Nerva did not esteem family relationship above the safety of the State' for 'he believed in looking at a man's ability.' Nerva is said to have declared, 'I have done nothing that would prevent my laying down the imperial office and safely returning to private life.'[40] He died of natural causes soon after retiring from his position and this probably explains why the Han were informed 'the ruler of *Da Qin* who has been dismissed, quietly accepts his demotion without anger.'[41]

The reports of *Da Qin* suggested that Rome might be a rich and powerful ally for the Han Empire. Therefore in AD 97 the Protector General Ban Chao sent a Chinese envoy named Gan Ying to establish direct diplomatic relations with the Roman government. Gan Ying set out from the Tarim Protectorates along the caravan routes that led from the Pamirs into Afghanistan. Crossing Iran, Gan Ying reached a region called *Tiaozhi* (Characene) which was 'next to a large sea' (the Persian Gulf), 'on the western frontier of *Anxi*' (Parthia). Chinese intelligence suggested that Roman territory lay somewhere beyond the western edge of the Indian Ocean and Gan Ying therefore reasoned that 'leaving *Tiaozhi* and heading south, you should embark on the sea to reach *Da Qin* [Roman territory].' This view oversimplified the maritime route as the Chinese had no knowledge about the intervening Arabian Peninsula.

When Gan Ying asked to 'sail to Rome', he got confusing responses from the sailors of Characene who spoke unfamiliar languages. Some of the sailors offered him passage to Roman Egypt via the Red Sea, while others assumed that he wanted to reach the city of Rome by sailing around Africa. The sailors said to Gan Ying: 'The ocean is huge. Those making the round trip can do it in three months if the winds are favourable. However, if you encounter winds that delay you, it can take two years.' Gan Ying was also told that he would have to pay for large-scale provisions since 'all the men who go by sea take stores for three years.' When he heard this, Gan Ying abandoned his plans to reach Rome by sea and began the long journey back to the Chinese held Tarim protectorates. He did not realise that Parthia and Rome shared a common land border and the city of Characene was only forty days distant from the Roman frontier in Syria.

Gan Ying reported to the Protector General Ban Chao that 'the vast ocean urges men to think about their homeland and they become homesick. Some of them even die.'[42] Ban Chao therefore concluded that Rome was too distant to assist the Chinese in their efforts to control Central Asia. Had Gan Ying been successful in his mission to Rome, he would have been brought before the military Emperor Trajan in the first year of his reign (AD 98). But this failed enterprise was the only known attempt by the Han regime to make contact with the Roman Empire.

Roman Knowledge of the Tarim Regions

The earliest Roman references to the Seres describe Tarim communities rather than Han Chinese populations. Strabo reports that in the third century BC the Greek kingdom in Bactria extended 'as far as the Seres' and this is probably a reference to the Tarim regions, perhaps Kashgar.[43] Strabo thought that the Asian landmass ended just beyond the Ganges and writing in AD 44 the Latin geographer Mela shared this view. Mela located the Seres somewhere between India and the homelands of the mounted Scythians on the Central Asian steppe. He writes, 'The most eastern parts of Asia are inhabited by the Indians, the Seres and the Scythians – the Indians and Scythians occupy the two extremities and the Seres are in the middle.'[44]

Mela also emphasised the extreme distance involved in journeys to the Tarim territories and the numerous threats along the route. He describes how Central Asia was home to mounted steppe warriors known as the Sakas and nomad Scythians who lived in places 'separated by territories that are uninhabited because they are full of wild animals'. Mela concludes, 'beyond this place there are more monstrous beasts that render vast regions unsafe all the way to Mount Tabis, which extends to the sea and the Seres.'[45] Pliny believed that the Asian landmass ended just beyond the Malay Peninsula and therefore located the Seres north of India 'above the Himalayas'.[46]

The second century Roman geographer Claudius Ptolemy calls the Land of the Seres, 'Serica' and places their territory above India in a region that covers the Tarim kingdoms.[47] This is appropriate since his information dates to a period when the Tarim Basin was subject to the Han Empire (AD 100). Consequently, the city that Ptolemy calls 'Sera; the capital of the Seres', could be the Han capital Louyang in northern China.

The Tarim population continued to be known as the 'Seres' throughout the Roman period. Writing in the late fourth century AD, Ammianus Marcellinus identified the Seres as the most distant population known to Roman authorities. He reports that 'east of the two Scythias, there is a country called Serica which is surrounded by a ring of high mountains.' Ammianus was possibly describing oasis territories belonging to the Tarim kingdoms. He also reports that Serica has 'fertile soil and covers a considerable area' and the 'encircling mountains' could be the Tien Shan and Kunlun mountain ranges. Ammianus explains that 'to their north the tribal Seres share a border with the Scythians, on the east they look towards snow and deserts; towards the south they extend as far as India and the Ganges.'[48]

Ammianus lists thirteen cities or population groups around the land of 'Serica' and these could be any of the thirty-six kingdoms mentioned in Chinese accounts of the region.[49] The Chinese *Hou Hanshu* describes how some of the larger Tarim kingdoms were able to form small regional empires during periods when Chinese or Xiongnu authority was weak. For example, during the mid-first century AD, Yarkand was able to claim authority over thirteen other Tarim kingdoms. Perhaps Ammianus is describing one of these Tarim empires or repeating antiquated information in his description of Serica. Ammianus suggested that there were lands beyond Serica, but he had no definitive information about the core Chinese Empire.

Indian merchants regularly travelled to China through the Tarim kingdoms and people from these oasis states displayed elements of Indian culture due to the spread of Buddhist religion along the silk routes. To further complicate matters, Roman merchants found it difficult to distinguish between Scythians and Indians as these two populations merged in the Indus territories.[50] Roman writers also had insufficient racial templates to be able to clearly define Tarim population types, or categorise indistinct cultural and ethnic origins. They knew the Tarim region was occupied by Xiongnu settlers who lived alongside pale-skinned Scythians from the Russian Steppe. But these interchanges created confusion and Roman authorities struggled to make sense of merchant reports regarding the Seres. Pausanias explains that 'some say the Seres are not Ethiopians (dark-skinned), but a mixed race of Scythians and Indians.'[51]

Pliny offers the fullest description of the 'Seres' who traded with Indian merchants near the Ganges. He writes, 'The Seres are above normal height, their hair is golden-red, their eyes are blue, the sound of their voices is rough and they exchange no words with merchants.'[52] Pliny reports that these red-haired Seres offered oriental steel, Chinese silk and animal furs imported from the Eurasian steppe.[53] To the Romans it seemed remarkable that these people eschewed a settled lifestyle, yet had access to metals and fabrics that were superior to the products used by the most advanced western civilization.

These Europoid 'Seres' are well-known to archaeologists due to the discovery of ancient burials in the Taklamakan Desert near the southern Tarim kingdoms of Loulan and Cherchen. The burials contain desiccated bodies that have been naturally 'mummified' by the extreme desert heat. The arid climate has also preserved their possessions and clothing, including furs, leather and soft felted materials that confirm their steppe origins. Although the human remains are thousands of years old, their distinctive natural skin coloration and hair pigmentation remain. These people belonged to a European population that probably migrated into the Tarim Basin from somewhere near the Caspian Sea during the third millennium BC. The earliest Europoid burials in the Tarim Basin date to about 1,800 BC and consist of tall individuals with angular faces and recessed eyes. They had distinctive fair or reddish-brown hair which they wore long and sometimes braided. One well-preserved burial found near Qiemo has become known as the 'Cherchen Man'. The burial, dated to 1,000 BC, consisted of a 6 foot 6 inch man with red hair, high cheekbones, aquiline nose and full beard. His skin was tattooed with yellow and purple pigments and he wore a red twill tunic with tartan-patterned leggings.[54] In an era when the average height of Mediterranean people was about 5 feet 5 inches tall, this population would have seemed 'larger than normal height'. This feature helped to foster a belief that the Seres might possess other attributes, including an ability to live far beyond a normal human lifespan.[55]

Another burial group at Cherchen included a tall man with light-brown braided hair buried next to three women and a twelve-week-old baby, all of whom could have died during an epidemic. The dominant woman in the group had facial tattoos and light brown hair gathered into two long braids. She was almost 6 feet tall and wore a red dress and white deer-skin boots. The baby was dressed in a blue felt bonnet and had tiny turquoise stones placed over his closed eyelids.[56] This might verify Pliny's statement that the ancient Seres had distinctive blue eyes.

The appearance of these Europoid people is confirmed by Chinese cave frescoes dating to the ninth century AD. They depict a Tarim people known to modern scholarship as the Tocharians. The frescoes are preserved in Buddhist monasteries cut into rock-faces at important sites along the southeast end of the silk routes. Images of Tocharians from Bezeklik and the Thousand Buddha Caves near Turfan show large individuals with tanned-skin, thick beards, reddish hair and striking blue eyes. They are depicted wearing Iranian-style riding clothes, or elaborate silk robes similar to the ceremonial fabrics worn by the Han Chinese. These figures appear in the frescoes as Buddhist benefactors and their presence confirms that the Europoid populations in the Tarim Basin were involved in the transfer of oriental fabrics.[57]

In Roman times, red-haired Tocharians were probably present at Khotan and active along an offshoot of the southern Silk Route that led through the Himalayas to the Ganges in northeast India. Indian merchants sought out the Tocharians at their seasonal grazing grounds when they put their horses out to pasture and pitched temporary settlements at river sites near the foothills of the Himalayas. The Romans received information about this commerce from a Sinhalese ambassador named Rachia who came to Rome from the Anuradhapura Kingdom in the reign of Claudius (AD 41–54). Pliny reports, 'The Sinhalese know of the Seres through commerce and Rachia's father has travelled to the place where the Seres hasten down to the beach to meet the traders.' This beach was probably the banks of a river chosen as a landmark boundary between territories. The exchanges between the Seres and the visiting merchants were staged as 'silent barter' agreements that were conducted in the open using gesture to communicate intent. Pliny explains, 'The details confirm what our Roman businessmen say, that commodities are deposited on the opposite bank of a river beside any goods offered by the Seres and if the exchange is appealing, the Seres take up what is offered.'[58] Mela confirms these reports when he describes the Seres as 'a race eminent for integrity and well known for trade'. He was told that the Seres 'allow transactions to be conducted without interference and in these encounters they lay out their wares in an exposed location'.[59]

Roman authorities also refer to the belief systems of the Seres and this subject was discussed by Christian philosophers when criticising pagan practices. A second century Christian theologian named Origen refuted the views of a Pagan named Celsus who tried to argue what might be 'normal' or 'natural' about religion. The Seres are included in a list of people who could not 'tolerate temples, altars, or images'. Celsus claimed that 'the nomadic tribes of Libya [Berbers], the Scythians, and the Seres worship no god.'[60] This is probably a reference to desert and steppe peoples engaged in shamanistic religions that did not require man-made temples dedicated to the worship of personified gods.

Some of the people known to the Romans as Seres were probably under Chinese rule during periods when the Han Empire controlled the Tarim kingdoms. However, the first definite Roman reference to Han China appears in the *Periplus of the Erythraean Sea* in about AD 50. The author of the *Periplus* was based in Egypt and involved in oceanic trade voyages to the main city-ports in western India. He believed that the Asian landmass ended somewhere near Malaysia, but he reports that 'at its northernmost point, where the sea ends on the outer fringe, there is a very great inland State called Thina' (China).

In this era Roman ships did not generally sail beyond the Tamil kingdoms on the southern tip of India, so only the land route to China was known. By this period the Central Asian trade routes were transporting large amounts of silk across the Tarim territories, but few merchants were making the entire journey from India to China. The *Periplus* warned, 'it is not easy to get to this Thina; for rarely do people come from it and they are only a few.'[61]

During this period, Indian merchants expanded their overland trade ventures through the Tarim Silk Routes to reach inner China. Chinese records describing the death of the Emperor Guangwu in AD 57 record that Indian merchants were among the foreign people who established a commemorative shrine at Louyang.[62] Buddhist missionaries accompanied these businessmen and in AD 68 they established the White Horse Monastery in the capital.[63] They told Roman merchants about these matters and passed on the Sanskrit name *Cina* (Sinae) to describe Han China. This became 'Thina' in ancient Greek pronunciation.

CHAPTER SIX

The Kushan Empire

After they were defeated by the Xiongnu in 174 BC, the Yuezhi had fled their homelands on the Chinese frontiers and escaped westward.[1] Over several decades they migrated almost 2,000 miles across the Eurasian Steppe and seized new territories on the upper reaches of the Oxus River. Near the Ili River they defeated a steppe nation called the Sakas who fled south into the disintegrating Greek kingdom of Bactria (centred in northern Afghanistan). In 124 BC, the Yuezhi tried to expand their domain into Iran, but their mounted armies were resisted by the Parthians.[2] They then began the occupation of neighbouring Bactria which, following the collapse of Greek rule in the region, had remained a well-urbanised and revenue-rich territory with fertile plains suitable for agriculture or horse-breeding. By 100 BC, the development of the Tarim Silk Routes meant that Bactria became the centre of a vast commercial network that connected the economies of India and Iran to the distant Chinese Empire. In Bactria the Yuezhi established a kingdom known as the Kushan regime which developed into one of the ancient world's leading empires.

Early History of Bactria

There was a strong Greek legacy in ancient Bactria that survived into the Kushan period. According to Strabo 'Alexander founded eight cities in Bactria and Sogdia' (331–323 BC).[3] These cities were *polis*-like civic communities populated mainly by retired soldiers, mercenaries and Greek attendants from the Macedonian army. They were established in locations that had a strategic value controlling resources, productive agricultural lands, overland routes or territorial frontiers. The political philosopher Plato thought that the ideal *polis* should include 5,000 male citizens and if Alexander had followed this practice he might have settled up to 40,000 Greco-Macedonian subjects in Bactria and Sogdia.[4] Diodorus reports that when the Greeks occupying these regions staged an uprising against the Macedonian regime in 323 BC, they were able to field 20,000 infantry and 3,000 cavalry.[5] Casualties in this conflict were high, but Macedonian generals recruited further Greek mercenaries to replace their losses in Bactria.[6] The Greco-Macedonian King Seleucus I Nicator (312–281 BC) continued this practice and Appian claims that he established over thirty cities in his kingdom, stretching from Syria across Iran to Sogdia and the Jaxartes frontier.[7]

One of the most significant cities in this Greek settlement was 'Alexandria in the Caucasus' (Bagram) which was positioned in the southern foothills of the Hindu Kush controlling the main passes that led into India. According to Curtius Rufus this new Hellenic city was founded by a community that included

7,000 Macedonians, camp followers and a large number of Greek mercenaries who volunteered to be settled in the region.[8] The city became an important outpost for Greek rule when the Indus Kingdoms and neighbouring Arachosia (southern Afghanistan) were claimed by the Mauryan Empire of ancient India (322–185 BC).

The ruling Greek presence in Bactria was small compared to the Iranian population which included about a million people.[9] But the Bactrian Greeks could raise significant fighting forces and when they ceded from Seleucid rule around 250 BC they were able to claim authority over Hellenic cities in neighbouring Sogdia.[10] They could also recruit native Bactrians who could provide a force of up to 7,000 cavalry.[11]

Over time the Greco-Macedonian settlers in Bactria married local women, but their descendants preserved the original culture of their fathers down through the subsequent generations. Their cities had Greek-style theatres, gymnasiums, temples and colonnaded buildings that displayed Hellenic architecture, decoration and themes. The surrounding countryside was planted with distinctive Mediterranean crops including olive groves and vineyards. Their descendants spoke and wrote in Greek and followed Hellenic religious practices.

One of these Greek cities was excavated at the modern site of Ai Khanoum in eastern Afghanistan. The ancient name of the city is not known, but it was established on a tributary of the Oxus River flanking routes leading to the Hindu Kush mountain passes and the northern Indus kingdoms. Ai Khanoum had a classical theatre that could accommodate 5,000 citizens, a large gymnasium, avenues lined with Corinthian columns, a fortified acropolis and a palace-centre that incorporated architectural elements from Persian culture. Long stone ramparts encircled the city to protect its inhabitants from attack and a monumental cemetery with Greek inscriptions was situated nearby. Various shrines and temples in the city were devoted to Greek gods including a temple housing a seated statue of Zeus. But this temple had the solid enclosed walls of a Zoroastrian fire cult building instead of the column-lined porticoes of a traditional Greek place of worship. The Greeks had a long tradition of displaying large cult statues, but as Bactria lacked marble, the inhabitants of Ai Khanoum used clay and plaster to fashion their sculptures. Archeologists excavating Ai Khanoum found olive presses, Hellenic jewelry, metal statuettes and fragments of ancient papyrus with Greek philosophical texts. Numerous Greco-Bactrian coins were recovered from the site including a batch of ten blank silver disks which suggests that the ancient city had a state mint. Inscriptions from the palace treasury reveal that the senior administrators had Greek names, while the lower officials were Bactrian.[12]

During the third century BC, Ai Khanoum was one of several leading Greek cities that dominated political affairs in ancient Bactria, but the entire region was under threat. In 208 BC the Seleucid King Antiochus III warned the Bactrian Greeks that conflict between the Hellenic kingdoms was weakening Greek rule in Asia. He suggested that the Scythians (Sakas and Kangju) who occupied the Transoxianan steppe were in a position to overrun Bactria if they were not opposed by sufficient Greek forces. Antiochus told his opponent the Greco-

Bactrian King Euthydemus, 'If you do not concede to my terms, neither of us will be safe, because great hordes of nomads are massing nearby and they will endanger both of us. If these hordes enter Bactria, the country will be completely barbarized.'[13]

During this period Greco-Bactrian armies could probably muster up to 30,000 Hellenic troops including a large cavalry contingent. In 208 BC King Euthydemus was able to deploy 10,000 cavalry to oppose King Antiochus III, but he could not prevent his capital city Balkh (Bactra) being placed under long-term siege.[14] In the second century BC, the Greek rulers of Bactria crossed the Hindu Kush and began conquering the Indus region. Strabo reports, 'the Greeks who caused Bactria to revolt grew so powerful because of the fertility of the country, that they became masters of both Ariana [eastern Iran] and India.'[15] It was claimed that these conquests gave the Greek king Eucratidas authority over 1,000 cities.[16] But soon after these conquests began, the Greco-Bactrian regime split into rival factions. Some of its leading generals seized power in the new subject territories and established independent Indo-Greek kingdoms. These Greek kings raised large armies from their subject nations and the Indo-Greek King Demetrius II is said to have commanded 60,000 soldiers in a war against the Bactrian King Eucratides I.[17] These conflicts further reduced the military capacity of the Greco-Bactrian kingdom. Strabo confirms that the Parthians took the opportunity to seize western territories from the weakened Bactrian kingdom.[18]

In response the Greco-Bactrian kings began recruiting armoured Saka warbands into their armies to fight rival Greeks, Parthians and other eastern adversaries. A second century ancient administrative document found in Bactria confirms Greek payments to Saka warbands. It records: 'In Amphipolis near Karelote the forty Scythians introduced as mercenaries have been paid 100 drachmas of coined silver.'[19] The Saka could mobilize up to 20,000 riders, but when their steppe homelands were seized by the Yuezhi a large part of this population fled south and attacked their former Greek allies in Bactria (145 BC).[20] The *Hanshu* reports, 'When the Great Yuezhi went westward they defeated and drove away the *Sai* (Saka) king who fled southwards.'[21] Strabo confirms that Bactria 'was occupied by the Sakas' through a series of 'raids' that 'crossed lands adjoining their own country and reached distant regions'.[22]

The city of Ai Khanoum was destroyed by steppe invaders sometime around 145 BC when the Sakas attacked the weakened Greek regime in Bactria. Storerooms were looted and many of the main buildings in the ancient city were destroyed during this period as permanent occupation ended at the site. Remains of Saka-style military equipment were found in the Greek city, including bronze arrowheads and fragments of segmented iron leg-sleeves that protected heavily armoured riders.[23] The appearance of these armoured Saka cavalry is confirmed by an ancient bone plaque found at a grave-site in Sogdia called Orlat. The plaque depicts battle scenes with riders dressed in long-sleeved coats of chain mail armour that extends below their knees. They wear domed helmets and metal-plated corselets that have a distinctive high collar at the back. The Orat warriors carry bows and fight with lances and long swords.[24]

When the Yuezhi conquered Bactria the mounted Sakas fled west into Arachasia and crossed the Hindu Kush to occupy the Indus territories. The *Hanshu* reports that 'the Sai nation was divided and dispersed, and everywhere they formed kingdoms.'[25] During the first century BC, one branch of the Sakas conquered the remaining Indo-Greek kingdoms in the Indus region. Their kings adopted Greek titles and motifs because this was the culture of the established elite. They seized the Greek city mints and began issuing their own silver coins that showed Saka kings wearing their distinctive domed helmets and high-armoured collars. Some of these coins had images of the new Saka rulers depicted as armoured cavalrymen. The Sakas ruled the Indus territories for several decades until 10 BC when Parthian princes conquered the region and made themselves overlords in the Punjab and Sindh.

The Yuezhi in Bactria

The Yuezhi forces that conquered Bactria fought as mounted archers supported by heavily armoured spearmen. Archaeologists have excavated part of a Yuezhi (Kushan) palace at Khalchayan in the valley of Sukhan Darya which flowed into the Oxus in northern Bactria (now Southern Uzbekistan). The building, which dates to the first century BC, had a large reception hall with clay sculptures covering the walls. Panels depict a Kushan royal court and a mounted military procession riding into battle. The mounted archers have their bows drawn and wear light tunics and riding trousers that are characteristic of the steppe. The spearmen wear sophisticated armour including cap-like helmets and metal suits that cover their legs and sleeves with concentric armoured bands. Their horses also wear coats of scale or chain mail armour. The Kushan men depicted in the Khalchayan sculptures have prominent moustaches and long hair tied back with ribbons worn across their foreheads. The warriors have a reddish skin-tone and facial features that suggest a Far Eastern ethnicity.

The sculptures from Khalchayan probably depict the Yuezhi (Kushan) nation progressing from warriors to victorious commanders and then regional kings. A further panel from Khalchayan shows a female radiating light and standing on a classical chariot. This could be a Yuezhi version of the Greek goddess Athena. Next to her stands a group of Yuezhi men who, although they are still armed with swords, have removed their protective armour.

The central panel from Khalchayan depicts a king and queen seated on thrones. They are flanked by other aristocratic couples including women dressed in long draped clothing. Positioned to their right is another seated pair who might be the crown prince and his wife. The king wears a traditional steppe riding costume, but he holds an ornate riding crop and wears a low-cap that could be a symbol of his rank.[26]

Thousands of gold items have been found at a first century BC Yuezhi-Kushan funeral site called Tillya-Tepe in northern Afghanistan. Tillya-Tepe was only a short distance from the Bactrian capital Bactra (Balkh) and its contents indicate the wealth of the conquering Yuezhi nation. Most of the 20,000 gold items recovered from Tillya-Tepe included decorative elements that had been sewn into the clothing of a high-ranking man and five women buried at the site. The gold items included diadems, necklaces, bracelets, belt-buckles and daggers along with turquoise and other precious stones. Other objects of interest were Greek-style cameos and intaglios, Parthian coins and fragments of Chinese bronze mirrors. The Yuezhi artefacts found at Tillya-Tepe were influenced by Greek, Iranian, Indian and Scythian (Saka) artistic styles. One decorative gold clasp depicted a Greek infantryman in a *cuirass* breastplate carrying a spear and an oval shield.[27]

During the Tang Dynasty (AD 618–906), a Chinese scholar decided to update the Han description of the Kushan recorded in the *Shiji*. He wrote: 'Riding horses are always numerous in the land of the Great Yuezhi (Bactria) and they number several hundred thousand. The layouts of their cities and palaces are similar to those of the Romans (*Da Qin*), but their people have a reddish-white skin tone. They are skilful at archery from horseback. Even India cannot compare with this region for its products, rare commodities and treasures.'[28]

The Kushan Empire

When the Yuezhi conquered Bactria their nation was divided into five separate tribes each led by its own *xihou* ('Allied Prince') who established a separate royal residence within a subject walled city.[29] Chinese reports reveal that in about AD 50, a Yuezhi prince named Kujula Kadphises (Qiujiu Que) 'attacked and murdered the other *Xihou*'. He then established himself as king of the entire Yuezhi nation and united their domains to form the Kingdom of *Guishuang* (Kushan).[30] These events were reported to Roman businessmen and the *Periplus of the Erythraean Sea* describes the Kushan as 'a very warlike people' and reports that these 'Bactrians are now ruled by a single king'.[31]

The Chinese sources describe the formation of the Kushan Empire and record how Kujula Kadphises attacked Parthia and captured the strategic site of Kabul in eastern Afghanistan. The *Hou Hanshu* records that '*Qiujiu Que* [Kujula Kadphises] invaded *Anxi* [Parthia] and took the *Gaofu* [Kabul] region.' The *Hou Hanshu* explains that the population of Kabul was considered 'weak and easy to subdue', but the territory had economic significance since the people were 'excellent traders, who are very wealthy'.[32] The capture of the strategic Kabul Valley gave Kushan forces a route into India. This conquest also separated the Indo-Parthian princes from their allies in Iran.

The Chinese estimated that there were perhaps 400,000 Yuezhi within the Kushan nation, including up to 100,000 men capable of bearing arms.[33] Prior to the Yuezhi invasion the population of Bactria was estimated to include over a million people.[34] The Yuezhi were therefore a significant occupying force among a population that included large urbanised communities comprised of Iranians and Asiatic Greeks. Most Kushan armies fought in the traditional style of their steppe ancestors as mounted horse archers, but their elite forces would have included *cataphract* cavalry as confirmed by the frescoes at the Kushan palace at Khalchayan.[35] To place this military force in context, the Romans maintained a total of 300,000 soldiers across their entire Empire. When the Emperor Trajan began his eastern war against Parthia in AD 114 he assembled a total of eight legions (80,000 troops).[36]

The Han envoys estimated that the Parthian frontier was about 49 days march from the Kushan capital Bactra in central Bactria.[37] As cavalry forces could cover this distance in about 21 days, this made the Kushan nation an imminent threat to the Parthian Empire. The Jewish historian Josephus records a sudden eastern attack on Parthia which occurred in AD 55. It came at a time when the Parthian King Vologases had taken his army westward into Assyria to attack a small subject kingdom called Adiabene that had defied his authority. But as Vologases prepared to attack Adiabene, he received reports that the eastern frontier of his Empire was being plundered by mounted invaders who Josephus describes as the 'Sacae' (perhaps Kushans who occupied the former Saka territories). It was said that this nation despised the Parthian king and had been joined by other steppe forces known as the 'Dahae' who inhabited lands to the east of the Caspian Sea.[38] Vologases was able to repel the Kushan-led invaders, but Parthian prestige was damaged by the incident. This episode demonstrated how the Parthian Empire found it difficult to conduct wars fought simultaneously on more than one frontier.

According to Chinese accounts Kujula Kadphises (*Qiujiu Que*) lived until he was more than 80 years old and died around AD 80. His son Vima Takto (*Yangaozhen*) formed an alliance with the Han Empire at a time when the Chinese were regaining their dominance over the Tarim kingdoms. The *Hou Hanshu* records how the ruler of the oasis kingdom of Kashgar in the western Tarim Basin rebelled from Han authority and summoned mounted Kangju allies from Sogdia to support his insurrection. The Chinese Protector General Ban Chao sent messages to the Kushan in Bactria proposing military cooperation. When the Kangju learned about this alliance they feared that their homelands might be attacked by Kushan armies and withdrew from the Tarim region. Ban Chao reclaimed Kashgar, but the Kushan sought further political recognition and demanded that the Chinese government present a Han princess to their king in a formal marriage treaty. When Ban Chao refused this request the Kushan king mobilized 70,000 horsemen led by a senior commander. In AD 90 this mounted Kushan army crossed the Pamir Mountains to attack Ban Chao and expel the small Chinese-led force occupying Kashgar.

Before the enemy arrived, Ban Chao brought all food stocks in the Kashgar region within the fortified main city and destroyed the rest. Kashgar was besieged by the Kushan army, but they failed to breach the city walls during several assaults. When their provisions became scarce, the Kushan general sent a detachment eastward to find food in the next oasis settlement several hundred miles distant from Kashgar. But Ban Chao had anticipated this and had positioned a force of Chinese-led troops between the oasis territories to ambush and kill most of the Kushan riders. Without adequate provisions, the Kushan general was forced to abandon the siege of Kashgar and ride back to Bactria with the remainder of his army.[39]

After this incident the Kushan King Vima Takto concentrated his efforts on expanding his dominion south into India. During this period Vima Takto led mounted armies through the Hindu Kush to conquer the Indus region. He defeated the warring Indo-Parthian princes who ruled this territory and took possession of Indus trade ports visited by Roman merchant ships making voyages across the Indian Ocean. The ancient Indus kingdoms covered a land area about the size of Asia Minor (modern Turkey), so these conquests almost doubled the size of the Kushan domains and established the regime as a major empire. The *Hou Hanshu* describes how Vima installed generals to 'supervise and lead' the Indus realms and after this conquest the Kushan Empire became 'extremely rich'. According to Chinese reports, 'all the foreign kingdoms call this regime the *Guishuang* (Kushan), but the Han call them by their original name, the Great Yuezhi.'[40]

Han accounts describe northwest India (*Tianzhu*) as a land flanking a great river (the Indus) in a region that was 'low-lying, humid and hot'. It was reported to be populated by a people 'who practice the Buddhist Way, not to kill or wage war'. The original inhabitants of *Tianzhu* had war elephants, but their forces were no match for an army of mounted Kushan archers and the *Hou Hanshu* describes Indian armies as militarily weak. The Chinese called India '*Juandu*' and describe how the country contained several hundred urban centres and many kingdoms, each with its own king.

The Kushan King Vima Kadphises (AD 100–127) conquered northern India and seized a series of kingdoms between the Indus and the Ganges. In the captured territories Indian rulers were replaced by steppe warlords and the *Hou Hanshu* records that the Kushan 'killed their kings and installed generals to govern them'.[41] The new administrators sent revenues to the Kushan court and were authorised to levy local troops if fighting forces were required to defend or further expand the Empire. The *Weilue* describes how the population of eastern India 'ride elephants and camels into battle, but currently they provide military service and taxes to the *Yuezhi* [Kushans]'.[42]

Chinese records indicate the range of valuable resources that became available to the Kushan regime after its Indian conquests. The *Hou Hanshu* lists 'elephants, rhinoceroses, turtle shell, gold, silver, copper, iron, lead and tin'. Additional new trade resources included 'fine cotton cloths, excellent wool carpets, all sorts of perfumes, sugar, pepper, ginger and black salt'. The Kushan also had control over important maritime trade routes which connected India to Egypt and gave them access to Roman goods. The *Hou Hanshu* explains that '*Tianzhu* communicates with the Roman Empire (*Da Qin*) and precious things from Rome can be found there.'[43]

The Kushan also developed a controlling interest in the oasis kingdom of Kashgar which was strategically positioned at the western edge of the Tarim Silk Routes. This occurred when the king of Kashgar died and the Kushan offered to support his brother Chen Pan in his bid for the sovereignty (AD 114–119). Chen Pan returned to the Kashgar royal court with a guard of Kushan soldiers and requested that the king's son should immediately abdicate in his favour. Conflict was avoided because Chen Pan was a popular figure in his kingdom and was widely respected by his people. But the Chinese determined from these events that the people of Kashgar 'dreaded the Kushans'.[44]

The Kushan King Kanishka (AD 127–151) also extended his empire further into northern India towards the Upper Ganges and his coins and inscriptions have been found near the ancient cities of Mathura, Patna and Gaya. The *Rabatak Inscription* found near Surkh Katul in southern Bactria confirms the chronology of the early Kushan kings. The text is written in the Bactrian language, but uses Greek letters to record an edict of 'Kanishka the Kushan, the righteous, the just, the autocrat, the god' who revered the Iranian goddess Nana. The inscription also lists major cities subject to his dictates including Ujjain and Pataliputra in northern India.[45]

Ancient Buddhist traditions preserved in Chinese texts describe a war between Kanishka and the eastern Parthian king Vologases III (AD 105–147). These accounts claim that a Parthian king attacked the Kushan Empire with an army comprised of mounted bowmen, armoured cataphracts and infantry equipped as archers and spearmen. In response Kanishka launched a ruthless counter-offensive and a vast number of Parthian warriors were slaughtered in the ensuing battle when it became a brutal close-quarter mêlée. The tradition claims 'the king of *An-his* [Parthia] was cruel and obstinate. He marshalled his four classes of troops and attacked Kanishka. King Kanishka punished him severely and when the two armies joined battle they fought incessantly with swords and daggers.' Kanishka was victorious, but he was appalled at the scale of the suffering he had inflicted. He therefore repented and sought guidance from religious leaders.[46]

Other Buddhist traditions present Kanishka as an ambitious conqueror who sought power over the known world. Having expanded his empire on almost every frontier, Kanishka assembled a great army from his subject nations that included elephants from India. He planned to attack the Tarim kingdoms, but his foreign troops refused to cross the high and dangerous passes in the Pamir Mountains. According to the tradition, 'the king prepared his army for a punitive campaign in the east, sending out a vanguard of foreigners on white elephants to lead the way, while he followed with his army. But when they entered the Pamirs and were about to cross a steep pass, the elephants and horses of the vanguard were unwilling to advance.' It was said that this was the moment that Kanishka had his religious revelation and rejected violence.[47]

Kushan Culture

The Yuezhi spoke a language called Tuharan, but they learned Greek and Iranian (Arian) from their subjects in Bactria. Tuharan did not have a written script, so the early Kushan used Greek letters to announce their titles, names and edicts. This new Greco-Kushan script included one additional glyph required to pronounce the '*sh*' sound used in the Tuharan language. Many Kushan texts were written in Bactrian (Iranian) using the Greco-Kushan script, but some Kushan coins and inscriptions also promoted the regime with a text known as Kharoshthi. Persian-based Aramaic letters were used to convey a form of Indian Prakrit spoken in the Hindu Kush. The regime also occupied parts of northern India around Mathura were the Brahmin script was common.

The Kushan adopted other aspects of culture and belief from their subject peoples in Inner Asia, Iran and India. Some Kushan kings followed an Iranian cult called Zoroastrianism, while others promoted Buddhism, or depicted Greek and Indian gods on their coins. Evidence from coin issues suggests that the Kushan King Vima Kadphises (AD 100–127) was a devotee of a Hindu sect called Shaivism that celebrated Shiva as the Supreme Being.[48] His coins proclaim him as a 'Worshipper of Shiva' and a Kharostani inscription found near Mat, close to the city of Mathura in northern India, commemorates the king as 'steadfast in the true law and on account of his devotion, receiving the kingdom from Shiva'.[49]

Evidence of changes to Kushan religion comes from the remains of a Hellenic temple at a site called Dilberjin near the Bactrian capital Balkh (Bactra). This temple honoured the Greek gods Castor and Pollux who were known as the Dioscuri (Twins). The Dioscuri were considered to be divine sons of Zeus that assisted mankind and protected travellers. In the Greek world they were associated with horses, promoted hunting on horseback and patronised athletic contests. In the second century AD, Vima Kadphises converted the Dioscuri cult space at Dilberjin into a Hindu shrine with murals to celebrate Shiva and Parvati, the goddess of fertility.[50]

The second century Kushan also built temples to honour their royal dynasty. The *Rabatak Inscription* records how Kanishka ordered dynastic statues of Kushan rulers to be displayed in major temples subject to the regime. Kushan royal temples have been excavated at Surkh Kutal in central Afghanistan and at Mat in northern India. Although the Surkh Kotal temple was a hillside stronghold ascended by a great staircase, it had elements of Hellenic architecture and inscriptions written in Greek script.[51] By contrast the brick-built Mat Temple was influenced by local Indian designs and had inscriptions in Kharoshthi.[52] The two temples were about 1,000 miles apart, but they were furnished with similar royal statues. The larger-than-life statues from the Mat Temple depicted dismounted royal riders dressed in knee-length coats with ornate belts, loose trousers and heavy riding boots. The figures also have their feet turned outward in the distinctive stance of steppe riders who, before the invention of the stirrup, gripped the flanks of the horses with their thighs and knees.[53] The statues were recovered in a fragmentary state with their portrait heads removed or destroyed. Only one of these heads survived and it depicts a Kushan king wearing a peaked cap or helmet.

Later Kushan kings promoted the Zoroastrian religion of Iran and the coins of Huvishka celebrate 'the royal fire' and 'the royal splendour' (AD 151–187). Subsequent kings are depicted on their coins wearing cataphract-style parade armour with conical helmets and metal corselets complete with sleeve and leg guards comprised of interlocking metal bands. This armour might have been made from bronze, gilded iron or Indian steel.[54]

But the Kushan also altered the culture of the subject civilizations. They built infrastructures to enable trade, travel and communication across their vast empire. They also transferred people between regions for the purposes of war or to exploit their construction skills. A Bactrian inscription from the Shiva Temple at Dilberjin near the Bactrian capital records that Vima had specialist workmen brought from the distant Indian city of Ujjain to help construct water conduits at this site.[55] The *Rabatak Inscription* found near Surkh Kotal records state-led efforts to supply abundant clean water to the new royal sites in southern Bactria. A canal was built 'by an officer of the King who buttressed the channel with stones so that the water would flow in a pure stream'. When this water system failed, Kanishka 'had a buttressed well dug and the overseer took good care of the well and the entire stronghold'.[56] The effort was justified since this arid region in southern Bactria was crucial to the Kushan regime as it led into the Hindu Kush region and allowed passage to India.

Under the rule of the Kushan Empire, the Gandhara region between the Indus and Bactria became a centre-point for commerce and cultural exchange. The region was a thoroughfare for Indian merchants heading north to the silk routes and travellers from Central Asia journeying down to ports on the Indian Ocean. Consequently this region developed its own style of art and architecture taking inspiration from both Greek and Indian culture. Gandhari art merged these influences with traditional Iranian art forms and blended motifs from Kushan steppe culture into a visual dynamic of artefacts and architecture. The subject matter often portrayed Buddhist themes, but Roman sources confirm that these eastern cultures also maintained a familiarity with Greek legends. Dio Chrysostom reports, 'It is said that Homer's poetry is recited in India, where people have translated it into their own language and dialect.'[57] A well-known relief sculpture from Gandhara is believed to depict a scene from the Trojan War with a female figure raising her arms in protest as a wheeled-horse effigy is being dragged into a city.[58] The woman is portrayed as an Indian princess, but she could represent the classical heroines Helen or Cassandra. The men are depicted in short Greek-style tunics which suggest the survival of Hellenic culture in ancient Bactria. The horse motif probably had additional significance for the mounted Kushan nobility who conquered the urbanised Indo-Greeks.

Greek and Kushan culture merged near the ancient Indian city of Taxila on the Upper Indus. Taxila controlled strategic routes leading across the Hindu Kush and when the Greco-Bactrian king Demetrius invaded the Indus region in 180 BC, he established a Greek centre called Sirkap near the Indian city. Sirkap was a Greek walled city built on the river bank opposite Taxila, but the two centres shared administrative duties and the royal mint remained in the Indian capital.[59] A Greek philosopher from the Roman Empire named Apollonius was said to have visited this region in about AD 44. He was received by an Indo-Parthian prince who was fluent in Greek and governed Taxila from the Hellenic site. The city was said to be 'fortified fairly well in the manner of Greek cities'. Apollonius is reported to have seen a city 'divided up into narrow streets in the same irregular manner as in Athens. From the outside many houses appear to be one story high, but if you go into them you find cellars.'[60] When the Kushan conquered this region they established a third administrative capital at a site called Sirsukh close to Taxila. This city was strongly defended with a stone wall that included projecting circular bastions for archers.[61]

Evidence of Kushan era Greek culture was unearthed during excavations at Taxila. The dome of one of the early Buddhist stupas (relic temples) in the city was decorated with sculptures of upside down acanthus leaves. The acanthus is a Mediterranean plant that is not indigenous to the region, but it does feature as decoration on Greek styled Corinthian columns.[62] Stone panels from a temple stairway in the nearby Swat Valley depicted men and women dressed in Greek-style belted tunics, but some wear trousers and boots instead of sandals. They are engaged in festive scenes, playing musical instruments and drinking wine from Greek-style jars (*kraters*) and serving bowls.[63]

The Kushan regime probably managed the Ganges territories from Mathura. The summer capital of the Kushan king was at Kapisa (Bagram) in northern Afghanistan near modern Kabul. But the royal court probably moved to the walled cities near Taxila in the less humid winter months.[64]

Kushan Contacts with the Roman Empire

Vima Kadphises (AD 102–127) might have been the first Kushan king to send envoys to meet a Roman Emperor. The Kushan probably attended the victory events that were staged in AD 106 to celebrate Trajan's triumph over the mountainous Transylvanian kingdom of Dacia. Dacia was positioned north of the Danube River and represented the first major acquisition of new territory since the Roman invasion of Britain over sixty years earlier. The annexation of Dacia had involved five years of conflict and the participation of units drawn from at least thirteen legions.[65] This conquest was celebrated as a major achievement for the Roman Empire and Dio explains that after the Dacian victory, 'upon Trajan's return to Rome many embassies came to him from various foreigners including the Indians.' The celebrations lasted 123 days and included numerous wild beast fights in the Colosseum. Dio reports that 'during these spectacles the ambassadors who came from the various kings sat in the senatorial section.'[66] The Kushan ambassadors would have considered their regime as an eastern equal to the Roman Empire. During the third century AD, the Kushan king Kanishka III referred to himself as the *Kaisara* (Caesar) on an inscription displayed near the Ara River in Punjab.[67]

Writing during the reign of Trajan, Dio Chrysostom refers to the Kushan when he describes Bactrians seen in Alexandria as 'excellent at horsemanship who practice this skill for the defence and independence of their empire'.[68] Kushan subjects were also seen in Rome when Dio Chrysostom describes the appearance of foreign peoples in the city wearing 'the turbans and trousers of Persians and Bactrians'.[69] Roman crowds who saw these exotic foreigners in the company of senators and imperial officials probably wondered where their emperor might be planning his next campaign.

The Roman Empire and the Kushan considered the Parthian regime to be a common adversary. They were positioned on opposite sides of the Parthian Empire and therefore each had an interest in containing, or diminishing, its power and influence. Perhaps the Kushan kings envisaged an alliance with the Romans that resembled their political agreements with the Han Empire in the Tarim territories (AD 90). This would have involved simultaneous border campaigns to divide Parthian attention and force them to split their army between battle fronts.[70] Tacitus suggests there was precedent for this kind of cooperation dating back to an Armenian war between Rome and Parthia early in the reign of the Emperor Nero (AD 58–63). During this conflict envoys from the secessionist realm of Hyrcania told the Romans that their forces had delayed the Parthian army in eastern Iran 'as a pledge of goodwill' towards the Roman cause.[71]

The Kushan probably conquered northern India with an army of about 70,000 mounted troops. This was the size of the campaign force that they mobilized in AD 90 to launch an attack on the Tarim territories against the Chinese General Ban Chao.[72] The news of these engagements may have reached Roman subjects and rekindled classical interest in the possibility of distant conquests. By the second century AD, the Kushan had conquered the Indus kingdoms and were extending their empire across northern India as far as the central Ganges. They had therefore surpassed the eastern achievements of Alexander the Great with his Greek-Macedonian army and certain Romans may have believed that further conquests could be made by their own empire as the western successor of Greek civilization.

During this period, there was renewed interest in Alexander and in studies that reconsidered his conquest of Persia and expeditions into India. New biographies of Alexander were composed by the Latin writer Curtius Rufus and the Greek authors Plutarch and Arrian. Arrian's work is of particular interest for military observations because he served as the governor of Cappadocia, a strategic Roman province positioned on the Black Sea coast near Armenia. Plutarch also introduced the theme of eastern conquests when he wrote about the civil wars of the late Roman Republic and the final battle between Julius Caesar and Pompey at Pharsalus in 48 BC. In his account of the battle he laments that Roman commanders fought civil wars during this period rather than expand imperial rule further into Asia. Plutarch questions, 'What Scythian horsemen, Parthian arrows, or Indian riches, could possibly resist 70,000 well-armed Roman soldiers under the command of generals like Pompey or Caesar?'[73]

Trajan seized the opportunity for an eastern war in AD 113 when the Parthians placed their own candidate on the Armenian throne without Roman approval. The Emperor annexed Armenia and began to conquer the Mesopotamian kingdoms claimed by Parthia. The Parthians were defeated in Babylonia, but in AD 116 many of the newly captured Mesopotamian territories revolted and there were uprisings against Roman rule in Palestine and Egypt. Worn out by his advancing age and the hardships of military command, Trajan suffered a stroke and died the following year. His successor Hadrian decided to withdraw Roman forces from Mesopotamia and allowed the Parthians to reclaim Babylonia.

During his twenty year reign the Emperor Hadrian received a number of Kushan embassies who requested alliance (AD 117–138). But the Emperor avoided further conflict with the Parthian regime and used these international contacts to enhance his imperial prestige. The *Historia Augusta* reports that 'Bactrian kings sent supplicant ambassadors to Hadrian begging for alliance.'[74] The Roman government remained in contact with the Kushan Empire during the reign of Antoninus Pius (AD 138–161) when imperial interest in eastern affairs included further dealings with the Hyrcanians. These were a people on the east coast of the Caspian Sea who sought independence from the Parthian Empire.[75] Contacts were enhanced by imperial propaganda and Aurelius Victor reports 'the Indians, the Bactrians and the Hyrcanians, all sent ambassadors to Antoninus Pius, because they had heard that this great Emperor maintained a spirit of justice demonstrated by his handsome and grave countenance and his slim and vigorous figure.'[76] Some of these ambassadors could have been sent by the Kushan King Kanishka I who came to power in AD 127.

International Commerce

Storerooms from a Kushan palace or royal treasury have been excavated at Bagram in northern Afghanistan. The finds included many valuable foreign objects that had been accumulated over more than a century. In the storerooms there were ivory plaques, figurines and carvings from India and fragments of ornate lacquered tableware from Han China. The Roman finds comprised bronze figurines depicting classical deities, steel weights and colourful glassware including multi-coloured *millefiori* bowls, blown-glass ornaments, painted vases and cut-glass goblets. The goblets were painted with classical scenes including the Pharos Lighthouse at Alexandria, Roman gladiatorial combat, a battle of Alexander, a duel between Hector and Achilles and a Greek hunting scene with mounted riders. These objects probably reached the Kushan Empire aboard Roman merchant ships that visited the Indus ports.[77] According to Strabo at least 120 Roman ships were involved in this commerce during the Augustan era. If each of these vessels carried only 300 tons of cargo then thousands of tons of merchandise were being shipped between the empires.[78]

As well as acting as intermediaries in foreign trade, the Kushan also maintained their own distant commercial dealings. The landscape and climate of southern Asia, including most of India, did not suit horse breeding. Merchants from the Kushan Empire therefore organized the export of Bactrian horses to distant kingdoms that required cavalry. The animals were brought down to the Indus ports and from there conveyed by ship to lands beyond India. A third century Chinese envoy named Kang Tai reported that Yuezhi subjects 'are continually sending horses by sea to Jiaying (Sumatra)'. These ships sailed around southern India and voyaged across the Bay of Bengal to reach Burma and the Malay Peninsula. The Chinese were informed that 'the king of Jiaying buys all the horses and if any have died during the voyage, it is sufficient for the grooms to present the head and hide to the king and he will pay them half price.'[79]

Kushan Coinage

The first century *Periplus of the Erythraean Sea* describes how Roman merchants brought imperial coins to the ports of northern India to pay for valuable spices, fabrics and gemstones.[80] Roman money was minted using pure bullion, so they commanded good exchange rates when offered against regional Indian currencies, which were usually made from silver debased by significant amounts of bronze or lead. The result was an outflow of gold and silver bullion from the Empire which enriched the northern Indian kingdoms. Describing conditions at the Indian port of Barygaza in Gujurat, the author of the *Periplus* reports that 'Roman money, gold and silver commands an exchange at some profit against the local currency.'[81] This coinage included large amounts of silver denarii that had been issued by the Emperors Augustus and Tiberius (27 BC–AD 37).

The Kushan regime must have received large amounts of revenue from taxing the international commerce conducted between the Indian Ocean and the Tarim Silk Routes. Writing in AD 75, Pliny reports that the Roman Empire exported more than 50 million sesterces of precious metal to India every year.[82] An ancient Indian guide to statecraft, called the *Arthashastra*, advised rulers to impose a one-fifth tax on foreign imports.[83] There were three main trade destinations for Roman ships during the era of the *Periplus*: the Indus, Gujurat and the Tamil kingdoms. By conquering the Indus region, the Kushan might have controlled a third of this commerce with revenues worth tens of millions of sesterces.

The Kushan were familiar with Roman coins from a time when their kingdom was confined to Bactria. The founder of the dynasty, Kujula Kadphises (AD 30–80), issued base metal coinage that copied the portrait image from Augustan or Tiberian denarii (27 BC–AD 37). These copper coins show the head of a classical emperor wearing a Roman laurel, but the text and titles are in Greek letters announcing 'Kujula Kadphises, Ruler of the Kushans'. Perhaps Kujula wanted to present himself as an overlord of the Bactrian Greeks and the image of a Roman Emperor provided a classical western model that indicated status and position.

Other coins issued by Kujula display the portrait of a Hellenic king with the image of the Greek demi-god Hercules on the reverse. These coins have titles and text in Kharoshthi script and announce Kujula as the 'Ruler' and 'Dharmathidasa' (follower of Indian doctrines). His successor Vima Takto (AD 80–102) conquered the Hindu Kush and seized territory from the Parthians who occupied the Indus region. Vima Takto acknowledged the residual Greek communities in this region by issuing bronze coins depicting a traditional image of a Hellenic king wearing a royal headband. On these coins he describes himself in Greek letters as 'King of Kings' and *Soter Megas* or the 'Great Saviour'. These are Greek motifs, but the reverse of the coin follows the Saka practice of depicting a royal figure mounted on a horse.

Mountain streams in Gandhara produced large amounts of gold dust. During the fifth century BC, the Persian Achaemenid Empire received over 13 tons of gold from this territory per annum.[84] This formed one third of Persian income and was enough precious metal to mint 1.5 million gold coins with a Roman currency value of 150 million sesterces (the annual cost of fourteen legions). As a comparison, the Persians received silver tribute payments from Bactria, equivalent to about 11 million sesterces.[85] Strabo verifies that 'gold dust is carried by the Indian rivers' and later sources confirm this prosperity.[86] Writing in the second century, Dionysios Periegetes refers to territory near Taxila 'where swift streams, the Hypanis and divine Margaros, carry down shining flecks of gold'.[87] Apuleius also refers to 'the marvellous stories told about India' including its 'streams of gold'.[88] Also when the Chinese monk Xuanzang visited the Indus region in the seventh century AD he reported that 'this country produces large amounts of gold.'[89]

In AD 64, the Roman Emperor Nero reduced the gold content of imperial aurei as part of his currency reforms. The weight of new aureus was reduced from 8 to 7.3 grams and the coin was issued as a smaller-sized piece to avoid altering the purity of the metal. This meant that Roman merchants could still use these new coins as export bullion, but they preferred to deal in older Julio-Claudian issues. Both coins had the same monetary value in the Empire, but in real terms the older aurei contained up to 9 per cent more gold. In terms of bullion, 40 old aurei were needed to gather 1 Roman pound of gold, while 45 of the new coins were required to amass the same quantity of precious metal. These extra 5 aurei would be worth 500 sesterces in Roman markets and represent enough wealth to buy more than thirty amphoras filled with wine.[90] Roman merchants engaged in eastern trade therefore did all they could to select the older, larger coins for export.

Dacia was rich in gold and the Roman conquest brought significant new wealth into the Mediterranean economy in the form of booty and captured royal treasures.[91] The imperial regime also seized gold mines in the Carpathian Mountains and this greatly increased the amount of precious metal entering circulation in the Empire.[92] As a consequence, the value of gold in Roman markets fell in relation to silver. During this period Roman currency valued gold to silver at a rate of about 1:11 (1 quantity of gold worth 11 quantities of silver). However, evidence from Egypt suggests that soon after the Dacian conquests gold became so plentiful that its price in export markets such as Coptos was temporarily reduced to a ratio of almost 1:8. An Egyptian papyrus dated to AD 110 reports: 'gold bullion which was selling at 15 (drachma) has fallen in value to 11 (drachma).'[93] The kingdoms of northern India placed a relatively high price on gold (1:10), so Roman merchants could buy gold at a diminished price in the Empire and, by exporting the metal, gain valuable purchasing power in Indian markets. During this period Roman merchants probably began exporting larger shipments of gold and this wealth further enriched northern India.

Vima Kadphises (AD 102–127) was the first ruler to mint a gold currency for the Kushan Empire. This new Kushan coinage was closely modelled on Roman aurei and matched the size and weight of Julio-Claudian coins (8 grams).[94] The dominant design depicts Vima in traditional steppe attire, dressed in a long riding coat and wearing a high-domed helmet with trailing ribbons. On the reverse is an image of the Greek sun god Helios next to a Kushan monogram known as the *tamgha*. Following the production of these gold issues, the Kushan do not seem to have minted significant amounts of silver coin. From this period onward their currency system was dominated by high-value gold issues and large bronze coins.

During the second century AD, Roman merchants continued to export gold and silver to northern India, but as bullion rather than coin. This was because Trajan reformed Roman currency by reducing the silver content of the denarius until it represented a silver-to-gold value that was similar to price ratios in India (1:10). One consequence of this action was that new Roman coinage lost its exchange rate advantage in the money markets of northern India. This meant that many Roman traders switched from coin to bullion, especially when supplies of older coinage became insufficient to meet export demands. Pausanias reports that 'The sailors on ships that go to India say that the Indians will only give produce in exchange for a Greek [Mediterranean] cargo,' and confirms, 'these Indians have an enormous quantity of their own gold and bronze coins, so they do not appreciate Roman currency.'[95] The lasting consequence of this international commerce was that the Kushan Empire increased its bullion wealth, but at the long-term expense of the Roman economy.

Changing Religious Practices

The Kushan King Kanishka (AD 127–151) is depicted on his coins in the clothing of a steppe warrior with a long riding coat, trousers and heavy boots. As symbols of his military prowess he is armed with a curved sword and a lance for mounted combat. On some of his coins he is depicted making an offering over an altar while a sacred fire burns behind him. But despite his military reputation, Kanishka became a benefactor of Buddhism and helped to promote and patronize Buddhist teachings across his empire. Some of his gold coins therefore depict an image of the standing Buddha with the Greek text 'Boddo'. The Buddha wears loose flowing robes similar to a Greek *himation*, but his feet point outward in the stance of a steppe rider.

Buddhism originated in the sixth century BC from the teachings of a religious leader named Shakyamuni who came from an urbanised kingdom in the mid-Ganges region. By the first century BC, the religion was practised in many regions of India alongside traditional Hinduism. Early Buddhist principals were conveyed by narratives called *Jatakas* that taught moral messages. These teachings promoted commerce and it was said the Buddha encouraged wealthy people to spend a quarter of their income on living expenses, save a quarter for future needs and invest the remaining half-share in business.[96] This explains the popularity of the Buddhist religion among prosperous merchant communities.

During his reign Kanishka convened an important Buddhist council in Kashmir and saw to it that leading religious texts were translated from the Gandhari vernacular into more accessible and commonly read forms of Sanskrit.[97] Kanishka also funded the construction of a monumental stupa near Purushapura (Peshawar, north of Taxila) that was larger than most other temple-complexes in India. Chinese missionaries who visited the site in late antiquity describe an enormous domed building made from ornate wood. According to these accounts a spike-like pillar rose from the centre of the dome and extended several hundred feet into the air.[98] Only the foundations of this building remain, but modern archaeological inquiry suggests that this circular stupa had a diameter of about

286 feet.[99] The central wooden dome of the building was therefore almost twice the size of the concrete roof that Hadrian provided for the circular Pantheon in Rome.[100]

Kanishka could have employed Greek artisans to work on the construction of his great stupa. This was confirmed by archaeologists who found an ancient reliquary in a small deposit chamber under the building. The casket has an inscription written in local Kharoshthi script, but the artisan bears the Greek name Agesilas and he dates the work to the first year of Kanishka's reign (AD 127). The inscription reads, 'The servant Agisalaos, the superintendent of works at the *vihara* of Kanishka in the monastery of Mahasena'.[101] Agesilas was possibly an Indo-Greek convert to Buddhism, but his community could have hired Greek artisans from the Roman Empire who would have travelled to India to find employment as craftsmen. Shipwrights at the Red Sea ports in Roman Egypt were able to construct vessels over 100 feet long so they could easily have transferred their joinery and craft-working skills to Indian projects. The *Acts of Thomas* describe how a royal agent from the Indus region visited the Roman Empire to acquire skilled artisans to help build an ornate palace in northern India. According to tradition one of these craftsmen was the apostle Thomas who brought Christian teachings overseas.[102]

Traditional Buddhism did not depict its teachers and deities as icons or sculptures, but in Gandhara the new artistic style portrayed the Buddha in statue form. This development may have been influenced by Greek artisans who had a pre-existing tradition and format for depicting their gods. Early depictions of the Buddha from Gandhara show a figure with a Greek-style aureole or halo and dressed in a *himation* or light robe similar to a toga.[103]

During the second century AD Buddhist merchants and missionaries from the Kushan Empire made journeys across the silk routes to China. They brought Buddhist teachings to the Tarim kingdoms and helped promote Buddhist principles in the major Chinese cities. But Buddhist ideas were also reaching China via sea-route connections with India and the developing civilizations of southeast Asia. One of the early Chinese converts to Buddhism was a Han prince named Liu Ying who was a younger half-brother of the Emperor Ming (AD 58–75). Liu Ying was presented with a royal command in the Chu district of southeast China where he began following Buddhist philosophies. In AD 65 his character and beliefs were investigated by the imperial government who could find no certain evidence of subversion against the Empire. Nevertheless, the Emperor Ming sent an envoy overland to India to investigate the character and origins of this foreign doctrine.[104] The envoy returned to China in AD 67 with two Indian monks named Moteng (*Kasyapa Matanga*) and Zhu Falan (*Dharmaratna*) who entered Louyang with religious texts (*sutras*) and sacred images carried on white horses. Consequently, the Buddhist monastery they established on the outskirts of the capital came to be known as the 'White Horse Temple'.[105]

The *Hou Hanshu* records that the Emperor Ming gave his approval to the religion and, soon after, 'paintings and statues [of the Buddha] appeared in China'.[106] Later the Han Emperor Huan was said to have 'devoted himself to sacred things and often sacrificed to the Buddha' (AD 146–168). His piety inspired others and 'people gradually began to accept Buddhism until they became numerous.'[107]

One of the leading monks in the transfer of Buddhist beliefs to China was a Kushan missionary from Gandhara named Lokaksema who taught at the Han capital Louyang. Lokaksema was accepted into the Han court in AD 150 and he remained in Louyang until about AD 189. While there, he translated important Buddhist texts into Chinese including a religious work called the *Prajnaparamita Sutra* or *The Practice of the Path*.[108] A famous third century Chinese Buddhist named Zhi Qian claimed descent from Kushan migrants. It was reported, 'he was a descendant of the Great Yuezhi Kingdom and his grandfather Fadu immigrated into China with hundreds of his countrymen during the reign of the Emperor Ling' (AD 168–189). Fadu was offered an official post in the Han administration which gave his family local respect and influence.[109] Due to these long-term cultural influences Buddhism eventually became one of the three main philosophical and religious systems in central China alongside Daoism and Confucianism.

The Kushan King Huvishka (AD 151–187) patronized Brahmin institutions, but his coins also depict Hindu divinities associated with Shivaism. In addition, Huvishka promoted Hellenic deities and the Greek-Egyptian god Serapis appears on his coinage as 'Sarapo'. This is significant because the cult of Serapis was devised in Egypt by the Ptolemaic Regime and the deity was not part of the established Indo-Greek pantheon. This could be additional evidence for the seaborne exchange of ideas. Further issues display the image of a classical goddess standing with the legend 'Riom' recorded in Greek letters beside her. This 'Riom' might be a personification of Rome, portrayed as a power honoured by the Kushan Empire.[110]

Eastern kingdoms were well-informed about political developments in the Roman Empire. For example, the Parthian King Artabanus sent letters to Rome accusing the Emperor Tiberius of political murders, cruelty towards his subjects and practices that led to 'a shameless and dissolute lifestyle'.[111] When the young Emperor Elagabalus assumed power in AD 218 he tried to replace traditional Roman religion with an esoteric Syrian cult involving the worship of a mysterious black stone. This cult caused widespread revulsion in traditional Roman society and the Kushan responded by sending a group of religious envoys to the Roman Empire which included Buddhist missionaries. A Syrian gnostic named Bardaisan met these envoys near Emesa on their journey to meet the Emperor. He questioned the envoys and used their statements to compose an account of Indian religions that only survives in fragments quoted by later scholars.[112] Although Han China was receptive to Buddhist philosophies, the cult endorsed by Elagabalus opposed the Buddhist principles of merit and moral action and the Kushan envoys failed in their mission.

CHAPTER SEVEN

The Sogdian Intermediaries

In ancient times, an Iranian people called the Sogdians became one of the leading intermediaries in Silk Route commerce between China and Rome. The Sogdians were an urbanised population who farmed fertile lands in Central Asia to the northeast of Bactria (northern Afghanistan). Their homelands lay between the Oxus and Jaxartes rivers (Tajikistan and Uzbekistan), near where the Ferghana Valley led into the Pamir Mountains and the Tarim Basin. Sogdia covered an area more than twice the size of Spain and this well-administered territory had once been a *satrapy* (province) in both the Persian and the Seleucid empires. The *Hou Hanshu* describes Sogdia as a land that 'produces superb horses, cattle, sheep, grapes, and all sorts of fruit. The water and soil of this country are excellent, that is why their grape wine is so famous.'[1] The Sogdians organized long-distance caravans from their capital at Samarkand for merchant expeditions travelling out across the Tarim kingdoms to acquire exotic goods from the distant Chinese Empire.

The Sogdians maximised their profits by transporting Indian and Persian goods to Chinese markets to secure silk and other eastern valuables. To facilitate their long-distance trade networks the Sogdians established merchant communities in the leading Tarim cities. Sogdian dealers and agents also began to settle in the Han Empire, especially in the militarized Hexi Corridor which facilitated direct passage into inner China. By the end of the first century AD there was a significant Sogdian community residing in the Han capital Louyang. These trade networks helped to spread influential new religious and cultural ideas across Inner Asia, including Buddhist teachings which became well-established in China during this period.

The Early History of Sogdia

Sogdia was part of the Achaemenid Empire of ancient Persia which had dominated the Middle East for more than two centuries from 550–330 BC. It had formed a satrapy in the northeast corner of the Persian Empire where the settled lands merged into the steppe wilderness. When King Xerxes invaded mainland Greece in 480 BC, Sogdian troops were levied into the Persian army to fight against the Greeks. Herodotus describes how the Sogdian troops were armed with cane bows and short spears similar to the equipment carried by Bactrian units.[2]

A blue semi-precious stone called lapis lazuli could be found in the foothills of the Pamir Mountains in southern Sogdia and mines in the region also produced valuable red garnets. These gemstones furnished the great Persian palace built by Darius I at Susa.[3] Herodotus reveals the wealth of ancient Sogdia when he lists the tribute that the Persian King Darius received from the peoples of his Empire (522–486 BC). The Sogdians paid tribute along with the Parthians in eastern Iran and the Arians who inhabited lands near Herat in neighbouring Afghanistan. These nations contributed almost 390 silver talents to the Persian regime, equivalent to approximately 2.3 million drachma, or over 9 million sesterces in Roman currency. At this time the satrapy of Syria and Palestine was paying 455 silver talents to the Persian Empire, so the territories of Central Asia were almost as revenue rich as those of the Mediterranean zone.[4]

When Alexander defeated the Persian Empire in 330 BC, he led his armies east into Sogdia to subdue the furthest territories of the former regime. In 329 BC the Macedonians captured Samarkand, known to them as Maracanda, and advanced as far as the Jaxartes River to establish the frontier city of Alexandria Eschate ('Alexandria the Furthest'). But the Sogdians and their Bactrian allies occupied a series of strongly-defended cliff-top fortresses and Alexander found native resistance in this region hard to eliminate. After a prolonged campaign including several sieges, Alexander secured an alliance with a Bactrian warlord named Oxyartes. To confirm the arrangement, Alexander married his daughter Rokhshana. Sogdia was then joined with Bactria to form a single satrapy under Macedonian rule with military outposts established in the region using retired Greek veterans as garrison troops and colonists.[5]

After the breakup of Alexander's Empire, Bactria and Sogdia became the most easterly provinces of the Seleucid Kingdom. Then in about 250 BC a governor named Euthydemus denounced Seleucid rule and established himself as regent of an independent Greek realm centred on Bactria. Euthydemus seized control of neighbouring Sogdia on the far side of the Oxus and extended his rule north to Alexandria Eschate on the Jaxartes River.[6] Sogdia was under the rule of this Greco-Bactrian kingdom for almost a century, until a time of civil war and foreign conflicts allowed mounted steppe nations to invade and occupy the entire region. When the first Chinese agents reached Transoxiana in 128 BC, the Sogdians were under the rule of a steppe nation called the Kangju that occupied lands on either side of the Jaxartes valley (the Syr Darya).[7] These were the same Kangju who supported the Xiongnu rebel Zhizhi when he established a fortress on the steppe lands to the north of Sogdia and defended his citadel against a Chinese-led army in 36 BC.[8]

The Roman writer Pliny the Elder describes Sogdia as an independent region, but his knowledge of the territory was based on Greek accounts concerning Alexander. He explains that 'beyond the Bactrians are the Sogdians and the town of Panda (Samarkand). On the furthest limits of their territory is Alexandria (Eschate) which was founded by Alexander the Great.' For Greek and Roman authorities the Jaxartes was the limit of the civilized world and not even the classical gods or semi-legendary kings were said to have advanced beyond this frontier. Pliny reports that on the edge of Sogdia 'there are altars set up by Hercules and Bacchus, by Cyrus and Samiramis and by Alexander. For they all found their limit in this region of the world confined by the Jaxartes River.'[9]

The Sogdian Silk Routes

The formation of long-distance caravan routes through the Tarim kingdoms created significant new opportunities for the Sogdians. Their territory had previously been thought to lie at the periphery of the known world, but by 100 BC new routes leading to China placed them at the centre of international affairs. Sogdia suddenly became the strategic midpoint of trade routes that connected China and the Tarim kingdoms with India and Iran. Sogdian merchants could therefore interact with three of the world's largest economies and develop their country as a conduit for long distance commerce. Sogdian noblemen engaged in commerce first began sending their sons to China in the first century BC. These envoys were concerned with commerce, but they offered political pledges to gain Han state assistance and receive diplomatic gifts. The *Hanshu* reports 'the Kangju send their sons to attend the Han court because they desire commerce, but their political assurances are a pretence.'[10] A Chinese pilgrim named Xuanzang visited Sogdia in the seventh century AD and describes Sogdia as 'completely enclosed by rugged land and very populous. The precious merchandise of many foreign countries is stored here.'[11] The contemporary *Xintangshu* reports that the Sogdians 'excel at commerce and love profit; as soon as a man reaches the age of 20, he leaves for the neighbouring kingdoms. They go to every place that profit can be earned.'[12]

The city of Samarkand was situated on the main route between Ferghana and the oasis territory of Merv on the frontier of the Parthian Empire. But the Parthians did not permit Sogdian caravans to travel into Iran and it is likely they also restricted foreign access to Merv. The Parthians had settled thousands of Roman prisoners of war at Merv in 53 BC and it was in their interests to isolate this community.[13] Parthian merchants would have passed through Merv on route to Samarkand, but Sogdian caravans did not make a similar journey westward. The Roman prisoners who were repatriated from Merv by a political agreement in 20 BC provided a detailed account of the routes across Iran, but they knew very little about the territories and peoples to the east.[14] Even a Roman invasion route presented in a work known as the *Parthian Stations* detours south at Merv and does not enter Sogdian territory. At that time Sogdia was ruled by people that the Romans called the Mardi (the steppe nation known to the Chinese as the *Kangju*).[15]

However, Sogdian caravans could bypass Parthian territory by following a river tributary from Samarkand down to the Oxus valley. The Oxus River flowed from Sogdia northwest through the steppe to the edge of the Aral Sea. At this location, deals were concluded with a steppe nation called the Alani who occupied grasslands extending around the northern shores of the Caspian towards the Caucasus Mountains. Some of these Central Asian trade networks combined river transport with caravan travel and the Sogdians operated small craft along navigable stretches of the Oxus. Connecting caravans transferred merchandise between these waterways and brought trade goods to the Caspian shore. Local sea-going vessels would then ship cargo west to the small kingdom of Caucasian Albania, which was positioned between the Caspian and the Black Sea. This provided an alternative route for eastern goods to be transported from Transoxiana into the Roman Empire.

The Karakoram Route into India

The Sogdians extended their trade operations south by sending caravans into neighbouring Bactria. It was a relatively easy journey from Bactria through the Hindu Kush to reach markets in the Upper Indus. But Sogdian caravans favoured another route to India that involved travel to the oasis city of Khotan on the southern part of the Tarim Basin. There was a route south from this city that led through high-altitude passes in the snow-capped Karakoram Mountains to reach valleys in the Upper Indus near Kashmir. This was a cold and arid region where caravans trekked along bleak rocky paths covered with rubble-like grey gravel. Some paths followed narrow precipices that led along cliff faces descending into steep rock-strewn valleys. Other routes crossed narrow gorges along suspension bridges made from knotted ropes and wood planks hung over steep chasms. The Chinese called these bridges 'suspended crossings'.[16] It was a 600 mile journey from Samarkand to Khotan and a further 400 mile crossing through the mountains to reach the Punjab.

This Karakoram route was known to the Chinese from an early period. In the first century BC merchants from Kashmir would reach the Han controlled Tarim kingdoms and request passage to China. Some of these merchant parties were conveyed to the Han capital at state expense and received valuable tribute in exchange for their diplomatic 'gifts'. A Han official observed, 'there are no members of the royal family or noblemen among those who bring the gifts. They are all merchants and men of low origins. They wish to exchange their goods and conduct commerce on the pretext of presenting gifts.'[17]

Ancient Sogdian inscriptions written in Aramaic have been found on desolate rock-faces in the Karakoram Mountains near the Swat Valley (northern Pakistan). The writing appears at devotional sites where travellers believed they could secure divine protection by carving their names into the rocks beneath the glacial mountains. Travellers also sketched religious motifs into the stones and many of these carvings depict the distinctive domed roofs of Buddhist stupas or the horned heads of the wild ibex goats that roamed the landscape. Sogdian messages have been documented at more than seven sites in the Karakoram Mountains.

There are more than 1,000 names and 700 petroglyphs carved into rock-faces near Shatial where an ancient bridge is believed to have spanned an upper tributary of the Indus River. Many of these short inscribed messages are in Indian languages written in ancient Brahmin and a northern form of Prakrit called Kharoshthi. Just under half of the messages are written in Sogdian script and record the names of Iranian travellers who passed through this region from the second to seventh century AD. By contrast only nine of the surviving inscriptions were written in the Bactrian language and only two inscriptions could be identified as Parthian. A single inscription from Shatial used Chinese characters and a single piece of ancient Hebrew script was carved into a rock-face at nearby Campsiote.[18]

The Sogdians travelled with Indian colleagues and a Brahmin text from Shatial mentions a Sogdian named Pekako who accompanied two Indian travellers.[19] There were over ten names recorded at this site that were probably Sogdian, but they were written in Brahmin script. The majority of ancient inscriptions found on the Karakoram route record only a single name, but some travellers mention family members who were accompanying the caravan, or who they hoped to see at their destination. One of the longest surviving inscriptions was written by a Sogdian with the surname Nanai-Vandak who was travelling through the Karakorams from India to an outpost near the Pamirs called the Stone Tower (Tashkurgan). He writes, 'Nanai-Vandak, son of Narisaf, passed here on the tenth and requested this favour from the holy presence at Kart: may I reach Kharvandan (Tashkurgan) quickly and see my dear brother in good health.'[20]

Some of the Sogdian names recorded along the Karakoram route identify the writers as adherents of the Zoroastrian faith. This ancient cult was prominent across Iran and was one of the leading religions in the empire of Achaemenid Persia (550–330 BC). Zoroastrianism had survived the Macedonian conquest of Transoxiana and during the period of Greek rule it remained a leading religion in Sogdia. Some Sogdian merchants also adopted aspects of Buddhist faith from India and spread these beliefs into the Tarim kingdoms. Many of the petroglyphs carved into the rock-faces along the Karakoram route therefore relate to Buddhism and were inscribed by Indian or Sogdian travellers who practised this faith.[21] Perhaps some of these travellers were missionaries, but many more would have been merchants funding their distant ventures through the profits of international trade.

Other evidence of silk route traffic comes from a collection of ancient documents found in the desert ruins of Khotan on the southern Tarim Basin. During the third and fourth century AD, people from the Hindu Kush travelled through the Karakoram passes to settle in this oasis-city. They introduced the Gandhai language and the Kharoshthi script to the region and wrote reports and records on paper, strips of leather and thin wooden slips. Many of the surviving documents are judgements, instructions and orders issued by the Khotan government. *Khotan Document 35* refers to a debt due on silk materials, but the agreed amount could not be paid until up-to-date information on the market value of the fabric could be acquired. The text states: 'The debt of silk is to be investigated when the merchants arrive from China. If the dispute persists, the matter will be decided at the Royal Court.'[22] Other orders concern supplies of grain and wine that were to be sold, if the market value of gold made the transaction profitable. *Khotan Document 140* explains, 'Attention must be paid to the price of gold in this place and if the conditions are good the products are to be sold.'[23] Several documents indicate that silk was in common use at Khotan. *Khotan Document 149* lists objects seized from 'the fugitive Masaga' including 'three woollen cloths, one silver ornament, 2,500 *masa* (coins), two jackets, two *somstamni*, two belts and three Chinese robes'.[24] *Khotan Document 225* is a household inventory of agricultural activities and goods received. The scribe records the delivery of two silk bundles and notes that 'a slave of Samgaparana entered the homestead to (deliver/take) three rolls of silk.'[25]

Silk Route Buddhism

Ancient Buddhism profited from commerce and Buddhist institutions assisted the development of trade. Buddhist monasteries established close to major trade routes were equipped with hostels. The resident devotees provided material aid to travellers in return for donations. Large Buddhist temples often owned and managed considerable wealth and assets, including estates that produced income from cash crops. Often these resources had been presented to the monasteries by local rulers wishing to obtain religious approval. Some monasteries propagated this wealth by offering loans to local industries or regional merchants who could repay the amount with interest. The wealth accumulated by the monasteries was displayed as adornments and stored in the form of *Sapta Ratna* or 'Seven Sacred Treasures'. These treasures included traditional Indian forms of wealth such as gold and silver, pearls, crystals and gemstones. But later *Sutras* included Red Mediterranean coral and vivid blue lapis lazuli from northeast Afghanistan among the accumulated treasures.[26] Chinese silk came to be venerated as a Buddhist treasure and monasteries in India and Inner Asia were festooned with coloured canopies, bright flags and banners fashioned from this sought-after material.[27]

During the first century AD, a new form of merchant-sponsored Buddhism called *Mahayana* ('The Great Vehicle') began to spread across the silk routes towards China. *Mahayana* teaching explained how certain Buddhists had obtained enough merit to transcend the normal circle of birth, life, death and reincarnation. But rather than receive Nirvana, these spiritual beings, known as Bodhisattras, remained in existence as intermediaries who could assist other souls on the path towards attainment. Some Bodhisattras had their own personal paradises where their devotees could obtain peace and sanctuary before their reincarnation closer to the eventual goal of Nirvana (full enlightenment). One particular Bodhisattra, named Avalokitshvara, was favoured by merchants who travelled the silk routes and crossed the Indian Ocean. It was believed that Avalokitshvara operated a Great Vehicle that could retrieve his followers and rescue anyone in peril who invoked his name before their moment of death. Businessmen could not take wealth into the afterlife, but they could accumulate and transfer merit between reincarnations, either by performing beneficial actions, or facilitating good deeds by funding religious institutions.[28] The concept of safe-havens between destinations appealed to many commercial travellers and they readily accepted the idea that merit could be purchased and transferred as if it were a physical commodity or investment. Consequently, Buddhist institutions devoted to Avalokitshvara received significant patronage from wealthy merchants and this encouraged the spread of this belief system across the silk routes.[29]

East to Niya

The oasis kingdom of Niya held an important position on the southern silk routes used by Sogdian merchants. Niya was on the route east of Khotan and its ancient remains have been preserved beneath layers of dry desert sand. The kingdom was heavily influenced by silk route traffic and its early coins have Chinese characters on one side and Kharoshthi script on the reverse.[30] The houses at Niya were wooden-framed buildings with walls constructed from sun-dried brick and painted plaster interiors. The discovery of a Han dynasty mould for making state seals confirms that a Chinese 'Office for Propagating Agriculture' operated at the oasis during an early stage of its development.[31]

Kharoshthi documents discovered in the desert ruins of Niya include details of commercial transactions, land deed records, state orders and accounts concerning legal disputes. Chinese people resident at Niya were generally given the surname 'Cina' in these records to distinguish them from the local inhabitants. A third century text known as *Niya Document 324* mentions a resident with the surname Yonu. Yonu could be the Kharoshthi word for 'Greek' since the Persians called Hellenic people 'Yona' (Ionians) and the name was also used in northern India to describe Greek culture. This Yonu who lived in Niya became involved in a legal dispute when one of his slaves was stolen by steppe raiders and sold to a Chinese man named 'Sgasi' for two gold coins. Sgasi had made a legal purchase, but Yonu recognised his own slave and wanted him returned. The local judge ruled that Sgasi had to put the slave up for sale and Yonu would have to pay in order to regain his property.[32]

The surviving documents from Niya confirm that fabrics formed an important part of the wealth owned and managed by the inhabitants of the site. In particular, silk functioned as an alternative to coinage when wealth and funds had to be transferred or stored. By the third century AD there was a significant Buddhist monastery at the oasis. Its representatives assisted the community by serving as independent arbitrators in disputes, witnessing agreements and storing legal contracts. For example, *Niya Document 419* records that two brothers with Buddhist connections sold a small vineyard plot to a man with the Indian name Ananda for one gold *stater*.

The Chinese government issued passports to silk route travellers to ensure that any people who joined the caravans were on legitimate business and had paid the required tolls. These passports were checked by authorities in the oasis kingdoms and at the Chinese garrison outpost at Niya. A small collection of these passports was found at the oasis, having been confiscated by the authorities when they detained certain travellers. One of the passes is dated to AD 269 and the rest seem to be contemporary with this date.[33]

The Niya passports give a physical description of the traveller including identifying features and approximate age. One pass issued on a wooden slip reads, 'thirty year old, medium build, black hair, big eyes, moustache and beard'.[34] Some passes describe clothing, for example one traveller wore 'cloth breeches and hemp shoes'.[35] Other passes mention ethnicity and one of the Niya documents belonged to a Kushan man described as 'Hu Zhizhu of the Yuezhi Kingdom, middle-aged, 49 years old, dark-skin'.[36]

Some of the passports list the route on which the individual was permitted to travel through Chinese controlled territory. One pass records a journey out of

China and lists fortified towns along the Hexi corridor including 'Wu-wei, Xiping, Zhangye, Jiuquan and Dunhuang'.[37] Another wooden slip lists a route around the northern Tarim Basin including 'Shanshan, Yanqi, Qiuci and Shule' (Loulan, Karasahr, Kucha and Kashgar).[38] Perhaps the holder of this pass had been unsure which route he would take to reach Kashgar due to uncertain conditions. He bought two passes in China, but at Loulan he decided to follow the more arduous southern course through Niya, rather than take the northern route which was vulnerable to steppe raids. Chinese passport details did not usually include information about trade goods or the purpose of travel. Only one pass mentions coins, while another records that the traveller was conveying Indian ginger, elm wood, pepper and sugar.[39]

The remains of Buddhist buildings dating to about AD 400 were excavated at the ancient town of Miran on the southern silk route between Cherchen and Loulan. These ancient ruins were buried beneath many layers of desert sand that had smothered the oasis during late antiquity. The religious buildings at this site contained coloured murals with Sogdian motifs including paintings of winged Iranian deities. Fragments of Kharoshthi script were found at the site containing prayers for the wellbeing of religious donors. One of the murals in an outlying stupa depicted the young Buddha in a scene framed by cherubs and wreaths. The artist signed his name as 'Tita' in Kharoshthi script which could be interpreted as an oriental version of the Latin name Titus.[40] If this is the case, then perhaps Tita was descended from a Greek or Roman artisan who had taken employment in the Kushan Empire. If so, he had established a lineage that travelled to the Tarim territories and settled at Niya. East of Niya was the large oasis kingdom of Loulan where the northern and southern silk routes joined.

East to Loulan

The Chinese had significant political interests in the city-state of Loulan which had been sinicised by long-term cultural contacts with Han China. Ancient Chinese texts were found in the ruins of a small fortified station near Loulan which guarded and monitored the main route east to Dunhuang. The ancient Chinese were familiar with paper, but they considered the material flimsy and the authorities preferred to issue orders written on thin wooden slips. These slips were laced together so that they could be read in sequence and stored as rolled-up bundles. The Chinese documents excavated at Loulan include hundreds of these wooden slips thrown into refuge heaps or abandoned in derelict storerooms. The wooden slats eventually collapsed into a disordered jumble as their binding ties decayed. The documents are mainly military data with security and logistical details, but some commercial information is included. The earliest document in the collection of wooden slips dates to AD 252 and the latest was written in AD 331.[41]

The Loulan documents confirm that the Chinese government employed merchant caravans to transport materials and used trade opportunities to acquire commodities. A wooden slip dated to AD 330 is marked with the seal of two Chinese officials and records how a Sogdian-owned caravan leaving China delivered 150 tons of grain and 200 coins to the station at Loulan.[42] A fragmentary document dated to AD 319 records how the Chinese authorities approved the exchange of 4,326 bolts of coloured silk for cavalry horses or camels.[43] Another partial text records that the Chinese garrison 'traded at Dunhuang, value 20,000 coins'.[44] The garrison also had records concerning Chinese merchant companies who operated on this frontier. These private companies adopted adversarial names including *Tun Hu*, *Po Hu*, *Yan Hu* and *Ling Hu*. These titles can be broadly translated as 'Those who supress the Foreigners', but the terms convey concepts such as crushing, oppressing or consuming the wealth of non-Chinese people.[45]

Over fifty documents written in Kharoshthi script have been found at Loulan, including texts that record Sogdian names. Most document minor transactions, for instance a Sogdian named Nani-Vadhag acted as witness in the sale of a camel by Vag'iti-Vandak to Khvarnarse. These are Iranian names and the document was dated using Khotan regal years.[46]

North through Yanqi

Tarim caravans taking a northern route to China could bypass Loulan by following a course through the oasis state of Yanqi (Karasahr) which lay between Kucha and Turfan. Wooden slips found at this ancient site confirm payment details and reveal commercial dealings conducted by garrison troops. Two Chinese slips from the first century AD confirm that Han soldiers were due a wage of 600 coins per month.[47] However, it seems that this state salary was often paid using a bolt of silk that could be sold for local cash or exchanged for supplies and equipment. An archaeologist and explorer named Aurel Stein discovered two strips of undyed silk in a refuse heap beneath a watchtower in Yanqi. The strips were from a bolt of state-issued silk stamped with a Chinese seal verifying the origin, quality and size of the fabric roll. The roll was about 20 inches wide, over 12 feet long and weighed 12 ounces (area: 20 square feet). The bolt was stamped with the official value of 618 coins, so it was probably intended for an officer on a slightly higher pay-scale (a 3 per cent bonus).[48] It was delivered to Yanqi sometime between AD 84 and AD 137. Perhaps the officer in charge of the watchtower decided to cut up the fabric into more convenient 'payments' and this would explain the scraps in the refuse heap.

Events in the second century AD suggest the scale of the silk payments reaching Chinese garrisons in the Hexi and Tarim regions. In this period a Chinese prince gave 10,000 silk rolls to the Han government to assist with payment costs on the northwest frontiers.[49] Texts from the Tang era record that two state-organized caravans delivered 15,000 bolts of silk from Dunhuang to a frontier military warehouse 400 miles to the east.[50] Despite these troop payments, there was still a large market demand for silk in the main Tarim kingdoms. One of the early Yanqi documents is a contract slip issued by a Han merchant who was supplying silk clothing to the oasis kingdom. In 60 BC he offered credit on a Han robe to a non-Chinese army officer with the full 1,300 in cash to be paid at the end of the month.[51]

East to Xuanquan

The Chinese outpost at Xuanquan in the Pass of the Jade Gate was the main route from the Tarim territories into the Hexi corridor. It offered caravans a final halt before they reached the frontier city of Dunhuang. The station had military stables and operated as an outlying base for the state-run postal system which used official riders to rapidly convey orders and correspondents across China. Tens of thousands of ancient documents have been recovered from this site with notices written on cheap bamboo slips or small inexpensive tamarisk panels.[52] These texts include correspondences between officials and announcements concerning fugitives and runaway prisoners. Any imperial edicts and orders were written on higher quality pine wood that did not warp with age and the surface ink could not be easily removed or altered by scratching.

Ancient documents found at Xuanquan and the nearby city of Dunhuang included travel permits issued to foreigners planning to travel through official Chinese territory. These permits specified destinations and listed the towns and cities that could be visited along the selected routes through the Hexi corridor into inner China. Travellers were not allowed to deviate from their itineraries and the documents registered the number of pack-animals accompanying the pass-holder. Foreigners who were issued with a permit to visit the Chinese capital Louyang for trade purposes were generally expected to be back at Dunhuang within six months. Most visiting foreigners left China with their permits, as these documents outlined and approved their return routes through the Tarim territories. However, some of the foreigners residing long-term in Dunhuang would discard their passes once they had reached the frontier. These documents were recovered for modern study. Some of these Chinese travel permits describe the pass-holders as 'Parthian' or 'Kushan' subjects who had business at Louyang. As at Niya, they include details that would identify the pass-holder, including stature, skin-complexion and ethnic clothing.[53]

In the late fourth century AD Chinese authorities became concerned that the Buddhism practised in their homelands had diverged from its original teachings and practices due to unreliable translations and missing texts. To address this problem the Chinese sent religious envoys and pilgrims to India to find and copy original Buddhist texts held in Indian temples and monasteries. The first of these envoys was a Chinese monk named Faxian who travelled overland to India in AD 399 and wrote a detailed account of his travels.[54] This has survived into modern times and provides an important account of conditions in Central Asia. Later Chinese pilgrims collected valuable donations of silk from wealthy patrons and conveyed offerings to Buddhist institutions along the route. In the sixth century two Chinese monks named Songyun and Huisheng counted more than 10,000 silk banners displayed on a Buddhist stupa near the southern Tarim city of Khotan. They estimated that at least half of the banners had been made in northern China. Their own caravan carried imperial gifts for Buddhist institutions in India and included 1,000 coloured silk banners (each 100 feet long), 500 silk incense bags and 2,000 small silk standards.[55]

During the fifth century AD large Buddhist statues were carved into sandstone cliff-faces near Dunhuang on the eastern edge of the Tarim silk routes. The Yungang Buddhas were created by a monastic community that received imperial patronage and collected donations from the merchant caravans that passed along the route. The site grew to include a large network of sculptured grottos and cave-like alcoves that were decorated with Buddhist carvings, murals and statues.[56]

During the sixth century AD additional giant statues of the Buddha were carved into other landmark cliffs close to important caravan routes. A pair of these ancient statues once stood in Bamiyan Valley (Afghanistan) on routes leading through the Hindu Kush. The statues were carved from sandstone with details added in plaster and painted in vibrant colours. The larger statue depicting the robed Buddha was over 170 feet tall and marked the western terminus for the trade and pilgrimage routes that stretched from Afghanistan to the edge of China.

The Sogdian Network

During the first centuries AD, the Sogdians established a prominent commercial presence in the main Tarim kingdoms that connected with trade routes to China. The journey from Samarkand to China was about 1,500 miles, but because Chinese silk could be acquired in the intervening Tarim kingdoms, not all merchants travelled the entire route. The total distance between Samarkand and the Chinese capital was 1,900 miles and travellers required at least eight months to complete this journey.

Two Sogdian caravans probably left China every year, one following the southern route around the Tarim territories and the other taking the more direct northern route back to Samarkand.[57] An event in the late fourth century AD reveals the scale of caravan traffic on these silk routes. In AD 383 an Emperor of the Later Qin Dynasty sent a force of 70,000 troops to attack the northern Tarim kingdom of Kucha. The military expedition sacked over thirty urban sites on the route west and returned to China with the plunder loaded onto 20,000 camels.[58]

By the fourth century AD, Sogdian communities in some of the main Chinese cities included hundreds of merchants involved in forwarding commodities or providing accommodation for associates who travelled the silk routes. Ancient Sogdian letters confirm that there were Sogdian merchant communities at Louyang and Chang'an in central China. There were also communities in the towns of Lanzihou, Wu-wei and Jiuquan in the Hexi Corridor and at Dunhuang on the Chinese frontier. This Sogdian presence was well established by AD 227 when a Chinese army marching through the Hexi corridor was welcomed by 'the enobled leaders of the Yuezhi (Kushan) and Kangju (Sogdian) foreigners who greeted the military commander'.[59]

The size of the caravans is indicated by events in the sixth century AD when Chinese authorities stopped a foreign caravan that was heading west along the Hexi corridor to the town of Wu-wei. The caravan included 600 camels, 240 non-Chinese personnel and 10,000 rolls of multi-coloured silk. This quantity of silk represented only 4 tons of merchandise, but it would have been worth over 4 million sesterces (1 million silver denarii) in Roman markets.[60] Most of the

300-ton load capacity of the caravan would have included other commodities and various essential supplies and materials for the journey such as food, water, tents and bedding rolls.

Goods Trafficked to China

Ancient Sogdian letters reveal how these Samarkand traders transported low-bulk and high-value goods to China including Indian spices and specialist minerals such as the 'white lead' (ceruse powder) that the Chinese used in cosmetics.[61] When the Han Emperor Zhi died in AD 146, high-ranking ministers attending the imperial funeral service were accused of applying this foreign white powder to exaggerate their pallid appearance and emphasise their mourning.[62]

The Sogdians also trafficked a tree-product called camphor that was used for flavourings, perfumes and medicines. Sogdian caravans probably conveyed other Indian flavourings including pepper, ginger, saffron, sugar and cinnamon. Non-perishables made ideal commodities, in particular sandalwood perfumes and specialist metals including copper, tin and an alloy known as antimony. Chinese markets also sought clothing dyes and the Sogdians could provide plant-based blue indigo and red mineral cinnabar. Precious stones offered another high-value commodity for Sogdian merchants as their homelands could supply lapis lazuli and red garnets. Khotan also provided jade and Indian markets offered diamonds, sapphires and rubies. Translucent green and white jades were particularly valuable in Chinese markets where the stone was carved into amulets, ornaments and sculptures. Roman merchants also shipped valuable red Mediterranean coral to India and this material reached China via the Tarim Silk Routes.[63]

The Sogdians received gold from the Parthians along with woollen cloth, hemp, linen, white lead and purple dyes that came from the Roman Empire.[64] Indian and Chinese workshops were only capable of producing thick opaque glass that contained many impurities, but Mediterranean workshops had perfected specialized techniques to manufacture transparent glass that could be coloured with rare mineral pigments to create brightly coloured items. Western glassware was therefore valuable in the distant east and could be transported as ingots, vessels, or even broken shards that could be melted down and remade as small decorative gemlike orbs. Sogdian artisans also melted down the foreign gold and silver to create ornate metalwork that included filigree hair clasps and Iranian-style tableware. Sima Qian confirms, 'When they receive Chinese gold and silver, they make it into tableware in preference to money.'[65] These items were sent east where exotic precious metal ornaments were highly valued for their decorative designs.[66]

The Sogdians transferred the profits they made between markets in the form of silver bullion and kept accounts in silver coins called *staters* based on older Greco-Bactrian currency. Small amounts were sometimes calculated in 'coppers' which is probably a reference to the commonplace currency used in Chinese markets. Sogdian merchants could also transfer large funds between foreign cities by using an imbursement slip called a 'transfer document' which acted as a guarantee of payment from business associates in distant markets.[67]

The Return Journey

The Sogdian caravans that left China were loaded with light-weight silk materials which fetched high prices in western cities. Sogdian merchants called silk *pirchik*, a term derived from Khotanese, the language spoken in the southern Tarim city-state of Khotan. Records from the eighth century indicate that the market value of silk fabric could double between Dunhuang and Samarkand (14 to 28 silver coins per bolt).[68] In this period, a wealthy Sogdian merchant paid a ransom of 5,000 silk rolls to an Arab general during the Muslim invasion of his homeland.[69]

Other products taken west by the Sogdians included Chinese lacquerware, bronze mirrors and ingots of silvery-white nickel that could be used for decorative metalwork. Sogdians also traded the potent musk glands of certain deer species found near the Tibetan Plateau, Siberia and North Korea.[70] These glands were used as a fixative in potent and long-lasting Iranian and Indian perfumes. Tibetan musk glands reached Roman markets in the form of small hair-covered leather pods. Their appearance confused Roman writers and Jerome refers to women who used potent scents made from 'that mouse-like musk'.[71] He also mentions perfumes manufactured from 'fragrant skins from the foreign mouse'.[72]

The Sogdian Settlers

Some Sogdian caravans crossed along the entire Tarim Basin to pass through the Jade Gate on their way to the Han frontier city of Dunhuang. In Dunhuang they could acquire silks directly from Chinese suppliers and join Han caravans heading down the arid Hexi Corridor to inner China. As trade developed, many of the Sogdian merchants engaged in this commerce split their business into two sectors. One branch managed the transfer of goods across the Tarim kingdoms and the other handled the transport of merchandise from Dunhuang to inner China. Sogdian merchants specializing in the Chinese section of these operations acquired silks and stockpiled them at Dunhuang for their colleagues to traffic across Central Asia. Dunhuang was also the transfer station where merchants from incoming Sogdian caravans handed over their western merchandise for kinsmen and trade associates to transport into inner China.

The Sogdian title *Sabao* (Chief Merchant) was derived from the Indian *sarthavaha* meaning 'caravaneer', but the term probably entered the Sogdian language through spoken Bactrian.[73] In an ancient text known as *Sogdian Letter V* a businessman named Fri-Khwataw calls his superior in Khotan a *Sabao*, indicating a senior position in the Sogdian trade network. By the fifth century AD there were large Sogdian communities living in most of the main Chinese cities connected with the silk route commerce. In this era the Chinese decided to permit these communities autonomy in terms of local governance and the Sogdians in China began organizing themselves into districts led by their own officials who took the traditional title of 'Sabao'. The Sabao presided over merchant communities, performed ritual religious functions and adjudicated any disputes brought to his attention. Bilingual epitaphs on Sogdian funerary monuments found in China record the duties and ancestry of these district officers. A sarcophagus found at Xi'an has a Sino-Sogdian inscription honouring a *sabao* named Wirkak who died in AD 579 aged 86. His family had lived in China for many generations and his grandfather had been a *sabao*, but he records that his more remote ancestors were Sogdians from Kish near the city of Samarkand.[74]

Many Sogdians were converts to Indian religions including Buddhism. These men travelled the silk routes as merchants and pilgrims and in the Far East they helped to translate the Buddhist sutras into Chinese. The Chinese wrote hagiographies of Buddhist monks including Sogdians who are identified by the traditional forename 'Kang'. The Buddhist Kang began their missionary activities in the Hexi corridor and by the second century AD they were active in the main cities of central China including Chang'an. One of the hagiographies describes the life of a third century Buddhist monk named Kang Seng Hui who was the son of a Sogdian merchant family. The family had lived in India for several generations before moving to Tonkin on the southern edge of China. Kang Seng Hui was orphaned at a young age and he chose religion rather than commerce. He travelled as a monk to the east coast of central China where he propagated Buddhism in the Nanking region.[75] The *Liang Shu* contains the biography of a Buddhist monk named Kang Xun who claimed descent from a leading family from Sogdia. It was said that his ancestor arrived in China as a royal hostage, but was granted civil status and allowed to settle in Hexi.[76] This movement of missionaries along the silk routes continued for centuries and in later times Buddhist murals from the Tarim kingdoms depict Sogdian monks and businessmen as donors to the ancient shrines.[77] Their testimonies and the accompanying relics reveal that substantial overland commerce was conducted across enormous distances for many generations.

The Sogdian merchant network communicated important market information through the dispatch of letters written and received by colleagues and agents in distant commercial centres. These letters, written in a form of Aramaic script called Sogdianian, were forwarded between various trade centres from China to Samarkand. The correspondents informed their colleagues about market opportunities in distant regions and kept merchants advised of any risks and opportunities along the main trade routes.

The Sogdian Letters

In 1907 a Hungarian explorer-archaeologist named Aurel Stein was excavating the remains of a Chinese watchtower in arid wastelands 50 miles west of Dunhuang. In these frontier ruins he found a postbag containing a collection of ancient Sogdian letters dating to a period of renewed conflict between China and a resurgent Xiongnu faction.[78] These documents had been confiscated in AD 313 by Chinese border guards who probably thought the letters revealed sensitive and strategic information about affairs in inner China.

The letters were written on paper in a cursive Sogdian script. They were then folded and enclosed in protective linen coverings which had the name of the intended recipient written on the reverse. This text included the name of a contact in the northern Tarim city of Loulan who guaranteed that the letters would reach their western destinations. *Letter II* was sealed in a special silk-cloth wrapping, perhaps because it was destined for an important official. Each of the letters reveals important personal details about the people who lived in the merchant communities operating along the ancient silk routes.

Letter II was written by a Sogdian merchant named Nanai-Vandak who was based in the walled Chinese town of Wu-wei on the Hexi Corridor. Nanai-Vandak addressed his letter to his business superior in Sogdia and wrote on the covering sleeve: 'Send this letter to Samarkand so that the noble lord Varzakk should receive it complete – Sent by his servant Nanai-Vandak.' It seems that Nanai-Vandak was responsible for conveying merchandise from Dunhuang to the cities of inner China where large quantities of silk could be purchased at an affordable cost. He informs Varzakk that 'linen cloth is selling well and anyone who still has not taken his unmade cloth to market can now sell all of it.' Varzakk would therefore ensure that the next caravan destined for Dunhuang was loaded with linen fabrics.[79]

At this time the Xiongnu war was interrupting contact with inner China and the Sogdians were having difficulty acquiring silk and transferring the fabrics to Dunhuang. But Nanai-Vandak was ready to transport a valuable consignment of Tibetan musk from China to Samarkand. He tells Varzakk, 'under my supervision Wan-Razmak has sent 32 units of musk (800 grams) to Dunhuang. These belong to Takut and I am delivering them to you.' Based on recorded seventh century prices from Turfan, this amount of musk would have been worth perhaps 27 kilograms of silver in foreign markets.[80] This is equivalent to almost 8,000 denarii or 32,000 sesterces in the early Roman currency system.

Nanai-Vandak also gave instructions as to how the profits from this merchandise were to be divided up, with three shares held in trust for his young son Takhsich-Vandak. He tells Varzakk, 'When the goods are handed over, you should divide them into five shares. Takhsich-Vandak should take three shares, and Pesakk should take one share, and you should also take one share.' Nanai-Vandak wanted the three shares owned by Takhsich-Vandak to be invested in further merchant dealings, so that the boy would be financially secure when he reached adulthood. He tells Varzakk, 'You should withdraw this deposit and you should both count it. Add interest to the amount and put the cash in a transfer document so that this money may increase.'[81] This is probably a reference to loan agreements, so it seems that Nanai-Vandak wanted to provide an income for his son by lending funds to other merchants at profitable interest rates.

Nanai-Vandak tells Varzakk, 'If you need further cash you should take either 1,000 or 2,000 *staters* out of the money.' Fourth century Sogdian *staters* contained 0.6 grams of silver, so this figure was perhaps equivalent to between 175 and 350 Roman denarii.[82] Most of the Sogdians who engaged in caravan ventures would have found it more lucrative to convey their profits in rare goods rather than coin. For example, only fragments of Sogdian *Letter VI* have survived, but in one of these scraps the author asks the recipient to buy silk. He advises that if the required silk is unavailable, the funds should be spent acquiring camphor.

Nanai-Vandak explains how Xiongnu attacks were limiting opportunities for trade with central China. The commercial supply-lines had been interrupted as

Chinese cities were besieged and sacked by Xiongnu armies. He reminds his superior Varzakk: 'it is eight years since I sent Saghrak and Farn-Aghat into inner China. It has been three years since I last received a message from them saying that they are well. I have not received a reply from them since that last evil event occurred and I do not know how they have fared.'

A few years earlier Nanai-Vandak had sent a subordinate named Artikhu-Vandak to manage his interests at Louyang. But the region was becoming a war zone and all communications with Artikhu-Vandak had stopped suddenly without explanation. Eventually news came from an associate named Wakhushakk. Nanai-Vandak reports, 'Wakhushakk went with the caravan from Wu-wei, but when they reached Louyang they found that all the Indians and the Sogdians there had died of starvation.'

Nanai-Vandak tells his superior that the situation was critical for China and the Sogdian merchants who made their livelihood from eastern commerce. He explains: 'The last Emperor fled Louyang because of the famine, his palace was burnt and the city destroyed, Louyang is no more! ... We do not know whether the remaining Chinese were able to expel the Xiongnu from Chang'an or whether they invaded the country beyond.' The text is fragmentary, but Nanai-Vandak confirms that the Sogdian network was in critical decline. One Sogdian community had been reduced to a few hundred freemen and another had only forty remaining associates.

Nanai-Vandak describes how 'many Sogdians were ready to leave China', but Chinese frontier garrisons were preventing foreign caravans from leaving the Empire. He travelled to Dunhuang to confirm the situation and found that an associate named Ghawtus was trying to find a way around the impasse. Nanai-Vandak tells Varzakk, 'I would have remained at Dunhuang, but the Sogdians there are destitute.' Perhaps the worsening situation in China explains why Nanai-Vandak was sending instructions for the long-term financial security of his son. He instructs Varzakk, 'When Takhsich-Vandak is grown up, find him a wife and do not send him far away from yourself.' Nanai-Vandak concludes, 'From day to day we in China can expect only robbery and murder.'[83]

Letter V was written by a Sogdian businessman from Wu-wei named Fri-Khwataw and addressed to his superior at the oasis kingdom of Khotan on the southern Tarim Silk Routes. The letter is addressed: 'To the noble lord Aspandhat who is *Sabao* [Chief Merchant] – Sent by your servant Fri-Khwataw.' Fri-Khwataw was based at the Chinese frontier city of Guzang in the Hexi corridor near Dunhuang. He received incoming merchandise from Sogdian caravans travelling the Tarim caravan routes and stockpiled the wares for transfer to urban centres in inner China. The war was interrupting his business and preventing contact with the main cities in central China where other Sogdian dealers waited to receive and sell incoming merchandise. Fri-Khwataw tells the Chief Merchant at Khotan in western China: 'In Guzang there are four bundles of 'white lead' powder waiting for dispatch. There are also 2,500 measures of pepper for dispatch' (88 pounds).[84]

Fri-Khwataw was also safeguarding 'half a weight of silver' which might have weighed thirty kilograms if he was referring to Babylonian talents. It was more profitable to transfer bullion funds from Iran to China in silver rather than gold as early Roman currency undervalued silver in relation to gold (1:12). By contrast the Han economy placed a premium value on silver and considered one measure of gold to be as valuable as ten measures of silver (1:10).[85] The half-talent of silver held by Fri-Khwataw probably had a bullion weight of nearly 8,750 drachma and was worth 35,000 sesterces in Roman currency.

Fri-Khwataw also had to tell the Chief Merchant about his involvement in the repayment of a debt due at Khotan. In China, a Sogdian businessman named Kharstrang owed money to the Chief Merchant and was repaying the debt to his business associates including Fri-Khwataw and a man named Aspandhat. Fri-Khwataw writes: 'I heard that Kharstrang owed you twenty *staters* of silver and he promised to send it to you. He gave me the silver, but when I examined it I found there were only four and a half *staters*. I asked him, if twenty *staters* were due, then why did he give me only four and a half *staters*? He said: "Aspandhat found me and I gave him the rest owed."'[86]

A fee of twenty *staters* seems to have been the cost of caravan passage between Samarkand and China. Perhaps senior merchants would lend these sums to fellow Sogdians travelling to work in China to finance their own commercial dealings in the intervening cities. Twenty Sogdian *staters* of pure silver weighed 345 grams and was equivalent to 100 denarii.

Another letter in the ancient postbag was written by the wife of a Sogdian merchant named Miwnay to her absent husband. Miwnay had moved to Dunhuang to be with her husband Nanaidhat, but when he got into financial difficulties he had fled the city, abandoning his wife and young daughter. Miwnay asked several Sogdian businessmen in Dunhuang for a loan so that she and her daughter Shanyn could return to Samarkand, but they were unable, or unwilling, to help her. They avoided destitution by becoming servants and tending sheep on a Chinese farmstead. Over the course of three years Miwnay had five opportunities to leave China with departing Sogdian caravans, but she could not afford the 20 *staters* required to secure passage to Samarkand. But it seems that the Sogdian community had established a Zoroastrian Temple in Dunhuang and its priest offered Miwnay the means to return home. They gave her a camel, funds for travel and arranged for a man to accompany her on the caravan journey back to Samarkand. Miwnay's letter to Nanaidhat contains a message written in the margin by Shanyn. She described their hardships and asked her father why he had abandoned his family in China.[87] Miwnay included another letter in the delivery to let Chatis, her mother, know that they were at last on their way home to Samarkand.[88]

None of these letters reached their intended destinations and the fate of the correspondents is not known. The documents were confiscated by frontier guards in a Chinese watchtower shortly before the outpost was abandoned. But the letters have revealed important details about the lives of the merchants and businessmen who transported valuable commodities across some of the most inhospitable regions of the globe.

hinese mural depicting a blue-eyed Buddhist donor with red hair (Bezeklik Thousand Buddha aves, Temple 9: Ninth Century AD).

ɔld Greco-Bactrian coin. Obverse: King Eucratides (170–145 BC). Reverse: Dioscuri riding large rgana/Bactrian horses.

Chinese Terracotta Solider depicted wearing lamellar armour (Tomb site of the First Emperor, third century BC).

Painted terracotta statuettes depicting Han soldiers (Yangjiawan Tomb offerings). Cavalryman on a 'Heavenly Horse' and two spear-armed guards with chest armour/shield.

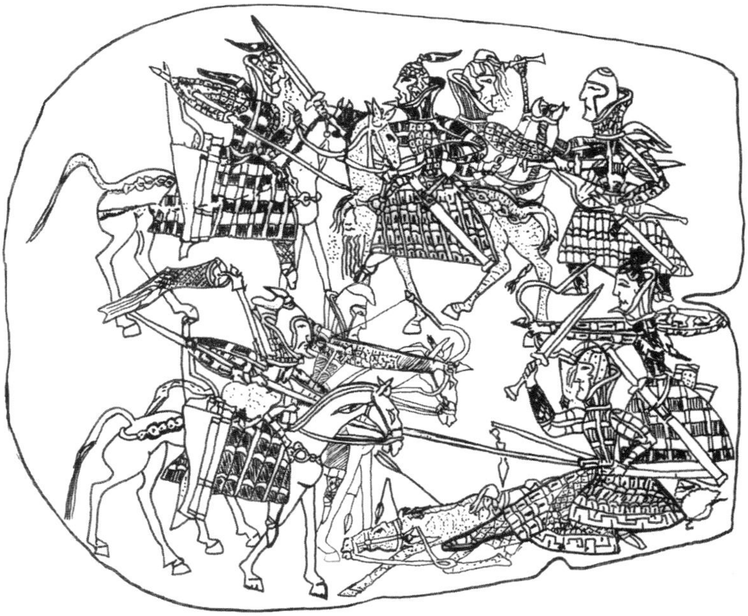

one plate carved with a
epiction of armoured
akas/Kangju in combat
Orlat plate, Uzbekistan: first
ntury AD).

lver coins issued by Saka King Azes with Greek script (Gandhara: 50–10 BC). Reverse: Greek
oddess Athena with shield.

Embroidered image of an armoured Kushan warrior dismounted in a meadow (textile fragments from Noyon uul Barrow 31: first century BC).

Stucco frieze depicting Yuezhi warriors and nobles (Kushan Palace at Khalchayan in Uzbekistan: first century AD).

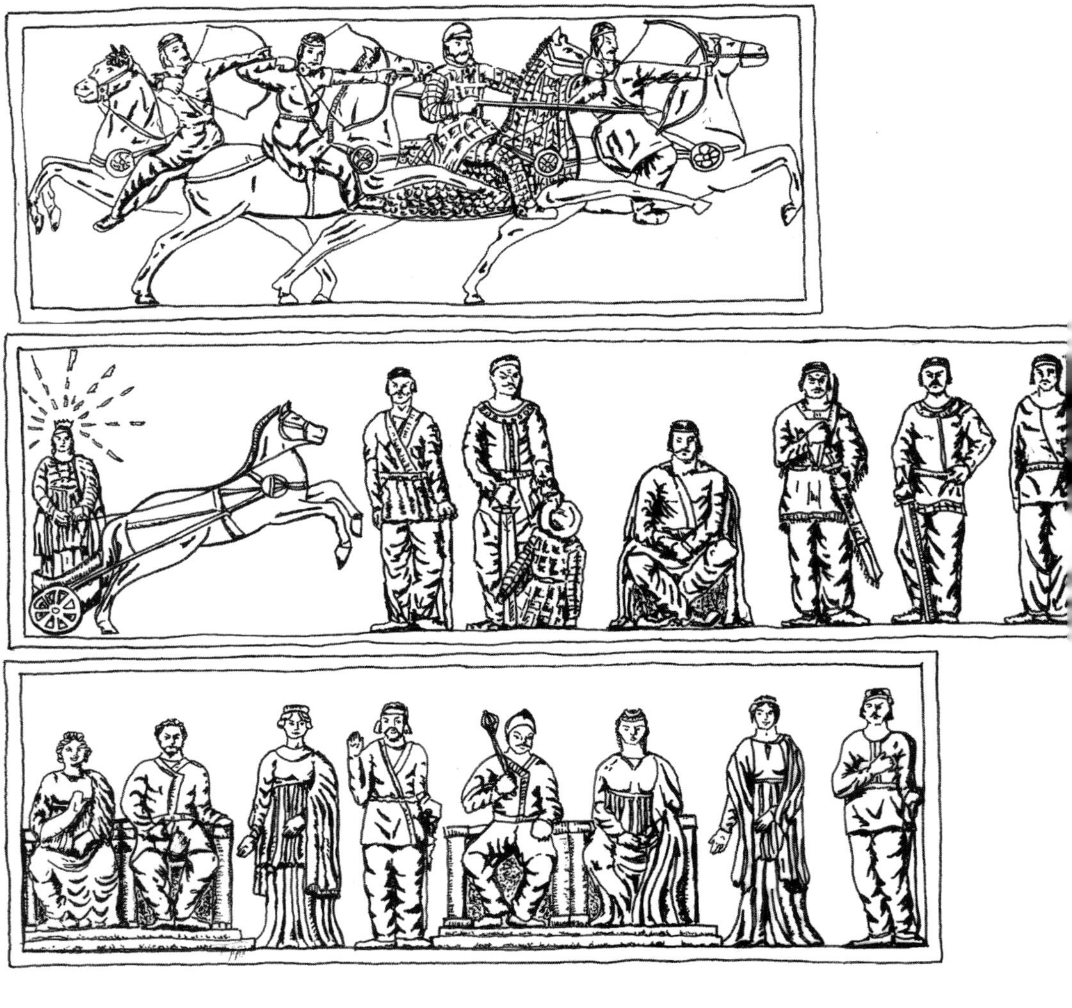

Centerpiece of a gold clasp depicting an armoured Greco-Bactrian solider (Yuezhi burial at Tillya Tepe in Afghanistan: first century BC).

oins of Kujula Kadphises with Greek text (AD 30–80). (*Top*) Silver tetradrachm depicting the king
s a Kushan chief. Reverse: dismounted next to horse and crowned by Nike. (*Middle*) Kadphises
epicted as a Greek King. Reverse: Hercules with club. (*Bottom*) Kadphises depicted as a Roman
mperor: Reverse: seated on *curule* chair wearing Parthian regalia.

Gold Kushan coins modelled on Roman aurei. (*Top*) Emperor Kanishka in steppe costume (AD 127–151). Reverse: Buddha and Greek text. (*Middle*) Armoured Kushan King. Reverse: Shiva and Bull Nandi. (*Bottom*) Huvishka mounted on battle-elephant (151–187). Reverse: Hercules and Bactrian text.

Kushan relief depicting the legendary Trojan Horse (Gandhara: second century AD).

old Kushan coins. (*Top*) Portrait of Huvishka wearing Iranian-style crown. Reverse: four-armed
niva and Bactrian text. (*Middle*) Huvishka wearing Indian regalia. Reverse: the Greek god Hermes
ith coin purse. (*Bottom*) Reverse: armoured female deity with shield (*Riom* – Rome).

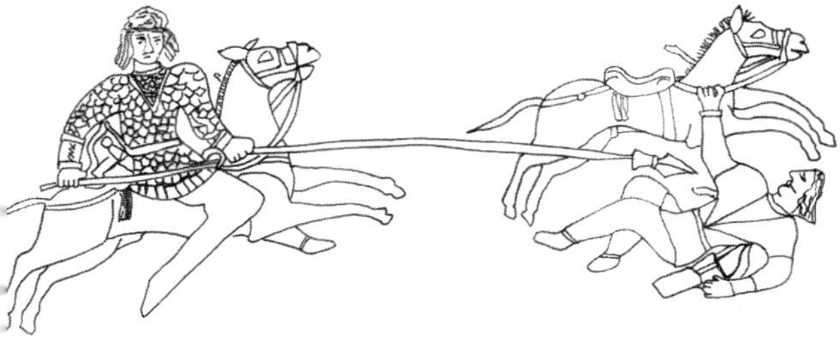

Image carved into a vase depicting an armoured Sarmatian lancer in combat with a mounted archer.

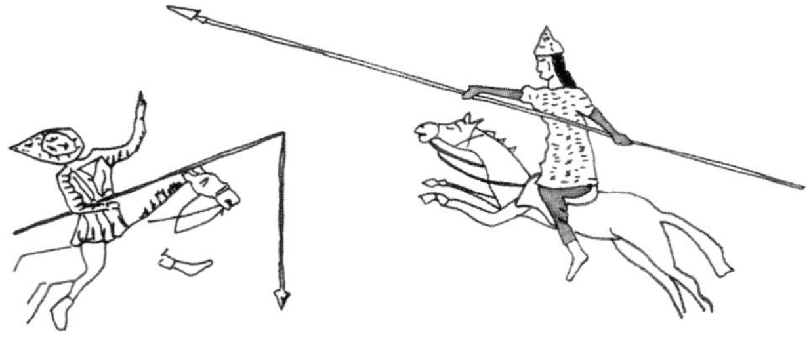

Tomb painting from Panticapaeum depicting a duel between mounted Sarmatians.

(*Left*) Relief depicting an armoured Sarmatian (Tanais: second century AD).
(*right*) Stele depicting a Hellenic solider from the Crimea (Panticapaeum: first–second century AD).

Scene from Trajan's Column showing Roman cavalry pursuing armoured Sarmatians (Dacian War: second century AD).

CHAPTER EIGHT

Caspian Routes and the Crimea

Chinese texts confirm that Roman access to Iran was restricted by the Parthians in order to monopolise the lucrative overland trade in silk fabrics between Transoxiana and the Mediterranean.[1] Roman subjects were able to freely enter Babylonia, but they were barred from joining Parthian caravans heading east through the mountains and deserts of Iran to join the silk routes of Central Asia. However, there was a way to bypass Iran by transporting goods through the northern steppe territories outside the control of the Parthian Empire. The Oxus and Jaxartes Rivers flowed from sources in Central Asia northward into the Aral Sea. The Jaxartes (Syr Darya) had tributaries in the fertile Ferghana Valley and the river formed a barrier between Sogdia and the Steppe as it flowed into the Aral. Further west, the River Oxus flowed between Bactria and Sogdia on a winding course into this same sea. Both rivers therefore became major trade routes and merchants from Transoxiana could follow these conduits northward, using caravans and river craft to carry their cargo.

In ancient times the Aral and the Caspian Seas were larger than their present dimensions and the distance between their shores was shortened by a vast oval lake which filled the Sarygamysh Depression. The Sarygamysh Lake covered an area over 100 miles wide and 50 miles across. This lake was filled by a large river which flowed between the seas, but due to extreme environmental change in recent centuries, this ancient watercourse now only exists as an arid river bed known as the Uzboy. The existence of a watercourse in ancient times meant that most classical authorities did not consider the Aral to be a separate body of water and concluded that the Oxus River simply emptied directly into the Caspian (Hyrcanian Sea). Strabo explains that 'the Oxus divides Bactria from Sogdia and it is said to be so navigable that any Indian merchandise carried over the mountains [Hindu Kush or Pamirs] is easily conveyed along this river to the Caspian Sea.'[2]

A Roman governor named Arrian used the reports of Macedonian generals to describe the ancient Oxus. The river was more than half a mile wide along its main course and its deep waters could not be easily bridged since 'the riverbed is sandy and the water flows in a rapid stream.' Arrian considered the Oxus to be the largest river in Asia, discounting the Indus and the Ganges.[3] Sailing speeds along the ancient Oxus are unknown, but Pliny reports that Alexander was able to travel at least 75 miles downstream along the Indus River per day.[4] At this speed it might have taken 20 days to travel the entire 1,500 mile length of the Oxus River, but many Bactrian or Sogdian travellers probably began their riverine ventures midway along the watercourse.

The fourth century Roman writer Ammianus Marcellinus confirms that the Jaxartes was an important watercourse for trade through Sogdia. He explains that 'two rivers that are navigable by ships, called Jaxartes and Dymas, flow through Sogdia. These streams rush headlong over mountains and valleys into a level plain where they form a long and broad lake called the Oxia.'[5] Strabo explains that the Jaxartes flowed into the Hyrcanian Sea (Aral-Caspian expanse) through two divergent watercourses that were about 6 miles apart.[6]

Sogdian merchants brought their goods to the shores of the Aral Sea to negotiate deals with a steppe people called the Aorsi who were part of the Alani nation. The Alani controlled lands around the eastern shores of the Caspian and they also received Parthian caravans coming from Iran loaded with goods from Armenia, Babylonia and the Persian Gulf. It was said that the Alani became rich from hosting this traffic and by supplying goods to steppe nations north of the Caspian. Strabo reports that 'the Aorsi rule over much of the Caspian coast and they receive Indian and Babylonian merchandise on camels. They import this merchandise from the Armenians and the Medes and because of this wealth the Aorsi wear gold ornaments.'[7] By the late first century AD, the Alani had expanded their homelands westward to the north coast of the Black Sea and Josephus describes the nation as 'Scythians inhabiting Lake Meotis' (the Sea of Azov).[8] According to Ammianus many of the Alani were tall in stature and had fair hair.[9]

The Han Chinese called the Pontic-Caspian Steppe 'Yancai' (Vast Steppe) and reckoned that it was about 500 miles from the territory of the Kangju in Sogdia. The *Shiji* records that 'Yancai is 2,000 *li* northwest of Kangju. The people are nomads and their customs are similar to Kangju people.' It was reported that 'the country has over 100,000 archer-warriors and it borders on a great lake of unknown dimensions' (the Caspian).[10] The *Hou Hanshu* calls the population of Yancai the *Alanliao* (Alani) and records that they paid tribute to the Kangju.[11] Chinese records from the third century AD record that the Alani had become an independent nation whose lands bordered *Da Qin* (the Roman Empire).[12]

Between the Caspian and the Black Sea were the formidable Caucasus Mountains which the early Greeks believed to be 'highest and greatest of all mountain ranges' before they learned about the Himalayas.[13] According to Pliny the River Kura which flowed through the Caucasus Mountains formed the traditional boundary between Armenia and the small landlocked kingdom of Caucasian-Iberia (Georgia) which stretched along the southern part of the mountains.[14] East of Iberia was the small coastal kingdom of Caucasian-Albania (Azerbaijan) which controlled mountain territories near the place where the Kura River flowed into the Caspian. Tacitus reports that the 'Iberians and Albanians inhabit a densely wooded country and their soldiers are accustomed to hardship and endurance.'[15]

The Caucasus Mountains form a vast overland barrier between the Black Sea and the Caspian coast. Two major mountain belts run roughly parallel to one another and are joined by several smaller interconnecting mountain ranges. The Greater Caucasus forms the larger belt and consists of a broad range that stretches in a diagonal line almost 700 miles from east to west and is almost 100 miles across at its widest extent.

The Caucasus Mountains were created when the Arabian Teutonic Plate collided with the Eurasian landmass and the area is still subject to earthquakes and landslides. Due to their size, the Caucasus Mountains contain a series of different climatic zones and distinct ecosystems. To the north of the Greater Caucasus there are broad steppe lands with grasslands rising up into forested hills covered with oak and ash trees. Above these low hills are pine forests and alpine meadow slopes that lead into a landscape of permafrost with snow-capped mountains and high glacial peaks. The lower slopes of the western Caucasus Mountains are heavily forested and descend into marshlands near the Black Sea coast. By contrast the eastern ranges of these mountains tend to be drier with barren terrain that is mostly treeless.

Some 60 miles south of this major mountain belt there is another long linear range known as the Lesser Caucasus. Between these high mountain landscapes there was a broad, lowland territory called Colchis, hemmed in by the intersecting Likhi Mountains. These mountains divided Colchis and Caucasian-Iberia from the Kura-Aras Depression (Azerbaijan) and the Caspian Coast. Both territories were encircled by the Lesser Caucasus Mountains which extend south into the steppe-like grasslands of northern Armenia on the edge of Asia Minor (Turkey).

The route across the Caucasus Mountains was a difficult passage through rough terrain subject to severe seasonal weather, including heavy snowfalls during the long winter months. But the low-lying belt between the Greater and Lesser Caucasus Mountains offered a viable route from east to west for travellers who were prepared to cross the Likhi range. In ancient times certain river valleys and mountain passes led through the Likhi Mountains from the Absheron Peninsula on the Caspian shore to the Greek-colonised coast of the Black Sea and the frontiers of the Roman Empire. The Greek geographer Strabo was born in the Pontic city of Amasia on the Black Sea near Trapezus and he was well informed about this commerce. He writes that 'from the Caspian Sea, Indian goods are brought by various rivers to the successive regions beyond and by this means they reach the Pontus.'[16]

The profits to be gained by commerce made this a worthwhile journey and the mode of travel was significant. In the ancient world shipping goods by river was up to five times less expensive than the cost of using road networks.[17] This meant that with ideal conditions, river systems and sea lanes provided a more cost-effective course for commerce than the land-based routes.

The Caspian Sea

In ancient times the Caspian Sea was the largest enclosed body of water in the world. It stretched from northern Iran into the vast Eurasian steppe that spread across southern Russia. The sea filled a depression that was more than 640 miles long and 270 miles across at its widest extent. It therefore covered an area greater than the entire Italian Peninsula.

The Caspian could be categorised as a giant lake since it is filled by rivers and its salinity is one third that of most seawater, but many ancient authorities considered it to be a sea due to its immense size and significant salinity. The Caspian is a closed basin so there is no natural outflow for its waters except from evaporation. Over 130 rivers provide inflow to the Caspian, but the Volga is the greatest source and provides four-fifths of the incoming water.

In pre-modern times the Volga River drained about one fifth of the European land area as it flowed through western Russia along a course that covered nearly 2,300 miles. It emptied into the northern Caspian Sea through a broad delta that stretched almost 100 miles along the coast. This was the largest river estuary in Europe, but due to severe winters at this northern latitude, the surface water remained frozen solid for at least three months of the year. The surrounding steppe land was arid and exposed to strong and persistent winds creating linear dunes.

The northern part of the Caspian was shallow as it flowed across the submerged Caspian Shelf. In this region the average depth was less than 20 feet and the shallow water froze easily due to its limited salinity. Towards the Middle Caspian the seabed descended into a wide depression where the average depth increased to more than 600 feet. Ancient ships sailing the Southern Caspian would have glided over a maritime expanse that was over 3,000 feet deep and largely free of ice except in severe winters.

The early Greeks gained information about the Caspian Sea from Persian authorities who suggested the scale of its expanse. Herodotus reports that 'the Caspian is separate and self-contained. Its length [north-south] is a voyage of fifteen days using oars and at its broadest [east-west] it can be crossed in a voyage of eight days.'[18] The Macedonian generals who succeeded Alexander the Great took possession of the Caspian shore adjoining Iran in a region known as Hyrcania. Pliny reports that Seleucus I Nicator (306–281 BC) and Antiochus I Soter (281–261 BC) authorised ship-borne expeditions to explore the Caspian coast.[19] Both rulers tried to rename the expanse as the 'Seleucian' or 'Antiochian' Sea, but the old name the 'Hyrcanian Sea' remained the preferred option.

One of these early Greek explorers was an admiral named Patrocles who charted the Caspian coasts during the 280s BC. Patrocles probably commanded trireme galleys that were powered by oars or a centrally placed mainsail. Support vessels could have included oared *penteconter* vessels that could carry extensive cargo. But it seems that Patrocles did not sail into the shallow Caspian Shelf and if he reached the Volga delta, he did not understand the true nature of the inrushing water. Patrocles assumed that the northern Caspian shore was an oceanic inlet similar to the Red Sea or the Persian Gulf. According to his theory the Caspian Shelf, or the Volga Delta, might be a vast icebound passage connecting the Caspian to the world ocean that encircled Eurasia. Strabo explains: 'The Hyrcanian Sea is a gulf which extends from the ocean south through a narrow entrance that widens as it advances inland.'[20] He also comments, 'Not everyone agrees that it is possible to sail from India into the Hyrcanian Sea, but Patrocles states that it is possible.'[21] However, in this era no Greek ships entered the Volga to test the theory due to the extreme distance, severe seasonal cold and high risk involved in entering unexplored territories.

The Romans acquired a more strategic understanding of the Caspian Sea as it bordered the lands adjoining their empire. Pliny based his description of the region on a map commissioned before 12 BC by a leading Roman general named Agrippa. He explains that 'the Caspian borders Armenia, adjoins the Chinese (Seric) Ocean and is bounded on the west by the Caucasus Mountain ranges.' Roman cartographers called the shallow northern part of the Caspian Sea the 'Scythian Gulf' since it was controlled by horse-riding nomads 'who communicate across the narrows'. Excluding this expanse (the Caspian Shelf) they estimated that the sea was 480 miles long, 290 miles broad, with a circuit of 2,500 miles. Information gathered by Agrippa suggested that with the exception of the Kura River mouth, the whole Caspian coast facing the Caucasus Mountains was 'formed from very high cliffs that prohibit landing for 425 miles'.[22]

Colchis and the Chersonesos

The Black Sea is about 730 miles across at its widest point and extends more than 160 miles from north to south. It covers an area almost the size of modern Spain, if inlets such as the Sea of Azov are included in the measurements. The Black Sea was about a fifth the size of the Roman Mediterranean, but most of the surrounding territories were relatively wild and underdeveloped due to their more northerly latitude. The upper coast extended north to the Eurasian Steppe and the western shores faced the mountainous forest-covered core of Central Europe.

Mediterranean ships entered the Black Sea through the Bosporus passage, a narrow strait 17 miles long and less than 2 miles wide. In Greek myth this was the location of the Cyanean Rocks which clashed together and crushed incoming vessels. Apollonius of Rhodes imagines 'the narrow winding passage through the strait, hemmed in by rugged cliffs. The eddying underwater current washes against the incoming ship and forward progress is made in dread. Now is heard the resounding thud of the crashing rocks.'[23] The rocks 'rushed together and clashed as they impacted, sending a mass of foam upwards like a cloud and causing the sea to thunder with a terrifying roar'.[24] It was believed that the Greek hero Jason piloted his ship the *Argo* safely through the Cyanean gap by releasing a dove. The bird triggered the clashing reefs and gave his crew time to row through the passage as the rocks withdrew. These stories were probably inspired by early Greek knowledge of the dangerous reefs near the entrance to the Black Sea. Strabo explains that 'the men of Homer's day regarded the Black Sea as a kind of second Ocean and they thought that those who voyaged there sailed beyond the limits of their world.'[25]

When the Persian king Xerxes led his army against Greece, he crossed from Asia to Europe by constructing a temporary bridge over the narrow Bosporus Passage (483 BC). The bridge was a pontoon structure raised across anchored transport ships secured in parallel rows by long cables. According to Pliny this bridge was 1,500 feet long and although it was dismantled soon after its construction, it was still considered a phenomenal achievement in the history of engineering.[26]

The early Greeks estimated the size of the Black Sea by using information about the length of voyages between its outlying ports. Herodotus had heard that the voyage from the entrance of the Black Sea to Phasis on the extreme east coast was a sailing of nine days and eight nights. By contrast a voyage to the northern limits of the sea in Crimea could be completed in three days and two nights. Herodotus estimated that in the best sailing conditions 'a ship will generally accomplish 70,000 *orguiae* [70 miles] in a long day's voyage and 60,000 *orguiae* [60 miles] by night.'[27] But sailing conditions were slower in the Black Sea and Herodotus overestimated its size by using optimum sailing speeds. Based on accurate modern measurements, early Greek ships crossing the Black Sea must have been sailing at about 3 knots (nautical miles per hour) which is half the top speed of ships in the Mediterranean.

The Romans knew the approximate size and shape of the Black Sea which they understood to be a relatively flat southern shore facing an arc-shaped northern coast. Pliny explains that 'the Black Sea intrudes on a large area of the continent, with a coast formed from a great bend that curves back as though it were horns and stretches out on either side to produce the shape of a Scythian [steppe] bow.'[28]

Two territories on the Black Sea coast had special significance to classical civilization because of their trade and resources. These were the heavily forested territory of Colchis on the east coast and the agriculturally rich Crimean Peninsula to the far north. Colchis was at the frontier of classical civilization and its landscape was defined by myths and legends dating back to the time of Homer and the eighth century BC. The territory therefore had special significance in the classical mindset as a destination for dangerous voyages to the limits of the known world.

The main sea-port in Colchis was an ancient city called Phasis founded by Milesian Greeks from Asia Minor in the sixth century BC.[29] At that time this was the most easterly coast that could be reached by seafaring Greek explorers. The forbidding snow-capped mountains in this 'edge of the world' territory entered Greek myth as the place where the immortal Titan Prometheus was chained by the god Zeus as a punishment for giving mankind the secret of fire. Bound to a rock, it was said that a great eagle tore at his innards every day until he was the freed from his agony by the intervention of the Greek hero Hercules.[30] Ancient Colchis was also immortalized in the story of Jason and the Argonauts who sought the Golden Fleece in these same lands.[31] The remoteness of Colchis with its inhospitable terrain meant that this legendary reputation prevailed in popular Roman imagination, even after the area became part of the Empire.

In ancient times Colchis was sparsely populated and although it was rich in natural resources, it had few urban settlements. But the region was positioned along a sailing route that led to another important territory that was also subject to early Greek influence. By the Roman era there was a small Hellenic kingdom in the northern reaches of the Black Sea positioned on the Crimean Peninsula. This peninsula was known in antiquity as the Chersonesos and it had such a narrow connection to the northern coast that it was considered to be almost an island. The region was settled by Greek colonists in the sixth century BC and they became wealthy from farming its rich agricultural land. By the fifth century BC, their cities were under the authority of local Greek tyrants who established dynastic rule over most of the region.[32]

At its widest extent the Crimean Isthmus is almost 200 miles across and stretches nearly 100 miles from north to south. The landmass therefore covers an area larger than the Mediterranean island of Sicily. The Greek geographer Strabo was approximately correct when he estimated that the Chersonesos was about the same size as the Peloponnese which formed the southern third of Greece.[33] The southeast coast of the Crimea was flanked by a narrow range of steep-rising mountains, but most of the interior of the isthmus consisted of steppe-like prairie land ideal for growing grain. The mountains on the eastern seaboard shielded the isthmus from incoming cold weather and the northern coast of the Crimea was warmed by Black Sea currents and mild winds from the south. Consequently, the Crimea enjoyed a temperate climate throughout much of the year and its coast was well suited to receive foreign shipping with many small peninsulas, headlands, inlets, bays and natural harbours.

The Crimea was an important producer of grain and a leading centre for trade goods acquired from the adjoining Eurasian Steppe. Strabo explains, 'except for the mountainous district extending to Theodosia, the land is everywhere flat, fertile and extremely favourable for the production of grain. It yields a thirty-fold harvest when furrowed by any sort of a digging-instrument.'[34] North of the Crimea (Chersonesos) was an enormous area of grassland known as the Pontic-Caspian Steppe, occupied by a horse-riding population who the Greeks called 'Scythians'.[35] The Black Sea routes therefore offered Greek and Roman merchants the opportunity to trade with steppe populations. This was significant since shipping goods by water was less expensive than the cost of using road networks.[36]

At various times the Scythians gained influence or dominance over parts of the Crimean Peninsula, but they were prepared to allow the coastal Greek cities to manage their own affairs in return for a share of their wealth delivered as annual tribute. Strabo explains that, 'the nomads have a diet of meat and horse-flesh and they savour a specially prepared form of sour mare's milk.' Their fighting skill was respected and Strabo confirms: 'They are warriors rather than brigands, but they go to war for the sake of the tributes due to them. They offer their land to those who want to farm it and are satisfied with moderate tribute because their assessments are based on acquiring necessities rather than gaining abundance. But if the land occupiers do not pay, the nomads go to war with them.' For this reason the Scythians were regarded as 'just' but 'resource-less'. Strabo explains that only communities 'who are confident that they are powerful enough to easily ward off these attacks, or prevent any invasion, will not regularly pay the tribute'.[37]

The first Greek dynasts to rule ancient Chersonesos were from a royal household called the Spartocids. During the fifth century BC they gained control over the small cluster of Hellenic cities occupying the Crimean Peninsula and the neighbouring Asiatic coast.[38] The early Spartocids became wealthy by shipping large volumes of grain to Athens at a time when the city ruled a powerful maritime empire surrounding the Aegean Sea. In gratitude the people of Athens granted honorary Athenian citizenship to their Spartocus allies in Chersonesos.[39]

It was a 700 mile voyage from the Crimea to Athens and although this trade route was developed to transport staple goods, it was also used to convey specialized craft products and regional luxuries. Fifth century Athens was enriched by lucrative silver mines and its citizens produced craft products that attracted foreign traders to the city. The Athenians therefore maintained a military fleet of war galleys in the Aegean to protect essential trade networks from the intervention of rival regimes.

Ancient sources confirm the scale of the Crimean grain trade that supplied Greek cities in the eastern Mediterranean. In 355 BC the Athenian statesman Demosthenes explained, 'the Athenians have relied on imported grain more than any other nation.'[40] He reports that 'the grain they import from the Black Sea is equal to all the grain that comes to Athens from other places' and confirms that Athens received 400,000 *medimnoi* (16,000 tons) of grain from the Chersonesos per annum.[41] It would have required more than 213 merchant ships with a cargo capacity of 75 tons to transport this amount of Crimean grain to Athens.

Demosthenes refers to a twenty-oared merchant ship that had a cargo of 300 amphora jars (75 tons) and this size of trade vessel could have been typical of Greek ships in this era.[42] Salt was an important preservative in the ancient world and as there were valuable salt works on the Crimean coast, this important product was also shipped to Athens. The holds of these Greek cargo ships would have been filled with other commodities including salted fish from the Sea of Azov, a large inlet on the northern shore of the Black Sea formed by the eastward projection of the Crimean Peninsula and a spur of land on the opposite Asiatic coast. In ancient times the Azov Sea was known to the ancients as Maeotis Lake and as its salinity was diluted by the incoming River Don, it had plentiful stocks of fish. Strabo explains, 'In early times the Greeks imported their supplies of grain from the Chersonesos and they imported their supplies of salt-fish from the lake.'[43] These waters contained unique species including the large sturgeon that produces caviar (salt-cured fish eggs).

Further ancient evidence confirms the size of the Greek fleet that sailed from the Crimea to Athens. In this era the Greek merchant fleet left the Crimea in summer when the new grain harvest was loaded aboard. They sailed to the Bosporus where they anchored along the shore of Asia Minor opposite the Hellenic city of Byzantium to await a military escort from the Athenian navy before entering the Aegean Sea. In 340 BC King Phillip II of Macedon attacked the assembled merchant fleet and captured 230 vessels. From this fleet he released fifty non-Athenian ships, but he detained the 180 trade vessels owned and crewed by Athenians.[44] The crews were enslaved or ransomed, their ships broken up to make siege engines and the cargoes sold. From this venture Philip raised 700 talents indicating that the average cargo and personnel value of each ship was 3.9 talents (94,000 sesterces).[45]

The scale of Crimean grain production is revealed by events in 360 BC when the grain crops failed in central Greece and Athens was threatened with famine. A ruler of the Chersonesos named Leuco intervened to assist his Athenian allies by sending a vast quantity of grain to the city-state. The Athenians redirected all available cargo vessels to the Black Sea to receive this shipment. According to Strabo, 'Leuco sent from Theodosia to Athens 2,100,000 *medimni* (84,000 tons).[46] This could have been the entire surplus harvest from the Crimea and it represented 1,120 cargo loads of 75 tons. It was enough grain to feed over 200,000 people for a year and more than the Athenians required. Demosthenes records that the Athenians sold the surplus grain at a profit of 15 talents (360,000 sesterces). Usually a *medimni* of grain was priced at 5 drachma so the surplus probably included 796 tons of grain.[47]

The Kingdom of Chersonesos kept its independence until 108 BC when Scythians from the neighbouring steppe threatened to overrun the region. The Spartocid dynasts sought help in Asia Minor and successfully petitioned the Pontic King Mithridates VI for military assistance.[48] But when the King of Chersonesos was killed in a subsequent battle with the Scythians, Mithridates sent his youngest son Pharnaces north to claim the kingdom. Strabo records that the Kingdom of Chersonesos paid a large annual tribute to Mithridates including 180,000 *medimni* (7,800 tons of grain=106 ships) and 200 silver talents (4.8 million sesterces).[49]

Strabo confirms the scale of ancient trade between the Black Sea and the Aegean when he describes port facilities at the harbour city of Cyzicus on the east coast of Asia Minor. Cyzicus was midway between Greece and the Crimea and was sited close to the Bosporus Strait which allowed passage into the Black Sea. Its port offered winter docking for merchant ships with extensive onshore storage and repair yards. Strabo reports that in adverse weather 'the city has two harbours that can be closed and more than two hundred ship-sheds.' When the Roman Empire gained power in Asia Minor, Cyzicus was made a free city exempt from tribute payments in return for a guarantee of support.[50]

Roman Intervention

The Romans first become interested in the Caucasus region during their final war against the Pontic King Mithridates VI (conflict: 75–63 BC). When Mithridates was defeated in Asia Minor he fled north to Colchis where he hoped to raise an army from tribal allies on the eastern shore of the Black Sea. In response, the Roman general Pompey marched his legions across the Lesser Caucasus Mountains and invaded the neighbouring kingdom of Caucasian-Iberia adjoining Colchis. This action ensured that Mithridates was confined to the Black Sea region and when Pompey captured the royal city of Mtskheta, he made the king of Caucasian-Iberia swear allegiance to the Empire as a vassal ruler. Pompey then crossed the Alazani River and defeated armed forces subject to the neighbouring kingdom of Caucasian-Albania (Azerbaijan). But although he expressed interest in reaching the Caspian coast, Pompey proceeded no further. Instead, he marched his forces west into Colchis where he captured the Greek city-port of

Phasis and made contact with the Roman fleet operating in the Black Sea.[51] According to Appian, Pompey was eager 'to gain knowledge of the country visited by the Argonauts, Castor and Pollux, and Heracles. He especially desired to see the place where they say that Prometheus was fastened to Mount Caucasus.'[52]

Pliny records how Pompey was interested to find that Indian commodities were available at the Black Sea port of Phasis. He therefore ordered enquiries to be made and these revealed an important trade route across Central Asia. Pompey was told, 'The journey from India to Bactria takes seven days and from a tributary of the Oxus called Bactrus, Indian merchandise can be conveyed across the Caspian Sea to the Cyrus River.' The Cyrus (Kura) is fed by streams of melted snow running down from both expanses of the Caucasus Mountains and flows along the broad depression that separates the ranges. Travellers from Caucasian-Iberia followed the Kura upstream from the broad delta where it discharged into the Caspian Sea. They journeyed more than 300 miles inland to the intersecting Likhi Mountains and then undertook a five-day trek to the headwater of the Phasis River (Rioni) in the Greater Caucasus. Once there, they could follow the river about 200 miles downstream to the eastern shores of the Black Sea and the port of Phasis.[53]

Some merchants from India and Bactria travelled the entire route and the Greek author who wrote the *Periodos to Nicomedes* in 100 BC describes Phasis as the place where 'people from sixty nations meet, all speaking different languages, including foreigners from India and Bactria'.[54] Some Indian travellers might have acquired ships or joined Colchian crews on voyages to the west coast of the Black Sea and the estuary of the Danube River. Pliny reports that in 63 BC a Roman governor in Gaul named Metellus Celer was presented with a group of Indian captives by a king of the Germanic Suebi nation. The Suebi inhabited inland territories to the north of the Danube River, but could have received slaves that included Black Sea sailors shipwrecked on hostile shores. Many leading ports in India were situated on river estuaries, so perhaps an Indian craft entered the Danube looking for signs of urban civilization. Pliny was informed, 'The Suebi king presented Metellus Celer with certain Indians, who had travelled from India for the purpose of commerce and while sailing they had been driven by storms into Germany.'[55]

At Phasis eastern cargoes were transferred onto seagoing vessels and conveyed through the Black Sea to cities on the Pontic coast. Strabo reports that the voyage from Phasis to the coastal cities of Amisus and Sinope took only two or three days. This was a distance of about 235 miles that must have been sailed at the relatively fast speed of about 4 or 5 knots.[56] From these Pontic Greek cities maritime trade routes continued around Asia Minor to the Bosphorus sea lanes that led into the Aegean Sea and the eastern Mediterranean.

Pompey had confirmed the existence of a route into Transoxiana that bypassed the Parthian Empire and offered the Romans the possibility of direct contact with India. But he was anxious to secure Roman interests in Asia Minor, so as soon as the allies of Mithridates were defeated, Pompey left Colchis.[57] Mithridates had sought refuge from the Romans in the Crimean kingdom of Chersonesos, but his son Pharnaces II staged a military uprising and besieged his father in the walled citadel of Panticapaeum. When Mithridates committed suicide, Pharnaces sought peace terms with the Romans who allowed him to remain in power in the Chersonesos as a client king allied to their empire.[58]

During the Roman civil war which began in 49 BC, King Pharnaces II seized the opportunity to invade neighbouring Colchis and occupy Pontus. Julius Caesar conducted the sudden and decisive Roman retaliation and it was here that he summarized his brief military campaign with the famous words, 'I came, I saw, I conquered' (*veni, vidi, vici*).[59] Pharnaces fled back to the Chersonesos where he was murdered by a member of the ruling aristocracy named Asander. Asander then seized power in the Chersonesos and submitted to Rome as a client-king with his royal status recognised and secured by the first Emperor Augustus.

Strabo describes how Asander decided not to pay tribute to the surrounding Scythian tribes. He ordered the construction of a large barrier to prevent mounted steppe warriors raiding the field systems and fortified Hellenic cities of the southern Chersonesos. These defences consisted of a wall and deep ditch to impede cavalry forces approaching from the surrounding steppe. Strabo reports that the wall included up to 10 'towers' per *stadium* (100 towers per mile), but given their density these elevated features must have been no more than narrow firing platforms.[60] The Scythians then threatened the harbours near the wall and the outlying forts that guarded the lagoon-based salt works. The Scythian army filled the outer trenches with straw so that their warriors were able to assault the walls. In spite of this, the defenders prevailed. But they had to abandon their garrison points on outlying capes, burning the bridges and connecting causeways on their strategic retreat.[61]

The Emperor Augustus entrusted the management of the Black Sea region to his senior commander Agrippa. There were disturbances in 14 BC when a dignitary named Scribonius married the widow of the former ruler and claimed the Chersonesos kingdom for himself. Agrippa ordered the client king of Pontus to land his forces on the Crimean Peninsula while a Roman army was mobilized to reclaim the territory.[62] This force assembled at the harbour town of Sinope in the central part of the Black Sea on the Pontic coast facing the Crimea. The ships included troops and war vessels sent by the Jewish king Herod who ruled the client kingdom of Judea.[63] But before the Roman invasion could be launched, the Crimean population rebelled against their self-appointed king and surrendered the region to the Empire. Eutropius confirms that following this display of force, 'all the maritime cities of the Black Sea submitted to Augustus.'[64] Tacitus confirms that several Roman cohorts, perhaps 1,500 soldiers, were posted to the Kingdom of Chersonesos to ensure its loyalty. In AD 49 this small force assisted a young prince named Cotys when he was challenged by a rebel army raised by a rival royal candidate. The cohorts probably had their own transport vessels including war-galleys docked at some of the main city-ports in the region. Tacitus describes how a group of Roman soldiers were returning from successful military operations in AD 49 when they were forced ashore by adverse weather.

He reports, 'They were returning by sea, but a few of the ships were forced onto the Taurian coast and surrounded by barbarians. The prefect of one cohort was killed along with many of the auxiliaries.'[65]

The Roman Empire controlled the Black Sea, Pontic and Colchic territories with a relatively small military force. By the first century AD the Pontic harbour city of Trapezus had become the main base for the Roman fleet stationed in the Black Sea (*Classis Pontica*). Describing events in AD 66, Josephus reports that these regions 'are subject to 3,000 soldiers and forty galleys keep this sea peaceful'.[66] An inscription from Trapezus records the name of a Roman *navarch* (admiral) named Gaius Numisius Quirina Primus who was a priest of the imperial cult and a town councillor at the nearby coastal city of Sinope.[67] Strabo reports that Sinope 'has at present received a colony of Roman citizens and they own part of the city and the surrounding territory'.[68]

During this period the Empire used Crimean grain shipments to support its garrisons in Asia Minor. When the Roman legions campaigned in Armenia, these grain shipments were diverted towards the forts and garrison points near the extended battlefront (AD 58–63). Tacitus describes how 'our supplies were coming in from the Black Sea and the town of Trapezus. The Armenian King could not attack the supply-line because it was carried across mountains to our occupation forces.'[69]

Throughout the early Roman period the Kingdom of Chersonesos continued to export large amounts of grain to densely populated cities in the eastern Mediterranean. The slave trade was also significant and markets in Chersonesos received captives from the Pontic-Caspian steppe who were sold in Mediterranean ports. With the wealth derived from this commerce, the kingdom became rich enough to mint its own coinage including gold Greek *staters* bearing portraits of the Roman Emperor and the reigning Chersonesos king.

In the imperial era, Roman interests in the Black Sea region also extended through the Caucasus Mountains to the small kingdom of Caucasian-Iberia. This kingdom remained under the rule of its own kings who were considered allies, rather than subjects of the Roman Empire. A stone inscription from Mtskheta written in Aramaic commemorates King Mihdrat I (AD 58–106) as 'the friend of the Caesars' and ruler 'of the Roman-loving Iberians'.[70]

Trade across the Caucasus

Strabo describes how trade was conducted across the Caucasus Mountains between the Black Sea and the Caspian. River-craft followed the Phasis River upstream to an outpost in the mountains called Sarapana described as a 'fortress capable of admitting the population of a city' (Surimi Pass).[71] This was probably a large fortified compound built to keep travellers and merchandise safe from bandit raiders or any hostile tribal war-bands who occupied the surrounding mountains. Pliny mentions a fortified caravan station in the Eastern Desert of Egypt that could accommodate up to 2,000 travellers and Sarapana probably performed a similar function for the Caucasus.[72]

From Sarapana goods were transferred onto ox-wagons to follow a paved road that crossed through mountain passes to a station on the frontiers of Caucasian-Iberia near the head of the River Cyrus (the Kura).[73] After completing this four-day overland passage, merchandise was loaded onto cargo craft to follow the Cyrus River downstream to the Absheron Peninsula on the Caspian shore of Caucasian-Albania (Azerbaijan). There goods were loaded aboard cargo ships designed for maritime travel across the Caspian Sea. The journey between the Caspian and Black Sea coasts covered at least 420 miles, but Strabo underestimated the distance stating that it was only 300 miles.[74] This was probably because the rivers allowed rapid downstream progress which shortened expected journey times.

Augustus made the regional rulers of Asia Minor subject to the Empire as client kings whose sons were 'hosted' in Rome. These kings were permitted to raise and deploy their own militia to keep order in their respective kingdoms, but they remained subject to the overall dictates of the Roman regime.[75] In AD 63, the Emperor Nero forced the Pontic King Polemon II to abdicate and his kingdom on the southern shores of the Black Sea was placed under the authority of a Roman governor. The Pontic troops stationed in Colchis were put under the direct command of Roman officers, or replaced by legionary garrisons.

During this period Colchis remained the eastern limit of direct Roman rule. Across the mountains the neighbouring kingdom of Caucasian-Iberia was permitted to remain as a vassal state subject to imperial demands. The kings of Caucasian-Iberia paid homage to Rome in return for the prospect of military assistance against nearby mountain tribes or other aggressive nations that might threaten their territory. In particular, Caucasian kingdoms were vulnerable to attack by the mounted raiders who inhabited the vast steppe lands beyond the mountains.

Any Steppe invaders who breached the frontiers of Caucasian kingdoms had the potential to destabilise the entire region if they moved south into the neighbouring kingdom of Armenia. Rome and Parthia both claimed Armenia as a vassal state and would mobilize in defence of this strategic frontier territory. From Armenia steppe invaders could ride directly into Roman Asia Minor or enter the Parthian Empire through its vulnerable northern frontiers.

Nero had plans for the Caucasian kingdoms which involved control over the north-south passes that led into this territory. Mid-way through the Greater Caucasus range was a steep and narrow gorge called the Darial Pass where the River Terek surges through steep rock-faces at the base of Mount Kazbek. The Darial Gorge was known as the Caucasian Gates because it was one of only two major routes through the mountains leading from the north down into Armenia. Pliny reports that 'maps of the region sent home from the Roman conflict in Armenia had the "Gates of the Caucasus" written on them.'[76] He describes these Gates as 'an enormous work of Nature – as though the mountains had been suddenly rent asunder'. The pass was blocked by 'gates with iron-covered beams under the centre of which flows a river that emits a horrible odour'. On the Iberian side of the pass was 'a rock on which stands the fortress called Cumania, erected for the purpose of barring the passage of innumerable tribes'. Opposite this fortress was the Iberian town of Hermastus, protected by the gates which seemed to 'divide the world' and mark the limit of settled civilization. The route had been measured by Roman surveys and, according to Pliny, 'it is practically certain that the distance from the Gates of the Caucasus to the Black Sea is 200 miles.'[77]

Suetonius describes Nero's plans for the region when he reports that 'he prepared an expedition to the Caspian Gates, after enrolling a new legion of recruits, all of Italian birth and each 6 feet tall, which he called the "Phalanx of Alexander the Great".'[78] Nero was possibly planning to annex the Caucasian kingdoms and conquer Sarmatian territories in the lands beyond to give Rome greater access to the Caspian Sea. Pliny explains, 'it is said that the expedition threatened by the Emperor Nero was going to penetrate the Caspian Gates. This refers to the pass that offers a road from Iberia into Sarmatia, since the mountain barrier provides limited access to the Caspian Sea.'[79] Tacitus describes how the Caspian campaign was to be directed against the 'Albani' which suggests the conquest of Caucasian Albania and control over the Derbent Pass. He reports that the Legion was on route to the Caspian Gates when it was recalled back to Italy to oppose the provincial rebellions that ended Nero's reign.[80]

During the Roman civil war of AD 69, Pontus and Colchis were involved in a brief uprising against imperial authority organized by a former admiral of the royal Pontic fleet. The admiral named Anicetus had lost his position when Rome annexed the region and native troops had been brought under provincial command. Anicetus announced his support for the short-lived Emperor Vitellius and refused to transfer his allegiance to the eventual victor Vespasian. By offering the prospect of plunder, Anicetus summoned support from the Colchic region and launched a sudden seaborne raid on the Roman fleet harboured at the Pontic cityport of Trapezus. Tacitus explains that the harbour was unguarded as the best Liburnian war-galleys had been transferred to Byzantium along with most of the long-serving Roman garrison. Anicetus burnt the ships that had remained and 'destroyed a cohort, previously part of the Royal Guard'. According to Tacitus these local soldiers 'had been granted the privileges of Roman citizenship and received Roman arms and standards, yet still retained the indolence and ill-discipline of Greeks'.

After this raid Anicetus withdrew to the Colchis to launch further attacks on the Pontic coast by using specially enclosed weather-resistant boats called *camarae*. These native craft were 'built with narrow sides and broad bottoms with hull planks joined together without brass or iron fastenings'. During rough weather the crews could raise the bulwarks with additional planking to resist the higher waves. Tacitus reports that further planks could be added until 'the vessel is enclosed like a cabin and they can roll about on the billowing seas'. These craft had 'a prow at both extremities and oar-banks that can be reversed so they could be propelled in either direction without difficulty'. But Colchic ships were no match for large fast-paced Roman war-galleys and imperial naval reinforcements easily overtook and captured the craft. After safeguarding the Pontic coast the

Roman navy threatened a seaborne assault on Colchis itself. Fearing severe retaliation, the Colchic people surrendered Anicetus to the Romans in return for monetary rewards. Anicetus was then executed as a traitor.[81]

When Colchis was brought back under imperial authority, it was placed under the direction of the Roman governor of Galatia (Central Asia Minor). Roman troops were posted at the main towns on the eastern seaboard of the Black Sea and imperial garrisons took control of fortresses in the mountain passes. There were no cities in the rugged interior territories of Colchis and the region was relatively underdeveloped. The population were mostly tribal peoples and there were no sizable Hellenic communities in the inland zone. Strabo summed up the situation when he reported that 'the Colchic tribes all speak different languages because of their stubbornness and ferocity' and 'they live in scattered groups and do not communicate much with one another.'[82] But despite the savage reputation of these mountain people, the Caspian-Colchis trade route remained an important trade conduit between the Roman Empire and eastern civilisations.

CHAPTER NINE

Black Sea Voyages

By AD 81 control over the Colchis region had been transferred to the Roman province of Cappadocia in central Asia Minor. Cappadocia bordered on Armenia and the provincial governor was assigned two legions to protect this frontier. This force was also responsible for garrisoning Colchis and assisting the allied kingdom of Caucasian-Iberia.

In AD 132, the strategically-minded Emperor Hadrian appointed a Greek named Arrian as Roman governor of Cappadocia. This posting included responsibility for the Caucasus and the Armenian frontier. The governor of Cappadocia commanded the XII Fulminate Legion based at Melitene and the XV Apollinaris at Satala to safeguard routes into Roman territory from Armenia and the neighbouring Parthian Empire.[1]

In addition to his military career Arrian had written a history of Alexander the Great that included a detailed account of his campaigns in India. He had also composed a ten volume account of Trajan's eastern wars against the Parthian Empire which has not survived into modern times.[2] During his term as governor, Arrian composed a tactical report called the *Array against the Alani* which described how the Roman army in the province of Cappadocia ought to be formed up for battle if a steppe people called the Alani breached the Caucasus Mountains and invaded Roman territory.

Hadrian paid particular attention to frontier defence and was responsible for Hadrian's Wall, the 80-mile long barrier that divided Roman Britain from Caledonia (Scotland). He was also fond of touring the Roman provinces, so Arrian prepared a special report for the Emperor about conditions along the Black Sea coast.[3] The work is composed in the style of a Greek sailing guide known as a *Periplus* (a circuit) which describes coastlines and sailing routes for mariners. Most of the document, known as the *Periplus Ponti Euxini* (*Periplus of the Black Sea*), is based on direct experience or details gathered from Roman informants. Arrian admired a fifth century BC Athenian historian named Xenophon who helped command a mercenary force of 10,000 Greeks in a military expedition against the Persian Empire. He therefore adopted the name 'Xenophon' as his literary identity.[4]

The *Periplus of the Black Sea* was written in Greek at a time when most educated Romans were fluent in this language and well-versed in Hellenic culture. The *Historia Augusta* confirms that Hadrian 'was so deeply devoted to Greek studies in his youth that some people called him the "Greekling".'[5] In his report Arrian describes the entire circuit of the Black Sea, including places subject to Rome, regions ruled by allied regimes and territories controlled by independent nations.

The *Periplus* includes details about ports, landmarks, marine hazards and sites that would have attracted foreign visitors.

Parts of this unique *Periplus* deal with Roman frontier administration and imperial defence strategies, but the report also suggests the progression of Greek trade routes around the Black Sea coast. It confirms that the Caucasus produced large amounts of high-quality timber, an essential resource for the seafaring communities of the Roman Mediterranean. It also verifies the export of linen to be woven into high-quality sailcloth and hemp used for ropes and rigging. The Roman economy was dependent on seafaring, so these resources were important in maintaining maritime connections across the Empire.

As the *Periplus of the Black Sea* is not a commercial document, it does not include business details about the trade ports, or the commodities offered in these places. It focuses instead on strategic and topographical information of interest to an emperor with a passion for educated Greek culture. Perhaps the Emperor Hadrian was reconsidering frontier security in preparation for further conflict in the region, or was planning a tour of inspection along the Black Sea coast. It is also possible that Hadrian enjoyed reading 'travel literature' and had an interest in military strategy as one aspect of this study. The *Historia Augusta* reports, 'He was fond of travelling and eager to learn from experience all that he had read concerning the different parts of the world.'[6]

Whatever his intention, the *Periplus of the Black Sea* allowed Arrian to demonstrate to the Emperor that he was an effective and efficient governor who took a direct interest in the issue of frontier defence. His work reveals how the Roman government controlled and protected various ports and strategic positions associated with maritime traffic. It also contains practical information such as distances between harbours and the political status of local populations. In addition, Arrian included interesting historical and cultural details about the region.

The Voyage to Colchis

Arrian begins his *Periplus of the Black Sea* with an address to the Emperor Hadrian, then starts the narrative as though he were a traveller heading out from the Roman naval port of Trapezus on the south-east corner of the Black Sea. Trapezus was a prominent Greek city, but some of its civic amenities had fallen into disrepair due to the neglect of the contemporary population. The port was near the historical frontier of Colchis and Arrian reminds Hadrian that this was the coastline reached by the Athenian general Xenophon when he led 10,000 Greek mercenaries out of Persia in 401 BC. On seeing these waters, the battle-weary and exhausted Greek soldiers cried out in thankful exclamation – 'The Sea! The Sea!'[7]

Trapezus was the main base for the Roman fleet on the Pontic shore and Arrian had selected a number of military craft for his voyage along the Colchis seaboard. These ships were probably light-weight *liburnian* galleys which had a single centrally placed mainsail and a bank of sixty oars (thirty oars on each side). In addition to the rowers, each of these ships could carry an on-board unit of between thirty and sixty infantry troops. The vessels could either be rowed by the trained oarsmen or make way under sail when wind conditions were favourable.

There were no cargo ships in the squadron assembled by Arrian, but the *liburnians* sailed with a large trireme galley which operated as the command vessel. This trireme could have had up to 180 rowers and it carried heavy military equipment including cumbersome ballistic weaponry. But triremes had limited cargo space and were difficult to manage in adverse weather.[8]

It was customary for Greek and Roman travellers to perform carefully prescribed embarkation rituals before undertaking a risky sea voyage. Incense was often offered to the gods at harbour altars to ensure divine assistance for a safe sailing and Arrian explains how at Trapezus he had repaired and enhanced some of the ceremonial features connected with these practices. Rough and weathered stone altars standing near the harbour had been replaced with white marble replicas inscribed with the correct Attic Greek in place of the corrupted script used by the local Hellenic community. A statue of the Emperor had been erected at the harbour, but Arrian informs Hadrian, 'though your statue has a pleasing pose, gesturing out to sea, the sculpture is not a good resemblance or particularly attractive.' Arrian reports that he had ordered another statue to be commissioned and sent to the port, so the monument might better convey the dignity of the Emperor and the authority of Rome.[9]

Trapezus had a prominent temple devoted to the Greek god Hermes, the deity associated with trade and travel. This temple was reported to be in good condition, but Arrian thought the existing Greek statue was not adequate given the significance of the site and requested that Hadrian send him a replacement image of the god at least 5 feet tall. He also asked for a smaller statue of the local god or divine hero called Philesios that shared the temple. Philesios was said to be a descendant of Hermes and travellers usually sacrificed to both deities before leaving on voyages around the Black Sea. Arrian had an ox slaughtered to fulfil his obligations and when the entrails were examined on the altar and showed no corruption, a perfumed libation was poured on them as an offering to the gods. Arrian and his soldiers said prayers to the Emperor and then headed down to the harbour where the ships were awaiting their embarkation.[10]

On leaving Trapezus, the Roman squadron sailed east to a garrison post named Hyssou Limen that was less than a day's voyage away. Hyssou Limen (Arakh Carsisi) was near the mouth of the Kara Dere River where ancient remains have been discovered including a rectangular fort measuring 650 feet by 985 feet with a gatehouse in each wall.[11]

Arrian had been approved for command by the Emperor, so his attention to military matters fitted the interests and practices promoted by Hadrian. The *Historia Augusta* reports that 'although Hadrian desired peace more than war, he kept the soldiers in training just as if war were imminent.' When the Emperor visited soldiers on the German frontiers, 'he inspired them by proofs of his own endurance and lived a soldier's life among the units.' It was said that Hadrian would march up to 20 miles a day while dressed in regular unadorned military gear, and while engaged in practice manoeuvres he would personally select sites for military camps. During his military inspections Hadrian re-established camp discipline, offsetting any harsh treatment by 'bestowing gifts on many and honours on a few'. He improved the arms and equipment of military units, promoted experienced soldiers worthy of higher rank and dismissed men still collecting wages who were too old or weak for combat. At garrison points and frontier camps Hadrian also 'made it his practice to be acquainted with the soldiers and to know their numbers'.[12]

When Arrian inspected the garrison at Hyssou Limen he had its infantry soldiers perform military manoeuvres with a display of javelin throwing to demonstrate their combat readiness. The garrison had a small cavalry contingent of twenty mounted troops and this was considered sufficient for keeping order in the area. The squadron under Arrian's command left Hyssou Limen in the early morning, taking advantage of the cold winds that blow down from the surrounding coasts. When the wind dropped, Arrian ordered the oarsmen to row the vessels along the Pontic seaboard. Then, with little warning, dark clouds rose up from the horizon and the squadron was caught by a sudden storm. As waves threatened to swamp the low-lying decks of the war galleys, the Romans stowed their sails and tried to row out of the turbulence. Arrian reports that the squadron was saved when a violent offshore wind suppressed the waves and pushed the heavy surf back from the struggling vessels. He writes, 'Having suffered much, we arrived at Athenai.'[13]

Athenai was a small deserted settlement named after an ancient temple that was dedicated to the goddess Athena. It was also the site of an abandoned fort that the Roman authorities had decided not to garrison. The site had no harbour, but there was a relatively safe mooring place close to the shore that could accommodate a number of ships and offer shelter from the strong winds blowing along this coast from different quarters. However, that particular night violent thunder and lightning woke the troops and signalled that another storm was approaching. As the wind rose, Arrian realised that the mooring place was no longer safe and by the light of torches and lamps he ordered his men to immediately beach their ships upon the shore. Ropes and cables were used to haul the *liburnian* vessels up onto the beach, but Arrian ordered the trireme to take its chances afloat. The trireme was needed to haul the smaller galleys back into the water with tow cables so its survival was essential. Out at sea the crew threw down heavy anchors and cabled the vessel to an offshore rock to ride out the storm. But before the last *liburnian* was dragged ashore the full force of the storm hit and Arrian reports that the 'sea turned completely savage'.[14]

Only one vessel was destroyed in the storm. It was a *liburnian* galley that had been caught broadside by a wave as it had turned on its mooring to make the dash onto the beach. The vessel tumbled over and was smashed against the shoreline by the pounding waves. The crew escaped and swam ashore, but the galley was broken up on the beach. Two days later when the storm had calmed the Roman troops were able to salvage the wreck. Arrian reports that 'everything was retrieved; including the sail, the rigging, the nails and even the sealing-wax was stripped off the vessel.' He adds that when the task was completed, 'none of the fittings remained except for the ship's timber, which you know is an abundant resource in the Black Sea region.' As the storm subsided the ships were refloated and spent the following night at their mooring. Arrian reports that 'towards morning we struggled against the waves coming over the sides of our ships,' but when a northerly wind arrived, the squadron were able to depart Athenai on a calm sea.[15]

From Athenai it was a 25-mile sailing east to a well-fortified Greek city called Apsaros (Gonio in Georgia) at the mouth of the Coruh River. This was the site of a large Roman garrison consisting of five cohorts, or about 2,500 troops. The walled city had a hippodrome for horse racing and a theatre which would have been of particular interest to Hadrian as he was an admirer of Greek theatrical culture. An inscription reveals that there was a community of veteran soldiers resident in Apsaros who had decided to remain in the city after receiving their discharge retirement bonuses.[16] Pliny estimated that Apsaros was about 140 miles from the fleet base at Trapezus.[17]

Apsaros controlled an important east-west route from Armenia into Pontic Asia Minor. So the stone-built Roman fort at Apsaros was more heavily defended than other military outposts on this frontier. It occupied a rectangular area (635 feet by 800 feet) with a gatehouse on each wall flanked by adjacent towers. There were four corner towers on the fortress walls and a series of five square and three rounded towers positioned around the perimeter to maximise sight-lines and firing positions.[18] Arrian was to make this fortress his command post in AD 135 when an army of mounted Alani warriors breached the Caucasus Mountains and threatened to invade Roman territory. The Cappadocian legions were summoned to Apsaros and Arrian repelled the Alani in a successful military engagement that he personally oversaw and commanded.[19]

When Arrian visited Apsaros in AD 132, he came to inspect the serving troops and assess the local defences. He informs Hadrian, 'I gave the army its pay and inspected their weapons.' He reviewed 'the walls and its trenches, soldiers on sick-leave and the garrison food supplies'. Arrian tells the Emperor that he has included a full report on the condition of the defences and garrison at Apsaros.[20] This report was not written in Greek like the rest of the text, but in Latin as this was the appropriate language for military dispatches. Unfortunately, because the Latin section was offered in a separate document, it has not survived into modern times.

Apsaros was supposedly named after a legendry Colchic prince named Apsyrtos who was killed at this site by the Greek hero Jason. It was said that when Jason seized the Golden Fleece from Colchis, he fled on board his ship the Argo with the sorceress-princess Medea. In some stories Apsyrtos led the Colchic fleet in pursuit of Jason and cornered him at this site, but when Apsyrtos agreed to parley with the Argonauts, he was murdered.[21] In other legends Apsyrtos was the infant son of King Areetes who was abducted by his sister Medea and dismembered by her as their father approached with the Colchic fleet. King Areetes was paralysed with grief when he saw the remains of his murdered son and ended the pursuit at this site.[22] According to Arrian, whichever version of the story visitors to the city chose to believe, they would all be shown the same ancient tomb of Apsyrtos.[23]

Strabo suggests that the voyage along the Colchic coast was a relatively easy sailing since 'the shores are soft and the coast has river outlets.' The region was renowned for its shipbuilding resources, including 'large quantities of timber brought down on its rivers, linen made by local peoples and supplies of hemp, wax and pitch'. Strabo reports that Colchic linen production was 'famous across a wide area, for they export it to foreign places'.[24]

From Apsaros, Arrian sailed with the Roman squadron north to the port of Phasis on the east coast of the Black Sea. Arrian describes the strange properties of the Phasis River (Rion) which flowed down through the Caucasus Mountains. The Phasis was the largest river in the region and it discharged a vast quantity of unusual water into the Black Sea. This water was fresher and lighter than the contents of other rivers and had the appearance of being tainted by tin or lead. The outflow from the Phasis river did not mix easily with the surrounding seawater and was seen floating above the marine currents. Arrian observed how local people could take their cattle down to the shore to drink, because the river had greatly diluted the salinity of the adjacent sea. These odd properties encouraged a superstition amongst sailors who would pour away all stored water when they reached the river and took onboard fresh Phasis water. Arrian reports that 'it is said that those who do this will encounter favourable sailing conditions.'[25]

The Phasis River was a major communication route for riverine travel and Pliny reports that 'it receives other tributaries remarkable for their size and number'. At one stage the river had numerous bridges and a considerable number of towns along its lower course. This included an urban settlement called Aea which was located 15 miles inland near where two large tributaries joined the river. However Pliny reports that by the late first century AD, the only remaining town in the inland region was Surium which was located about 38 miles inland. Ships of all sizes could navigate the Phasis upstream as far as Surium, but from this point onward smaller vessels had to be used to convey cargo into the Caucasus. According to Pliny these smaller craft followed the river a long way into the mountains.[26] Strabo cautions that some upper stretches of the Phasis passed through chasms as it flowed along a winding course and these sections of the river became a 'rough and violent stream' during seasonal heavy rains.[27]

Somewhere inland was the fortress called Sarapana where river cargoes were transferred to wagons to be conveyed to the River Cyrus (Kura) which flowed into the Caspian.[28] Strabo describes Sarapana as 'a Colchian stronghold' located near a gorge that formed one of the main routes through the mountains.[29] Pliny reports that some Greek and Roman authorities thought that the isthmus that separated the Black Sea from the Caspian was less than 375 miles wide. The Emperor Claudius claimed that only 150 miles of land separated the two seas and this could be a reference to the route between the upper Phasis and Cyrus rivers. It was claimed that close to the time of his death (281 BC) the Seleucid King Seleucus I Nicator was 'contemplating cutting a channel through this isthmus' that might have linked the two rivers.[30]

To the Greeks, Colchis was a forbidding region, 'shut in by rocks, strongholds, and rivers that run through ravines'.[31] Strabo describes Phasis as the 'farthermost voyage' and reports that 'the great fame of this country in early times is revealed by the myths which refer in an obscure way to the expedition of Jason.'[32] Apollonius Rhodius imagined how the Argonauts stored their sails and manned the oars to enter 'the broad flowing Phasis' in search of 'the shady grove of Ares where the glaring serpent, a monster terrible to behold, watches over a Golden Fleece spread over an oak tree'.[33] Appian had a theory concerning the Golden Fleece of Greek legend and he describes how 'many streams issuing from the Caucasus carry fine gold-dust that is almost invisible'. The mountain people placed sheepskins with shaggy fleeces into the stream to collect the floating particles. Appian suggests that these fleeces might have been the prize sought by Jason.[34] The Phasis River is also mentioned by Virgil and listed by Aelius Aristides as one of the prime points on the Roman frontiers alongside the Euphrates, Ethiopia and Britain.[35]

Near the gates of Phasis port there was a large statue of the patron goddess Phasiane that personified the town. She was depicted holding a cymbal and seated on a throne with lions at her feet. Arrian thought that the statue resembled Rhea, the Earth mother of the Greek pantheon. The main anchor from Jason's ship the Argo was on display in the town centre as a monument to the ancient myth. Arrian wrote with frankness about this object and explained that 'it is made of iron and although it does not look old to me, the shape is unusual and it is not the same size as modern anchors.' There were also some old fragments of a stone anchor on display and Arrian believed that these objects were more likely to be the remnants of the anchor that Jason had aboard the Argo.[36] Apollonius Rhodius confirms this tradition that the Argo carried stone anchors.[37]

Strabo calls Phasis the emporium (commercial centre) of Colchis and explains that the site had good natural defences, 'protected on one side by the river, on another by a lake, and on another by the sea'.[38] The town had a Roman fort garrisoned by a small and well-equipped force of 400 'select troops'. Arrian describes how the fort had a double-ditch perimeter and its original inner wall was made from banks of earth and a wooden palisade guarded by two flanking towers. The site was being upgraded by replacing the wooden defences with walls and towers made from brick-blocks. He inspected the foundations to ensure that the new battlements were sturdy and also reviewed the war engines in the fort to confirm that they had sufficient ammunition. These weapons probably consisted of catapults and large two-manned 'scorpion' bolt-throwers designed to launch long-distance harpoon-like javelins. These weapons could outrange the hand-held bows or slings used by the mountain tribesmen or any steppe hordes that managed to infiltrate the region. Arrian concluded his inspection with the statement that the new fortress 'is fully equipped to prevent any of the barbarians from approaching and will certainly protect the garrison from sieges'.

Arrian had also given thought to the protection of the surrounding community which included many merchants and ex-soldiers. He reports, 'The mooring-place for the ships and the whole area outside the fort must also be secured because it is settled by veterans and various merchants.' In assessing the situation, Arrian ordered the perimeter of the town to be fortified by a double-ditch stockade that extended from the fort to the river and fully enclosed the harbour and surrounding houses. He concluded that the town would soon be highly secure and become a 'very convenient and safe place for those who sail this route'.[39]

Roman merchants operating at Phasis received Indian cottons, pearls and black pepper by way of the Caucasus mountain passes. Chinese silk would also have reached the town by way of Sogdia and the Oxus trade routes that carried Indian merchandise into the Caspian region. These trade contacts came through the Kingdom of Caucasian-Albania (Azerbaijan) and products from this connected territory would also have been carried across to Phasis, along with valuable Chinese and Indian goods. Large quantities of locally obtained shipbuilding products including timber, linen and hemp were also exported from Phasis. Native slaves may have been another export, along with stocks of salt that served as an important additive to preserve meat and fish.[40]

Arrian describes the native people who lived in the mountain districts around Phasis. The Trapezuntines and the Colchoi controlled much of the region, but they were threatened by the Saimoi who are described as being 'very warlike' and living in 'fortified places'. The Saimoi were a tribe without a king who gave tribute to Rome as a symbol of their subject status. According to Pliny this tribute included a quota of beeswax gathered in their forested territories. These forests produced honey and the Roman authorities would have demanded tribute payments from this product, except that there were rumours it was harmful due to the presence of poisonous flowers in the region.[41] Strabo was better informed about the region and simply comments that the honey was avoided because it 'generally tasted bitter'.[42] Arrian reports that the Saimoi had recently reneged on their tribute payments and turned to piracy. But he assures Hadrian, 'soon they will pay their tribute, or we will exterminate them.'[43]

Within the Caucasus there were five native rulers who sought recognition from Rome as regional 'kings'. Their authority either extended over tribal settlements in the mountains, or covered rural populations near the coast. Some of these rulers had received imperial confirmation and grants of power from the Roman Emperor Trajan (AD 98–117) and Hadrian had approved at least four of these rulers as 'kings'. Another tribe in the region called the Zydritai were subject to King Pharasmanes II who ruled the nearby kingdom of Caucasian-Iberia.[44] The cooperation of these kings and their native communities was crucial to maintaining the security of coastal Greek cities.

North of Phasis the Colchis seaboard curved west towards the Crimea and the upper reaches of the Black Sea. Arrian explains that the squadron were no longer sailing in the direction of the setting sun as they followed a coastline overshadowed by the Greater Caucasus. On this sailing the summit of an enormous landmark named Strobios came into view amongst the distant mountains (Mount Elbrouz). The snow-covered peak of its formidable summit was pointed out as the place where 'according to legend, Prometheus was strung up by Hephaistos, on the orders of Zeus' to endure an eternal punishment.[45] Apollonius Rhodius imagined what the crew of the Argo might have seen as they sailed 'past the steep-rising crags of the Caucasian Mountains, where Prometheus had his limbs bound to hard rocks by the galling of bronze shackles'. They might have heard 'a load whirr, near the clouds as their sails shook with the fanning of huge wings' and seen 'long-wing-feathers like polished oars' and heard 'the screams of Prometheus as his liver was torn away'.[46]

From Phasis it was a voyage of 63 miles along this coast to the site of a fortified Hellenic city named Sebastopolis. Sebastopolis used to be known by the name Dioscurias and the city had been founded by Milesian Greeks in the sixth century BC. Dioscurias was a thriving trade post in 270 BC when a Greek navigator and geographer named Timosthenes reported that 300 tribes, all speaking different languages, traded at the site. Strabo corrected this figure and characterised Sebastopolis as a Colchic city and 'the common emporium of the surrounding tribes; the meeting place for seventy populations'. By the Augustan era there was a large steppe presence near Sebastopolis including many Sarmatians. Strabo reported that the Colchic tribes and the Sarmatian incomers 'all speak different languages due to their stubborn ferocity, for they live in scattered groups, without frequent contact with one another'.[47] Pliny the Elder had heard that during the late Republic, 'Roman traders carried out business in the city with the help of a staff of 130 interpreters.' However, he reports that in his own time the city had declined dramatically and much of the merchant community had abandoned the site for more profitable ports and markets on the Black Sea coast.[48] Parts of the city might have been abandoned, but the fortress remained intact and well-guarded.

It was almost midday when Arrian sailed into the port of Sebastopolis (Sukhumi). The surrounding lands were occupied by a Colchic population called the Sanigai who were ruled by a chief named Spadagas. The Emperor Hadrian had conferred the title of 'king' on Spadagas, but the Romans were still concerned about security and the threat of invasion from the steppe. On his arrival Arrian arranged for the Roman garrison to assemble for inspection and receive their regular pay in coined money. The Roman force posted in this frontier city included a large cavalry contingent that Arrian called upon to perform complex field manoeuvres. He observed the drills designed to demonstrate the combat-readiness of the troops before examining the horses and weapons to ensure they were well maintained. Arrian knew that it was important for the governor to know the actual fighting capacity of the garrison, so he took a tally of those excused active service due to sickness or injury. He then verified that the supply stores were sufficient and toured the city walls to confirm that the circuit and ditch were adequate for defence purposes.[49] The remains of stone towers and walls that have been found on the seabed near Sukhumi could be these Roman defences submerged by coastal erosion, seismic activity or dramatic changes to the sea level along this shore.[50]

Roman traders visited Sebastopolis to procure slaves and shipbuilding materials, but merchants could also make a profit by supplying the well-paid Roman garrison with various supplies and amenities. Arrian calculated that it was about

226 miles from the fleet base at Trapezus to the city of Sebastopolis.[51] This was not a great distance for Greek and Roman cargo ships involved in coastal trade circuits and the sailing could be completed in three days if conditions were favourable. After visiting Apsaros, Pontus and Sebastopolis, many trade vessels would have followed the Black Sea coast north to the Crimean Peninsula to conduct further commercial deals with ports adjoining the Scythian Steppe.

The Chersonesos and Scythian Steppe (AD 131)

In the imperial period the kings of Chersonesos were expected to send annual tribute payments and status reports to the Roman government. In the second century their closest contact was the governor of Bithynia on the Pontic Coast. When Pliny the Younger was governor of Bithynia he received an ambassador sent by the King Sauromates I (AD 90–123). The ambassador carried a sealed letter addressed to the Emperor Trajan with a request to be issued with a permit to obtain state assistance on his journey through the Roman provinces.[52] The land journey from Pontus to Rome would have taken up to two months, but the route could be travelled in winter when the Mediterranean sea lanes were generally closed.

Annual tribute payments from the Chersonesos were sent to Bithynia aboard special delivery ships before being transported to Rome. Lucian took passage aboard one of these vessels as it sailed from Rome past the western coast of Greece near Corinth. He reports: 'There I encountered some men from the Bosporus [Chersonesos] who were voyaging along the coast. They were ambassadors from King Eupator travelling to Bithynia, to collect the yearly payment.'[53] King Rhoemetalces (AD 132–153) of Chersonesos was summoned to Rome by the Emperor Antoninus Pius to defend himself against charges brought by an imperial commander and on this journey he might have travelled aboard one of these tribute delivery vessels. Rhoemetalces was successful in his defence and was permitted to return to his kingdom.[54]

When Arrian undertook his voyage around the Black Sea, he sailed only as far as Sebastopolis, on the frontier of direct Roman rule, because this was the limit of his provincial command. After inspecting the mounted troops in this outlying city, he returned with his squadron to the naval base at Trapezus. However he thought it worthwhile to include information on the voyage to Crimea in his report to the Emperor Hadrian. The client King Kotys II had just died, so there was a possibility that Hadrian might choose to depose the dynasty and place Chersonesos under direct provincial rule. Arrian describes the region as the 'Chimmerian Bosporus' and explains, 'I have decided that it is my duty to explain the sailing routes as far as the Chimmerian Bosporus to you, so if you were planning something for the region you would know about the voyage.'[55]

Sailing north from Sebastopolis, Greek ships passed along a coastline that had many well-known mooring places and natural harbours. The inland region was ruled by a tribal people called the Zilchoi whose leader Stachemphax was recognised as a king by Hadrian.[56] From this place the coast curved north to form the Taman Peninsula which projected west towards the Crimea and enclosed the Sea of Azov. During Roman times the Taman Peninsula was part of the Crimean Kingdom of Chersonesos. It was an important grain producing territory with a diverse population and a regional capital called Phanagoria that had Greek origins.

Many trade vessels visited the city of Panticapaeum on the western edge of the Crimean Peninsula (the Chersonesos). Panticapaeum controlled the Strait of Kerch between the Crimean and the Taman Peninsulas and ships could sail through this passage to enter the enclosed Sea of Azov. Strabo refers to Panticapaeum as the metropolis (capital) of the Chersonesos and Pliny describes it as the strongest city in the region. The city was built around an acropolis and had a harbour with docks for about thirty ships.[57] Pliny estimated that the distance between Panticapaeum and Phanagoria on the far side of the strait was barely 4 miles and 'this is all the width that separates Asia from Europe'. He reports that the sea was frozen solid in winter allowing travellers to walk between the cities.[58] Fishing continued during these months when people cut into the ice with trident shaped tools to retrieve large sturgeon. According to Strabo the passage became an ice road in winter that could be crossed using wagons. The general sent by the Pontic King Mithridates IV to defend the Crimea was said to have won a naval victory on the strait during the summer and a cavalry engagement in the same place the following winter.[59]

The Sea of Azov was known to the Romans as Maeotis Lake and at its northern edge was the River Don which led deep into the Russian steppe. The sailing from the Strait of Kerch to the mouth of the Don was 180 miles, but Roman authorities overestimated this distance due to the slow and difficult sailing conditions.[60] Arrian considered the River Don to be the dividing line between Europe and Asia, but its northern reaches had never been fully explored by any Greek or Roman travellers.[61] Writing in the late first century AD, Pliny described the population living along the Don as Sarmatians who had expelled the native Scythians from the territory.[62]

Where the River Don flowed into the Sea of Azov there was a Hellenic trading city called Tanais. This had previously been a Greek colony established in the third century BC by Milesian settlers. Strabo reports that Tanais was second only to Panticapaeum on the Crimea, 'as the greatest emporium' for the non-Greek inhabitants of this region. It was visited by 'Asian and European nomads (Scythians and Sarmatians) and those who navigate these waters'.[63] Tanais was the most northerly and remote Greek outpost in the Black Sea, but its position offered unique trade opportunities. Merchants from Tanais could have dealt in mink and sable pelts similar to the products that Roman traders sought from the Indo-Scythians.[64] The Chinese *Weileu* reports that the Alani who inhabited the Pontic-Caspian steppe possessed 'large numbers of famous sables'.[65] Strabo also reports that 'the nomads bring to Tanais their products including slaves and hides to exchange for clothing, wine and other things that belong to settled civilisation.' He records that King Polemon (16–8 BC), who received the Chersonesos from the Emperor Augustus, had sacked Tanais because its inhabitants refused to obey his dictates.[66]

Pliny describes how the broad Crimean Peninsula was surrounded by sea and its east coast consisted of 'low-lying land rising to large mountain ridges'. Its population was diverse and included towns occupied by various native peoples, the descendants of Greek settlers and Scythian migrants from the steppe.[67] Arrian describes the sailing from Panticapaeum west around the Crimean Peninsula which the Romans called 'Taurica'. About 42 miles from Panticapaeum there was a former Hellenic city named Kimmerikon which had declined until it was little more than a village. Approximately 28 miles west from Kimmerikon, travellers sailed past the Greek city of Theodosia which had also become depopulated when commercial activities were redirected towards other ports. Strabo describes this region as 'everywhere productive of grain and containing villages' and the old harbour at Theodosia could accommodate up to a hundred ships.[68] These harbours might have remained in operation as places for ships to shelter from the 'furious storms from the north' that affected this coast.[69] Situated about 20 miles further west there was a disused mooring place or port facility that Arrian describes as the harbour of the Scytho-Taurians.[70]

Claudius Ptolemy records the presence of a military installation on the southern coast of the Crimea known as Charax (the Fortress). This site can be identified with a Roman fort which has been excavated on the top of Ay-Todor Cape. The site, now known as 'Castrum Charax', was possibly established when the Emperor Nero temporarily made the Chersonesos subject to full Roman authority and placed the kingdom under the control of the governor of Moesia on the west coast of the Black Sea (AD 63–68). An inscription from Rome records how the governor of Moesia, Tiberius Plautius Silvanus, sent an expedition to the Crimea to help defeat a force of Scythians threatening to invade the peninsula. The text records that he 'dislodged a king of the Scythians from the siege of Chersonesos' and 'was the first to add a great quantity of wheat from that region to the grain supply of the Roman people'.[71]

The Roman garrison at Charax may have been withdrawn when the ruling dynasty of Chersonesos was restored to power in AD 68. But the site was strategically important since it controlled sailing routes around the peninsula and occupied land near the shortest crossing point between the Pontus and Crimea. The fortress was reoccupied by Roman troops in the second century AD, receiving a garrison from the Legio I Italica and later the Legio XI Claudia who were based near the Danube frontier.[72] The remains at Castrum Charax include defences built using lime mortar, Roman brick-built bath houses with clay heating pipes, a cult building and altars with dedications to Jupiter and other Italian deities. The inscriptions include mention of military road builders who were probably tasked with improving routes to the main Crimean cities from the coast at Castrum Charax.[73] These roads were probably planned for rapid military deployment, but would have facilitated transport and trade.

Just beyond the southern tip of the Crimean Peninsula, archaeological work has uncovered the remains of city walls, defensive watchtowers, a Greek temple, a Roman amphitheatre and ancient farmland under civic authority (the *chora*).[74] Here there was a thriving Hellenic city named Chersonesos that had its origins in a Greek colony sent from Pontic Heraclea in the sixth century BC. Pliny reports that the city was encircled by 5 miles of wall and its inhabitants preserved a culture that was considered the most 'Greek' of all the cities in the region. He also reveals that the Romans had at that time made the city free from tribute payments.[75]

About 60 miles north was another Hellenic city called Kerkinitis and 70 miles from Kerkintis was a Greek town called Kalos Limen. From Kalos Limen, ships could leave the Crimean Peninsula and begin sailing along the northwest shore of the Black Sea towards the Dnieper-Bug Estuary.

The Dnieper-Bug Estuary

West of the Crimean Peninsula was the entrance to the narrow Dnieper-Bug Estuary which led 40 miles inland and received water from two major river systems. There was a Greek city called Olbia a short distance upstream on the River Bug which led inland to the forested territories of central Europe. Strabo reports that the Bug could be navigated 60 miles upstream and he describes Olbia as 'a great trading centre'.[76] About 4 miles west of Olbia was the Hellenic city of Odessos which had a good mooring for ships and was sited near the mouth of the Dnieper River. Rising in Russia, the Dnieper flowed over 1,000 miles down through the Ukranian Steppe to reach the Black Sea coast. The Bug, Dnieper and Don all formed important north-south migration routes for steppe peoples to move cattle and products between distant seasonal grazing lands.

Some 30 miles west of Odessos was the mouth of the Dniester River and the site of former Greek settlements known as Nikonion and Tyras. Rising in central Europe, the Dniester flowed through the Carpathian Mountains and formed the northern frontier of Dacia as it travelled down to the Black Sea coast. Goods from across these regions would have reached Odessos, including valuable amber from territories near the Baltic Sea.[77]

The Roman orator Dio Chrysostom visited the Greek community at Olbia (Borysthenes) sometime between AD 96 and AD 101. He describes it as 'an important trading centre' and reports that the sheltered estuary was marshy with slow moving river outlets. Consequently ships could run aground in the summer months, when the water level could fall to 12 feet in parts of the inlet. Dio warns that 'inbound sailors must judge the depth by the current.' He describes the coast as 'a muddy shore overgrown with reeds and trees, with many trees visible in the midst of the marsh resembling the masts of ships'. Pilots had to be alert, as 'sometimes those who were less familiar with these inlets have lost their way, supposing that they were approaching other ships.'[78]

There were a large number of salt works close to the Dnieper-Bug Estuary, 'from which most of the barbarians buy their salt, as do the Greeks and Scythians who occupy the Tauric Chersonese (Crimea)'. Dio Chrysostom reports that after the Sarmatians seized this coastline they established a fortified outpost near the estuary known as the 'Citadel of Alector'. The western steppe nations allowed women to acquire military commands and when Dio Chrysostom visited the region the citadel belonged to a wife of the Sarmatian king.

Many Greek cities on this part of the Black Sea had lost their autonomy when the Sarmatians overran the Pontic Steppe in the mid-first century BC. Dio Chrysostom records that after the takeover, 'some of the Greeks no longer united to form cities, while others had a wretched existence as their communities were joined by many barbarians.' Greek ships stopped sailing to the Dnieper-Bug Estuary when its cities were first captured by the Sarmatians. This was because the Sarmatians 'had no people of common speech to receive the merchants and had neither the ambition nor the knowledge to equip a trading centre of their own in the Greek manner'. The new rulers of Olbia managed to restore commercial traffic by permitting the Greeks in the city to form a distinct community that could manage civic regulations and social networks favourable to visiting merchants. Nevertheless, Dio Chrysostom thought that Olbia was in decline since the city did not match its historic reputation. This was due to 'its repeated seizure in wars' and the fact that the city had 'been in the midst of virtually the most warlike barbarians for a long time and constantly in a state of conflict'.[79]

By AD 96 many civic buildings in Olbia were in disrepair and the city had contracted into a smaller defensive area close to the best fortified stretch of its ancient circuit-wall. Dio Chrysostom reports that 'few towers remain on the wall and they do not match the original size or power of the city.' As the city contracted into this smaller district a new defensive façade was established with houses built in intervening spaces to create a wall-like barrier around the exposed part of the site. A flanking wall was built around these houses, but it was low and weak. Abandoned stretches of the former wall were dismantled for building materials leaving only the ancient towers as an indication of the city's former limits. When Dio Chrysostom visited the Greek community he saw evidence of former conflicts in the temples, shrines and public buildings. He records, 'not a single statue remains undamaged in the sanctuaries, all having suffered mutilation along with the funeral monuments.'[80]

Various Scythian groups continued to exist under Sarmatian dominance including a clan called the Black-Cloaks who are first described by Herodotus.[81] While walking outside the walls of Olbia, Dio Chrysostom was approached by a steppe horseman who dismounted and began a conversation. This steppe warrior was a Black-Cloak who carried a long cavalry sword and dressed in traditional Scythian costume including riding trousers. He adhered to his native customs, wearing black clothing and wearing a small thin cape.[82]

The Island of Achilles

Arrian reports that there was a strange white-coloured island in the sea near the Dnieper-Bug Estuary that was sacred to the Greek hero Achilles. It was said that the nymph Thetis gave the island to her son Achilles as an isolated retreat for exercise and training. The young hero made his home on the island and for this reason the place was known as the 'Isle of Achilles' or the 'Race Track'. The island was uninhabited and had no facilities except for a temple maintained by visitors who came to pay homage to an ancient wooden image of Achilles. Sailors visiting the island often captured a wild goat to sacrifice at the temple. It was said that the divine presence on the island signalled its satisfaction by rendering the goat unresistant to the blade. A great deal of wealth had therefore accumulated within the temple because landing parties had to keep offering goods until the animal ceased its struggles. People who made pilgrimages to the island brought selected offerings with them, but any ships that made unscheduled stops due to incoming storms had to devote items from their cargo. Arrian reports that all manner of votive offerings decorated the unguarded temple, including ceramic bowls, jewellery rings and expensive precious stones. These items give an indication of the kind of cargoes that were carried aboard the ships that sailed by this place.[83]

The island was well-known to Greek and Roman writers from this period. Pliny had heard that Achilles might be entombed on the island while the Greek travel writer Pausanias verifies that the temple contained the hero's statue.[84] Arrian confirms that the Isle of Achilles was believed to be a place of wonder with a supernatural influence that extended into the surrounding sea. Visitors to the site had carved inscriptions on the walls in Greek and Latin to honour Achilles and thank him for answering prayers asking for divine assistance. These inscriptions also honoured the legendary Greek hero Patroclus who was part of the Argonaut crew and a close comrade of Achilles in the Trojan War. There were a large number of wild birds nesting on the Isle of Achilles including cormorants and gulls. Arrian heard that they maintained the temple by flapping sea water from their feathers onto the paving stones every morning and cleaned the surfaces with their wings. Achilles was said to appear in the dreams of people visiting the island and the crew aboard nearby ships had night visions giving them instructions about the best place to land. Sometimes Achilles appeared to sailors who were wide awake and these men witnessed an image of the hero appearing on the sail or prow of their ships. Although Arrian considered himself to be a practical man concerned with military matters, he was unwilling to dismiss these stories. He had spoken directly to people who had landed on the island and concludes, 'These things do not seem incredible to me because I believe that Achilles was a divine hero and inferior to no-one.'[85]

The West Coast

Beyond Olbia and Odessos, the Black Sea coast continued south towards the marshy Delta of the Danube River. The Danube poured a large volume of fresh water into the Black Sea and its inland courses could be navigated. Pliny reports that 'the river has sixty tributaries, nearly half are navigable and it discharges into the Black Sea through six vast channels.'[86]

According to Arrian most of the Dacian coast 'was deserted and nameless', but south of the Danube River, Moesia and neighbouring Thrace were lined with cities and ports. This seaboard stretched down to the entrance of the Black Sea and was well integrated into Roman trade networks extending into the eastern Mediterranean. Arrian names six Hellenic cities on the coasts of Moesia and Thrace, with seafaring communities that probably sent their own trade vessels north to the Crimea.[87]

One of the most well-known ports in Thrace was Tomis, where the poet Ovid was banished by the Emperor Augustus. Inscriptions from Tomis reveal the existence of a significant Greek merchant community in this prominent city-port. The grave stele of a *naukleros* (captain or ship-owner) named Theocritos was carved with the image of a large merchant ship.[88] The merchants and ship-owners at Tomis who traded with particular Mediterranean ports formed mutual associations with their colleagues.[89] Visiting merchants also formed their own headquarters at the port, including ship-owners from Roman Egypt who established a temple to honour the god Serapis which was known as the 'House of the Alexandrians'.[90] An inscription by an Alexandrian wine merchant suggests that some of these traders were dealing in wine that could have been produced in Egypt, or reached Alexandria through its grain trade with Italy.[91] Other merchants operating at Tomis were citizens of prominent city ports on the coasts of Bithynia and Pontus on the southern shores of the Black Sea.[92]

At the southern entrance to the Black Sea was the narrow Bosporus Strait formed by the converging coasts of Europe and Asia Minor. The strait is 17 miles long, but less than 2 miles wide at its broadest point. The Bosporus was economically and strategically significant because all merchant shipping heading into the Mediterranean (Aegean Sea) had to sail through this narrow passage. On the European side of the Bosporus was the ancient Greek city called Byzantium which controlled commercial traffic passing through the strait. In AD 330 this city was selected to become the eastern capital of the Roman Empire and was renamed Constantinople by the first Christian Emperor Constantine. Constantinople inherited an empire from Rome's eastern provinces and this imperial regime survived into medieval times.

Arrian ends his account of the Black Sea at Byzantium on the European side of the Bosporus Strait. Neighbouring Asia Minor (including Bithynia and Pontus) was one of the most prosperous and well urbanised regions of the Roman Empire with a series of city-ports on the southern Black Sea coast.[93] These cities would have been significant staging posts for Roman trade voyages to Phasis and the Chersonese. They would also have been visited by Mediterranean ships carrying Black Sea cargoes out to the wider Roman world.

CHAPTER TEN

The Sarmatians

The steppe lands north of the Black Sea were inhabited by a powerful nation of mounted nomad warriors known as the Sarmatians. The Sarmatians were the cultural group that included the Alani and Aorsi population who occupied the northern Caspian region. Ancient Roman sources suggest that the Sarmatians were divided into at least five large sub-nations that shared common ethnic and cultural features, but each had their own rulers, territories and political interests. During the first centuries AD, the Sarmatians began to expand their range and power westwards across the steppe lands that led from the Ural Mountains in southern Russia into Central Europe. They conquered many steppe-dwelling Scythian populations and absorbed them into their wider culture.

By the end of the first century AD, the Alani and Siraces occupied lands stretching west from the Caspian Sea to the River Don.[1] On the north coast of the Black Sea the plain between the Don and the Dniester was claimed by a Sarmatian people called the Roxolani.[2] Beyond the Dniester was the territory of the Iazyges who moved west to the plains of Hungary and the Danube frontier of the Roman Empire. The Sarmatians were therefore in a position to control crucial population movements across the northern steppe and threaten Roman interests in Europe.

Greek and Roman sources suggest that the Sarmatians had a similar lifestyle to traditional Scythians (mounted steppe nomads). Herodotus describes the Scythians as having 'no established cities or fortresses, just house-bearers and mounted archers who live, not by tilling the soil, but by cattle-rearing and carrying their dwellings on wagons'. These customs made the steppe nations 'invincible and unapproachable'.[3] Writing in the Augustan era, Strabo describes how the Sarmatians 'spend their lives in felt tents fitted to wagons, while around them are the herds that provide the milk, cheese, and meat that provide them with sustenance'.[4] They did not store liquids in metal or fragile pottery vessels, as even bronze water jars would burst and fracture when their contents froze in the harsh steppe winters.[5]

The Sarmatians could establish fortified compounds, but most of their population had no fixed habitations and no sacred temples.[6] When Ammianus describes the Alani, he reports 'An unsheathed sword is fixed downward in the ground and they reverently worship it as their God of War and the presiding deity of the lands that they range across.' Pliny suggests that the early Sarmatians considered decorative tattoos to be a symbol of honour and reports that even their infants were marked with tattoos.[7] During the winter months the Sarmatians led their ox-driven wagons down to meadowlands near shores of the Black and Caspian

Seas. In summer they moved north again to graze their horses, cattle and sheep on the vast open steppe. Strabo explains, 'They follow the grazing herds. In time they move to other places that have grass, living in the marsh-meadows about Lake Maeotis (Sea of Azov) in the winter and the plains in the summer.'[8] Their wagons followed the course of rivers on seasonal journeys across the Eurasian steppe which meant that their routes were mainly along a north-south range. The old, infirm and the women remained with the wagons, while mounted bands of male warriors gathered for hunting, raiding or war. Writing in the fourth century AD, Ammianus describes how the Alani remained one of the leading Sarmatian groups and preserved their nomadic lifestyle throughout antiquity.[9]

Strabo describes how Sarmatian horses were comparatively small and difficult to control, but they were extraordinarily fast. The horses used for riding and war were castrated to better manage their temperament. This ensured that they remained silent and obedient when Sarmatian war-bands concealed themselves for ambush attacks.[10] On long-range expeditions, mounted Sarmatians rode with spare mounts and used a relay system to cover great distances at a relentless pace. Ammianus explains that 'they cover vast spaces in pursuit or retreat, on swift manageable horses, sometimes each rider leading one or two spare chargers, so they can preserve their strength by alternate rest periods.'[11] With this advantage Sarmatian armies might cover more than 50 miles per day.

Early Sarmatian warriors carried wicker shields and wore helmets and breastplates fashioned from thick layers of raw ox hide. They carried bows, but were also prepared for close combat with spears and swords. According to Strabo, in a pitched battle this light weaponry was not effective against a disciplined unit of well-armoured Greek infantry. He describes how in 100 BC, during a battle for control over the Crimea, a force of 50,000 Roxolani was overcome and massacred by a phalanx comprising only 6,000 Hellenic troops.[12]

During this period the Sarmatians served as mounted mercenary forces in foreign wars occurring close to the Pontic-Caspian steppe by various kingdoms and other factions. The chief of the Sarmatian Siraces was said to have mobilized 20,000 mounted warriors to support Pharnaces II of Pontus (97–47 BC). Strabo thought that the Aorsi (Alani) might be able to field over 200,000 horsemen in the defence of their own territories. He estimated that this number might be larger if the more distant steppe clans mobilized, 'for they held dominion over more land and rule over most of the Caspian coast'.[13] The Greek writer Lucian heard stories from the Chersonesos kingdom about wars fought with the assistance of steppe allies. In one of these accounts 20,000 Alani and other mounted Sarmatians were recruited by a Hellenic king to fight an enemy force including 30,000 Scythians.[14] These accounts suggest the scale of warfare conducted in the Pontic-Caspian region and Chinese records confirm that the Caspian Steppe (*Yancai*) could support over 100,000 mounted warriors.[15]

In the early first century AD the Romans probably considered the Sarmatians to be a manageable threat. In AD 49, Julius Aquila, a Roman commander stationed in the Crimea, had to deal with a rebellion in the Chersonesos kingdom led by a dignitary who summoned cavalry support from the Siraces. Pro-imperial forces included native troops equipped in the Roman military manner backed by a small number of Roman cohorts numbering several thousand soldiers. But this army required cavalry support, so Aquila consequently formed an alliance with a Aorsi chief named Eunones who offered horsemen to fight for the Roman cause. Tacitus reports, 'It was agreed that Eunones should engage the enemy with his cavalry and the Romans undertake the siege of towns.'[16]

The Roman-Aorsi army advanced against the rebel districts with the armoured cohorts and the native infantry forming the centre point of the battle line and the Sarmatian horsemen formed up along the front and rear. They assaulted a fortified rebel town called Uspe which was defended by moats and earthwork ramparts created by heaping layers of soil between wickerwork hurdles. The Roman army used spears and firebrands to drive back the garrison from their wooden towers and burn their wickerwork defences. By nightfall large parts of the defences were destroyed and the Roman army prepared to assault the town using ladders to scale the breached earthworks. Spokesmen from the town sought terms and offered the entire population of 10,000 people as slaves if their lives were spared. Tacitus reports that the offer was rejected since it would have been 'extremely difficult to maintain a cordon of guards round such a multitude. It was better they should die by the law of war.' When the inhabitants of Uspe were massacred, the shocked communities from surrounding districts quickly renounced their support for the rebellion.[17] This conflict demonstrated how quickly urban settlements on the northern coast of the Black Sea could transfer their allegiance and resources between dominant factions.

By this period the Sarmatians were adopting new forms of armour and equipment that greatly increased their military prospects. Mounted Sarmatians began to wear conical metal helmets and distinctive coats of scale-armour made from the hard plates of horse hooves strung together with strong sinew or sewn onto ox hide. When Pausanias visited Athens he saw Sarmatian armour displayed in the Temple of Aesculapius, the Greek god of medicine who was venerated with snake imagery. Pausanias describes this Sarmatian armour as being 'like a reptile' and fashioned 'like a closed pine cone'. He explains that 'Sarmatian breastplates are as well-crafted and sturdy as those of the Greeks, for they can withstand the blows of missiles.' It was confirmation that these 'foreigners are as skilled artisans as the Greeks'.[18] Ammianus confirms that horn-armour was still utilized in the fourth century AD when the Alani fought 'in cuirasses made from smooth and polished pieces of horn, fastened like scales to linen shirts'.[19] Some Sarmatian armour could have been crafted from small iron or bronze plates riveted onto leather or sewn onto heavy cloth. When Tacitus describes the Roxolani he reports that 'their princes and all their nobility wear iron scales and hard hide and although this armour is impenetrable to blows, it is difficult for the wearer to get up when thrown from his mount.'[20]

A first century Roman poet named Valerius Flaccus imagined an attack by 'fierce Sarmatians who thronged together with savage yells, their corselets ridged with flexible chain mail which also covered their steeds'.[21] Trajan's Column depicts the armour-encompassed Sarmatian mercenaries who fought for the

Dacian kingdom in their war against the Empire (AD 101–106). The reliefs show fleeing Sarmatian horsemen dressed in long-sleeved scale-covered coats and protective leggings with a barde that extends down to their horses' hooves. As this length of barde would have restricted the movement of the horse, these images must be based on inaccurate eye-witness descriptions.

The Sarmatian cavalry fought with long slashing swords and the remains of these weapons have been found on the steppe in small grave mounds known as kurgans.[22] Armoured warriors also began to carry long lances held in both hands to spear enemy combatants with a direct forward charge. When Tacitus describes Sarmatian warriors in AD 68 he reports that long-swords and two-handed lances of 'excessive length' were part of their standard arms and 'it is not their custom to use shields.'[23] Valerius Flaccus describes these lances as 'a pine-wood shaft that stretches out over the head and shoulders of their horse, which they rest firmly on their knees. The lances cast a long shadow over the field of conflict ready to be driven with the might of warrior and steed swift through the midst of the foe.'[24] Arrian reveals that the Romans called these lances '*contus*' and suggests that they were a particular innovation of the Sarmatians.[25] Tacitus explains that this combination of lance and heavy armour meant that 'when the Sarmatians charge on horseback, hardly any battle-line can withstand their assault.'[26] Sarmatian riders were also skilled in the use of lassoes and Pausanias reports that they could 'throw a lasso around any enemy, then by turning around on their horses take them off-balance'.[27]

Sarmatian armies rode into battle with *draco* (dragon standards) made from a hollow metal head with a long sleeve-like streamer attached made from brightly coloured silk. When the riders charged at an enemy these banners became dramatically animated. The wind whistled through the funnel head and the silk 'tail' thrashed about to resemble dragons flying above the heads of the riders. Scenes from Trajan's Column depict captured arms and equipment including *draco* standards with fish, wolves and dog-heads.[28]

The Late Roman army adopted Sarmatian-style standards for their own military units and Ammianus describes how the Emperor Julian addressed his troops in front of a carefully arranged display of gilded ensigns (AD 357). He was 'surrounded by gold and jewelled dragons, woven from purple fabric fixed to spear-poles. The broad mouths of the dragons were open to the breeze and they hissed as if animated by anger, as their tails wound in the wind.'[29] In his war against the Persians, Julian was able to rally a unit of Roman cavalry as they fled the battlefield. He rode into their midst with his distinctive standard and Ammianus reports, 'They recognised his purple dragon ensign, fitted to the top of a very long lance and spreading out like the slough of a serpent. The tribune of one of the squadrons stopped and although pale and shaken with fear, he rode back to renew the battle.'[30]

Ammianus had served as a soldier in the fourth century Roman army and he claimed that the Sarmatians were 'more suited to predatory incursions than to regular war'.[31] They did not maintain garrisons or conduct long-term sieges, but they became a substantial threat to the Empire due to opportunistic attacks that inflicted substantial losses on Roman armies and damage to imperial territory. Their expansion also caused population movements that created fear and disorder on the Roman frontiers.

Conflict with the Parthian Empire

The Parthian Empire ruled the Middle East with mounted armies and could mobilize up to 50,000 cavalry to fight conflicts with foreign powers.[32] The Sarmatians therefore represented a threat to Parthian military supremacy due to their expertise in mounted combat. In this period the various Sarmatian clans served as mercenaries who would fight for, or against, the Parthians depending on pay or political interests.

In AD 35 the Emperor Tiberius encouraged King Pharasmanes of Caucasian-Iberia to invade neighbouring Armenia and depose its Parthian-backed ruler Orodes. Iberian forces captured the Armenian capital Artaxata, but Orodes returned with a Parthian army to reclaim his kingdom. As both sides prepared for war, they recruited Sarmatian clans from the Pontic-Caspian steppe using payments that Tacitus calls 'bribes'. Pharasmanes formed an alliance with the king of Caucasian-Albania (Azerbaijan) to ensure that the Caucasus mountain passes were under his control. Then 'he suddenly surged his Sarmatians into Armenia by the Caspian route.' By contrast, the Sarmatian clans committed to the Parthians were blocked from crossing through the mountains due to the fact the Iberians and their Albanian allies controlled the passes.[33]

The mounted Parthian-Armenian army probably included more than 40,000 steppe archers supported by several thousand armoured *cataphracts* equipped with lances. They faced an enemy that included hardened infantry known for their endurance, supported by many thousands of Sarmatian riders equipped with lances and short-range bows. Tacitus reports that the Sarmatians 'encouraged one another not to begin the battle with volleys of arrows; but to anticipate the attack and charge into close-combat'. When battle commenced, the Parthians advanced and withdrew from the Iberian line in order to maintain a set distance. This gave maximum advantage to their archers who had a longer bow range than their adversaries. In response the Sarmatians stowed their bows and charged the Parthians with their lances fixed and their swords drawn. Tacitus describes how the battle ebbed and flowed with mass cavalry charges and retreats under the pressure of close combat fighting. Whenever the Albanian and Iberian infantry engaged the Parthian cavalry they 'seized the riders and hurled them from their steeds'.

At a crucial moment in the battle King Pharasmanes rode against Orodes and 'pierced his helmet with a sword-stroke'. The Royal Guard immediately protected their wounded prince, but the Parthian army, thinking their leader had been killed, began to withdraw from the fighting. This allowed the Iberians to claim a victory.[34] The conflict demonstrated how the Parthians were vulnerable to a well-led and determined army using steppe equipment and tactics. The Parthian Empire did not regain a controlling influence over Armenia until AD 53 when Tigranes, a brother of the Parthian King Vologases I, was installed as the new ruler of the kingdom.

The Derbent Pass

One of the main routes through the Caucasus Mountains was the Derbent Pass on the shores of the Caspian Sea in the Kingdom of Caucasian-Albania (Azerbaijan). Tacitus reports that this passage was difficult to traverse in summer when the shallows were flooded and the eastern winds blew strongly against the shore. But in winter the waters retreated and a flat area of land on the coast was exposed, allowing passage between the mountains and the sea.[35]

In AD 75 the king of Caucasian-Albania left the Derbent Pass unprotected and permitted a large Alani army to pass through the Caucasus Mountains. The Alani attacked and plundered the wealthy Parthian kingdom of Media which was poorly protected from this quarter. The unprepared Parthians could not organize an effective defence so their dispersed forces avoided open battle with the enemy. When the Alani rode west to plunder Armenia, its king Tiridates led an unsuccessful counter-attack in which he was almost caught and captured by a Sarmatian rider using a lasso. Josephus reports that an Alani warrior 'threw a rope over him from a great distance and would have pulled him in, if he had not cut the cord with his sword and fled to escape capture'. With this victory the Alani 'laid waste to the country, drove away a great multitude of people and cattle from both kingdoms and then retreated back to their own lands'.[36]

After this attack the Parthian King Vologases I appealed to the Emperor Vespasian requesting urgent Roman military assistance against the steppe invaders. The Romans had endorsed Tigranes as king of the Armenians, so the Alani presented a common challenge to both empires. Suetonius reports that Vologases asked for one of Vespasian's sons to 'lead a force of auxiliaries against the Alani'. It was said that Domitian tried to make sure that he was appointed in place of Titus, but this military expedition never occurred.[37]

Roman Defensive Measures

After the attack on Parthia in AD 75, Vespasian sent Roman forces to control the Caucasus routes that might allow steppe invaders to overrun Armenia and the revenue-rich Roman territories in Asia Minor. There is evidence that the Romans provided combat engineers and military labour to strengthen defences in the gorge-like passes that led through the Greater Caucasus Mountains.[38] A monumental inscription from the Iberian kingdom called the *Armazi Stele* records in Greek and Aramaic how the Emperor Vespasian sent engineers to fortify the capital city Mtskheta. During the reign of Domitian (AD 84–96) the mountainous Kingdom of Dacia, which lay north of the Danube River, also received Roman engineers, war engines and even annual cash subsidies as part of its frontier agreements with the Empire.[39] Perhaps the Kingdom of Iberia received similar support to lessen the likelihood that the Caucasus routes could be used as thoroughfares for armies of mounted steppe invaders.

The Roman Emperors also sent military support to King Mihrdat in Caucasian-Albania. Roman military involvement near the Derbent Pass is attested by the discovery of a Latin inscription near Mount Boyuk Dash (Qobustan, Baku). The inscription reveals the presence of a Roman centurion named Lucius Julius Maximus from the XII Fulminata who was in the region on the orders of the Emperor Domitian.[40] The centurion was from a legionary base at Cappadocia in Asia Minor and was operating more than 1,000 miles from his primary posting. He could have been a military diplomat, or a liaison officer overseeing Albanian efforts to fortify the northern frontier with a team of Roman engineers. Alternatively, he may have commanded a small Roman garrison posted near this strategic site. Whatever his role, he was at a foreign outpost hundreds of miles from the recognised frontiers of the Roman Empire.

During the imperial period Arrian considered the eastern Sarmatians to be a significant threat and wrote an account suggesting how the Roman army should engage the Alani if their armies tried to overrun Cappadocia (AD 135). The *Array against the Alani* explains the battle formations and fighting tactics that could be used against a mounted steppe enemy. This document is unique and offers extraordinary insights into Roman military deployment and battlefield planning from the viewpoint of a serving commander.[41]

Arrian was expecting the Alani cavalry to attempt outflanking attacks and to stage feigned retreats in order to create disorder in the Roman battle line. He planned to stop the frontal charge of Alani lancers with a dense line of heavily armoured legionaries equipped with long spears. The legionaries included a full complement from Legio XV Apollinaris (up to 5,000 soldiers) and a large detachment from the XII Fulminata. These troops would have formed a phalanx eight ranks deep with the first four ranks armed with pikes and rear lines equipped with javelins. Behind the legionaries were mass units of infantry archers, long-range catapults and horse archers who could quickly target fast moving threats. The auxiliary were posted on high ground flanking the legionary battle line in formation with pikes, javelins and archers that matched their unit organization. According to Arrian, Roman victory would depend on deterring, or withstanding, the high-impact Sarmatian cavalry charge.[42]

The Threat in the West

The western Sarmatians began to create difficulties for the Roman Empire in the mid-first century AD when a steppe nation called the Iazyges moved onto the Hungarian Plains between the Carpathian Mountains and the Upper Danube frontier. Many foreign tribes in territory close to the imperial frontiers had treaty arrangements with the Empire, but their homelands could not be protected by the Romans due to imperial troop commitments in the Armenian conflict (AD 58–63).

In AD 60 defeated native peoples from the Upper Danube region fled across the imperial frontiers to seek protection from the Roman Empire. An inscription from Rome honours the Roman governor of Moesia, Tiberius Plautius Silvanus, 'who conducted into the province and forced more than 100,000 trans-

Danubians with their wives and children, chiefs or kings' to pay tribute. By this grant of asylum he was able to safeguard his province and 'suppress a growing disturbance caused by the Sarmatians, although he had sent a great part of his army to the expedition against Armenia'. The sons of some Sarmatian chiefs were being hosted by the imperial government, so Silvanus returned these 'princes' to the Iazyges in the hope that they would promote pro-Roman attitudes among their ruling elite.[43]

In AD 69 the Roman Empire became engaged in its first civil war for almost a century and further troops from frontier regions were redeployed to fight for rival imperial factions. The Roxolani exploited this situation to cross the Lower Danube frontier in winter and raid Roman Moesia with a force of 9,000 mounted warriors. Tacitus reports that this war-band destroyed two cohorts (1,000 soldiers), but they were 'more intent on plunder than on fighting'. The Roman counter-attack was managed by Legio III Gallica and their auxiliary support who ambushed the Sarmatians as they were trying to return along rural trackways treacherous with melting snow. The Sarmatians were off-guard, out of formation and overburdened with loot while the Romans had 'everything ready for battle'.

Tacitus reports that in this engagement the Sarmatians could not charge with their two-handed lances as 'their advantage, the superior speed of their horses, was lost on the slippery surface.' When the Sarmatian riders were toppled from their mounts they struggled to fight under the weight of their armour and 'at the same time sunk deep in the soft and heavy snow'. By contrast the Roman infantry, clad in their breastplates, 'moved about unencumbered, throwing javelins at the enemy, attacking with spears and when the opportunity came, moving to close quarters to stab the vulnerable Sarmatians with short swords'. The survivors fled into nearby wetlands where most died from their wounds or succumbed to the severe winter weather.[44]

These events caused the Romans to reassess their arrangements with other Sarmatian groups including the Iazyges who occupied the Hungarian Plains near the Upper Danube. The Roman general Vespasian planned to withdraw Roman troops from this region in his bid to seize Italy and become Emperor in Rome. Tacitus reports that 'to avoid leaving the provinces in an unprotected condition, exposed to barbarous nations, the ruling chiefs of the Sarmatian Iazyges were called into service with the army.' The Iazyges probably offered cavalry forces to the Romans in return for pledges, bribes and army pay. Tacitus explains that Vespasian decided to decline the offer of military support fearing that if the Sarmatians were permitted into Roman territory, 'they might attempt some hostile enterprise, or abandon their sense of duty and accept higher offers from other quarters'.[45] Josephus reports that after Vespasian became Emperor he 'placed more numerous garrisons on this frontier so it was impossible for the barbarians to cross the river again'.[46]

The effectiveness of Sarmatian armies was confirmed in AD 92 when a force of Iazyges crossed the Upper Danube to raid Roman Pannonia. The attack occurred during a period when the Empire was facing increased threats from tribes in Dacia and western Germany. According to Suetonius an entire legion, probably

Legio XXI Rapax, was annihilated in the Sarmatian attack. The Emperor Domitian led a retaliatory expedition into Iazyges territory (Hungary), but he claimed only a minor victory commemoration for this achievement when he displayed a laurel crown in the Capitol Temple of Jupiter.[47]

Mounted Sarmatian mercenaries fought to defend the Dacian Kingdom from Roman invasion and are depicted on Trajan's Column fleeing before lightly armed auxiliary cavalry equipped with shields and spears (AD 101–106). When Dacia became a Roman province, the Empire occupied territories between the Iazyges and Roxolani which probably diminished the Sarmatian threat. During the early second century AD, certain Roman cavalry units also began to adopt Sarmatian-style arms and equipment, including metal scale-armour, horse barding and long two-handed lances (*contus*).[48]

The western Sarmatians resumed hostilities against the Empire in AD 169, at a time when a serious epidemic was devastating the Roman population and imperial forces were struggling to repel hostile German tribes. The Iazyges attacked Moesia (Serbia) in AD 169, defeated a Roman army in battle and killed the commanding governor.[49] At the same time a German tribe called the Marcomanni invaded northern Italy and besieged the city of Aquileia. The Emperor Marcus Aurelius was forced to conclude a peace agreement with the Iazyges so that Roman forces could concentrate on expelling the German invaders. The Sarmatians captured tens of thousands of Roman citizens in Moesia before returning to their homelands beyond the Danube.[50]

In the winter of AD 173 the Danube froze and the Iazyges launched a further plundering raid on Moesia. But this time the Roman forces were ready for pursuit and when the Sarmatians realised that an army was following, they prepared an ambush. They planned to scatter the Roman ranks as the legionaries crossed the treacherous flat, frozen surface of the Danube River. Dio reports that the Sarmatians 'awaited the oncoming Romans, expecting to overcome them easily, knowing they were not accustomed to the ice.' Some of the Iazyges charged directly at the Roman line while others rode around the legionaries as 'their horses had been trained to run safely over a frozen surface'. The Roman army formed a compact infantry square to face their opponents on all sides. As the enemy cavalry charged, many soldiers drove their shields into the brittle ground to create a solid defensive barrier which they braced their feet against. This prevented the soldiers from slipping on the ice and when the Sarmatian charge failed to break the Roman line, the infantry immediately counter-attacked, 'seizing the bridles, shields and spear-shafts of their assailants and dragging the men down'. The combined weight and ferocity of the Roman infantry 'pulled down both men and horses, since the barbarians could no longer keep from slipping due to their momentum'. But Roman soldiers also fell, often landing on their backs. Dio describes the close-combat struggle that followed, resembling a mass wrestling contest with the struggling legionaries grappling and biting at their opponents. The Sarmatians were defeated and the Emperor declared the Iazyges to be a prime enemy of the Empire.[51]

After the battle, the Emperor Marcus Aurelius rejected peace terms with the Iazyges, 'for he knew their race to be untrustworthy' and 'he wanted to utterly annihilate them.' But the Empire faced threats from other hostile populations and Marcus Aurelius could not commit the forces required to complete his objective. The Iazyges were collaborating with a German tribe called the Quadi and had received fugitives from the Marcomannian nation which was also in conflict with Rome. Therefore in AD 175, the Emperor set terms to ensure peace. Marcus Aurelius received Zanticus, the chief of the Iazyges, who appeared at the Roman camp 'as a suppliant'. The agreement stipulated that the Iazyges would not occupy lands within 10 miles of the Danube frontier, but the exclusion zone was halved if the nation were prepared to meet their peace commitments. As an incentive for compliance, the Iazyges were permitted to approach designated frontier towns to meet and trade with Roman merchants on certain prearranged days. In return for these privileges the Iazyges offered 8,000 warrior horsemen to serve in the Roman army. About 5,500 of these new Sarmatian mounted recruits were sent to the island-province of Britain, ensuring that they could not easily desert and ride back to their homelands.[52]

Dio reports that the peace agreement caused concern in Rome since it was evident that 'the Iazyges were still strong at this time and had inflicted great damage on the Romans.' This was demonstrated by the number of Roman captives that the Iazyges had seized during their raids and military victories. Dio claims they were able to 'return 100,000 captives that they still possessed after many others had been sold, died or escaped'. The Iazyges also delivered 8,000 warrior recruits to the Romans promptly and without difficulty. This confirmed that they still possessed a large armed force ready for immediate conflict. Dio suspected that it was only the revolt of a Roman general in Syria that had forced Marcus Aurelius to make immediate terms with the Iazyges 'very much against his will'. He notes that the Emperor did not report the terms of the peace to the Roman Senate as he had on previous occasions when campaigns were concluded.[53] These conflicts between Rome and the Sarmatians demonstrate how the Roman Empire remained vulnerable to attack by a well-led steppe army and how opportunities for trade were used as an incentive for peace settlements.

CHAPTER ELEVEN

The Parthian Empire

The Parthians established their empire almost a hundred years before Rome received its first Emperor Augustus. Between 148 and 138 BC mounted Parthian armies conquered Media and claimed Babylonia from the declining Seleucid regime. The Parthians then dominated the area now known as Iran for almost three centuries and played an important role in confining Roman rule to the Mediterranean seaboard (138 BC–AD 224).

The Romans and the Parthians understood that their respective empires incorporated territories that had once been ruled by a single regime. The Achaemenid Empire of ancient Persia had stretched from Asia Minor and Egypt across Iraq and Iran to Afghanistan and the Indus territories on the northern edge of the Indian subcontinent. This land-based empire had been divided into twenty revenue-generating provinces known as *satrapies*.[1] The Persian regime managed to maintain this political system for several centuries (550–330 BC) before their empire was conquered by Alexander the Great and subsequently divided between his Macedonian generals.

At the height of their power the Parthians governed about a third of the domain that had previously formed the Persian Empire. Their subject realms included the rich homelands of ancient Persia which lay near the Persian Gulf and over 1,500 miles of territory stretching from Mesopotamia in northern Iraq to the oasis outpost of Merv in Turkmenistan. By the first century AD, the Parthians also had a controlling interest in the Indus kingdoms ruled by allied Indo-Parthian warlords.

The Parthians governed their empire from three royal capitals: Seleucia-Ctesiphon in Babylonia, Hecatompylos in northern Iran and Nisa in their early homelands in Turkmenistan. They minted silver coins at Nisa and Seleucia-Ctesiphon based on traditional Hellenic issues and promoted their regime using Greek terms and titles. The Parthians installed *satraps* (governors) in certain districts, but in other areas that already had well-established kingdoms they permitted the existing dynasties to remain in power as subject rulers. These included the kingdoms of Persis and Elymais which where the homelands of the original Persians near the northeast shores of the Persian Gulf.

Writing in AD 77, Pliny records that the Parthian Empire had dominion over eighteen kingdoms that occupied lands between the Euphrates and the Indus Region.[2] This represented about 1 million square miles, including enormous tracts of desert, mountain ranges and large stretches of encroaching steppe lands. By contrast the early Roman Empire included just over 2 million square miles of subject territory subdivided into more than forty provinces and at least six significant client kingdoms.

The Rise of the Parthian Empire

The rise of the Parthian Empire in the second century BC was connected with the Mediterranean expansion of the Roman regime.[3] When the Seleucid King Antiochus III came to power in 222 BC, he campaigned in Parthia and Bactria to regain his authority over these distant territories.[4] Antiochus also expanded Seleucid rule into western Asia Minor and made plans to annex the Greek city-states around the Aegean that were either semi-independent or under the rule of rival Hellenic kings. In 192 BC Antiochus invaded Greece with an army of 10,000 soldiers and the support of a federation of Greek states called the Aetolian League.[5] This invasion brought the Seleucid Empire into conflict with the militarized Roman Republic and its formidable network of Italian allies. The Romans mobilized over 20,000 soldiers and after defeating the Seleucid army at Thermopylae, they pursued Antiochus into Asia Minor and sent a fleet to attack his naval forces.[6] The decisive battle in this war took place in 190 BC at Magnesia in western Asia Minor. According to Livy, the Roman legions achieved a battlefield victory with a force of 30,000 soldiers while facing a Seleucid army consisting of about 70,000 fighting men levied from all parts of their extensive realm.[7]

In 188 BC Antiochus III was forced to conclude a peace settlement with Rome that required all Seleucid forces to withdraw from Greece and most of Asia Minor. Seleucid armies were dependent on Greek mercenaries, but Rome prohibited the regime from recruiting new troops from any territories under Roman protection. The Romans also demanded war reparations from the Seleucid Kingdom to be paid in silver bullion. The annual figure was set at 1,000 talents (almost 26 tons) which was enough silver to mint 6 million Roman denarii.[8] To give context to this figure, by the first century a denarius represented a generous day's pay for a labourer.[9] This income greatly increased Rome's capacity for war, while stripping the Seleucid kingdom of the wealth and revenues it relied upon for its own stability. The loss of this income diminished Seleucid funds for employing soldiers, maintaining garrisons, hiring labour and purchasing foreign resources such as shipbuilding materials.

After its defeat by Rome, the Seleucid Kingdom began to disintegrate through a series of dynastic conflicts, local revolts and civil wars supported by rival powers. The Seleucid Empire finally collapsed when mounted Parthian armies attacked from its eastern flanks to invade Media and seize power in Babylonia (141 BC). In 138 BC, the Seleucid King Demetrius II Nicator was defeated in battle and taken as an 'honoured captive' to the Parthian capital Hecatompylos in eastern Iran. Meanwhile, his brother Antiochus VII Sidetes assumed the Seleucid throne in Syria and prepared a large force of Greek mercenaries to retake Babylonia. Ancient accounts claim that his army included 80,000 armed men which represented the largest force that the Seleucid regime had been able to assemble for several generations.[10]

Attacking in 130 BC the Seleucid army successfully retook Babylonia from the Parthians. But Seleucid soldiers imposed heavy requisition burdens on some Iranian communities and their actions encouraged pro-Parthian uprisings. During these disturbances an army of Parthian horsemen crossed undetected into Media and when the Seleucid King Sidetes entered the territory with his royal guard, he was intercepted and killed. The leaderless Seleucid army was expelled from Babylonia and the Parthians prepared to conquer Syria and extend their empire west towards shores of the Mediterranean Sea.[11] But the campaign had to be abandoned when Saka war-bands from the Central Asian steppe attacked the Parthian homelands in eastern Iran.[12]

Babylonia contained densely populated cities and its conquest brought immense wealth into the Parthian Empire. The walled city of Seleucia on the Tigris River had a population of up to 600,000 people which included Greeks, Jews, Arabs and Persians.[13] It had been one of the primary capitals of the Seleucid Empire and by the first century BC it was perhaps the third largest city west of India. In an effort to dominate Babylonia and further enforce their rule, the Parthians established their own royal capital named Ctesiphon on the banks of the Tigris, opposite Seleucia. Ctesiphon served as the western capital of their enlarged empire and the Parthian King spent the winter administering his realms from palaces in this monumental city. But every year before the onset of the hot and humid summer months, the king moved his royal court east to the cooler higher-altitude climate of Ecbatana where meadow greenery covered the hillsides around the ancient Iranian city.[14]

The Han Empire established its first diplomatic contact with the Parthians in about 100 BC. They called the regime *Anxi* since the Parthian founding dynasty was known as the Arsacids. The *Shiji* records that when the first Chinese envoys arrived on the eastern frontiers of Parthia they were greeted by a ceremonial guard of 20,000 horsemen. They were escorted 'several thousand *li* from the border and passed through several dozen cities inhabited by great numbers of people as they travelled to the capital [Hecatompylos].' The Parthian King Mithridates II (121–91 BC) reciprocated by sending his own envoys to China to ascertain the size and power of the Han Empire. The Parthians sent the Han Emperor unusual gifts from their homelands including court conjurers and ostrich eggs.

Chinese records from this period describe the Parthian Empire as 'by far the largest kingdom' and report that it possessed 'walled cities like the people of *Dayuan* [Ferghana] in a region containing several hundred cities of various sizes'. Even in this early period Parthia had long-range commercial networks, and the *Shiji* reports 'some of the inhabitants are merchants who travel by carts or boats to neighbouring countries, sometimes journeying several thousand *li*' (1,000 *li* = 310 miles). The Chinese also took an interest in Parthian coinage, noting that 'the coins of the country are made of silver and display the face of the king. When the king dies, the currency is immediately changed and new coins issued with the face of his successor.'[15]

First Contacts with Rome

During the second century BC the Roman Republic conquered the Kingdom of Macedonia and achieved full authority over ancient Greece. Then in 133 BC the Romans were bequeathed the small kingdom of Pergamon and the Republic gained a permanent presence on the Aegean coast of Asia Minor. This was the beginning of the Roman expansion into western Asia.

The first diplomatic contact between Rome and Parthia occurred in 97 BC when a general named Lucius Cornelius Sulla restored a deposed ruler to the throne of Cappadocia in eastern Asia Minor. Cappadocia was confirmed as a Roman protectorate and during these operations Sulla led imperial forces as far as the River Euphrates. On their arrival there, the Roman army received a Parthian envoy who had come to investigate recent political events and 'seek the friendship of the Roman people.'[16]

Sulla did not refer the matter to the Roman Senate and insulted the Parthians by arranging that their envoy take a submissive position close to the Cappadocian king in a publicly staged political meeting. The envoy was escorted to a chair beneath that of the Roman general in a scene that suggested that the Parthians were a foreign power subject to Roman dictates. But Parthian rule was dependent on maintaining authority over subject realms and when the Parthian king received news of this public dismissal, he ordered his envoy executed for defaming the regime.[17]

In 66 BC the Senate sent Gnaeus Pompeius (Pompey) to take charge of the Roman forces campaigning in Asia Minor. Pompey renewed the existing agreements with the Parthian Empire that promised non-aggression, non-interference and possibly acknowledged the Euphrates as the frontier between their domains.[18] Pompey then added a large part of Asia Minor and Syria to the Roman Empire and formed political intrigues with vassal rulers under Parthian dominion. This broke the terms of the existing treaty, but when Parthian envoys asked the general for an explanation, Pompey replied that 'he would observe any frontier that seemed fair to him.'[19]

These Roman conquests in western Asia gave the imperial government access to enormous new revenues. In 61 BC Pompey returned to Rome to celebrate his achievements with an elaborate triumphal parade through the centre of the capital. Written records were displayed to the Roman public showing how the new conquests had added 140 million sesterces to Republican revenues previously worth about 200 million sesterces per annum (50 million denarii).[20]

In this era it seemed possible that the Romans might claim all the territories that had once formed the Seleucid Kingdom. Many of the urban communities in Babylonia were still recognisably Greek and the Romans saw themselves as the natural successor to that civilization. These Greek communities paid regular tribute to the Parthian Empire in order to preserve a degree of localised political freedom and self-governance. But they could be antagonistic towards their Parthian overlords and might support Roman interests if the opportunities seemed favourable.

A Roman pretext for intervention came in 58 BC when the Parthian king Phraates III was murdered and his sons fought a civil war for control over his empire. One of the sons fled to Syria where he sought military assistance from the Roman governor Aulus Gabinius (57–55 BC). The sources suggest that Gabinius was prepared to support this Parthian prince with an invasion force that would seize the western capital Ctesiphon. But then Gabinius received a payment from the Ptolemaic king Ptolemy XII Auleles, who needed urgent Roman support to crush a rebellion in Egypt. Auleles is said to have offered Gabinius 10,000 talents (240 million sesterces) for his immediate assistance and his needs took precedence over Roman plans to seize Ctesiphon.[21]

Crassus and the Battle of Carrhae

In 58 BC Julius Caesar began the conquest of Gaul which extended the Roman Empire north as far as the Rhineland and the coasts of Europe facing Britain. Meanwhile, his political ally Marcus Licinius Crassus was allocated the governorship of Syria and prepared for the conquest of Babylonia. Crassus had gained military honours by brutally suppressing a major slave revolt in Italy led by a former gladiator named Spartacus (71 BC). By 55 BC he was the richest politician in Rome, but he craved the wealth and glory of foreign military conquests that would equal or exceed the achievements of his colleagues Pompey and Caesar.[22] Crassus therefore planned to emulate Alexander by invading Persia before leading his conquering armies east to the frontiers of India.[23]

The Roman conquest of Persia seemed feasible since the Republic had overcome all rival powers in the eastern Mediterranean, including the Greek and Macedonian successors of Alexander. As Livy claimed, 'The Romans have repulsed a thousand armies more formidable than those of Alexander and his Macedonians and if the peace is broken, they will do so again.'[24] The steppe armies of the Parthians seemed to be a manageable opponent since in 68 BC the legions led by a general named Lucius Licinius Lucullus had easily defeated mounted archers and armoured cataphracts in Armenia at the Battle of Tigranocerta. In this battle, Lucullus ordered his lightly-armed auxiliary cavalry to charge the Armenian cataphracts and keep them occupied while several hundred legionaries rushed forward to surround their position. The legionaries were instructed to strike at the unprotected legs of the armoured horses causing the riders to tumble from their heavy mounts.[25] Plutarch explains the Roman soldiers commanded by Crassus 'were fully persuaded that the Parthians were the same as the Armenians and the Cappadocians, whom Lucullus had robbed and plundered till he was weary of the effort. They thought that the most difficult part of the war was going to be the long journey and the pursuit of an enemy who would avoid close quarter fighting.'[26] However, Plutarch claims that many Roman politicians opposed a conflict with Parthia because 'they were displeased that anyone should wage war on men who had done the Roman State no wrong and were held in established treaty relations.'[27]

When Crassus took command in Syria in 54 BC, he sent Roman troops into northern Mesopotamia to claim several frontier towns on the Upper Euphrates.

Greek communities from the walled cities of Babylonia also sent spokesmen into Syria to negotiate terms with the Romans and offer them support against the Parthians. As Crassus awaited the arrival of reinforcement Roman cavalry from Gaul, he spent his time reviewing the revenues and treasury reserves of subject populations in Syria and Palestine.[28]

Crassus sent word to the Armenian King Artavasdes II requesting allied troops for his planned conquest of the Parthian Empire. But Artavasdes cautioned Crassus not to invade Babylonia via the northern Euphrates, as this meant crossing desert plains where the Parthian cavalry had an advantage over Roman infantry. He urged the general to proceed through Armenia and Media where rugged terrain would impede the Parthian horsemen. The Armenians offered to provide abundant supplies and significant military support to Roman forces using this route and Artavasdes pledged 6,000 royal horsemen, 10,000 armoured cavalry and 30,000 infantry to assist the legions.[29] Crassus rejected the offer, perhaps reasoning that the Euphrates River Valley would provide a more direct invasion route into the Parthian domain and offer better supply and communication lines for the Roman advance. He expected the Greek cities of Babylonia, including Seleucia, to support the Roman cause and when he captured the Parthian capital at Ctesiphon, this would provide him with greater wealth and glory.[30]

In the summer of 53 BC, Crassus led an army of 40,000 Roman troops across the Euphrates frontier into the territory of the Parthian King Orodes II. This Roman force was almost the same size as the army that Alexander led to victory against the Persians almost three centuries earlier.[31] Crassus commanded seven legions consisting of 35,000 armoured infantry, 4,000 light-armed auxiliaries, 4,000 cavalry and 1,000 Gallic horsemen sent by Julius Caesar.[32] The cavalry forces were under the command of Crassus' son Publius, a well-respected leader who had served with Julius Caesar in Gaul.[33]

Crassus had high expectations of success, but even before the campaign began, disturbing reports reached the Romans regarding Parthian tactics and armaments. Roman garrison troops posted in northern Mesopotamia reported that during the winter they had been attacked by Parthians riders equipped with arrows that could pierce through any protective armour. The reports suggested a type of missile-weaponry that was superior to any previously encountered equipment, but Crassus dismissed these claims as 'exaggerated terror'.[34]

Further concerns were raised when the legions crossed the Euphrates River. Crassus was met and challenged by a Parthian envoy named Vageses who accused him of being led by greed to cross the agreed boundary between their empires. Vageses warned Crassus that he was breaking political treaties agreed by previous Roman generals and if he continued with an invasion in search of Parthian gold 'he would instead find himself burdened with Seric iron.'[35]

The term 'Seric iron' would not have alarmed Republican Romans who knew little about the distant Seres or 'Silk People'. In this era the Romans were unaware that the Parthians were connected to an overland supply chain that was equipping their warrior-horsemen with superior armour and weaponry. Small samples of Chinese silk had probably reached the Mediterranean soon after the Han Empire secured the Hexi Corridor and established a route through the Tarim territories (104 BC), but during this period supplies of superior oriental steel were highly-prized by steppe peoples and this metal was not reaching markets in the Mediterranean in any great quantity.

As Crassus began his march down the Euphrates Valley, reports arrived that the main Parthian army had crossed from Media into Armenia. The Parthian King Orodes II probably hoped to distract Crassus from his invasion route by threatening Roman interests in the allied Armenian kingdom. But Crassus ignored Armenian requests for assistance in favour of continuing his planned attack on Babylonia.[36] He probably reasoned that, with the Parthian king and main army absent in Armenia, the territory would be poorly defended.

King Orodes had left the defence of Babylonia to a Parthian prince named Surenas who had raised a force of horsemen from his subject realms in eastern Iran. Orodes knew that Surenas could harass and delay the Roman invasion, while the main Parthian forces made military gains in Armenia. But Surenas planned a full engagement with the Roman army using the well-known strategies and ambush tactics of steppe warfare. His force was small, highly mobile and carried steel-enhanced weaponry including lances, armour and arrowheads.[37]

Surenas was in command of approximately 9,000 lightly-armed mounted archers and 1,000 heavily-armoured cataphracts. These mounted lancers wore steel-strengthened mail-clad armour with conical-style plumed helmets with their warhorses protected by a blanket of chain mail.[38] The archers carried composite horn and wood bows and wore belted tunics, wide trousers and long riding boots that allowed fast flexible movement. To provision this mounted battle-force, Surenas brought his personal caravan of 1,000 camels. By comparison the Roman infantry force were equipped with chain mail shirts, cap-like protective headgear, large oval wooden shields, short-swords suited for stabbing and several weighted javelins for single-use ranged attack. The spear-equipped Roman cavalry carried large shields and were armoured with mail shirts and helmets. Crassus had not made any arrangements for supply columns to replenish his stock of spent weaponry.

As the Roman army began its march down the east bank of the Euphrates, the forward scouts reported that the cavalry tracks of horse-riders had been sighted. They reasoned that these had been made by enemy cavalry retreating back into the nearby desert. Although Crassus was again warned not to proceed by Armenian envoys, he took advice from an Arab leader named Ariamnes who recommended immediate pursuit.[39] Crassus marched his army into the desert without adequate water supplies or suitable cover from the scorching summer sun. Plutarch describes a landscape that had ‘no branches, streams, hillocks or greenery, just an expanse of sand which might encompass the army’. After hours of marching, the Roman army sighted a force of several thousand Parthian cavalry. At first the Roman army tried to extend their ranks into a long defensive line, before new orders were issued and the legions drew into tight infantry blocks and prepared to engage the mounted enemy.[40]

Surenas placed part of his army in front of the Romans, assembling them in a formation that concealed their full numerical strength. The cataphracts hid their bright armour beneath animal skins and dull leather cloaks, so that the Romans would be unprepared for an assault by heavy cavalry. Crassus appeared to be engaging a weaker enemy force, but as the Romans advanced, Surenas gave a signal to mounted drummers in the Parthian line. They began to rhythmically pound the large hide-skin drums fixed to their horses. These drums were hung with bronze bells and produced a deep reverberating tone that filled the desert plain with a roaring sound like the approach of wild animals, or an oncoming thunderstorm. This noise caused fear and alarm in the Roman ranks. The resultant tumult made it difficult for Roman forces to convey orders along their battle-line. Breaking into a canter the Parthian formation began to spread out along the plain, then charged forward in a full gallop towards the legions. At this moment Surenas signalled his cataphracts to discard their dark coverings and reveal the full splendour of their encompassing armour. The Romans suddenly saw the gleam of polished armour plates and the steel of the enemy lances.[41] As the Parthians began their charge forward, they unfurled colourful banners made from a strange ethereal fabric that streamed out behind them in the desert breeze. This was said to be the first time that Roman soldiers had seen Chinese silk.[42]

The legionaries had formed themselves into dense infantry squares to resist the cavalry charge, but the Parthian horsemen suddenly broke off the attack before they reached the Roman line. They paced along the front ranks keeping their distance from the legionaries. The cataphracts were screening a larger force of Parthian archers who rode the length of the Roman lines, firing lethal volleys of arrows into the densely packed legionary formations. These Parthian bows outranged the Roman javelins which were one-shot weapons designed to buckle and break on impact so that they could not be reused by the opposition. There were a few units of Roman archers with the legions, but they did not have the numbers or weapon range to match the powerful bows of the fast-moving Parthian riders.[43]

The Romans raised their shields and held them together in a shield-wall formation known as the *testudo* (the tortoise). The front ranks interlocked their shields into an outer barrier, while the inner rows lifted their shields above their heads to create a shell-like roof designed to deflect missile fire. But the piercing steel of the Parthian arrows punched through their wooden shields and tore through their chain mail chest armour.[44]

Crassus ordered his Roman skirmishers to charge the Parthian horsemen, but the lightly-armoured auxiliary troops were driven back into the legionary ranks by a dense hail of arrows. As they scrambled for protection, they caused further fear and disorder amongst their fellow soldiers. Riding around the Roman positions, the Parthians spread out into a wide formation and shot their arrows into the legionary ranks from multiple quarters. These highly skilled warriors could fire on the gallop and wheel around in the saddle to shoot at targets behind them – a manoeuvre known as the 'Parthian shot'. Any of the legionary ranks who tried to charge the Parthian archers found that the enemy fled before them, maintaining their distance, but still firing to the rear at their now exposed pursuers.[45]

By this stage it was clear to the Roman officers that the Parthians were equipped with a superior form of weaponry that was causing unexpectedly high casualty rates amongst the legionaries. But Crassus still expected the enemy either to withdraw, or commit to decisive close-quarter combat once their arrows were exhausted. Close combat would favour the Romans with their superior numbers and proven expertise in brutal short-range engagements. However, this hope was thwarted when Roman observers realised that Parthian archers who had emptied their quivers were returning to the front line fully restocked. Heavily laden camel teams were carrying new bundles of the lethal, steel-tipped arrows into the offensive.[46]

The fake retreat was a well-known tactic in steppe warfare, used to divide and exhaust any over-eager enemy cavalry. In 120 BC the Han general Li Guang faced similar strategies when he fought mounted Xiongnu warriors in Mongolia. In response, he placed his son Li Gan at the head of a small cavalry unit with orders to charge towards the enemy and provoke the expected feigned retreat. Li Gan galloped out from the Chinese ranks and when the opposing horsemen fled towards their ambush site, he returned immediately to the main army. This allowed his father to boost Chinese moral by proclaiming the Xiongnu to be 'cowards'.[47]

The Parthians expected the Romans to be unfamiliar with this tactic. When Crassus realised there would be no imminent end to the Parthian missile fire he ordered an assault using the Roman cavalry he had kept in reserve. He sent his own son Publius to lead the breakout in command of Caesar's mounted Gallic auxiliaries. Publius was a popular figure amongst the troops and as he rode through the front ranks of the Roman army, a large section of the surrounding infantry ran forward to support his assault. At that moment the Parthian horsemen suddenly wheeled around and fled the battlefield in what appeared to be full-scale rout. The Roman cavalry pursued them with several thousand infantry joining the headlong rush after the fleeing enemy. This forward charge took the cavalry far from the sight of Crassus and the protection of the main Roman army. Publius did not realise that he was entering a trap until the retreating Parthians wheeled around to face their pursuers and were joined by further battle-lines of steppe horsemen. Surenas had prepared a killing-ground some distance from the first battle site where the larger part of his army of 10,000 warriors waited to ambush and slaughter the most mobile units of the Roman army.[48]

Outnumbered and exhausted, the Roman infantry formed a wall of shields around Publius in an attempt to protect the cavalry. The Parthians rode around this isolated force launching volleys of arrows into the huddled mass. Their horses' hooves tore up the bare earth until a great cloud of choking dust engulfed the Romans and made it difficult for their officers to shout commands. The Romans were cut off from any retreat and their officers could not restore cohesion. After the haphazard chaos of the pursuit, intermixed divisions clambered through their own ranks to escape the unrelenting arrow fire. The battlefield was covered in low hillocks wich made it difficult for the Roman troops to form an effective shieldwall or assemble into rank formations. Publius urged his soldiers to charge forward into the enemy, but his infantry were already critically injured, their hands pinned to their shields by Parthian arrows, or their feet skewered to the ground.[49] To some, these injuries may have been reminiscent of crucifixion, the humiliating public death that Crassus had imposed upon the slave-captives who had supported the Spartacus rebellion.

When it was clear that no reinforcements would come to their aid, Publius led a final desperate cavalry charge out from the Roman ranks to engage the enemy in close-quarter combat. But his lightly-equipped Gauls were no match for the armour-encased cataphracts with their heavy steel-tipped lances. In desperation, those Gallic riders who had been thrown from their saddles tried to stab at the unprotected underbelly of the cataphract horses, only to be trampled to death in the attempt. The Gauls were quickly exhausted by thirst and the oppressive desert heat. Consequently only a few survivors managed to retreat back into the Roman infantry ranks, carrying with them the critically wounded Publius.[50]

Crassus still had more than 30,000 legionaries, but when the news came of the enemy ambush, he was overcome with conflicting emotion and could not decide on a course of action. By ordering an immediate advance to the new battle site he might have saved Publius, but this meant jeopardising the entire army. An urgent retreat back to the Euphrates would have condemned the Gallic cavalry to annihilation, but might have granted the main army enough time to escape. Crassus stalled and waited, before ordering his army forward to rescue Publius and the Roman cavalry.[51] But by then it was already too late.

As Parthian arrow-fire continued, the encircled Romans commanded by Publius realised that there was no possibility of rescue or further resistance. Many of the leading Roman officers began to commit suicide rather than face the ignominy of defeat. Those suffering multiple wounds were assisted to die by junior colleagues. Publius, who had his sword hand pierced by an arrow, had to be helped by his shield-bearer to force the blade into his own chest. When the Romans could no longer maintain their rank order amidst their crippled and dead comrades, the cataphracts charged, trampling the fallen and skewering the legionaries with their long-lances. Almost 6,000 Roman troops were butchered on the battlefield before Surenas called a halt to the killing and prepared his army to engage Crassus and the main Roman force.[52]

As the full Parthian army rode into view, they sounded their drums and spread out into a wide formation to relaunch their attack on the main Roman force. They galloped close to the Roman ranks and displayed the severed head of Publius to the horrified legionaries. Then with jeering insults they resumed their relentless arrow-fire. Without the support of the cavalry the Roman retreat back to the Euphrates Valley would involve hours of marching through dry featureless terrain with the infantry exposed to continuous missile attack. The Romans were forced to abandon any immediate prospect of retreat and formed ranks into infantry squares to withstand the Parthian arrows.

From that moment on, any Roman units who broke formation or tried to rush into close combat with the Parthian archers were charged by the cataphracts. These cataphracts could impale more than one man with a single powerful strike from their long steel lances and their manoeuvres forced the Roman ranks back into tightly packed formations. This maximised the impact of the Parthian archery volleys and caused greater distress and trauma to troops already crushed in by their comrades, or choked by dust. Stumbling over corpses, some legionaries succumbed to heat-stroke and exhaustion. Others caused themselves further injuries by tearing out the barbed steel arrowheads from their wounded bodies.[53]

In 101 BC, the Han general Li Ling had found himself in a similar situation against the Xiongnu. His small regiment had fought a disciplined retreat across the Mongolian steppe while being harassed by an overwhelming force of Xiongnu horsemen led by their Chanyu. When the Chinese troops had exhausted their arrows, Li Ling destroyed and buried his battle standards rather than have them fall into enemy hands. Then he waited until dusk and created a diversion that allowed many of his remaining soldiers to escape back to the well-guarded Chinese frontier.[54]

By contrast, as night fell Crassus had been reduced to utter despair before the Parthians finally broke off their attack due to fatigue and poor visibility. Centurions took charge of the situation and prepared their units to retreat in silence under the cover of darkness. They abandoned any wounded soldiers who could not keep pace, but when their colleagues began to shout out appeals for help, this caused widespread alarm. The retreating force was thrown into confusion by the fear of further Parthian attacks and they fled in disarray to a nearby fortified town named Carrhae. Carrhae had a sympathetic Greek population and a Roman garrison, but this outpost was not provisioned to withstand a protracted siege. The following night Crassus escaped the town with his command staff in the hope of finding safety in Syria or Asia Minor. The remaining Roman troops took their chances to leave the town in small groups setting out at nightfall to evade the Parthian cavalry and their Arab allies, who were patrolling the surrounding countryside ready to kill or capture any survivors.[55]

But before Crassus could reach the Mediterranean coast, the Parthians caught up with him. The general was compelled by his own troops to go forward and meet the enemy and discuss terms. When the Parthians tried to seize Crassus, there was a violent scuffle with his bodyguards and the general was fatally stabbed. The battle-standards of the legions defeated at Carrhae were taken to Ctesiphon as trophies and Surenas sent the severed head of Crassus to the Parthian King Orodes in Armenia. The Parthians believed that Crassus had been motivated by plunder and it was said that they poured melted gold into the mouth of his severed head as a symbol of his greed.[56]

From an army of 40,000 Roman troops less than a quarter were able to reach safety. More than 20,000 men were killed and 10,000 legionaries were taken prisoner.[57] This was the greatest loss of men that the Romans suffered in a single battle and the largest number of citizen-soldiers ever captured by a foreign regime. The entire episode demonstrated how devastating steppe tactics and weaponry could be when used against unprepared infantry.

The Crassus campaign had taken almost all the available Roman troops out of Syria, so the Parthians were able to plunder the region and claim full control of Armenia. Prince Surenas exploited his victory at Carrhae to reinforce Parthian authority in Babylonia. He prepared a parade through Seleucia that further humiliated the Romans by imitating an imperial triumph. The procession was complete with prisoners of war and military trophies, including the legionary battle-standards captured during the retreat. One Roman captive who resembled Crassus was forced to wear a woman's purple dress to mock the appearance of a triumphal toga. He was accompanied by a guard of prostitutes and musicians who ridiculed Roman courage and battle prowess.[58] This exhibition sent a powerful message to the Greeks of Babylonia that Parthia was the military superior of Rome. After this degradation, the surviving Roman prisoners were taken to be settled at Merv on the eastern frontier of the Parthian realm (Margiana in modern Turkmenistan). Rather than conquerors of the east, they had become prisoners in exile on the borders of the steppe far from their Mediterranean homelands.

The Oasis Outpost at Merv

The oasis settlement at Merv was the site of a Hellenic city called Antiochia Margiana which had been founded by the Seleucid King Antiochus I Soter (281–261 BC).[59] Merv was on the eastern edge of Iran at a location more than 1,500 miles from the frontiers of Roman Syria. The settlement lay east of the Caspian Sea and was positioned on the main desert route leading from Iran to the steppe lands of Transoxiana. It was therefore a crucial site for the defence of Iran and by the first century BC it was the strategic eastern frontier of the Parthian Empire. It was here that Chinese envoys had met with representatives of the Parthian Empire in 100 BC.[60]

Merv spread out across a wide oasis area that was hemmed in by fertile hills with valleys that produced wine from locally-grown grapes.[61] Some of the thousands of former legionaries who were settled in this region were probably set to work upgrading the local irrigation systems, but others might have been given limited military responsibilities as guards or garrison troops. The district around Merv was surrounded by a vast circuit of sand and bleak flat-land terrain, so there was little prospect of mass escape for the Roman settlers. Anyone who planned to return to Roman Syria would have to travel through the heartland of Parthia where more than fifty Iranian caravan stations were under the direct control of their captors.[62] Dio Cassius suggests that some Roman soldiers may have escaped further east and reports that among the captives at Merv many 'took their own lives out of shame, or managed to escape detection and hid themselves in remote places'.[63]

Any legionaries who could not reconcile themselves to Parthian rule could have escaped east to Afghanistan by following the Murghab River, or by undertaking a journey to the Oxus River about 300 miles away. Travellers on foot might cover this distance in about twenty days, providing they could carry sufficient provisions and remain undetected by Parthian patrols. If they reached the Oxus River they could escape into the cities of Sogdia which were under the rule of steppe warlords that the Chinese called the Kangju.

Roman captives who escaped east into Sogdia would have found themselves at the forefront of further conflict. At this time the rebel Xiongnu chief Zhizhi was using labourers from Sogdia to build his fortress complex on the Ili River and he possibly employed mercenaries from neighbouring territories. When the Chinese army attacked this fortress in 36 BC they observed a strange infantry division formed up in what they called a 'fish-scale formation'.[64] If a Han observer had seen a Roman *testudo* he might have compared the pattern to the scales of an oriental carp. It is therefore possible that bands of Roman fugitives escaping Parthian captivity could have found service with Zhizhi and his fugitive Xiongnu.[65] If captured, their testimonies would have added to growing Han knowledge of the wider ancient world that extended from China to beyond the Caspian steppe.

CHAPTER TWELVE

Parthia and Rome

After the defeat of Crassus, the Romans expected a Parthian invasion to overrun and claim the poorly defended territories of the eastern Mediterranean. Instead, the Parthians launched plundering raids into Syria and Asia Minor that undermined, rather than vanquished, Roman authority in these regions (53–52 BC). The death of Crassus destabilised Roman politics and in 49 BC Julius Caesar was drawn into a civil war with a political faction led by his former friend and colleague, Pompey. When Caesar emerged victorious and was declared Dictator, he prepared the Roman legions for a further campaign against Parthia. His plan was to avenge Crassus by conquering the Parthian Empire and extending Roman rule as far as the Oxus River.[1] But Caesar's autocratic rule had alarmed traditionalists in Rome who conspired to have him assassinated before he could begin his war against the Parthians (44 BC).

The death of Caesar caused another civil war as Mark Anthony joined with Caesar's nephew and adopted son Octavian to establish their own joint rule over the Roman Republic. They achieved a decisive victory over the pro-republican faction at the Battle of Philippi in Macedonia in 42 BC. Octavian then assumed power in Rome and Antony took authority over the Roman commands in the Eastern Mediterranean. The responsibility therefore fell on Antony to enact Caesar's plans and conquer the Parthian Empire.

Antony invades the Parthian Empire

Antony utilized the Egyptian city of Alexandria as his new political headquarters and with the support of Roman client kingdoms in the Near East he prepared for a new war against the Parthians. He mobilized an army of 100,000 soldiers including up to 60,000 legionaries from sixteen legions and 10,000 cavalry.[2] The allied forces included 20,000 Hellenic troops provided by Queen Cleopatra VII of Egypt and several other kingdoms in the Near East subject to Rome. The King of Armenia also offered 6,000 cavalry and 7,000 infantry to support the Roman conquest. A convoy of 300 wagons was organized to transport essential siege machinery including an 80-foot long battering ram. The wagons also carried crucial food stocks for the campaigning army.[3] Antony believed that this force was sufficient to defeat a Parthian army that could probably mobilize about 40,000 mounted troops including 4,000 armoured lancers commanded by their new king Phraates IV.

In 36 BC the Roman army crossed the Upper Euphrates and invaded the large kingdom of Media Atropatene which dominated the northwest quarter of the Parthian Empire. Their first target was the Median winter capital Phraaspa

(Maragheh) which was almost 300 miles, or three week's march, from the Euphrates frontier. The Roman soldiers were equipped with slings that had proved effective in countering volleys of enemy arrows. Dio reports that 'the numerous slingers routed the enemy because they could shoot farther than the Parthian archers.' A hail of lead sling-stones could inflict 'severe injury on all Parthians including men in armour', but this weapon rarely killed and the enemy could quickly retreat if overwhelmed or injured.[4]

Antony achieved a rapid advance by marching ahead of the slow-moving train of accompanying wagons which were guarded by at least two Roman legions and a large force of allied Hellenic troops. But the Parthian army ambushed the convoy, massacred its guard of 10,000 legionaries, plundered the Roman supplies and burnt the siege equipment. Plutarch explains that this was a decisive point in the war and 'the king of Armenia, despairing of the Roman cause, withdrew his forces and abandoned Antony.'[5]

Antony reached Phraaspa with a force of more than 50,000 legionaries, but the fortified city was well-garrisoned and provisioned to withstand long-term siege. The Roman siege machinery that had been destroyed could not be replaced using local timber or the palisade wood that the legionaries carried to fortify their camps. The Romans therefore began to build a large earthen mound next to the city wall to surmount the defences and provide a platform for attack. This was a time-consuming, labour-intensive effort and as their supplies dwindled large parts of the army were left immobile. The Parthian army appeared outside the legionary camps arrayed in full battle formation to yell repeated challenges and insults which badly affected Roman morale. Antony was concerned that this 'dismay and dejection would increase through inactivity,' so he assembled ten legions and with the support of his cavalry he marched into the countryside to seize all available food supplies. This he hoped would draw the Parthians into a decisive battle.

Leaving a retaining force near the city walls, Antony marched his army a day's journey from Phraaspa. The following day, the Parthian army including up to 40,000 mounted warriors appeared within sight of the Roman legions. They waited for the Romans to renew their march then gathered a crescent-shaped formation to attack the legionary columns from their flanks. But at a given signal the marching legionaries began a complex manoeuvre to bring columns of men into rank formation and face the Parthian army in a combat-ready battle-line. Plutarch describes how the Parthians 'were awed by Roman discipline and watched the men maintain equal distance from one another as the marching lines rearranged in silence without confusion. Then soldiers brandished their javelins.' Antony had issued orders that the Roman cavalry were to ride against the Parthians if they came within range of a legionary charge.

The Parthians interpreted these silent manoeuvres as the early stages of a Roman withdrawal and were not alarmed when the space between two armies narrowed. But at a given signal, 'the Roman horsemen wheeled about and rode against the enemy with loud shouts.' The shocked Parthians did not have time to unleash a full volley of arrows as 10,000 Roman cavalry charged into their midst.

The larger Parthian force was able to withstand and repel the Roman charge, but the delay gave the legionaries time to dash forward and reach their enemy. Plutarch describes how battle was joined with shouts and the clash of weapons, but 'the Parthian horses took fright and broke contact, and the Parthians fled before they were forced to fight the legionaries at close quarters.' The legionaries pursued the Parthians for up to 6 miles, then the Roman cavalry continued the chase for 18 miles, but the enemy did not regroup for battle.

This engagement was considered a Roman victory, but when the legionaries took a tally of the battle they counted only eighty Parthian casualties and thirty prisoners. Plutarch explains that 'Antony had great hopes that he might finish the whole war or decide a large part of the conflict in that one battle.' But the tactics and casualty figures suggested otherwise, especially as the Roman army had already lost 10,000 legionaries in the earlier ambush. Plutarch reports that 'all were affected with a mood of despondency and despair. They considered how terrible it was to be victorious, yet have killed so few of the enemy, when they had been deprived of so many men when they themselves had suffered defeat.'[6]

The following day the Roman legions began the march back to Phraaspa. But the Parthian army had rallied and reappeared, 'unconquered and renewed, to challenge and attack the Romans from every side'. Plutarch explains that the Romans only reached the safety of their siege camp after 'much difficulty and effort'. When they saw the condition of the returning Roman army, the defenders of Phraaspa launched a successful sortie to destroy the improvised siege-works and put the guards to flight. To maintain discipline Antony ordered an immediate 'decimation' where one in ten of the soldiers in the disgraced units were selected for summary execution by their colleagues.[7]

By this stage famine was imminent as Roman supplies were depleted and any troops sent on foraging parities suffered heavy casualties. Furthermore, winter was approaching and both armies knew that severe cold and frosts would soon cover this exposed landscape. Antony had no choice but to abandon the siege and withdraw to Roman territory. Plutarch reports that 'although Antony was a natural speaker and could command armies with his eloquence, he was overcome with shame and dejection and did not make his usual speech to encourage his troops.'[8] The Roman retreat was announced by a sub-commander who perhaps reminded the legions that Armenia was now considered to be hostile territory, since its king had changed his allegiance.

Antony chose an alternative route back to Roman territory that crossed hills rather than the open treeless stretches of plain which would have been favourable to pursuing Parthian cavalry. The hill route passed through well-provisioned villages, but the Parthians were prepared and 'seized passes before the Romans approached, blocked routes with trenches or palisades, secured water-sources and destroyed pasturage'.[9] On the third day of the march the Parthians breached a dyke and flooded the ground in preparation for an ambush. But the legions were quick to form defensive formations with slingers and javelin-throwers launching missiles. The forward march continued and Antony ordered his troops not to leave the marching column to pursue the enemy. On the fifth day a detachment of light-armed troops guarding the rear disobeyed his orders and followed a Parthian attack force away from the main column. The detachment was immediately surrounded by Parthian reinforcements and Antony fought a fierce battle to retrieve his troops. Almost 3,000 Romans were killed and a further 5,000 soldiers suffered serious wounds in this single engagement.

The following day the Parthians again rode against the Roman rear-guard and encountered several units formed up behind a wall of shields (the *testudo*). They assumed that these immobile ranks were units that had abandoned the march prior to surrender. The Parthians therefore dismounted and approached on foot. But the legionaries counter-charged and cut down the first ranks of the enemy with their short-swords.

As the march continued the weather worsened with severe frosts and driving sleet further hampering the Roman retreat. Many wounded Romans had to be carried or supported, and the accompanying pack animals began to die from exhaustion and exposure. Provisions were almost exhausted and the troops became ill from eating harmful wild plants. But the Parthians still followed the retreating Romans, guarding any nearby villages that the legionaries might try to seize for shelter or supplies.[10]

Antony considered leaving the hills, but he received a Parthian deserter who warned that the Roman column would be annihilated if it ventured onto the open plains. One source suggests that this man was a survivor from the campaign by Crassus who had undertaken to serve his Parthian captors, but could not bear to see his countrymen massacred. Florus reports, 'The gods in their pity intervened, as a survivor from the disaster of Crassus dressed in Parthian costume rode up to the camp. He uttered a Latin salutation, inspired trust by speaking their language and told them of imminent danger'. Florus asserts that 'no disaster had ever occurred comparable with the one which now threatened the Romans.'[11]

The Parthian deserter warned Antony that the hill route was taking them across a district where there was no fresh drinking water. Antony therefore instructed his soldiers to fill all available leather-skin containers and carry additional water in their upturned helmets. The Romans began the 30-mile march across this district at night with the mounted Parthians still in pursuit. By morning the Romans had reached a clear, cold-running stream that was heavily saline. Despite direct orders from Antony, many thirsty soldiers drank this harmful water and were debilitated by a sudden sickness. After miles of further forced march, the exhausted legionaries finally reached shade and clean drinking water, but they were only permitted a short rest. Their guide promised Antony that they were close to a boundary river and rough terrain that the mounted Parthians would not cross in pursuit.[12]

The night before they reached the river there was a large-scale disturbance in the Roman camp. A group of deserters killed comrades who had been guarding the pay and precious metal artefacts carried by the legions. The Parthians saw the disorder and attacked. Antony feared that a breakdown in the Roman formations would cause a mass rout, so he ordered a member of his personal guard to kill him if his capture seemed imminent. The freedman was instructed to cut the head from Antony's corpse so that it could not be taken and displayed as a Parthian trophy.[13] But Roman training and discipline held enough of the ranks together to repel the enemy throughout the night. In *testudo* formation the Roman column finally reached the banks of the boundary river the following day. The cavalry formed a guard as the sick and wounded were brought across the river to safety in the territory that lay beyond.[14]

It had been twenty-seven days since Antony had abandoned the siege at Phraaspa and begun the retreat back through the hill country. Since then, his army had fought at least eighteen defensive engagements and suffered heavy casualties due to enemy action, exposure, sickness and fatigue. According to Plutarch the Romans lost 20,000 legionaries and 4,000 cavalry on the return march alone.[15] To these figures can be added the two legions (10,000 troops) destroyed with the siege equipment on the outbound expedition. Florus claims that barely a third of the expedition force (23,000 troops) reached safety, meaning that 12,000 were captured or killed at Phraaspa. Roman casualties were over 40,000 men, the size of the entire army led by Crassus.[16] Antony had probably lost two-thirds of the soldiers taken on campaign.[17] This reduction in Antony's forces proved significant when Octavian successfully challenged and defeated Antony to gain control over the entire Roman Empire (32–30 BC).

Augustus and Parthia

In 27 BC Augustus (Octavian) formally accepted the position of Emperor and became the uncontested ruler of the entire Roman Empire. But important political legacies of the civil war period were still unsettled. Julius Caesar had planned the conquest of Parthia in revenge for the Roman defeat at Carrhae and Antony had suffered humiliating setbacks in his failed campaigns against the Parthian Empire. Augustus was expected to rectify this situation and restore Roman honour in the Middle East.

But eastern conquests were not an easy prospect for the Augustan regime. Two Roman armies had been almost annihilated attempting first the Euphrates invasion route and secondly the Median route into Parthia. Furthermore, any invasion of Parthian territory would take large numbers of Roman troops far from the centre of their Mediterranean Empire at a time when Augustus needed to be near Rome to oversee political affairs and guarantee the dictatorial reforms that he had introduced. Any Parthian campaign needed to be undertaken by generals that Augustus could trust to pursue conflicts in distant regions far from his direct supervision. Alexander had been able to conquer the core territories of the Persian Empire in just three years (331–328 BC), so perhaps the Romans could expect similar progress if everything in their high-risk invasion plans were to succeed. Appian records that even Caesar's invasion plans had set out a three-year schedule for the conquest of the Parthian Empire.[18]

The Latin poet Horace reveals the prevalent Roman attitude during this period (30–20 BC). In one instance he refers to 'the Parthians, threatening Rome' and in another context suggests that the Roman army needed to develop a cavalry corps equipped with long lances to counter the tactics of mounted Parthian forces.[19] He asserted that 'our youth should learn how to use the steed and lance to impose fear on the Parthians.'[20] This is probably based on popular debate as to how to prepare the legions for the prospect of eastern wars.

Other comments by Horace promote Roman supremacy, for example, 'The Roman soldier fears the deceptive retreat of the Parthians, but Parthia dreads Roman dominance.'[21] Elsewhere he comments, 'who fears Parthian or Scythian hordes, or dense German forests, while the Emperor lives?'[22] The view that the Romans might be about to attack Parthian territory is also conveyed by his statement that 'Rome, in warlike pride will stretch a conqueror's hand over Media.'[23]

Rock Crystal

Among the reasons that Rome wanted to conquer the Parthian Empire was the revenue wealth provided by its subject territories. This included tribute paid by subject kingdoms and profits made by exploiting valuable natural resources including quartz (rock crystal). Gemstones were an important revenue source for many ancient regimes and an Indian guide to statecraft called the *Arthashastra* recommended that rulers stocked their treasuries with jewels.[24] The Romans mined emeralds in the Egyptian desert and when the Latin poet Statius described the imperial treasury he identified 'transparent crystals' as a major revenue source.[25] Rock crystals were one of the most desirable and costly items in Roman consumer society. Quartz could be found in Europe, but the material was scarce and difficult to access. Pliny explains, 'I can confirm that rock crystal is found in the Alps, but it is located in such inaccessible places that it has to be removed by men suspended from ropes.'[26] European quartz also lacked the vivid colour ranges of the crystals found in India and in the eastern deserts of Iran.

The earliest coloured crystals seen at Rome were exhibited by Pompey in his Syrian Triumph (60 BC). During the victory parade onlookers were astonished by the sight of vases carved from multi-coloured quartz.[27] Later, Queen Cleopatra sent love letters to Mark Antony with her words carved into six delicate crystal tablets. Anthony became obsessed with these objects and it was said that he would rather gaze upon these exquisite letters than engage in state business, or conduct important negotiations with foreign kings.[28] The largest rock-crystal that reached Rome in this period was a 50-pound block of unworked quartz acquired by Livia, the wife of the Emperor Augustus. She donated this prized object to the Capitol where it was placed on display in its unique natural state for the Roman public to view.[29]

During the imperial period large quantities of quartz were imported from India and entered Roman markets via Alexandria. This gave artisans in the city a valuable monopoly in the production of certain crystal objects. Alexandrian craftsmen catered for fashion styles popular across the Empire and could replicate the traditional types of vessel favoured in particular provincial markets. Athenaeus explains, 'The Alexandrians have a particular way of working crystal to form it into various shapes of goblets and they can imitate the form of any earthenware cup from any country.'[30] The high prices paid for quartz objects were increased by the specialist artisan skills involved in cutting and carving the crystal into delicate forms. Crystal goblets and wine decanters were a focal point in Roman feasts and these objects offered the elite an opportunity to display their wealth and show their appreciation for artisan skills. However, not all quartz was used for decoration and some crystals were polished into lenses that could focus the rays of the sun into intense points of heat. These devices were used to treat open wounds and Pliny explains that 'doctors believe that the most effective method for cauterizing flesh is to use a crystal sphere placed to intercept the rays of the sun.'[31]

Indian quartz was valuable, but the most sought-after and expensive crystal in Roman society was fluorspar (fluorite) gathered from the deserts of ancient Iran. Fluorspar, known as *myrrhine* to the Romans, was a highly translucent crystal displaying an unparalleled range of vibrant colours that naturally blended together to create unique effects. Although fluorspar was fragile, it was relatively easy to carve and Roman artisans engraved the surface of fluorspar cups with intricate scenes from classical mythology or traditional pastimes. Each fluorspar item would be unique and irreplaceable because of the shifting colour combinations present within the crystal. Furthermore, some fragments of fluorspar had fluorescent properties and appeared to shimmer in dim light, especially when placed in contact with warm acidic liquids, including wine.

Parthian caravan merchants offered blocks of fluorspar to Roman traders visiting Ctesiphon on their way into Babylonia. The rock-crystals were sold to Roman workshops where the best gem-cutters carved the product into the finest possible decorative pieces. The labour-intensive work by an artisan further increased the value and exclusivity of the piece. The finest crystals were exquisitely carved with emblems associated with the Greek god of wine Dionysius, who was known to the Romans as Bacchus. Achilles Tatius described a distinctive myrrhine vessel that had tiny grape-vines engraved around its rim and these seemed to tumble down the surface of the goblet. When this cup was empty, the bundles of grapes appeared green, but when wine was poured into the vessel the clusters became dark-red as though they had suddenly ripened within the vessel.[32]

During the early imperial period, table-sets of translucent vessels made from eastern quartz were very expensive and the finest Iranian fluorspar goblets might cost the owner more than a city mansion.[33] Pliny recommended, 'crystal vessels are used for cold drinks and myrrhine-ware for both hot and cold liquids,' but only the wealthiest men could afford these luxuries.[34] Martial describes an affluent man named Rufus who offered his guests the finest wines served from expensive crystal and myrrhine vessels.[35] It was said that one woman, engaged in procuring girls as courtesans, would entice them to work for her with stories of the luxuries they would enjoy, including the chance to sip the best of wines from '*myrra* cups coloured with the flames of Parthia'.[36] Propertius emphasised his commitment to courtship with the claim that love mattered more to him than 'drinking from carved gems'.[37]

As this fashion intensified, other items began to be fashioned from crystal including display stands, decanters, ladles and other utensils. Romans imagined that wealthy Indians might wish to possess entire dinner services made of crystal.

Philostratus expresses the view that 'Precious stones imported from India are used in Greece for necklaces and rings because they are small, but among the Indians they are turned into items such as decanters and wine coolers.'[38]

Pliny confirms that the Roman demand for crystal wine serving sets was part of an escalating trend. He describes how 'expenditure on this fashion is increasing every day' and 'crystal provides yet another example of our mad addiction for excess.' As an example of these practices he reports that 'only a few years ago a respectable married woman, who was by no means rich, paid 150,000 sesterces for a single ladle.'[39] This item cost a hundred times the annual wage of a labourer, but it brought the woman notoriety. Every guest at her exclusive dining parties wanted to view this prized object as her slave ladled choice wines into their goblets.

During the reign of Nero the expense of home banquets was taken to new levels of competitive excess by the political elite in Rome. Pliny heard reports about an exceptionally large block of Indian rock-crystal that had been carved into a goblet with a capacity of four pints.[40] Ostentatious emperors could surpass the elite citizen in the expense of their banquets and the range of their dining equipment. Pliny reports that Nero paid 1 million sesterces for a single crystal bowl simply to outdo everybody else.[41]

Many wealthy Romans developed a special attachment to their favourite crystal drinking vessels. One ex-consul paid 70,000 sesterces for a single fluorspar cup that could hold three pints. The man became so enamoured by the object that he would 'gnaw at its rim; but the damage he caused did not greatly detract from its value'.[42] The Emperor Lucius Verus was said to have named his favourite crystal goblet in honour of a popular race horse called *Volucer* or the 'Flyer'. It was said that Volucer could hold more wine than any other crystal vessel in the Roman Empire.[43] At one famous feast Lucius Verus allowed his guests to keep the priceless crystal vessels in which their drinks had been served. These included 'myrrhine goblets and cups of Alexandrine crystal'. The cost of this one banquet was reported to have been at least 6 million sesterces at a time when Rome was at war with the resurgent Parthian Empire. When the frugal Marcus Aurelius heard about the banquets staged by his co-ruler he was said to have groaned in dismay and muttered concerned words about the fate of the Empire.[44]

The value of fine crystal vessels was enhanced by their susceptibility to fracture and Pliny reports that 'once it has been broken, crystal cannot be mended by any method whatsoever.'[45] Seneca describes an incident when the Emperor Augustus was dining with a wealthy adviser named Vedius Pollio. A young slave accidentally broke a valuable crystal goblet and Vedius immediately ordered the boy to be seized and fed alive to the carnivorous eel-like lampreys that he kept in the fish ponds on his estate. These lampreys have funnel-shaped mouths lined with teeth and the dinner guests expected to see the creatures tear the living flesh from the terrified boy. But the Emperor was shocked by this savagery and when the young slave broke free and fled to him for mercy, he took pity. Augustus rebuked Vedius with the words, 'Would you really have a person torn to pieces for a broken cup?' and he ordered all the crystal vessels at that dinner table to be smashed. To ensure that there would be no future opportunity for such cruelty, the Emperor ordered Vedius to fill his fish ponds with earth from the garden.[46]

In later times, wealthy men subjected to an imperially-decreed death sentence would often smash their own crystal vessels as a final act of defiance to prevent them passing into the hands of their enemies. When Titus Petronius was charged with treason, he shattered a crystal ladle worth 300,000 sesterces before taking his own life. He thus prevented Nero from obtaining this prized artisan piece for his dining table.

As a young man Pliny visited a display of confiscated crystal dining-sets that Nero had exhibited in his private theatre. Pliny was amazed to see a smashed goblet arranged in a casket as though it were the body of a king lying in state for mourners to pay their respects. He recalled seeing the shards of a single broken cup with the pieces displayed 'like the body of Alexander the Great, in a kind of catafalque, to show the sorrows of the age and the ill-will of Fortune'.[47]

It was said that when Nero's own overthrow was imminent, he roamed the empty imperial palace looking for his missing attendants, companions and supporters. Finally, in despair, he smashed two of his favourite crystal goblets on the ground. Pliny viewed the destruction of these priceless cups as 'the last vengeance of someone who wished to punish his whole generation, by making it impossible for anyone else to appreciate these items'.[48]

The Emperor Galba tried to recover some of the wealth that Nero had spent from the Roman treasury. Tacitus claims that Nero squandered 2,200 million sesterces in gifts, but Galba discovered that only a fraction of this sum could be reclaimed. According to Tacitus, 'Nero's favourites had hardly one-tenth of the money remaining, for they had wasted these funds on the same extravagances that had depleted their own wealth. The most worthless and depraved had neither lands nor investments, but only the apparatus of their greed.'[49] The figure of 2,200 million sesterces was more than double the annual state costs of the entire Empire, but most of this sum had been spent on luxuries, including the consumption and display of expensive eastern products.[50] At any time in this period the capture of quartz-producing territories in eastern Iran would have been a valuable source of revenue for the Roman government and would have lessened its long-term financial concerns.

CHAPTER THIRTEEN

Roman Invasion Plans for Parthia

Ancient sources reveal the extent of Roman plans to add Parthia to their empire during the first decades of Augustan rule (27 BC–AD 14). The preparations involved intelligence gathering and the creation of itineraries to map possible invasion routes through Iran. These accounts confirm the veracity of Roman ambitions and verify the scope of military preparations being considered by the Emperor Augustus.

During the first decade of Augustan rule there was a resurgence of Roman interest in eastern campaigns and Latin poets took the subject as inspiration to introduce dramatic situations into their narratives. For example, Propertius explored ideas of distant military service and the feelings of a Roman wife separated from her soldier-husband who was fighting in Bactria. The verse takes the form of a letter with the wife appealing to her husband not to be reckless in the pursuit of glory when Roman forces lay siege to Bactrian cities and take silks as plunder from the steppe hordes. She writes, 'I beg you not to set so much glory in scaling Bactrian walls, or seizing fine fabrics from their perfumed chieftain, especially when the enemy launch the lead shot from their slings and fire their bows with such cunning from their wheeling horses.' Propertius imagines that the soldier-husband would return when 'the lands of the Parthian hordes are overcome' and the Oxus River was established as a new imperial boundary. However, he hints at even more distant locations. The Roman wife expects her husband will be seen amid 'the dark-skinned Indians who are pounded by the eastern waves'.[1]

These ideas could have been prompted by the arrival of Indian envoys in the Roman Empire who might have offered the prospect of military alliances (26–20 BC).[2] In another work, Propertius addresses a lover with the possible scenario, 'What if I were a soldier detained in far-off India, or my ship was stationed on the Ocean?'[3] In this period it must have seemed possible that well-led Roman armies could exceed the eastern conquests of Alexander.

There are also some indications that the scenarios suggested by Propertius could be based on genuine military planning. Propertius mentions charts being circulated that mapped Parthian territory and provided details concerning enemy logistics. The wife reveals that she 'studies the course of the Oxus River which is soon to be conquered and learns how many miles a Parthian horse can travel without water'. She also 'examines the world depicted on a map and the position of lands set out by the gods to be sluggish with frost, or brittle with heat'.[4] These details suggest that imperial authorities were gathering geographical and logistical information about the east in order to determine the practical prospects for conquest.

The *Parthian Stations*

The Romans knew the size and geography of Persia from Greek histories, including accounts written by authorities who followed Alexander. From these historical descriptions Roman commanders reconstructed hypothetical invasion routes as 'itineraries' listing the directions and distances between strategic sites. These itineraries might have been represented pictorially on charts containing geographic detail including mountains, lakes and rivers. But other documents were descriptive texts that explained the character of strategic locations and itemised possible invasion routes.

The Romans had supporters in the main Greek cities of Babylonia and these communities were in continual contact with Mediterranean merchants who travelled back and forth across the Euphrates frontiers. In particular, the Romans had a network of collaborators in the city-port of Spasinu Charax near the head of the Persian Gulf. Spasinu Charax was originally a military outpost established by the Seleucids, taking its name from the Greek word 'Charax' meaning 'palisaded fort'. This fortified Hellenic town developed into a commercial city that was well-protected from siege or cavalry attack by the floodplains of the Tigris River. When the Parthians conquered the eastern half of the Seleucid realm, the local Greek commander Hyspaosines took the title of king and founded a new Hellenic dynasty at Charax to govern a region called Characene (127 BC). The new kings of Characene accepted Parthian suzerainty, but with a well-defended capital they could assert their independence and challenge outside interests.[5]

Spasinu Charax was positioned at the junction between riverine and maritime travel. The city received traffic coming down the Tigris River from the heartlands of Babylonia, but it was also a staging post for maritime voyages into the Persian Gulf. Spasinu Charax therefore received trade goods from Arabia and India and served as a meeting place where Persian and Greek traders could engage with eastern merchants from distant lands. Consequently, the city was an ideal location to gather intelligence about political developments in the distant east and use as a base from which to reconnoitre possible invasion routes into foreign territories.

Pliny reveals how Greek operatives from Spasinu Charax provided Roman authorities with accounts of eastern geography and politics in preparation for a planned military action against the Parthians. He explains that 'the most recent writer to have dealt with the geography of the world is Dionysius who was born in Charax and sent to the East by the Emperor Augustus to write a full account of this region.' Pliny explains that Dionysus was given this responsibility sometime before 2 BC and 'shortly before Gaius Caesar travelled into Armenia to take command against the Parthians'.[6] The work has not survived, but it probably included the type of information suggested by Propertius when he described Roman charts recording the distance between Parthian watering-stations and the condition of the surrounding landscapes.[7]

An ancient account known as the *Parthian Stations* could also be a product of these early intelligence gathering operations. The *Parthian Stations* was written by a Greek author called Isidore who also came from Spasinu Charax. Sometime before 10 BC Isidore charted a route through Parthia for the benefit of Roman authorities. If Augustus had ordered the conquest of the Parthian Empire, the route was intended for Roman forces to follow during their military campaign.[8] Isidore also described valuable resources produced in Parthian territory, including pearls that contributed large revenues to eastern treasuries.[9]

The Invasion Route through Parthia

The *Parthian Stations* gives an itinerary of ancient sites leading across ancient Persia from the frontiers of Roman Syria to the eastern edge of Iran. Isidore mentions distances between strategic locations and provides information about the character of prominent settlements. He maps out a possible route for Roman legions that follows the Euphrates River into Babylonia and then out across the Iranian Plateau to reach the eastern frontiers of Parthian jurisdiction in Arachosia (southern Afghanistan). Isidore mentions which settlements are fortified and notes which districts have access to the main wells. He records sites that were founded by the Macedonian regime and on several occasions includes details as to whether an urban population could be considered 'Greek' and thereby, by implication, pro-Roman.

Isidore suggested the invasion route should begin at the Syrian town of Zeugma on the Euphrates frontier. Zeugma controlled a large bridge that spanned the Euphrates, but he advised the main Roman force keep to the western bank so that any intercepting Parthian cavalry would need to cross the river to launch an attack. From Zeugma, the Roman army would march south through a line of fortified Greek towns and walled villages that had been founded by Alexander or the Seleucid kings. Isidore also notes the site of several 'Royal Stations' in this region that had been established by the Persian King Darius as part of an ancient Royal Road that connected his domains in the fifth century BC.[10] It is possible that the Romans planned to ship supplies and personnel down the Euphrates on river craft and Isidore therefore notes any sailing hazards. At one point he warns, 'Here the flow is dammed with rocks in order that the water may overflow the fields, but in summer this same barrier will wreck the boats.'[11]

A village named Phaliga on the Euphrates occupied a strategic position in the invasion plans. Isidore records that the settlement lay almost halfway between the Syrian capital Antioch and the main city of Seleucia in central Babylonia. Downstream from Phaliga a tributary river flowed into the Euphrates near a walled village called Nabagath. At this point Isidore recommends, 'Here the Legions cross over to territory beyond the river.'[12] This was the site where the Romans expected to bridge the Euphrates in order to advance down the east bank of the river.

There were Parthian garrisons guarding river outposts on the east banks of the mid-Euphrates and the Romans needed to occupy these locations in order to control this part of Mesopotamia (northern Iraq). Isidore mentions two Euphrates islands that the Parthians used as secure bases to store treasury funds. When a renegade Parthian Prince named Tiridates II temporarily took control of Babylonia in 26 BC, he was able to take these sites from King Phraates IV. Isidore noted that Phraates ordered his men to 'cut the throats of the concubines' when the exiled Tiridates had surrounded the loyalist outpost. This incident reminded the Romans that the Parthians would kill hostages and destroy property if they believed defeat was imminent.

Beyond the treasury island of Thilabus there was another island midstream in the Euphrates where the city of Izan was located. The Romans required river transports to seize these sites and Isidore mentions that the nearby city of Aipolis had bitumen springs used to waterproof ship-hulls. This material could repair any Roman transports damaged by sailing downstream, or perhaps the imperial invaders planned to construct new vessels at this site. Meanwhile, Roman land forces could advance towards the city of Besechana which had a prominent temple dedicated to the Syrian goddess Atargatis. Beyond this city the course of the Euphrates came close to the Tigris with a short canal connecting the two rivers. After capturing the Hellenic city of Neapolis, the legions would follow the path of this canal east to Seleucia on the banks of the Tigris River. The vast city of Seleucia was heavily fortified, but the Romans could expect support and assistance from its largely Greek population.[13]

The twin capitals of Seleucia and Ctesiphon were positioned on opposite sides of the Tigris River, so the Romans needed to commandeer or build river craft to make a crossing to this monumental Parthian city. The Romans probably surmised that once Ctesiphon was captured, the Parthians would relinquish control over Babylonia, including Spasinu Charax at the head of the Persian Gulf. Isidore therefore suggests that the next stage in the Roman campaign was the invasion of Iran and the capture of Ecbatana, the second royal city of the Parthian Empire.

Babylonia was densely populated with wide well-irrigated field systems and relatively short distances between the leading urban sites. But the cities of Iran were separated by arid and mountainous tracks of land and this created difficulties for the invading force. Isidore uses a new terminology to describe sites on the route through Iran, including positions that he calls *stathmoi* or 'stations'. These sites might have been caravan supply-stations (caravanserai), military installations, or communication posts used by Parthian administrators to relay government orders. It is also possible that many of these locations fulfilled multiple roles for travellers and because the Parthian regime depended on cavalry, these outposts were crucial in maintaining cohesion across their empire. As the ruling Parthian court wintered at Ctesiphon and spent the summer months in Ecbatana, the thoroughfare between these two cities was well maintained for official travellers. It therefore provided the Parthian rulers with a fast and effective escape route if the Romans sized Babylonia. Isidore describes Ecbatana as a metropolis that housed the Parthian treasury and reports that it also had a major temple dedicated to the Iranian goddess Anaitis.[14]

The route from Ctesiphon to Ecbatana headed northeast to the Iranian Plateau. Leaving the banks of the Tigris, the Roman force would pass a Greek city named Artemita on the edge of Babylonia. From this point onwards the legions had to cross open terrain through a series of rural villages equipped with caravan stations. On route to the Zagros Mountain range they would pass through another Greek city named Chala before crossing into Media.[15]

The legions needed to travel through ten villages in Median territory, each equipped with stations (*stathmoi*) for travellers. After these positions were secured, the Romans would reach a mountain city named Bagistana that controlled passage to the city of Concobar with its famous temple to the Greek hunting-goddess Artemis. By then the Roman army were close to the centre of Parthian rule in Media and if they marched further east they were advised to capture a custom station known as Bazigraban which controlled caravan traffic moving between Babylonia and Iran. Close by there was a royal summer palace named Adrapana which had surrounding parklands for the Parthian nobility to hunt game and engage in other equestrian sports.[16]

From Adrapana it was suggested that the legions marched onward to capture the nearby capital Ecbatana. Ecbatana was crucial to the conquest of Media and after this city had been captured, Isidore recommended a further route through the region to seize three important caravan stations, ten villages at strategic locations and five additional cities. This part of the campaign route ended near a city called Rhaga which had a population larger than Ecbatana. Nearby was the city of Media-Charax which had developed around a fortified installation where the Parthians had settled some of their steppe allies known as the Mardi (176–171 BC).[17] The city of Media-Charax was positioned beneath a mountain called Caspius and it controlled the main approach to the southern Caspian Gates. This location marked the edge of Media, so the capture of the city would have brought the western realms of the Parthian Empire fully under Roman dominion. According to Pliny, Ecbatana was 750 miles from Seleucia and 20 miles from a strategic pass known as the Caspian Gates.[18]

Hostile deserts of salt-encrusted sediment filled large stretches of eastern Iran. These were the remains of ancient prehistoric seas that had entirely evaporated to leave broad wastelands between the mountain ranges that encircled the country. In order to capture the remaining Parthian territories, Roman forces needed to follow a course across Hyrcania, a fertile region that stretched around the southern shores of the Caspian Sea.[19] This open coastline included grasslands, but inland there were deciduous broadleaved forests and upland alpine meadows that provided a habitat for the now extinct Caspian tiger. Leopards, lynx, brown bears, wild boars and wolves were hunted in these forests and its grassland peripheries.

However, to enter Hyrcania, the Romans had to pass through a narrow gorge known as the Southern Caspian Gates that cut through the Alburz Mountains. The legionaries taken prisoner at Carrhae had been marched through this bleak mountain pass, so the Roman authorities already had harrowing eyewitness accounts of the region. Pliny describes how the pass had been cut through the rock by Persian engineers, but the 8-mile roadway was scarcely broad enough for a single line of wagon traffic. He reports that the gorge was 'overhung on either side by crags that look as if they had been burnt by fire and the narrow passage through the gorge is only interrupted by a salt-water stream'. Roman reports suggested that the surrounding country was almost entirely waterless for a range of 28 miles. The permanent mountain streams were saline and fresh water could only be obtained with the melt of winter snows. Consequently, the region would present serious challenges to any infantry-based Roman army trying to capture this strategic position from Parthian cavalry forces. Pliny concludes, 'The Parthian kingdom is effectively shut off by passes.'[20]

Pliny had read Roman itineraries that used information from Alexander's campaigns to chart invasion routes through Iran. The Southern Caspian Gates was a central strategic point in these studies since it was estimated to be almost 600 miles from the River Jaxartes (the Syr Darya) where Alexander fixed the northern limits of his conquests in Sogdia. The gorge was also calculated to be about 450 miles from the Bactrian capital Balkh and 2,000 miles from the northern frontiers of ancient India.[21]

A modern survey of these routes has confirmed the accuracy of these ancient figures. Pliny reports that the distance from the Caspian Gate to the Parthian capital Hecatompylos was 133 Roman miles (122 modern miles). The distance measured using modern techniques is close to 125 miles along a course that probably deviates only slightly from the ancient pathways.[22]

Isidore outlined a route into the fertile lands of Hyrcania for any Roman forces that captured and held the Caspian Gates. Beyond the Gates, the legionaries would arrive at a narrow valley that led to the Iranian city of Apamia. From there, the invasion course had to turn east and occupy another line of villages equipped with caravan stations that probably operated as Parthian military outposts. There were no cities in this region and the Romans would travel through thirty-five villages with *stathmoi* (stations) on their route through Hyrcania. Only then would they reach the frontiers of the region known as Parthia and the original homelands of their enemy.[23]

An Iranian city called Asaac (Arsak) was on the western frontier of Parthia. It was here on the southeast shores of the Caspian Sea that the founder of the Parthian regime, Arsaces I had been proclaimed king by his steppe followers after they had settled the region (250–211 BC). Isidore reports that Asaac was an important centre for an ancient Iranian religion known as Zoroastrianism and a sacred everlasting fire was maintained in the city temples.[24]

Near Asaac was the fortified city of Nisa (Parthaunisa) which was the location of ancient royal tombs belonging to the earliest Parthian rulers.[25] Excavations at this site, near Ashgabat in Turkmenistan, recovered carved ivory drinking cups or ceremonial libation cones known as *rytons*. Other finds from the city include thousands of fragmentary administrative records from the Parthian regime written on clay tablets in Persian script. These texts document deliveries of wine and other produce to the Parthian administrators at Nisa.[26] They also record military titles including Border-Wardens and Fortress-Commanders who oversaw the conveyance of cash crops to the royal centre.[27]

There were no travel-stations in this part of Parthia because the region already had sufficient cities to accommodate caravans and facilitate the movement of mounted armies. North of Parthia was the Eurasian steppe, but the lands to the south were covered by desert. This meant that any Roman invasion route had to pass directly through the region. Isidore lists a series of Parthian cities that would have to be captured on any campaign through this territory, including Gathar, Siroc, Apauarctica and Ragau. This would complete the anticipated Roman conquest of Parthia, but further east there were other territories subject to Parthian rule that might also be claimed for the Roman Empire.

Beyond Parthia

Isidore outlined a route from Parthia east into Margiana that would have allowed Roman forces to take possession of the oasis site of Merv. The territory around Merv was almost entirely devoid of any settlements, but there were two Parthian villages on route to the oasis.[28] Here Roman commanders expected to find the captive legionaries who had served under Crassus (53 BC) and Mark Antony (36 BC). By the 20s BC many of these prisoners would have spent most of their adult lives under Parthian governance.

The Romans received reports that Merv was enclosed by mountains that formed a 187-mile circuit around the oasis. Beyond the mountains was a large expanse of desert that extended for at least 120 miles to the east.[29] The oasis at Merv received water from the Murghab River which flowed more than 500 miles from mountains on the edge of northwest Afghanistan into the Karakum Desert in Turkmenistan. Curtius records that Alexander the Great established six Hellenic towns on hill sites near Merv, 'spaced only a short distance apart so that they could seek mutual aid from one another'.[30] Pliny claims that Alexander also established a city near the river, but the settlement was abandoned or destroyed by enemy forces. Antiochus I Soter reclaimed the oasis by founding a walled Hellenic city called Antiochia Margiana close to the river (281–261 BC).[31] He enclosed the countryside surrounding this city with a wall measuring almost 8 miles in circumference.[32]

Archaeological remains and records from later eras suggest the appearance of this ancient territory. A Chinese soldier visited the city of Merv (Mulu) in the eighth century AD after he had been held captive by Iranian forces. He saw a caravan city surrounded by walls that were 3 miles in circumference and had iron gates. When he returned to China he reported that the 'walls of the city are high and thick and the streets and markets are tidy and well-arranged'.[33] The remains of ancient clay-wall barriers have been found stretching across certain northern districts of Margiana.[34] These defences were probably built to protect the territory from mounted raiders, but the remains cannot be securely dated. They could be Hellenic, Parthian or perhaps Sassanid defences (AD 224–651) built or repaired by native peoples, or perhaps foreign prisoners of war.

Pliny describes how Margiana was 'famous for its sunny climate' and received recognition as one of the few territories in Parthia where grape vines were cultivated.[35] Strabo emphasises the wine production at this site and describes fertile soil suitable for viticulture. He reports that 'vine stocks are found that require two men to girth [10 feet circumference] and bunches of gapes grow to 2 cubits

[3 feet].[36] This suggests that viticulture might have been well established when the first Roman captives were brought to Merv in 53 BC.

Many of the Roman captives were probably settled as agricultural labourers in towns near the city of Antiochia Margiana. Some of these Italian captives might have had pre-war experience in viticulture which was a valuable skill. One of the Parthian clay tablets recovered from the royal city of Nisa records wine deliveries from the oasis (before 40 BC). The delivery was arranged and overseen by two 'Tagmadars', a Greek title that designated unit officers. These men had the Parthian names Frabaxtak and Frafarn, but they could have commanded labour teams of Roman workers assigned to royal vineyards.[37] A further possibility is that some Roman captives adopted Parthian culture and received the titles and responsibilities of their new regime. Horace asked his reader to imagine their fate: 'Are the soldiers of Crassus, men of Marsi and Apulia, living under Median rule, joined in shameful marriage to foreign wives?'[38]

Merv was the eastern limit of Parthian rule in inner Asia and the oasis would have been a formidable frontier outpost for Rome. Any advance further east towards the Oxus River would have brought the Romans into conflict with other steppe peoples including the Mardi (Kangju) in Sogdia and the Tocharians (Yuezhi-Kushan) in Bactria. These steppe populations were developing into powerful regimes that could field mounted armies as large as their Parthian rivals. Pliny explains that 'these people are numerous enough to live on equal terms with the Parthians.'[39] War with these nations would be a significant challenge for Rome, so a better prospect for conquest was for Roman armies to march south and claim a contested desert region in eastern Iran called Aria (western Afghanistan).

Strabo describes Aria and Margiana as 'the most powerful districts in this part of Asia because they are populated plains enclosed by mountains'. These wide plains were intersected and irrigated by large rivers that made the land fertile, suitable for viticulture and capable of supporting large cities. Strabo estimated that central Aria occupied an area about 200 miles long and 30 miles across.[40]

In this period Aria was ruled by Parthian princes and Isidore outlines the route from Merv that would lead an invading army through the main cities in this region. These included Candac, Artacauan and a capital called Alexandria Ariana, which was founded by Macedonian military colonists. Isidore also mentions 'a very great city' known as Phra and five further cities named Bis, Gari, Nia, Parin and Coroc. The existence of this urban network meant that Roman armies would be capturing cities rather than village-based caravan stations.[41] But the area was remote from Babylonia and Isidore had few details about the actual condition of the cities of Aria.

The conquest of Aria would have extinguished Parthian rule in ancient Iran and if they continued south, the Roman legions would provoke conflict with other nations. East of Aria was the territory of Arachosia (southwest Afghanistan) which was under the rule of a steppe people who Isidore calls the 'Scythian Saka'. These Saka were subject to the Parthians, but they could be encouraged to become allies of the Roman Empire as vassal rulers or client kings. Isidore lists a route through Arachosia to bring Roman forces to the cities of Barda, Min, Palacenti and a capital called Sigal, where these Scythian-Sakas had their royal residence. Nearby was a part-Hellenic city called Alexandropolis which was another legacy of Macedonian military colonisation.[42]

According to Isidore, the Parthians referred to eastern Arachosia as 'White India'. This was probably because its Iranian population had been part of the Mauryan Empire of ancient India during the third century BC. Consequently, Arachosia preserved strong elements of Indian culture within its civic administrations. Arachosia controlled certain approaches to the Hindu Kush and the mountain passes that led to the Indus kingdoms. Isidore charts a route through this region that would have taken Roman forces through several important cities including Biyt, Pharsana and Chorochoad. He also records the existence of a Hellenic city named 'Demetrias' that was probably established by the Greek King Demetrius of Bactria who conquered this region in about 180 BC.[43] The itinerary outlined by Isidore ends at the city of Alexandria Arachosia (Kandahar) which was another Macedonian foundation established by Alexander and his generals. Isidore explains that the city was considered 'Greek' and 'as far as this place, the land is under the rule of the Parthians.'[44]

If they had accomplished all these conquests, the Romans would have occupied every Hellenic city in the Parthian realm and brought the frontiers of their empire as far as Bactria and Gandhara. Beyond Arachosia were the Indus kingdoms who were at that time subject to the Indo-Sakas and their overlord King Azes. Azes sent envoys to Augustus in 26 BC proposing a political alliance. Suetonius records that these 'Indo-Scythians' (Sakas) 'were from nations previously known to us only through hearsay and they petitioned for an alliance (*amicitia*) with Augustus and the Roman people'.[45] In earlier times the Sakas had been able to field 20,000 mounted archers, but Azes probably commanded only a fraction of this fighting force.[46] Orosius suggests that the Saka ambassadors expected a western war against Persia and came 'to praise the Emperor with the glory of Alexander the Great'.[47] To emphasise his connection to Hellenic culture, Azes issued currency displaying images of the goddess Athena and used Greek titles referring to himself as 'The Great King of Kings'. He sent further envoys to the Emperor in 22 BC who delivered a royal letter written in Greek pledging that Azes was 'ready to allow Augustus passage through his country, wherever he wished to proceed and co-operate with him in anything that was honourable'. The king confirmed that he held the allegiance of 600 minor sovereigns in northern India and 'was anxious for an alliance with Caesar Augustus'.[48] Dio reports that earlier proposals were formalised and a 'treaty of friendship' (*amicitia*) firmly agreed between the two sovereigns. Augustus emphasises the military aspect of these meetings in his memorial testimony when he records that 'to me were sent embassies of kings from India, who had never been seen in the camp of any Roman general'.[49] Respecting this alliance, the military itinerary provided by Isidore assumes that Roman aggression would end in Arachosia near the frontiers of the allied Saka kingdom.[50]

Augustus may have given Azes the honours due to a Roman Consul (supreme magistrate) including the gift of a *curule* chair. Curule chairs were distinctive campaign stools that consuls would sit upon when they made formal diplomatic or judicial rulings. Consequently the object symbolised the political and military authority of senior imperial commanders operating outside Rome. Livy describes how the Numidian king Masinissa was given this honour in 203 BC when the Romans required military allies to fight the city-state of Carthage in North Africa. The Roman general Scipio presented Masinissa with imperial insignia including 'a golden crown, curule chair, an ivory sceptre, a purple-bordered toga and a tunic embroidered with palms'.[51] The Senate approved these gifts and bestowed further symbols of Roman rank on the foreign king including 'two purple cloaks with golden clasps, two tunics embroidered with the *laticlave* [senatorial purple stripe]; two richly caparisoned horses and a set of equestrian armour with cuirasses; two tents with the military furniture appropriate for Consuls'.[52] The remains of a folding iron stool similar to a *curule* chair were found during excavations at the Saka capital of Sirkap near Taxila.[53] The object became a symbol of political authority in the Upper Indus that was claimed by the Indo-Parthians. When Kujula Kadphises conquered this region in the late first century AD he depicted a subject Parthian prince seated on a curule chair.

The Peace Settlement

Augustus reasoned it was not an opportune time for Rome to begin a war against the Parthians and consequently no invasion scheme was launched during the first decade of his reign. However an opportunity for war occurred in 20 BC, when the Armenians asked the Romans for assistance to remove an unpopular king who had aligned himself with the Parthians. Augustus arranged for a replacement ruler to be selected from amongst the eastern princes that were resident in Rome. He chose an Iranian noble named Tigranes and in 20 BC Roman armies entered Armenia and Tigranes III formally received his crown from Tiberius, the step-son of Augustus. This was a provocative act given that the previous Armenian king had been appointed by the Parthian King Phraates IV. But the Parthians were involved in eastern wars against the Sakas and chose not to immediately retaliate, or further escalate the situation in Armenia. It was in their interests to maintain peace on their western frontiers, even if that meant that Armenia was brought under increased Roman influence.

In 20 BC Augustus secured a long-term peace agreement with the Parthian King Phraates IV. This agreement allowed both rulers to concentrate their military activities on other frontiers and thereby enlarge their respective empires. In 19 BC Roman armies completed the conquest of northern Spain and eliminated the remaining outposts of resistance in the Alps. By 12 BC the Romans had annexed Pannonia and secured the Danube frontiers that safeguarded the main land-routes between Italy and Greece. Then the legions began campaigns in Germany to capture territory beyond the Rhine. In the east the Parthians over-ran Saka-controlled territories beyond the Hindu Kush and installed allied war-lords as princes in the rich Indus kingdoms. These eastern conquests were complete by 10 BC, when the Parthians deposed King Azes and the remaining Saka warlords fled south to form a new ruling dynasty in Gujarat on the west coast of India.[54]

The political settlement agreed in 20 BC required Phraates IV to return the legionary battle-standards lost by Crassus and repatriate Roman prisoners of war who had been settled in Merv. Augustus granted his stepson Tiberius an imperial commission to collect the battle-standards from the Parthians and return them to Rome where the political settlement was presented as a Roman triumph. Dio Cassius reports that the Emperor 'received the standards as if he had conquered the Parthians in a war and took great pride in this achievement'.[55]

By returning the standards, Phraates IV removed a pretext for war and allowed Augustus to defuse the political pressure in Rome from those who sought further conflict and military revenge. The Parthian compliance was probably based on the goodwill achieved by covert diplomatic assurances, but Roman honour was satisfied with the suggestion that Phraates IV had been forced into submission by military threat. In his memorial testimony, Augustus records, 'I forced the Parthians to return to me the spoils and standards of three Roman armies and to seek, as suppliants, the friendship of the Roman people.'[56]

The Parthian diplomats may have suggested a marriage alliance in order to join the ruling dynasties of the empires. Augustus had a teenage daughter named Julia who had been married to a Roman youth named Marcus Claudius Marcellus. But when Marcus died suddenly in 23 BC, Augustus had to reconsider his plans for establishing a royal dynasty through Julia. Perhaps Phraates asked to marry Julia or some other leading Roman noblewoman, but the request was declined as it would have suggested that the two empires were equal in terms of international status. Augustus wanted to present himself as a citizen head-of-state rather than a dynastic king, so he preferred not to engage in the type of matrimonial alliances being practised by the rulers of other ancient empires. In 21 BC, Augustus arranged for Julia to marry his leading commander and most trusted political advisor Marcus Vipsanius Agrippa. Instead of an imperial princess, Augustus sent King Phraates IV the gift of an Italian concubine named Musa. Phraates IV married Musa and when she gave birth to a son named Phraataces, she was elevated to the position of leading consort. Eventually Musa became the Parthian Queen and was in a position to influence the royal succession.[57]

The political settlement agreed in 20 BC was presented as a full Parthian capitulation to Roman authority and the return of the battle-standards was celebrated in Roman iconography as a symbol of foreign submission. The larger-than-life Prima Porta statue of Augustus portrays the Emperor standing barefoot with his right arm empty of a sword, raised in a gesture of peace. His breastplate depicts the return of the standards with the image of a kneeling Parthian offering the captured emblems to a Roman commander, a scene also celebrated on imperial coins issued in 19 BC. It was decided that the restored standards would be placed on display in a new monumental temple erected in Rome to honour the war god Mars Ultor (Mars the Avenger).[58] The return of the lost battle-standards was also celebrated in imperial poetry with Ovid declaring 'You Parthians no longer hold the proofs of our shame.'[59] Horace addressed Augustus with the comments 'Throughout the whole world wars have been concluded under your auspices' and 'Parthia dreads a Rome led by your government.'[60]

Over the next decade, Augustus remained on good terms with Phraates IV and between 11 and 7 BC the Parthian King sent some of his older sons to Rome to be 'hosted' by the Emperor.[61] Phraates IV probably had personal motives for this action, as dissenters in the Parthian nobility often encouraged young princes to seize power from their fathers. So, by sending the young men to Rome, Phraates IV removed these candidates from court intrigues without having to deprive them of their royal position. The Parthian Queen Musa possibly encouraged this action, so that the succession route would be cleared for her own son Phraataces.

Strabo indicates the impact of imperial propaganda from this period when he explains that 'the Parthians are very powerful, but they have yielded to Roman pre-eminence and returned the military trophies which they took to memorialize their victory over Rome. Moreover, Phraates has entrusted his children and grandchildren to Augustus, obsequiously ensuring his friendship by offering hostages.'[62] Writing several centuries after these events, Orosius believed that 'the Parthians acted as if the attentions of the entire conquered and pacified world was focused upon them and the Roman Empire might direct their total strength against them.' For this reason, 'they voluntarily returned the standards that they had seized on the death of Crassus and after giving hostages, they obtained a lasting treaty by humbly promising to observe good faith.'[63]

The Roman governor of Syria, Marcus Titius, oversaw the transfer of the Parthian princes across the imperial frontier. They were conveyed to Rome with their families and their royal requirements financed by Augustus at the expense of the Roman state.[64] The exchange gave the Emperor an influence in the Parthian succession and further ensured that Musa's half-Italian son Phraataces could succeed as king. Augustus derived great political advantage from these Parthian princes who he presented in Rome as royal candidates subject to imperial authority. Their presence suggested that Parthia might eventually become a client kingdom of Rome and its rulers subservient to Roman imperial interests. Horace presents this impression by claiming that 'Phraates is now suppliant on his knees for he has acknowledged the laws and power of the Emperor.'[65]

Further Prospects for War

Another political crisis threatened the peace between Rome and Parthia in 6 BC when King Tigranes III died and the Armenians appointed his sons as joint rulers without first seeking the approval of Rome. This was seen as a dangerous statement of independence that challenged Roman authority in the region. To deter Roman aggression, the Armenians sought Parthian backing to guarantee their efforts to reassert regional autonomy. In 5 BC, Augustus sent a campaign force into Armenia to place a Roman candidate on the throne, who within months was deposed by a popular uprising. The pro-Roman faction was expelled and a prince named Tigranes IV obtained the backing of the Parthian King Phraates IV to establish himself as the new ruler of a sovereign Armenia. This was a political triumph for the Parthians who had acquired new allies to support their regime and extend their political influence towards the Black Sea.

But Augustus was not prepared to accept this outcome of the Armenian dispute and planned to restore Roman claims over the kingdom. The invasion of Parthia was reconsidered as a military option and Roman agents were sent east to gather further intelligence concerning the Parthian realms. In 2 BC Augustus gave Gaius, the eldest of his grandsons, a special command in the eastern empire with orders to settle affairs with Parthia either by diplomacy, or military force.[66] Gaius was in his early twenties, a similar age to Alexander when he had begun his conquest of Persia. The young general was well-liked by the Roman people and his command revived popular expectations that eastern victories were imminent.

During this period, dramatic public spectacles were staged in Rome to promote the prospect of Parthian wars and lead Roman opinion to expect new conquests. On one occasion the Emperor flooded part of the enormous plaza in the centre of the Saepta Julia building. From bleachers around the plaza the Roman crowds watched a specially staged mock naval battle recreating the victory at Artemisium when an Athenian-led Greek fleet triumphed over an invading Persian armada (480 BC). The combatants dressed in archaic costume and fought aboard replica ships.[67] The spectacle reminded Roman audiences of past victories by classical civilisations over the land-based powers of Iran. It suggested that these conflicts were about to be reignited by Gaius in a Roman struggle against Parthian aggressors.

Ovid describes the spectacle and records how 'the whole world seemed to be gathered in the city' and how many Roman men were 'beguiled by foreign romance'. After the excitement of the mock battle, even Ovid was enthusiastic for a war against the Parthian Empire. He explained: 'The Emperor is preparing to complete the conquest of the world. Far-off eastern countries will soon submit to our laws, including the arrogant Parthians. For they will be punished as they deserve.' Perhaps many Romans were unsatisfied with the previous diplomatic settlement and the appointment of Gaius offered them an opportunity for full revenge. Ovid wrote, 'Oh spirits of Crassus and his Eagle standards shamed by barbarian possession, now you will rejoice and be festive, for your avenger is ready!'[68]

Roman opinion was also encouraged by the prospect of receiving new wealth from the Parthian realms. Many would have recalled how Augustus granted large sums of money to Roman citizens after he had conquered Egypt and seized the royal treasures of the Ptolemies.[69] They expected similar exploits from Gaius, and Ovid proclaimed: 'Our righteous cause shall overcome the Parthians and our young hero will bring victory. The wealth of the Orient shall be added to the riches of Rome.'[70]

Victory over the eastern kingdoms would mean impressive celebrations in Rome and Ovid looked forward to witnessing these exciting public festivities. The highlight of these events would have been a military triumph with captured eastern treasures and prisoners of war paraded through the crowded centre of

Rome in carriage-mounted tableau displays. Ovid visualises the Parthian trophies and advises his readers to appear knowledgeable about foreign events, even if they know little about world affairs. He tells his male readers, 'a beauty might ask you to name that defeated monarch, or you might have to explain to her "what do these emblems mean?", "what country is that?" or "what does that mountain or river display represent?" You must anticipate her questions and answer with confidence, even if you have no real knowledge.' Ovid gives an example of the right response: 'That is the Euphrates with the crinkled crown, the figure with the sky-blue hair signifies the Tigris, those people are Armenians and that woman represents Persia.' He also suggests that the suitor should include impressive references to ancient Greek myths and exaggerate the significance of the foreign captives being displayed on the exhibits. Tell her 'they are captured generals and then invent their names.'[71]

But the prospect of war between Rome and Parthia was averted by the murder of King Phraates IV. News reached Rome in 2 BC that Queen Musa had poisoned her husband and successfully installed her 17-year-old son Phraataces on the Parthian throne as Phraates V.[72] As Gaius and his command staff made their way to Syria, Phraataces sent an embassy to Augustus explaining his concerns and requesting the return of any Parthian princes in Rome who might challenge his succession. Augustus denied this request and refused to hand over the royal candidates. He then escalated the situation by declining to acknowledge Phraataces as the Parthian 'King of Kings'.[73] By retaining the princes in Rome, Augustus reserved his right to interfere in the Parthian succession if Phraataces did not comply with future Roman policy.

When Gaius Caesar arrived in Syria he reaffirmed Roman claims to hold authority in Armenia and prepared the eastern legions for war. But he did not launch an immediate attack on Parthia and entered into political negotiations instead. In the autumn of 1 BC, Gaius and Phraataces assembled their armies facing each other on opposite banks of the Euphrates River. In a carefully staged pageant the two young men, accompanied by an equal number of attendants and political advisors, met on an island midstream. In full view of both armies, they deliberated over the details of a peace settlement and exchanged pledges to confirm the status and rights of their respective empires. Official celebrations were then conducted on each side of the river, with the Roman camp offering a reception for Phraataces and his nobles, and the following night the Parthians hosting a banquet for Gaius and his Roman commanders.[74] Once more, long-term peace and cooperation between Rome and Parthia seemed to have been secured, but within a few years each of these young generals had met their death.

The Euphrates Agreement guaranteed that if Rome were to restore its authority over Armenia the Parthians would not interfere. Roman forces launched a campaign in Armenia to reclaim the region and install a royal candidate favourable to Rome. By AD 4 a Roman victory seemed assured and Gaius agreed to meet an Armenian leader named Addon who was ready to discuss surrender terms. Addon claimed to possess important documents and requested a personal meeting to present them to Gaius. As Gaius leant forward to receive the documents, Addon thrust a hidden dagger into the young man and fatally wounded him. Gaius, who had been the favoured candidate to succeed Augustus as Emperor, died from this wounds aged just 24.[75]

By this time Augustus was 66 years old and there was no one else in the imperial family with the authority, popularity and esteem required to take charge of this special eastern command. With the death of Gaius, the reclusive middle-aged Tiberius became the most likely candidate to succeed Augustus as Emperor. But it was well-known that Tiberius had become estranged from the imperial family and had withdrawn from political and military service.

Meanwhile amongst the Parthian nobility, support for the half-Italian King Phraataces was wavering. In an effort to legitimise his foreign ancestry, he granted grand titles to his mother Queen Musa, but he could not quell the growing insurrection. In AD 4 he was overthrown by a rival Parthian regent named Orodes. On seizing the throne Orodes III had Phraataces put to death before launching a series of violent reprisals against large sections of the Parthian nobility. As a consequence Orodes was himself assassinated for his cruelty.[76]

In AD 6 the Parthians sent an embassy to Augustus requesting the return of another son of Phraates IV named Vonones who was still living in Rome as a hostage prince. Augustus obliged and Vonones I was crowned as the Parthian King in AD 7. Strabo indicates Roman expectations that Parthia could be made a vassal state. He comments, 'At present the Parthians have gone to Rome seeking a man to be their king and are now about ready to put their entire authority into the hands of the Romans.'[77] But Vonones had spent over two decades in Rome and his subjects considered his loyalties and mannerisms to be 'too Roman'. Vonones ignored Parthian formalities and did not demonstrate sufficient interest in the steppe pursuits of horsemanship and hunting which strengthened social bonds between the ruling nobility.[78] A revolt began in Media and by AD 12 a rival prince named Artabanus was proclaimed king in Ctesiphon.[79]

Gaius and Phraataces might have changed the political fortunes of the western world if they had lived long enough to secure their position as rulers of their respective empires. But as events turned out, Rome missed the opportunity to conquer Parthia and lost the political struggle to establish an allied dynasty in ancient Iran. This meant that a foreign regime continued to control the caravan trails that connected Rome, through the Middle East, to Transoxiana, the Tarim Silk Routes and the economic wealth of ancient China.

CHAPTER FOURTEEN

Roman Routes to China

Indian merchants provided Roman businessmen with some basic information about the location of China. Roman seafarers used the stars to determine the position of distant countries and plot the direction of sea crossings. Night journeys across featureless desert landscapes were also made using the constellations as a guide.[1] Greek pilots therefore tried to connect Indian information on China with star patterns that might reveal the global position of this distant country. The *Periplus of the Erythraean Sea* suggests that 'Thina lies right under Ursa Minor and must be on the same level as the outer parts of the Pontus (Black Sea) and the Caspian' (AD 50).[2] Based on this perspective, China was thought to be on the same latitude as the Caspian Sea in a location just slightly north of its true position.

As ocean commerce developed, Roman ships began sailing around the southern tip of India to reach city-ports in the Ganges and Burma. But these Roman voyages remained within the Indian Ocean since the 1,000-mile-long Malay Peninsula was a major barrier that hindered ventures further east. Roman ships were dependent on seasonal weather and once the northeast monsoon began to blow in November, it was time for them to sail back across the ocean to Egypt.[3] This timeframe discouraged any Roman voyages around the Malay Peninsula to investigate the lands that lay beyond.

In the early second century AD, a Greek sailor named Alexandros gathered details from Indian merchants who sailed to a site on the northern part of the Malay Peninsula called Tamala. From Tamala, travellers trekked 100 miles across the narrow Kra Isthmus and boarded other Indian vessels on the eastern seaboard. These ships were outfitted to cross the Gulf of Thailand and their Indian crews sailed to Cambodia and Vietnam in search of new trade opportunities. When they reached the southern tip of Vietnam some of these ships sailed south into the open sea and made the crossing to Borneo.[4] Ancient Borneo was an extensive jungle-forested island that was almost as large as Asia Minor (modern Turkey). Indian ships making landfall on the 700-mile-long northern coast of Borneo were therefore unsure if the landmass was an island or some southern extension of the Asian continent.

The *Periplus* written by Alexandros has not survived, but it provided Claudius Ptolemy with most of the geographical data he used to map the southeast edge of Asia. Using this information, Ptolemy locates 'Sinae' (Han China) in a narrow band of territory on the very edge of the Asian continent. However Ptolemy made errors in his reconstruction of the Far East. He theorised that the northern coast of Borneo was part of the Asian continent and therefore made the seaboard of Sinae extend southeast to enclose the entire southern ocean.[5]

The Maes Expedition

For centuries the overland Silk Routes around the Tarim Basin provided a conduit through which Chinese goods reached Bactria, India and Parthia. Only one Roman merchant group is reported to have ventured into Central Asia and followed the Tarim routes to the Chinese Empire. The group was sent by a Roman entrepreneur named Maes Titianus sometime around AD 100. But this contact was exceptional and was only made possible due to special circumstances that arose between the leading ancient empires.

In the late first century AD, the Han general Ban Chao restored Chinese authority over the Tarim kingdoms using a combination of diplomacy and military force (AD 74–97). By AD 84 Ban Chao had secured Kashgar and the Han could re-establish direct political contacts with the Yuezhi in Bactria (the Kushan Empire). Chinese rule created stability on the silk routes and prevented intervening regimes from hindering travel, or monopolizing various sections of the caravan trails that led across the Tarim territories. In AD 87 the Parthians responded to these developments by sending an embassy to China which was received by the Han Emperor Zhang.[6] They returned with oriental merchandise and brought new information about the Chinese Empire back to the Parthian capitals at Ecbatana in Iran and Ctesiphon in Babylonia.

These events probably motivated Maes Titianus to plan his own commercial venture into Central Asia. Sometime around AD 100 Maes arranged for a team of commercial agents to travel along the Parthian caravan routes that led from Iran into Afghanistan. This Roman group journeyed through the northern part of the Kushan Empire towards the Tarim territories. Somewhere near the Pamirs they were intercepted by Han authorities who took them eastward through the Tarim kingdoms to China. The bewildered Romans were delivered to the Chinese capital Louyang and brought before the Han Emperor He. On their return to the Roman Empire the group offered an account of their exploits to Maes who wrote a report for his business colleagues. This account was read by educated Greeks and Romans, including geographers who extracted names, distances and directions from the work. One of these geographers was a mathematician named Marinus who came from the Syrian city of Tyre. This is significant because Tyre was famous for its fabric industries and the city was a leading participant in the international silk trade.[7] The original report by Maes has not survived into modern times, but the data collected by Marinus was copied by Claudius Ptolemy. Ptolemy used the information from Maes to construct new maps of the Far East and determine the geographical position of the people that the Romans called the Sinae (the Chinese).[8]

Claudius Ptolemy describes Maes as 'a Macedonian who was also called Titianus and was the son of a merchant and a merchant himself'.[9] Maes was a Syrian name and the *nomen* 'Titianus' indicates that he came from a family granted Roman citizenship by a man called Titian. Therefore Maes Titianus was a Macedonian who spoke Greek, but he came from a family of businessmen who claimed elements of both Syrian and Roman identity. Maes could have inherited his Roman citizenship from an ancestor who served a leading politician named Marcus Titius.[10] Titius was the Roman governor of Syria in 13 BC and on the orders of the Emperor Augustus he helped facilitate an important peace settlement with the Parthians. This was the agreement whereby the Parthian King Phraates IV sent several of his young sons and grandsons to Rome as political wards of the Roman Emperor.[11] Strabo describes how Marcus received the four children, four grandchildren and two daughters-in-law of the Parthian King. He took responsibility for the safety and wellbeing of these Parthian royals from the time they crossed into Syria until their transfer to Rome.[12]

Marcus Titius would have sent trusted Syrian servants to the Parthian capital Ctesiphon to convey messages and arrange for the safe conduct of the royal family. Some these servants were probably granted Roman citizenship by Marcus and as freedmen they could have used their knowledge and political connections to create successful commercial businesses. They had high-status contacts in Ctesiphon who could acquire silk batches for dispatch to the cities of Roman Syria. Maes Titianus was probably from one of these merchant families, a Roman citizen with connections to the Parthian nobility, which ensured that his business requests would be granted. In this special context, he was able to arrange for some of his commercial agents to join a Parthian caravan as it headed out across Iran towards Bactria and the Kushan Empire.

Claudius Ptolemy explains the route taken by the Maes group. The first stage in the expedition was a journey across the Parthian Empire from the Euphrates frontier to Merv on the eastern edge of Iran. Before the onset of summer, Parthian caravans would have left the hot and humid city of Ctesiphon and headed east to the seasonal capital of Ecbatana in the drier and cooler climate of Media.[13] This was a journey of about 250 miles through passes in the Zagros Mountains which formed the outer fringe of the Iranian Plateau. Caravans followed this route in springtime when snows from the mountains melted and provided temporary streams of water for the benefit of travellers and their horse-mounted escorts.

The multi-walled city of Ecbatana offered accommodation and supplies to the Parthian caravans that crossed ancient Iran. From Ecbatana the route headed north across the Iranian plateau towards the coast of the Caspian Sea. This was a journey of about 200 miles through mountain valleys that descended towards the narrow seaboard of Hyrcania. Hyrcania was a 300-mile-long belt of low-lying territory between the mountains and the Caspian shore. This plain of fertile land was a vital corridor for east-west travel as it offered caravans a well-provisioned route around the eastern section of the Iranian Plateau. On the edge of Hyrcania the merchant caravans passed through the Iranian city of Hecatompylos. This was the first capital created by the Parthians (the Parni) when they migrated from the Central Asian steppe to settle in northeast Iran (238–209 BC).

The caravan route from Hecatompylos (Qumis) to the Parthian frontier at Merv covered more than 450 miles across arid terrain. Merv was the last major outpost of the Parthian Empire and from there caravans would have entered Kushan territory and headed 300 miles east to the Bactrian capital Bactra (Balkh). Centuries earlier Bactria had been part of a Greek kingdom that included an urban population descended from Macedonian colonists (256–140 BC). Perhaps the Maes group was able to exploit a shared Macedonian heritage to pass unhindered through this region.

In AD 100 there was peace between Parthian Iran and the Kushan Empire which ruled in ancient Afghanistan. This meant that caravans were able to pass unobstructed between their realms and the Parthian merchants that reached Bactra (Balkh) were permitted to travel eastward to the Pamir Mountains. It was a journey of about 500 miles between Bactra and a trade outpost on the Kushan frontier known as the Stone Tower (Tashkurgan). The Stone Tower was a meeting-ground for the steppe peoples that Claudius Ptolemy calls the 'Scythians'. Ptolemy calculated that the entire route from Ctesiphon to the Stone Tower covered about 26,280 *stadia*, which is equivalent to about 2,600 miles.[14] Caravans can travel up to 15 miles per day, but with frequent rest periods the journey would have taken up to six months.

The Stone Tower trade outpost in the Pamir Mountains was about 250 miles from the oasis city of Kashgar on the edge of the Tarim Basin. Perhaps the Roman merchants sent by Maes expected to conclude their trade dealings at this distant site and then begin the long trek home to Syria. But in AD 100 Kashgar was a protectorate of the Han Empire and Chinese observers were active on this new frontier. The Protector General Ban Chao was planning his retirement and wanted to impress the Han Emperor by returning to Louyang with a range of foreign peoples from western countries beyond the Tarim territories. By chance the Roman merchants were at the Stone Tower when Han agents were searching for foreign representatives who could give an account of their distant homelands to the imperial court. As a result the Maes group was brought to the offices of Ban Chao in the Tarim kingdoms where they accepted the opportunity to travel onward to Louyang.[15]

The Maes merchants spoke Greek and were found by Chinese agents near a country that had once been ruled by Hellenic dynasties (Bactria). They were also travelling with Parthian merchants and so did not identify themselves as Roman. This meant that Chinese authorities were not aware they were dealing with subjects of *Da Qin* (the Roman Empire). The Maes merchants were conveyed 600 miles across the Tarim kingdoms by a Chinese military escort and brought through the Jade Gate to the 600-mile-long Hexi corridor that led into inner China and the 400-mile route to Louyang.

This part of the journey revealed the true scale of eastern Asia to Roman geographers. Ptolemy reports, 'The distance from the Stone Tower to Sera, the capital of the Seres, is a journey of seven months, estimated at 36,200 *stadia*.'[16] This distance was about 3,600 miles and suggests that a journey from the Euphrates to central China could be completed in about twelve months, or a full year of travel. Consequently, anyone making the round trip would be absent from their homeland for at least two years.

Maes wrote a full account of the journey taken by his business agents, but only the briefest summary of this work survives in the map-based discussion given by Claudius Ptolemy. Ptolemy describes how the Maes group journeyed for seven months through lands that were previously unknown to any Greek or Roman authority. As they travelled through the Tarim territories the agents kept to a route 'subject to violent storms' until at the end of their journey they entered the capital of the Seres. This was the imperial city of Louyang and the Maes group found themselves in the company of dozens of envoys from Central Asia who had come to pay honour to the Chinese Court.[17]

The Chinese history known as the *Hou Hanshu* reveals the incident from the Han perspective and dates this encounter to AD 100. It seems that the Maes group described themselves as Macedonians and explained the long distance between their Syrian homelands and the Chinese Empire. This information was translated for the imperial court and the Chinese scribes entered in their records that the Maes group came from a previously unknown region called *Meng-chi Tou-le* (Macedonia–Tyre). The *Hou Hanshu* reports: 'the distant States of *Meng-chi* and *Tou-le* came to make their submission by sending envoys to bring tribute.'[18] The Chinese were informed that the route from *Meng-chi Tou-le* to the Han capital at Louyang covered a distance of more than 10,000 miles (40,000 *li*). This made these western territories the most distant region in contact with the Chinese regime and placed *Meng-chi Tou-le* within the Roman Empire.

The Maes merchants followed the protocol practised by foreign envoys and were permitted into the imperial palace to offer ceremonial submission to Emperor He. The group was carrying lightweight silks that had been rewoven in Syrian workshops and had some imperial gold coins that bore the image of the Roman Emperor. The *Hou Hanshu* reports that the representatives from *Meng-chi Tou-le* 'brought silks and the gold seal of their ruler'.[19] There were dozens of visiting envoys offering tribute at this time and the Maes group were accepted as just another party of exotic foreigners from a minor power on the western edge of Asia. They would have received the finest Han silks as diplomatic gifts before being escorted back to the Stone Tower to begin their long return journey to Syria.

The report written by Maes described a journey to the Far East that challenged the traditional view of Central Asia as a place occupied by monsters and cannibals. The expedition confirmed the existence of powerful and well-organized kingdoms on the eastern edge of Asia. This new awareness of China could explain a comment made by Juvenal when he complains that Roman women were interfering in traditional male interests by interrupting generals with the question, 'what are the intentions of the Chinese?'[20]

The Maes report suggested unique opportunities for the development of distant commerce and the advancement of Roman knowledge. For the first time Roman subjects in Syria and Egypt knew for certain that there was an oriental superpower in the Far East which manufactured large quantities of silk and steel. Reports of the Maes expedition spread through Roman Syria at a time when Roman Emperor Trajan was engaged in conquering Dacia (AD 101–106).

Perhaps knowledge of these distant contacts and the value of eastern commerce encouraged the Emperor to plan the conquest of Parthia.

The Antun Embassy

Chinese sources record that in AD 166 a Roman ship sailed around the Malay Peninsula and crossed the Gulf of Thailand to reach the South China Sea. The Roman crew then sailed north along the coast of Vietnam and docked at a Chinese military outpost called Rinan. Rinan was on the southern periphery of the Han Empire where the Red River flowed into the Gulf of Tonkin. Its Han commander allowed the Roman crew to come ashore and made arrangements for some of their personnel to be escorted to the Chinese court at Louyang.

This contact between China and Rome appears in a brief encyclopaedia-like entry in the *Hou Hanshu* in the section marked 'Da Qin'.[21] The author was interested in descriptive facts and did not think it was relevant to explain the purpose of this contact. Unfortunately, this brief account is all that survives regarding this first meeting between the Han court and representatives from Rome. This event was a prime opportunity for the exchange of important commercial, cultural and technological innovations between the two ancient civilisations. But the contact had no long-term impact and Chinese accounts provide the only record of these Roman representatives reaching Han China. This suggests that the Roman crew may not have made it safely back to Egypt on a sea voyage that would have spanned a quarter of the globe and crossed 8,000 miles of ocean.[22]

The arrival of Roman subjects in China was probably connected with events in AD 162 when the Parthian King Vologases IV invaded the Roman client kingdom of Armenia and installed his own candidate on the throne. In response the Roman governor of neighbouring Cappadocia, Marcus Sedatius Severianus, marched his legion into Armenia to restore imperial order. But the Roman army was outflanked, encircled and massacred by a large force of Parthian horsemen. This meant that Emperor Marcus Aurelius was forced to declare a state of war between their regimes. After almost fifty years of peace on the eastern frontiers, the Roman and Parthian Empires prepared for full-scale military conflict.[23]

As the situation escalated, the Romans probably decided to threaten Parthian interests by making direct contact with powerful regimes in the distant east. This would have included the Kushan Empire in Afghanistan and the Caspian kingdom of Hyrcania which had split from the main Parthian realm. The usual route chosen for this type of diplomatic contact was through Egypt and its Red Sea connection with India. Roman businessmen were probably given state messages to deliver to foreign rulers and envoys from distant kingdoms were offered safe passage on Roman trade vessels sailing to and from the Indus region.

These contacts had proved important in the reign of Nero when the Roman legions fought Parthian-backed forces for control of Armenia (AD 58–63). Roman successes in this war were aided by eastern conflicts that drew Parthian military manpower away from the Armenian campaign. Tacitus reports, 'Our successes were more easily gained because the Parthians were fully occupied with the Hyrcanian War. The Hyrcanians sent messages to the Roman Emperor asking for an alliance and as a pledge of goodwill they explained how they had detained the Parthian King in the east.' For their return journey, these envoys were given quarters on the Roman ships that sailed from Egypt to the Indus kingdoms. Tacitus explains how the Roman commander Corbulo 'was concerned that the deputies would be intercepted at the enemy's outposts when they crossed the Euphrates. So he gave them an escort and conducted them down to the shores of the Red Sea and they returned safely to their native lands by avoiding Parthian territory.'[24] These envoys would have travelled through the Kushan Empire from the Indus kingdoms to the northern frontiers of Afghanistan and from there to Hyrcania on the eastern shores of the Caspian Sea.

The Romans probably used this same merchant network in AD 163 to contact distant regimes opposed to Parthian rule. But this time it seems that the Emperor decided to contact the Seres (Chinese) and send Roman representatives to the Far East. Perhaps Marcus Aurelius wanted to establish contact with the mysterious steel-equipped empire described by Maes Titianus.

In the spring of AD 163 the co-emperor Lucius Verus arrived in Syria to prepare the Roman legions for war against Parthia. Around the same time arrangements were made for a Roman delegation to sail from a Red Sea port in Egypt to contact the Seres. Their first point of contact was the Kushan Empire which had dealings with China via the overland Silk Routes. But by this period the Tarim kingdoms were no longer subject to Han rule and the Kushan could not guarantee safe passage through Central Asia.

An alternative route to China was to cross the entire Indian Ocean and sail around the Malay Peninsula to reach the Gulf of Thailand and the South China Sea. Indian merchants had recently discovered this route when they explored the north coast of Vietnam. Han accounts record that in AD 160 a regent from one of the Indus kingdoms managed to send envoys to southern China using this new maritime route.[25] The discovery of this sea passage offered an important new avenue for long-range diplomatic and commercial contacts. The Roman envoys, who were probably senior merchants, were sent east by Marcus Aurelius to confirm the existence of this route and establish direct contact with the Han government.

The Romans spent the winter of AD 165 in an eastern port before resuming their voyage at the onset of the summer monsoon winds in AD 166. From Burma they sailed 1,000 miles down the Malay Peninsula and through the treacherous Malacca Strait to enter the Gulf of Thailand. From Thailand it was 500 miles to the southern tip of Vietnam and then a further 1,000 miles around the southeast coast of Asia to reach Rinan on the southern edge of the Han Empire. Rinan was a Chinese military outpost established close to where the Red River flowed into the Tonkin Gulf (near modern Hanoi). The Roman crew probably arrived at Rinan in the late summer of AD 166, after spending over fourteen months at sea or in various foreign ports.

Rinan was managed by a Han administrator who oversaw Chinese interests in the region and had authority over the local rulers. In AD 166 the Han government had just restored order in the Rinan Commandery following a brief series of military mutinies.[26] Consequently the Romans who arrived at the port would have seen numerous military personnel dressed in strange uniforms and carrying unfamiliar weaponry. The travellers must have realised that they were dealing with a large militarized empire similar to Rome.

The Chinese commander at Rinan recognised the significance of the Roman visitors and they were immediately dispatched under guard to Louyang, along with cargo samples removed from the ship. The journey from Rinan to Louyang was more than 1,200 miles which is almost the same distance as from Egypt to Italy. Travel across China was conducted mainly through a network of large roads and the Roman group would have been conveyed in official carriages accompanied by a small escort of Chinese cavalry. The main Chinese highways were over 50 feet wide which made them twice the size of the largest Roman roads. A paved lane in the centre of these highways was reserved for state carriages and dispatch riders. Postal offices were situated on the main routes and these managed the conveyance of messages and kept records of dispatches. Every 6 miles there were Cantonal offices staffed by soldiers who policed the area and monitored traffic. At 10 mile intervals, postal stations provided couriers and state officials with fresh horses and offered facilities for overnight accommodation.[27] But even with these advantages, the journey north to the inland capital of Louyang must have taken several weeks of fast-paced and relentless travel.

On their way north the Romans would have seen the tall watchtowers in the Chinese countryside which served as multi-storey grain silos. They also had an opportunity to observe the formidable defensive walls that surrounded Han cities. These cities had none of the monumental stone-built classical buildings that a Greek or Roman might expect to see in an important urban centre. Instead, the upper stories of the largest Chinese buildings were constructed entirely from ornately carved wood supporting bright terracotta tiles.

The Roman travellers would have noticed other cultural differences. In China thick silk fabrics were worn by poor people of low status, including orphans and widows who were offered basic clothing as handouts by the state. High quality steel was a rarity in the Roman Empire, but in China it was used both for battle-gear and common work tools. In Roman domains the image of the Emperor was widely produced on coins, army emblems and public statues. But the Chinese did not display reverence in the same manner. During their weeks of travel through China the Roman envoys might have wondered if the Han Emperor would be a soldier-general like Trajan, or perhaps a philosopher statesman like Marcus Aurelius.

When the Romans reached Louyang they were probably taken to an administrative headquarters within the imperial palace for assessment. China was managed by a vast civil service and the Han palace complex in Louyang resembled a self-contained city filled with scholars, archivists, ministers and bureaucrats. Han officials might have summoned translators from the Indian merchant community resident at Louyang, or perhaps asked assistance from one of the Buddhist temples that had been established within the city. There were also members of the Parthian nobility living in Louyang who were associated with Silk Route commerce and the propagation of Buddhism.[28] The sight of Han officials in the company of these Parthian nobles would have been highly disconcerting for the Roman envoys.

After careful questioning, the Roman delegates were granted an audience with the Han Emperor and summoned to the inner court. As part of this protocol the Han officials subjected the Romans to a list of stock questions designed to ascertain the scale and character of their regime. According to Chinese records the delegates claimed to represent '*Antun*' which is a reference to the ruling Roman household and the Emperor Marcus Aurelius Antoninus. The Chinese recognised that Rome had a ruling political family similar to the Han dynasty and shortened the dynastic name Antonine to '*Antun*'.

The Antonine delegates confirmed that there was a direct overland route to the Roman Empire that passed through Parthian territory. They told the Chinese that the Roman regime had been trying to send representatives to China, but their efforts had been blocked by the Parthians who wanted to maintain control of the overland silk trade. Further questions concerned the profits that Roman merchants made from their trade ventures to India. The Chinese probably asked the envoys about the military strength of the Roman Empire as this is an important feature in most Han reports concerning foreign powers. However the envoys did not reveal Roman military numbers or explain their methods of warfare. Maybe they thought it was unwise to disclose this information to a foreign power, or perhaps the presence of Parthians in the Han court inhibited their response.

It was customary for embassies to offer exotic and expensive diplomatic gifts to foreign rulers as tokens of respect and measures of prestige. Even trade delegations followed this practice in order to begin successful commercial negotiations with foreign governments. However it seems that the Antonine group had no valuable ambassadorial gifts to present to the Han court and no high-value Roman merchandise to hand over as diplomatic offerings. This cannot have been an oversight, so the Romans may have lost their prepared gifts during some previous encounter. Perhaps they were compelled to part with these items by some foreign ruler at one of the eastern kingdoms they had visited on route to China. This could have been the price they paid for a safe-harbour during the preceding winter.

In place of Roman gifts they offered the Han Emperor the cargo samples that had been removed from their ship and conveyed to the palace at Louyang. These items were a collection of ordinary eastern merchandise that disappointed the Han officials. Based on existing reports from the silk routes, the Han were expecting to receive gemstone jewellery, objects fashioned from delicate red coral, or exquisite western fabrics dyed vibrant colours. The *Hou Hanshu* records: '*Antun* the ruler of *Da Qin*, sent envoys from beyond the frontiers to reach us through Rinan. They offered us elephant tusks, rhinoceros horn, and turtle shell. This was the very first time there was ever communication [between our countries].'

The Antonine envoys offered no explanation for their lack of appropriate diplomatic gifts and this caused concern in the Han court. All previous reports collected by the Han government suggested that Rome was as powerful as the

Chinese Empire, so the absence of suitable diplomatic offerings was suspicious. This was viewed as a possible lack of commitment by the Romans, or a sign that their empire was not as wealthy as existing reports claimed. The *Hou Hanshu* comments, 'The tribute they brought was neither precious nor rare, raising suspicion that the accounts of Rome might be exaggerated.'[29]

In 1885 a German scholar named Friedrich Hirth translated this passage and assumed that the Chinese were 'suspicious' about the delegates. He suggested that the envoys were opportunist Roman merchants who offered trade cargo as diplomatic tribute.[30] But the Han court had protocols for assessing foreign groups and the passage in the *Hou Hanshu* suggests the diplomats were on a genuine mission from the Emperor. An accurate reading of the ancient text suggests that the meagre gifts made certain Chinese officials doubt established reports describing the wealth and significance of Rome. This exchange of gifts concluded the meeting and the Antonine envoys were escorted back to Rinan and their waiting ship.

The Antonine delegates probably expected to spend the summer of AD 168 in India with their return to Roman Egypt scheduled for November of that year. Given these schedules, the Chinese anticipated further contacts from the Romans in AD 170. But no one returned, not even opportunistic merchants exploiting lucrative new opportunities. Chinese officials sought explanations for the lack of contact by Rome and drew attention to the condition of the gifts offered by the Antonine group. They accepted that the diplomats were genuine, but concluded that Rome was not as wealthy or as politically ambitious as their foreign informants had claimed.

However, if the Antonine delegates had returned safely to Egypt they would have found the Roman Empire in the midst of an unprecedented crisis. In AD 165 the Roman legions successfully invaded the Parthian Empire, captured the city of Seleucia and occupied Babylonia. But an unknown disease broke out amongst the troops during the winter months and this lethal sickness soon reached high levels of infection. The Roman army was forced to abandon the war and retreat back to Syria with many men still infected by the outbreak. Dio reports that the co-emperor Lucius Verus 'lost a great many of his soldiers through supply shortages and disease, but he made it back to Syria with the survivors'.[31]

The returning troops spread the disease into the main cities of the Roman Empire. The *Historia Augusta* claims that 'it was his fate that a disease seemed to follow Verus through whatever provinces he travelled on his return, until finally it reached Rome.'[32] This disease, known to academics as the 'Antonine Plague', quickly reached epidemic levels in many parts of the Empire. Major outbreaks kept reoccurring in previously affected regions, causing further distress and death to the Roman population. In AD 168 the imperial physician Galen had to treat an outbreak amongst the Roman army in northeast Italy. He reports, 'When I reached Aquileia the infection was at a greater intensity than previous outbreaks. The Emperors immediately went back to Rome with a few soldiers, while the majority had difficulty surviving and most perished.'[33] In AD 169, the co-emperor Lucius Verus died suddenly due to an undisclosed illness that might have been the disease, or a sickness caused by the toxic effects of preventative medicines.[34]

Galen documented the symptoms and effects of the disease which seems to have been a virulent new form of smallpox. The infection caused many deaths since the Roman population had no inherited resistance to this lethal strain. Possible death rates are suggested by papyrus documents recovered from Roman Egypt. Tax records for Socnopaiou Nesos confirm that between September AD 178 and February 179, a village with 244 male inhabitants lost seventy-eight men due to the disease. This is almost one third of the male population in a six month period.[35] A bronze plaque from Virunum, near the Noricum iron mine, gives a membership list for a local temple devoted to Mithras. In AD 183, the Mithraeum lost five of its ninety-eight members during a fresh outbreak of the disease.[36] Modern strains of the smallpox virus can leave survivors visually impaired or infertile, so many who recovered from the infection were left with serious disabilities that made them dependent on others, or vulnerable to further illness.

As the legions succumbed to disease, the Roman defences on the northern frontiers were overrun by Germanic invaders. Marcus Aurelius spent the remainder of his reign campaigning to restore the Roman Empire and safeguard its European frontiers. Unknown to the Romans, the same disease was spreading through the Far East and inflicting a similar death rate on the Chinese Empire. The *Hou Hanshu* records that in AD 162 one third of the Han army stationed on the northern frontiers died or were debilitated during the early stages of this pandemic.[37] International trade declined and long distance communications were no longer feasible as both empires suffered severe damage to their manpower. Hopes of alliance between distant empires were no longer achievable as the governments of China and Rome fought for individual survival in a world were devastating disease reduced settled populations and crippled entire armies.

Roman contact with Southern China

In AD 184 the Chinese Empire was destabilised by a major political uprising known as the 'Yellow Scarves Rebellion'. The rebels mobilized Chinese peasants and rural militia who wore yellow fabric around their heads to identify their allegiance to a revolutionary Taoist sect that practised faith-healing. To restore order the Han regime gave greater political, military and tax-collecting powers to provincial governors, local rulers and Chinese generals. These new warlords suppressed the Yellow Scarves rebellion and then fought to claim power for themselves (AD 196–208). China was split into three rival kingdoms with a warlord named Cao Cao ruling the northern half of the country (the Kingdom of Wei). South of the Yangtze River the lower provinces of China were divided between the Kingdom of Shu in the west and the Kingdom of Wu in the east. The Han dynasty officially ended in AD 220 when the weak and ineffective emperor Xian was forced to abdicate by the son of Cao Cao.

During this era the Roman Empire also suffered a period of serious political and economic instability as the population declined and imperial revenues diminished. This crisis included a civil war that threatened to split the Roman Empire into three rival domains (AD 192–197). Clodius Albinus seized power in Gaul, Pescennius Niger claimed Syria, while *Septimius* Severus gained Pannonia and Italy. When Severus successfully defeated his rivals he founded a new imperial dynasty that stabilised the Roman Empire for several decades (AD 198–235).

A Chinese text called the *Liang-shu* records how a Roman merchant named Lun reached southern China in AD 226. Lun could be the Greek name Leon phonically simplified by Chinese scholars.[38] Lun, or Leon, arrived aboard a Roman ship that sailed from Thailand around Vietnam to reach the Chinese Kingdom of Wu. On arrival he was questioned by the Chinese Prefect of Tonkin (northern Vietnam) and identified himself as a merchant specializing in long-distance trade. The Prefect of Tonkin sent Leon to Wuchang (modern Ezhou) which was the inland capital of the Wu Kingdom and the court of the regional Emperor Sun Quan.[39]

By AD 226 the Kingdom of Wu had reached a political and military stalemate with the powerful Kingdom of Wei in northern China. But Sun Quan wanted to expand his domains and was interested in extending his rule south into Cambodia and Vietnam. He had maritime interests in the East China Sea and was preparing an armada with 10,000 troops to invade the nearby island of Taiwan (AD 230).[40] Sun Qian may have been surprised to learn that the Roman Empire was still intact and functioning as a unified state at a time when China had split into three rival kingdoms. The *Liang-shu* reports that Sun Quan 'asked Lun for details about his native land and its customs and Lun prepared a report in reply'. The prospect of establishing political and commercial contacts with Rome must have been intriguing. The *Liang-shu* records that Sun Quan selected a Chinese officer named Liu Hsien to accompany Leon on his return journey to the Roman Empire.

While he was present at the Wu court, Leon expressed interest in some very small dark-skinned captives that had been seized by Chinese forces in Southeast Asia. Leon remarked that these people were rare and valuable in Rome, so Sun Quan gave twenty of the captives to him as a gift, possibly hoping to ensure the return of further Roman merchants to the Wu Kingdom. Leon left China around AD 227, but there is no record that his ship ever made it safely back to the Roman Empire. The vessel may have been wrecked by storms, attacked by pirates in the Gulf of Thailand, or perhaps succumbed to the paralysing calms in the Straits of Malacca. The *Liang-shu* recorded that 'Lun returned directly to his native land, but Liu Hsien must have died on the way.'[41] The contemporary Roman sources make no mention of this contact, or the arrival of any distant foreigners at the court of Severus Alexander (AD 222–235). Once again, an opportunity to establish direct political and commercial contacts had been lost.

Conclusion: The Silk Routes and the Economies of China and Rome

Han China and Imperial Rome were the largest and most prosperous empires in the ancient world, but according to a direct measurement, their territories were more than 3,000 miles apart. The intervening lands were subject to extreme conditions with some of the most inhospitable terrain on earth, including the steppe-like Hexi corridor, the scorching Taklamakan Desert in the Tarim Basin and beyond that the snowbound Pamir Mountains which merge into the Hindu Kush and the Himalayas. The arid landlocked country of Bactria was at the centre of the ancient Silk Routes and offered routes south to the Indus kingdoms or west towards the desert plains of eastern Iran. Travellers crossing Iran had to journey through barren mountain passes as they ascended the well-guarded Iranian Plateau. Even the journey from Babylonia to Syria was not a simple venture, but involved desert crossings through contested territories. The actual distance from the Chinese border to Rome traversed more than 5,000 miles as the route wound across Central Asia between impassable deserts, steppes and mountain ranges.

Sections of these Silk Routes were dominated by other major empires including the Xiongnu on the East Asian Steppe, the Kushan in Afghanistan and the Parthians in Iran. As a consequence, land-based Roman traders could not reach Central Asia and Chinese merchants were unable to journey directly into Roman domains. Instead, Silk Routes operated in segments with merchants from particular nations managing transport and trade operations across large territories. This international network enabled Chinese silk to reach Roman markets through a series of intermediaries that included urban populations from the Tarim oasis territories of Central Asia and Sogdians from Transoxiana. Roman merchants from Syria received eastern silks from Parthian dealers in Babylonia, but silks also reached Rome via the Indian Ocean and the Roman ships that visited city-ports in India and returned to Egypt with oriental fabrics.

The value of this international commerce is arguably more significant than its scale or cultural impact. Strabo reports that 120 Roman ships sailed to India every year and a Roman legal document called the *Muziris Papyrus* records that the cargo of one of these vessels was valued at just over 9 million sesterces. This evidence suggests that the Roman Empire imported more than a billion (1,000 million) sesterces worth of eastern goods per annum.[1] An inscription from a second century Palmyrene tomb-tower records how foreign goods worth 360 million sesterces were assessed for tax as they passed into Roman Syria.[2] This commerce was highly significant because Roman government imposed a quarter-value tax called the *tetarte* on all goods crossing the imperial frontiers. Consequently, international commerce was a major contributor to Roman revenues.

Comparing Revenues

The Roman Empire was maintained by its legions and this military structure was paid for by revenues that included land and poll taxes. For tax purposes the Roman regime periodically conducted a census to ascertain the population size and the distribution of wealth in its subject regions. A well-known reference to this practice occurs in the Christian *New Testament* when the Emperor Augustus issued orders that a census should be taken of all Roman-controlled territories expressed as 'a decree from Caesar Augustus, that all the world should be taxed'.[3] Provincial population details were available to imperial governors and Pliny offers his readers select details about a census that was conducted in Hispania Tarraconensis while he was in office (AD 72–74).[4] Hardly any of these population figures have been preserved in the surviving classical sources and modern scholars therefore have to estimate the size of the Roman population using other evidence, including guideline figures from much later historical periods. Most current estimates for the population of the Roman Empire therefore range from 45 to 60 million people.[5]

The surviving Chinese texts provide more precise information about population sizes in the Far East. A Chinese census report assembled in 2 BC records that the Han Empire had a population of 59.6 million people, living in 12.4 million households and cultivating 827 million *mou* of land (over 147,000 square miles).[6] Confirmation comes from a collection of ancient documents written on bamboo strips that were found at Yinwan in the coastal Shandong province of northeast China. These documents include administration and tax records for the Donghai Commandery and date to 15 BC. They record that the commandery (province) had a population of about 1.4 million people living in 266,000 households with over 5,500 square miles of land under cultivation.[7] Donghai Commandery therefore represented about one twenty-seventh of the cultivated land and one fortieth of the population ruled by the entire Han Empire.[8]

Most Chinese subjects paid more direct tax to central government than their Roman counterparts. Adult males between the ages of 15 and 56 paid an annual poll tax of 120 cash to the Han government (a sum that could be earned in about four or five days of well-paid work).[9] Han authorities also collected a land tax of one thirtieth on agricultural harvests and this was often paid in grain. Every year about 500,000 men reached an age when they became eligible for military service, but the Han Empire needed only a fraction of this manpower for its regular army.[10] The government therefore allowed potential conscripts to purchase their freedom by paying an annual commutation rate along with their standard poll tax.[11] Merchants also had to pay higher-rate poll taxes, but the Han government did not impose expensive custom taxes on goods crossing their imperial frontiers.

A further source of Han state income was an annual gold offering made by fief-holders who had been granted titles and land by the imperial government, along with the right to collect taxes from subject rural communities.[12] The Han Empire also maintained monopolies on vital industries including the production of salt which was an essential element for the preservation of foodstuffs. In addition, in certain periods the early Han Empire managed the iron production required for the manufacture of most weapons, tools and agricultural implements.[13] These monopolies allowed the government to regulate prices and generate substantial revenues from market requirements.[14]

The Yinwan documents provide further information about provincial revenues in the Han Empire. The documents record that the annual revenue collected by Donghai Commandery was 266.6 million cash and 506,600 *shi* (16,474 tons) of grain. From this figure 145.8 million cash and 412,600 *shi* had already been spent in the commandery with the remainder to be stored, or forwarded to other administrative centres.[15] This meant that, after provincial costs were met, just under half of the cash and about one fifth of the grain gathered in the region would be transferred to central government.

In the first century AD, a Chinese courtier and philosopher named Huan Tan wrote a study called the *Xinlun* which records the revenues of the Han Empire. Huan Tan suggests that the Han government collected taxes worth more than 4 billion cash, with about half of this figure spent on paying the salaries of civil servants and the remainder stored in the treasury for ongoing state initiatives. According to Huan Tan, the Han Emperor also maintained his own imperial treasury which received an income of about 8.3 billion cash per annum.[16] This suggests that the total annual revenues of the Han Empire were about 12.3 billion in cash.

At a basic level, money could be viewed as a medium used to secure resources and human effort. Chinese revenue figures can therefore be converted into Roman equivalents by comparing the basic cost of hiring a soldier or labourer. In the early Roman Empire, one silver denarius was worth four large brass sesterces and this sum could buy a day's labour from an adult male.[17] Each sesterce contained about 28 grams of a bright golden-coloured brass called *orichalcum*. *Orichalcum* consisted of about 80 per cent copper and 20 per cent zinc. In Han China the main currency was a small bronze coin called the *wushu* and about twenty of these coins could secure a day's labour.[18] Each *wushu* contained 3.2 grams of bronze formed from 90 per cent copper and 10 per cent tin. This means that, as a rough calculation, Han revenues worth 12.3 billion in Chinese currency would be equivalent to about 2.5 billion Roman sesterces.

Classical evidence suggests that by the late first century AD the Roman regime had an income of about 1.1 billion sesterces per annum.[19] These calculations therefore suggest that the Han government was receiving revenues from their empire which were almost double the income of the Roman regime. But each empire had different costs and levels of responsibility for regional administration. For example, the Han government appointed administrators to manage tax collection and civic spending in provincial cities. By contrast, the Romans often left civic administration to the local elite in their subject provinces. These people would be responsible for taxing their own populations and, after extracting collection costs and profits, they would forward the agreed amount of tribute to the Roman government.

The Han government probably received sizable funds from most of its forty main provinces as many of these regions had been part of well-administered Chinese kingdoms for centuries. For example, the Han administration in Donghai Commandery collected the equivalent of 53 million sesterces of tax from its population. Cash equivalent to 29 million sesterces was spent locally with funds worth 24 million sesterces forwarded to Louyang.[20]

The early Roman regime had to operate under different conditions as large parts of its empire consisted of newly conquered tribal territories with little pre-established urban infrastructure. There were about fifty provinces in the Roman Empire, but ancient accounts suggest that once local expenses were met, most of these regions sent less than 4 million sesterces to Rome.[21] Celtic and German territories in northwest Europe had no long-term history of civic administration in monetised economies, so early revenues from these regions appear to have been comparatively low.[22] Furthermore, the Romans extracted only moderate revenues from most of the territories they captured in the eastern Mediterranean. Suetonius suggests that the Roman treasury received only about 5 million sesterces per annum from the small subject kingdom of Commagene in Asia Minor.[23] This is about a quarter of the funds that the Han government in Louyang could receive from a single Chinese province.

The Romans imposed tribute on subject peoples as a symbol of submission and they punished revolt by increasing their demands for money and materials. Tribute amounts were fixed by longstanding agreements, so this meant that the imperial regime did not necessarily derive greater revenues from a country that became more prosperous under Roman rule. The Roman regime imposed low-rate taxes of about one fortieth (2.5 per cent) on goods crossing provincial boundaries and this meant that internal trade did not raise large amounts of revenue.[24] For example, the provinces that comprised Gaul needed to export goods worth 40 million sesterces in order to raise 1 million sesterces for the Roman regime.

The ancient evidence suggests that the Romans demanded only a moderate amount of tribute from most of its subject territories. This meant that only a small amount of central government tax was taken from ordinary individuals. The *New Testament* suggests that the Roman poll tax (*tributum capitis*) paid by adult males was only 1 denarius per annum (worth 4 sesterces or a single day's labour).[25] This meant that 1 million men might raise only 4 million sesterces in poll tax revenue and population increases would need to be very large to significantly increase Roman revenues.

Property taxes also seem to have been comparatively low in most Roman provinces. Appian reports that Roman subjects in Syria had to pay an annual land tax (*tributum solis*) set at only 1 per cent of their assessed wealth.[26] Roman land taxes would have been collected as coin value or as an equivalent quantity of agricultural product that could then be transferred to nearby garrisons, or sold on the open market. Tacitus mentions grain taxes in Roman Britain and Josephus describes how rebels in Judea seized grain from 'imperial granaries' during the Jewish revolt of AD 66.[27]

Tribute levels were set by historic agreement and this meant that an increase in regional population or property wealth did not necessarily increase Roman revenues. Instead, an increase in regional agricultural prosperity or population meant that smaller contributions were required from each individual. Census reports revealed these demographic changes to central government, who then responded by reducing or removing some of the tax burden imposed on certain communities. Sometimes entire cities were offered exemption from these taxes as a special reward or privilege. In AD 70, Vespasian granted the inhabitants of Caesaria Martima exemption from *tributum capitis*, while his successor Titus removed their obligation to pay *tributum solis*.[28]

In the early imperial period, Roman citizens did not have to pay *tributum capitis* and soldiers who received their pay from the state were also exempt from this tax. This was significant because most of Hispania, Gaul and Britain had no towns or cities before the Romans conquered these regions. Northern Europe was urbanised by Roman occupation and many of the earliest towns and cities developed around forts and veteran colonies. Rome regarded tribute as money extracted from subject people for the benefit of Roman citizens. Consequently these new urban centres were not considered to be tax-producing assets by central government, even if they developed into cities.

The Roman economy also contained large-scale imbalances concerning food production. The Crimea produced over 84,000 tons of grain per annum which was enough to feed over 200,000 people.[29] Much of this grain was exported to large Greek cities in the eastern Mediterranean that could not otherwise have maintained their population size and density with locally grown produce. The city of Rome had a population close to a million, but this was sustained by a government-issued grain dole offered to select male citizens.[30] About 200,000 citizens were eligible for a dole that provided more than their basic needs and consisted of enough grain to feed 400,000 people in the capital.[31] The annual dole included 88,000 tons of grain shipped from farms on costal North Africa and the Nile Valley in Egypt.[32] According to Josephus, almost a third of this grain, 29,000 tons, was Egyptian produced.[33] As Tacitus observed, 'It is not a barren soil which causes distress in Italy. We prefer to cultivate Africa and Egypt, and trust the life of the Roman people to ships with all their risks.'[34]

The first interruption to this system occurred in the third century AD when a Germanic people known as the Goths migrated from forested lands on the Baltic coast of northern Europe to the upper Black Sea region. They occupied the Pontic steppe and settled near the Danube River where they introduced agriculture and adopted cavalry practices from the mounted Scythians. In the mid-third century AD the Goths launched ships to raid Roman ports on the Black Sea coast while their armies overran the Crimea and conquered the Kingdom of Chersonesos.[35] As a consequence the food resources and population potential of the Crimea were transferred from Roman to Gothic control. Between AD 322 and AD 336 the Emperor Constantine conducted campaigns against the Goths and Sarmatians to force these nations to submit to Rome.[36] As a result the new Gothic realms eventually became allies of the Empire, but they remained beyond direct Roman administration.

Roman Revenues

The best evidence for Rome's provincial revenues comes from the Late Republic. Plutarch records that the Roman state received a total income worth 340 million sesterces after Pompey annexed Syria and most of Asia Minor (60 BC).[37] This figure increased when Caesar imposed tribute payments worth 40 million sesterces on newly conquered Gaul (50 BC).[38] But ancient evidence suggests that the tribute received by Rome was moderate and did not greatly increase over time. As an example, Philostratus describes how the Romans extracted tribute worth 28 million sesterces from their province in western Asia Minor.[39] This is almost the same amount of tribute that the Persian Empire demanded from this region when they had ruled the territory six centuries earlier.[40]

The province of Egypt was an exception because it was treated as though it were an imperial estate. Its large population was intensively managed and the region produced high levels of transferable revenue. Strabo confirms that Ptolemaic Egypt produced revenues worth 300 million sesterces for its kings and even higher sums were extracted by Rome.[41] Josephus suggests that by the mid-first century AD, with the full development of Indian Ocean commerce, Egypt provided the Roman state with over 570 million sesterces of revenue per annum.[42]

Tribute could remain low in most provinces because the Roman government met its costs by minting coins from newly mined bullion. Strabo describes how state-owned mines in southern Spain provided the Roman Republic with more than 39 tons of silver per annum (worth 36 million sesterces).[43] Pliny records that by AD 73, Roman gold mines in Hispania were producing more than 7 tons of gold per annum (worth 80 million sesterces).[44] This suggests that the Roman state received more than 120 million sesterces worth of bullion from its mines. This bullion could produce enough precious metal coinage to pay the costs of ten Roman legions or about a third of the entire imperial army.[45]

Roman tribute levels could also remain low because the state received enormous profits from taxing international commerce. Maritime Indian imports worth more than a billion sesterces must have raised at least 250 million sesterces in Egypt as part of the *tetarte* tax. Goods brought through Palmyra worth 360 million sesterces would have generated revenues worth 90 million sesterces for Roman tax collectors at Antioch and other Syrian cities.[46] Added to these figures would be the tax value of Roman goods and bullion exported to Parthia, Arabia and India.

Comparing Expenses

There were other major differences in the state-systems that China and Rome developed to manage their empires. The Han regime paid salaries to a large bureaucratic staff to work for the central government in Louyang and serve in the provinces to collect tax and manage the administration of cities and rural communities. This civilian bureaucracy included more than 120,000 staff; as a comparison, the Roman army numbered 300,000.[47] This method of administration cost the Chinese government the equivalent of more than 400 million sesterces in wages per annum.[48]

In the Roman system, the Emperor's interests were managed by a large household-based network of citizen freedmen and administrative slaves. The Roman Empire also retained a senate consisting of about 600 ex-magistrates, each of whom met the required property qualification for office which was set at 1 million sesterces.[49] Outside Italy the Roman administration was primarily a military-based system with governors commanding the imperial forces in their designated territories. There were about 160 senior positions in the Roman provinces which were filled by senators and members of the lesser nobility known as *equites*, who had a property qualification of 400,000 sesterces.[50] These administrators were well-paid for their services, but they often used local military officials, or staff from their own households, to manage provincial affairs. Consequently, modern scholars calculate that the early Roman government could have spent as little at 75 million sesterces per annum on its 'civilian' employees.[51]

Recently scholars have estimated that the early Roman Empire spent at least 640 million sesterces per annum on its military.[52] This was the cost of about 300,000 career soldiers including legionaries, auxiliaries, the Praetorian Guard in Rome and the imperial navy. In total there were about thirty legions in the Roman army which, when at full strength, would have each consisted of about 5,000 legionaries and 5,000 auxiliary soldiers. Each legion cost about 11 million sesterces per annum to maintain, but a significant part of this cost was due to the generous discharge bonus paid to soldiers who had completed their twenty-five-years service contract. In the early imperial period the greatest concentration of Roman soldiers was on the Rhine frontier, which was maintained by eight legions at a cost of perhaps 88 million sesterces per annum. This is similar to the amount that the Chinese paid to the largest of the steppe nations as an incentive not to attack their northern frontiers.

The Han Empire spent less on its military institutions than its Roman counterpart. The Later Han Empire was divided into two main military forces known as the Southern and Northern Armies. The Southern Army was partly composed of Chinese peasants who were conscripted into short-term service. By contrast the Northern Army was structured around regiments of career soldiers who depended on conscript units for pre-planned offensive campaigns.[53] The Later Han also made extensive use of cavalry regiments formed from warrior-based steppe populations that had surrendered to Chinese authority and been permitted to settle on the frontiers.[54]

The Northern Army units that guarded Louyang included about 3,500 soldiers, compared with the nine cohorts of Praetorians stationed near Rome (4,500 troops).[55] Military bases on the Chinese frontiers could accommodate several hundred career soldiers and with the assistance of cavalry units, these troops were able to guard large stretches of the Han frontiers. Ancient documents found on the frontiers suggest that a force of 3,250 front-line career soldiers maintained the 620 miles between Dunhuang and Shuofang.[56] The northern frontier of China covered over 3,000 miles, so based on that density of troops, the Northern Army would have required 16,000 soldiers to protect this key frontier of the Han Empire. The Later Han also established several large military bases to monitor subject steppe populations settled close to the Chinese frontiers. The evidence suggests that each of these outposts included several thousand permanent soldiers.[57]

Infantry soldiers in Chinese frontier garrisons were paid about 600 cash per month.[58] Officers received considerably more and cavalrymen needed higher pay in order to maintain their horses. Some of these military wages might have been supplied as food or equipment, but the Chinese state still had to meet these expenses from resources raised by taxation or other means. A standing army of 25,000 career infantry would have cost at least 180 million cash per annum. This would be equivalent to 36 million sesterces in Roman currency, which represented the cost of almost three legions (30,000 men).[59]

When fully mobilized for war, a Chinese army including 200,000 conscripts would require pay and supplies worth over 1,440 million cash per annum (288 million sesterces). The cost of aggressive warfare was higher in the Far East because Chinese armies had to enter steppe lands or other remote territories to engage hostile nations who often fought as highly mobile mounted opponents. These campaigns involved the challenge of long-range supply issues and the huge costs involved in moving men and resources into marginal lands far from the productive core of the Empire. In the second century AD, the Han declared war against the Western Qiang who occupied lands on their Burma-Tibetan frontiers.[60] The total cost of this twelve-year war is attested as 24 billion cash or about 2 billion per annum.[61] This figure per annum is equivalent to about 400 sesterces in Roman currency, or about a third of the annual revenues that Rome received from its Empire.

Later sources suggest that the Emperor Diocletian significantly increased the size of the Roman army (AD 284–305). The Byzantine scholar John Lydus reviewed official figures from the fourth century AD and he reports that in this period the Romans had 389,704 soldiers and 45,562 troops serving in the fleet.[62] A list of Roman units contained in a work called the *Notitia Dignitatum* (*List of Offices*) suggests that the later Roman army might have had up to 500,000 soldiers if all its recorded units were active and at full military strength (AD 395–420).[63] By this period the Roman army was divided into static frontier troops based at garrison points and mobile field-armies able to conduct immediate campaigns.

Dominating the Steppe

The steppe nations were a serious threat to Chinese authority and frontier security. At its political height the Xiongnu ('Hun-nu') regime incorporated several leading steppe nations and was organized into twenty-four territorial divisions that could each provide up to 10,000 mounted warriors.[64] In times of war this manpower could be assembled into armies including several hundred thousand mounted warriors.

During two centuries of intermittent fighting the Han weakened the Xiongnu by conducting long-distance campaigns on the steppe to kill and capture the men and livestock that provided the regime with its military strength. Over time this diminished the regime allowing some of its more important subject nations on the outlying steppe to achieve independence. But the Han were not able to fully dominate the Xiongnu until the mid-first century AD when the nation was divided by a civil war and the southern faction requested Chinese aid. The Southern Xiongnu were accepted into Han service and eight of their clans, including up to 50,000 warriors, were allocated frontier territory in the Chinese Empire. The southern Chanyu Bei was ordered to establish his court under Han supervision in Xihe Commandery (Luliang, Shanxi). The newly subject Xiongnu offered military service in return for the guarantee of large-scale economic subsidies from the Han government including food, clothing and coined money.[65]

The Northern Xiongnu faction was destroyed in subsequent military action as Chinese commanders led further expeditions into the outer steppe. The decisive engagement, known as the Battle of Ikh Bayan, was fought in AD 89 near the Altai Mountains. In this battle a Chinese force of 46,000 cavalry, including 30,000 Southern Xiongnu allies, defeated the northern Chanyu and forced his surrender.[66] Further campaigns in the following years caused the remaining northern Xiongnu to flee westward into parts of the Central Asian steppe that were beyond the reach and knowledge of the Chinese Empire.[67]

After the collapse of the Xiongnu Empire, a steppe nation called the Xianbei became the leading regime in Mongolia. The Xianbei were former subjects of the Xiongnu who lived on the Manchurian prairies on the eastern edge of the Asian steppe. But as the Xiongnu Empire fragmented they gained independence and began to extend their range and influence across Mongolia. The *Hou Hanshu* records that 'ever since the northern Xiongnu fled, the Xianbei have become powerful and populous, seizing all the lands previously held by the Xiongnu and claiming to have 100,000 warriors.' It was said that the Xianbei had better bladed steel and superior horse breeds and consequently, 'their weapons are sharper and their horses are faster than those of the Xiongnu.'[68]

Another steppe nation called the Wuhuan had a prominent place in Chinese strategies to protect its frontiers. The Wuhuan also originated in Manchuria and the *Hou Hanshu* claims that 'the language and culture of the Xianbei are the same as the Wuhuan.' The Wuhuan gained independence from the Xiongnu in 121 BC and, forming an alliance with the Chinese, they were permitted to settle along the Han frontiers. Their chieftains were given economic subsidies in return for long-term military service to help protect the Chinese frontiers from other steppe nations.[69]

The Chinese Empire recognised that war was an expensive prospect and it was therefore better to avoid large-scale conflict. Therefore, to maintain peace on the frontiers, the later Han regime paid large subsidies to foreign nations to buy their manpower for military service or to deter attacks. By the first century AD the Chinese were paying 101 million cash per year to the Southern Xiongnu on the Han frontiers and 270 million to the Xianbei on the Mongolian Steppe. Similar payments were made to the border-based Wuhuan nation and the Western Qiang on the southern frontiers of China (Tibet-Burma).[70] Payments worth 740 million cash were equivalent to about 148 million sesterces in Roman currency. This sum would have paid the salaries of a large standing army, the equivalent of thirteen legions, except that the Han considered it safer and more economical to purchase peace.

The early Chinese and Roman Empires each faced different military, political and financial challenges. Both regimes had to raise substantial revenues in order to finance state administration and create a military infrastructure that could prevent internal unrest and deter foreign invasion. The Romans met these demands by spending large sums on a vast professional army while the Chinese maintained a smaller military structure and made tribute payments to external powers to ensure peace and stability on their frontiers. Silk produced in Chinese workshops had a unique international value and this gave the Han a valuable renewable resource, other than precious metal, to pay border troops and bribe foreign regimes.

The Chinese established a large and expensive bureaucracy that could manage the high levels of tax revenue extracted from its subjects. By contrast the early Roman Empire generated much of its required income from mining precious metal bullion and taxing the international commerce that developed between its territories and the eastern world. Commercial taxes financed the Roman regime, but the bullion that their merchants spent at trade centres in Babylonia, Arabia and India was a finite resource. Trade imbalances ensured that the Roman Empire could not sustain its original prosperity or adapt to the challenges of late antiquity. Crucially, the Roman military failed to master steppe warfare and consequently the appearance in Europe of a steppe nation from East Asia was to cause the collapse of their empire.

Xiongnu, Huns and the End of Empire

In the fourth century AD an offshoot of the Xiongnu (*Hun-nu*) nation moved west onto the Pontic-Caspian Steppe. This Xiongnu faction, known to the Romans as the Huns, defeated the Alani and conquered the populous Gothic realms in Eastern Europe. In the process they caused a major refugee movement into Europe which destabilised the Roman Empire. Over the following century the Huns launched devastating attacks on Roman territory that destroyed frontier defences and eventually caused the downfall of the Western Roman Empire (AD 476).

This westward movement of Xiongnu people occurred in a period of Chinese history known as the Sixteen Kingdom Era (AD 304–439). The Sogdian Letters record how the resurgent Xiongnu (*Xwn* = Hun) overran northern China in AD 312 and sacked the walled capital Louyang.[71] The attack was led by a southern Xiongnu faction who called themselves the 'Han Zhao' because their leaders claimed to be descendants of the Han dynasty princess that Chanyu Modu had received as his royal bride. With an army of 50,000 steppe warriors the Han

Zhao also sacked the former capital Chang'an, capturing two Jin Emperors during the course of their campaigns (AD 304–319).[72]

As a consequence the northern domains of China fractured into numerous small kingdoms formed from various nations and dynasties that had once been Chinese subjects. Some of these states and their successors existed in steppe territories ruled by warlords descended from the Southern Xiongnu. This included the Northern Lang in the Hexi Corridor, the Northern Tiefu of Inner Mongolia and the Kingdom of Xia in the Ordos Loop. Between AD 351 and AD 376, a powerful frontier regime known as Former Qin began to conquer its warring rivals, but it was the Northern Wei that achieved overall victory and established control over northern China (AD 386–534).

The Northern Wei governed with Chinese-style administration and promoted their regime using Buddhist ideologies. But their ruling dynasty was descended from Xianbei warlords so the regime possessed numerous skilled cavalry that could campaign on the steppe. Their rise to power prompted a migration of Xiongnu factions westward towards the Caspian steppe. A Chinese text called the *Weishu* (*History of the Northern Wei*) records that by the start of the fourth century 'the remains of the Xiongnu descendants' were to be found northwest of the steppe-dwelling Rouran who by that period occupied most of Central Asia.[73]

One of these Xiongnu groups called themselves the 'White' clan which was the symbolic colour of the West in their ancient culture.[74] The Roman historian Ammianus confirms that this subgroup followed a migration route into Transoxiana where they threatened lands subject to the Sassanid Persian Empire (AD 356).[75] The Persians called these invaders 'Chionites', but the Indians referred to them as 'Huna'.[76] The Chionites quickly overran Bactria and the Byzantine scholar Faustus records how in AD 368 the Persian King recruited Armenian troops into his armies to try to defend his eastern provinces.[77] Writing in the sixth century the Byzantine scholar Procopius calls these invaders 'the Hephthalite Huns, who are called White Huns' and reports that 'they do not intermix with any of the other Huns known to us.'[78]

Another subgroup of Xiongnu (Huns) first appear in Roman accounts in AD 370 when they arrived in lands to the north of the Caspian Sea and crossed the Volga River. Coming from unknown territories, these Huns rapidly conquered the Alani and Goths who occupied steppe lands north of the Black Sea (Scythia). Zosimus reports that 'a barbarous nation, which had remained unknown until this time, suddenly made its appearance and attacked the Scythians beyond the Ister (Danube).' He claims that the Huns did not seem to be 'Scythians' and had no 'regal government'.[79] Claudian confirms that the Huns came from somewhere beyond the 'extreme eastern borders of Scythia'.[80] Ammianus explains: 'A hitherto unknown race of men has arisen from some hidden recess of the earth and like a tempest of snows from the high mountains they seize or destroy everything in their way.'[81]

The Huns had migrated to seek land and they arrived on the Pontic steppe with their wives, children, horses and wagons.[82] Zosimus explains that their warriors 'were not capable of fighting on foot, rarely walked, could not fix their feet firmly on the ground, but live perpetually, and can even sleep, on horseback'.[83] According to Roman accounts they possessed superior horses, greater skill at archery and demonstrated more persistence in their attacks than other steppe nations.

Some Roman accounts suggest that the Huns had a Mongolian ethnic element. Jordanes, the sixth century Byzantine historian, describes them as being 'tanned with a large head that is not distinct. Their eyes are small resembling a pin head.' He reports that male Huns ritually scarred their faces with blades as displays of mourning enacted at funeral services.[84] Procopius also suggests that the Huns had a distinctive haircut that was copied by the riotous gangs who watched chariot races in Constantinople. The Hun haircut was achieved by 'clipping the hair short on the front of the head down to the temples, then letting it hang down in great length and disorder at the back'.[85]

Jordanes reports that the Huns were 'short in stature with fast physical movements, alert horsemen, broad shouldered and primed in the use of bow and arrow, with firm-set necks held erect with pride'.[86] Ammianus offers a similar account, describing the Huns as possessing 'compact bodies, strong limbs and thick necks'. He suggests they were disfigured by a lifetime of horse-riding and walked awkwardly when they dismounted.[87] Sidonius compared the Huns to the centaurs of classical mythology describing how they learnt to ride as soon as they could walk. He reports, 'You would think that the limbs of man and horse are fused together so firmly does the rider always move with the horse; other people are carried on horseback, but these people live there.'[88] Ammianus reports that even their war councils were conducted while mounted and 'when deliberation is required regarding important matters, they all consult as a common body on horseback.'[89]

Hunnic horses were considered superior to the western breeds used by Scythians on the Pontic Steppe and Roman cavalry in Europe. A Roman named Vegetius wrote a study on veterinary medicine in which he lists the characteristics of these horses. They had 'large hooked heads, protruding eyes, narrow nostrils, broad jaws, strong and stiff necks, manes hanging below their knees, overlarge ribs, curved backs, bushy tails, great strength in their cannon bones, small pasterns, wide spreading hooves, hollow loins, angular rumps without fat or muscles, a back stature that is long rather than high, drawn in belly and large bones.' This exactly describes the horses used by Central Asian steppe nations.

Roman horses were expensive to maintain since they had to be kept warm in stables and required frequent veterinary attention. Vegetius explained that Hunnic horses did not need stables and could endure greater cold and hunger without distress. They were also longer-lived and less prone to injury than their Roman counterparts. Hunnic breeds were also better able to bear wounds due to their quiet and sensible temperament. Therefore in the opinion of Vegetius they held 'first place among horse breeds in their fitness for war'.[90]

Hunnic Conquests

Skilled Hun bowmen could outpace and outmanoeuvre armoured Sarmatian riders who specialized in cavalry charges carrying cumbersome lances. Jordanes reports that the Alani 'equalled the Huns in battle, but had different cultures, manners and appearance. The Huns exhausted them by their incessant attacks and subdued them.'[91] Zosimus confirms that their warriors overcame the western steppe-dwellers with continual attacks and 'by the rapidity with which they wheeled about their horses, by the suddenness of their excursions and retreats, shooting as they rode they caused a great slaughter among the Scythians.'[92] Claudian refers to their attacks which seemed 'disorderly, but had incredible swiftness, allowing the Huns to often return to the fight when little expected'.[93]

Ammianus describes how Hunnic warriors rode into battle in wedge-shaped masses while 'their medley of voices makes a savage noise.' They were 'lightly equipped for swift motion and unexpected action, they purposely divide suddenly into scattered bands and attack, rushing about in disorder here and there, dealing terrific slaughter.' The Huns surpassed all other warriors in the skill of their archery, but when the opportunity came, 'they can gallop over the intervening ground and fight hand-to-hand with swords.' They also lassoed their enemies throwing 'strips of cord plaited into nooses over their opponents, entangling and binding their limbs so they cannot ride or walk.'[94] Unlike the Chinese who possessed sophisticated crossbows, the Goths and Romans had no projectile weaponry that could easily outrange and target mounted Hunnic archers.

Ammianus records that within a few years the Huns 'had overrun the territories of the Alani,' they 'killed and plundered many of them, then joined the survivors to themselves in a treaty of alliance.'[95] This gave Hunnic armies Sarmatian cavalry equipped with scale and chain mail armour. After suppressing the Alani, the Huns moved west to attack the Goths who by the fourth century AD were a populous nation inhabiting agricultural territories stretching from the Baltic coast to the northern Black Sea. The Goths on the Pontic steppe had adopted cavalry practices, but they fought with spears instead of the sophisticated reflex bows used by the Scythians. Procopius explains that Gothic bowmen 'entered battle on foot under the cover of heavily armed men'.[96]

Gothic spearmen could not ride faster than Hunnic warriors, and even in close combat Goth riders could find it difficult to overcome Huns equipped with helmets and lamellar armour. Procopius describes how an elite Hun soldier 'was surrounded by twelve Goths carrying spears who all struck at him at once, but his corselet withstood the blows and he was not seriously injured until one of the Goths succeeded in hitting him from behind, in a place where his body was unprotected, above the right armpit'. This Hun was only wearing a helmet and jacket-like coat of chain or lamellar armour, since another spear-thrust wounded his exposed thigh.[97]

Roman sources suggest that it was difficult to unseat or kill a mounted Hunnic warrior. Sidonius describes a Hun who was speared by a lance, 'transfixed, his corselet was pierced front and back so that blood came throbbing through the two holes.'[98] Some Huns carried shields and Sozomen describes a Hunnic warrior leaning on his shield, 'as was his custom when parleying with his enemies'.[99] Grave finds suggest that some Huns practised the steppe custom of artificial cranial deformation and by binding the heads of their babies they encouraged the infant's skull to develop in an elongated shape.[100] Some Romans assumed that this practice was connected with warfare, to flatten the face and make it easier for warriors to wear helmets with broad nose-guards.[101] A few wealthy Huns gilded their armour, perhaps emulating the customs of the Aorsi who wore gold ornaments.[102] Asterius of Amasia reports that 'the armour of the barbarians is ostentatious' and describes a steppe chief on the Black Sea coast who offered his gilded cuirass to a Christian representative.[103]

When the Gothic kingdoms were defeated by the Huns, tens of thousands of refugee Goths and Alani fled south to seek protection in the Roman Empire. Ammianus reports that, 'exhausted by a lack of necessities they looked for a new homeland far from the savages and after much deliberation they chose Thrace as a suitable refuge, because it has very fertile soil and because it is separated by the mighty flood of the Danube from the lands exposed to war.' The Gothic realms were allied to the Roman Empire and Ammianus records how a large part of the defeated nation suddenly appeared on the banks of the Danube asking admittance into imperial territory.[104] Zosimus reports, 'The surviving Scythians (Goths and Alani) were compelled to abandon their homelands to the Huns and cross the Danube, they therefore appealed to the Emperor to receive them, promising to serve faithfully as soldiers.' Tens of thousands of Goths and Alani were admitted into the frontier provinces along with their families, but despite confiscation orders, many were able to bribe officials and cross the Danube carrying weapons.[105]

These refugees were confined to camps near the frontier, but they were offered limited supplies while they were systematically exploited and mistreated by various Roman officials. As a result the Gothic refugees rebelled and overran the Balkan countryside with raiding parties (AD 376–378). In AD 378 the Eastern Emperor Valens marched against the Gothic army, but he was outmanoeuvred by their steppe cavalry at the Battle of Adrianople.[106] The Emperor was killed along with most of the Eastern Field Army while their enemies 'plundered the dead bodies and armed themselves with Roman equipment'.[107]

The Goths dominated imperial politics throughout the following century as their various nation-states crossed the Empire to seize territories from imperial control. They overran rich agricultural territories, demanded tribute from Roman cities and captured various armouries and imperial workshops. The Visigothic chief Aleric boasted that the Roman province of Thrace forged spears, swords and helmets for his warriors.[108] Meanwhile the Huns moved westwards towards the grasslands of Hungary on the Danube frontier. In a few decades they had conquered and occupied a territory stretching over 1,700 miles from the Roman Danube to the Volga River.

The Threat to Rome

Theodosius I was the last Emperor to rule a unified Roman regime. In AD 393 he placed his 9-year-old son on the throne of the Western Empire under the guidance and protection of a senior general named Flavius Stilicho. Theodosius was then succeeded by his eldest son Arcadius who ruled the Eastern Empire from a bureaucratic court, while the western government fell under the authority of generals assisted by Gothic and Germanic warlords brought into regular imperial service.

Authorities in the Western Roman Empire sought alliances with the Huns who occupied large parts of Eastern Europe and the Pontic-Caspian steppe. By contrast the Eastern Roman Empire was a target for Hunnic raids, aggression and extortion. In AD 395 the Huns sent an army through passes in the Caucasus Mountains to raid the eastern Roman Empire. Jerome describes the sudden terror of these attacks as 'everywhere their approach was unexpected as their speed overtook any rumour of their coming and they spared neither religion, rank nor age.' Hunnic armies entered Armenia and rode south to plunder Syria, as the population of Antioch and Tyre retreated into their cities. Roman authorities suspected that the Huns might be planning to plunder gold from Jerusalem and wealthy citizens fled onto ships to avoid capture or death.[109] Jerome confirms the impact of these raids when he writes that 'the soldiers of Rome who are conquerors and lords of the world are subdued, tremble and withdraw in fear at the sight of those who cannot easily walk on foot.'[110]

The Huns then turned their attentions west and subjugated populations in central Germany prompting a further movement of displaced Germanic peoples into the Western Roman Empire. In AD 405 tens of thousands of Suebians, Vandals, and Alani crossed the Rhine frontiers along with their families to settle in Roman Gaul. Up to 80,000 Vandals migrated through Spain and in AD 429 they crossed into North Africa to seize the rich farmlands that supplied grain to Rome.[111]

During this period, military leaders in the Western Roman Empire recruited Hunnic warriors into imperial service as the elite bodyguards of senior commanders. The Western Emperor Honorius (AD 393–423) maintained 300 Huns in the Italian capital Ravenna and Stilicho, the *Magister Militum* ('Master of Soldiers'), was protected by a personal bodyguard of Hunnic troops.[112] In AD 409, the Emperor summoned a mounted force including 10,000 Hunnic allies to help defend Italy from an army of Visigoths who were threatening Rome. Zosimus suggests that the Romans found it difficult to feed and supply this number of horsemen and the riders withdrew allowing the Visigoths to sack Rome the following year.[113] In AD 425 a Roman commander named Flavius Aetius requested the support of a Hunnic army to decide a succession dispute in the Western Roman Empire. He led 60,000 allied Hunnic warriors into Northern Italy before negotiating a peace that allowed him to claim the title *Magister Militum.*[114] By this period Hunnic armies incorporated the strongest military traditions of their subject peoples and Jordanes describes their varied appearance including 'Suebi (Germans) fighting on foot, Huns with bows and the Alani forming-up into a heavy-armed battle-line'.[115]

In AD 445 a chief named Attila was proclaimed king of the Huns and, after unifying his subject peoples, 'he gathered a host of the other tribes under his power.' Jordanes describes Attila as 'short of stature, with a broad chest and a large head; his eyes were small, his beard thin and greying; and he had a flat nose and tanned complexion'. He was said to be 'enthusiastic for war, but restrained in action, mighty in counsel, gracious to suppliants and lenient to those who were received into his protection'.[116]

Under the command of Attila, Hunnic armies reduced the political and military strength of the Roman regime and caused the collapse of the Western Empire. Like the Xiongnu, the Huns wanted to dominate and extract wealth from their imperial rivals, rather than conquer or destroy them. It was said that when Attila captured the Italian city of Milan he saw a painting of the Roman Emperors sitting upon golden thrones and Scythians lying dead before their feet. He ordered the image redrawn to depict 'Attila upon a throne and the Roman Emperors heaving sacks upon their shoulders and pouring out gold before him'.[117] Attila's funeral oration was reported to have praised him as the chief who 'held the Scythian and German realms, terrified both Roman Empires, captured their cities and placated by their appeals, took yearly tribute in place of plunder'.[118]

Attila's attacks on the Eastern Roman Empire began in AD 441 when Hunnic armies crossed the Danube frontier and plundered the Balkans. The Huns had with them Roman captives with the engineering skills required to bridge rivers. They also brought numerous battering-ram siege engines that they mounted on large steppe-wagons. If threatened by attack, these heavy timber wagons could be quickly drawn into formation to create a fortress-like wooden stronghold. Priscus describes the siege of a fortified Roman city called Naissus when the Huns drove 'a vast number of siege engines' against the walls. Archers fired from wicker and hide-protected portholes in these wagons, forcing the defenders from the battlements, as the battering-rams were rolled forward. These rams consisted of a large metal-headed beam fixed to chains so that it could be drawn back with ropes, then swung forward with pendulum force. The walls of Naissus were battered down at numerous points, allowing the Huns and their Gothic allies to scale the rubble with ladders and plunder the city.[119] These sieges were rapid operations conducted with overwhelming force and in AD 443 the Huns threatened, but did not attack, the heavily-fortified imperial capital of Constantinople (Byzantium). Tens of thousands of Roman subjects, including many skilled urban tradespeople, were seized in their raids and conveyed to the Hunnic homelands in Hungary and the Pontic steppe. A Roman chronicle describes the conflict as 'a new disaster for the east: more than seventy cities were sacked while no assistance came from the troops of the Western Empire'.[120]

The Eastern Empire bought peace terms with the Huns for 6,000 pounds of gold and an agreement that a further 2,100 pounds of gold per annum would be given as tribute (equivalent to 8.4 million sesterces of first-century currency).[121] In addition, thousands of Roman prisoners were returned at a ransom of 8 gold *solidi* per person.[122] According to Priscus, 'these tributes were very heavy, as many resources and the imperial treasuries had been exhausted.'[123] Priscus reports: 'The Romans pretended that they had made the agreements voluntarily. But because of the overwhelming fear which gripped their commanders, they were compelled to accept gladly every injunction, however harsh, in their eagerness for peace.'[124]

Despite these protests the Eastern Empire had the capacity to pay further tribute and John Lydus reports that in AD 457 the treasury preserved 100,000 pounds of gold, 'which Attila, the enemy of the world, had wanted to take'.[125]

In AD 449 Priscus was selected by the government of the Eastern Roman Empire to lead an embassy to the court of Attila. He travelled to one of the Hunnic capitals north of the Danube which resembled a vast wood-built village the size of a Roman town. Attila's royal residence was constructed from close-fitting polished timbers and ornamental wooden boards and, although it had a perimeter adorned with towers, the complex was built 'for beauty rather than protection'. Priscus reports that a Roman captive taken from the city of Sirmium had built a heated bath-house at the site, confirming the new engineering skills then available to the regime. Attila received envoys and petitions and oversaw legal cases in his royal hall. Priscus records that one of his royal secretaries was a Roman administrator named Rusticius who was another war-captive, employed by the Huns because of 'his skills in speech and composing letters'.[126] Attila was also promoting his regime using motifs from Sarmatian religion and claimed to have discovered the sacred sword of the classical war god Mars (Ares).[127]

Another incident indicates the Hunnic capacity for acculturation. Priscus met a former Roman merchant in the Hunnic capital who spoke fluent Greek, but was dressed in full 'Scythian attire' and cut his hair in their distinctive style. The Greek explained he had been a wealthy inhabitant of Viminacium near the Danube River, but when the city was stormed he was captured and brought into Hunnic service. He had 'fought bravely in battles against the Romans' and with the spoils 'he had obtained his freedom according to the law of the Scythians.' He could have returned to the Empire, but he married a Scythian woman, had children by his foreign wife and continued to serve the Huns.[128]

While Priscus was attending the Hunnic court he spoke to visiting envoys from the Western Roman government about the threat posed by Attila. They explained to Priscus that 'no one who ruled over Scythia or any other land has achieved such great things in such a short time.' They warned that Attila 'rules all of Scythia, makes the Romans pay tribute and is aiming at greater achievements for he wants to engage the Persians and enlarge his territories'. The envoys explained that Media was no great distance from the Hunnic territories and the Huns knew the main routes through the Caucasus Mountains. They believed that Attila, 'with little difficulty and only a short journey, would subdue the Medes, Parthians, and Persians and force them to submit to the payment of tribute. For he has a military force which no nation can resist.' One of the envoys from Rome named Constantiolus warned that if Persia fell to the Huns, then Attila would dictate ruling terms on the Western Roman Empire. Constantiolus claimed, 'At present we bring Attila gold for the sake of his rank, but if he overwhelms the Parthians, Medes, and Persians, he will no longer endure the rule of independent Romans.'[129] But contrary to Roman expectations the Huns did not engage the Persian Empire as their next military target.

In AD 450 Attila received a pretext for war against the Western Roman Empire. Honoria, the disgraced half-sister of the Emperor Valentinian III, sent a marriage proposal to Attila. This union would have given Attila controlling interests in the imperial succession, but the marriage was refused by the Roman court who insisted that Honoria marry an aging senator. At the same time the Eastern Roman Empire withheld the annual gold tribute that it had agreed to pay to the Huns. Priscus reports that 'Attila was undecided who he should attack first, but resolved to begin with the greater war and advance against the West, since his fight there would be against Goths and Franks' who had fled Hunnic rule for Roman protection.[130]

In AD 451 Attila attacked the Western Roman Empire with a Hunnic army supported by large numbers of subject Goths (Ostrogoths) and Germans. His invasion force would have included more than 60,000 warriors, making it the largest field-army operating in the western world. Attila plundered cities in Gaul and 'launched a fierce assault with his battering-rams' on the heavily fortified city of Orleans.[131] In response the Western Roman regime formed an alliance with the Alani, Franks and Visigoths who occupied large parts of Gaul and viewed the Huns as their traditional enemies. The two armies fought a large-scale engagement at the Battle of the Catalaunian Plains that ended with stalemate and the withdrawal of the Hunnic army from Gaul.[132]

The following year the Hunnic army crossed the Alps and sacked the major cities in northern Italy before threatening Rome itself (AD 452). On this occasion the Roman regime could not obtain support from their Germanic allies and the remaining imperial units were unable to manage an adequate defence. Jordanes describes how the Hunnic army attacked the fortified city of Aquileia: 'Bringing forward all manner of war-engines, they quickly forced their way into the city, plundered it, divided the spoils and so cruelly devastated the place that scarcely anything remained.' He claims that the invaders 'devastated the largest part of Italy' before approaching Rome.[133] Pope Leo was chosen as the envoy to Rome and the western government was forced to agree peace terms that made their empire tributary to the Huns. Attila also reasserted his claim to an imperial marriage alliance and demanded the government surrender the princess Honoria, 'with her due share of the royal wealth'.[134]

The campaign had exhausted the Roman capacity for war and the regime was open to invasion and exploitation by further foreign powers. With the Western Empire subdued, Attila returned with his army to his Hungarian realm to plan new campaigns against the Visigoths and Alani.[135] He was also anticipating conflict with the Eastern Roman Empire as it was withholding the promised tribute payments to the Hunnic court. But in AD 453, on the night of his marriage to a German princess named Ildico, Attila suddenly died from a brain haemorrhage.[136] The fate of Honoria is not known and she may have remained in Rome under imperial custody. The death of Attila caused subject nations to rebel and his empire disintegrated in a series of conflicts. The Hunnic threat diminished, but by this period large parts of the Western Roman Empire were under the direct rule of Germanic nations who had conquered important territories, or been given land in return for military service. The last ever Emperor of Rome was a boy named Romulus Augustus who was deposed by a Germanic king named

Odoacer in AD 476. It had taken less than a century for a major steppe incursion with an influx of foreign refugees to destabilize, undermine and destroy the Roman Empire.

In antiquity the Huns were the largest and most significant population group to have travelled across the steppe from the Far East to the Roman frontiers, a journey of more than 5,000 miles. But during the long history of the silk routes many other unnamed, impoverished or dispossessed individuals passed through the empires of Central Asia as the consequence of conflict, slavery or commerce. Archaeologists excavating the ancient site of an imperial estate at Vagnari in southern Italy unearthed the graves of slave workers who had been involved in textile production during the first century AD. DNA testing of skeletal remains revealed that one of the men buried in the plot had Far Eastern ancestry inherited from his mother.[137] In spite of all the wealth associated the silk routes, his sole possesion was a plain wooden food bowl, placed next to his body for use in the afterlife. Whoever this man was and however his ancestors had found themselves in the very centre of the Roman Empire, he had ended his days as a slave and was burried in a simple grave on a bleak hillside.

APPENDIX A

Economic Figures

Roman currency
- 4 brass sesterces = 1 silver denarius.
- 25 silver denarii = 1 gold aureus.
- 1 day's labour = 1 silver denarius.

Cost of a Legion: 11 million sesterces before pay increase by Domitian (AD 81–96). After pay increase: 15 million sesterces.
- 5,000 Legionaries paid 1,200 sesterces annually = 4.5 million.[1]
- 5,000 Auxiliaries paid 1,000 sesterces annually = 3.75 million.[2]
- 66 officers = 1 million sesterces.[3]
- Discharge bonuses = 2 million.[4]

Military pay (per month)
- Rome: 1 gold aureus = 100 sesterces or 30 silver denarii = 120 sesterces.
- China: 1 silk bolt = valued at 600 cash.[5]
- 100–120 sesterces (Rome) = 600 cash (China).

Revenues (per annum)
- Han Empire: 12,300 million cash (= 2,500 million sesterces).[6]
- Roman Empire: 1,000 million sesterces (modern estimates based on state spending).

Roman state spending: 1,000 million sesterces (per annum)[7]
- Military: Legions and Auxiliaries, Praetorian Guard in Rome and Roman navy (300,000 soldiers) = 640+ million sesterces.
- Civilian employees (160 officials) = 75 million sesterces.
- Imperial hand-outs including *donatives* (occasional cash gifts to soldiers) = 44 million sesterces.
- Imperial building projects = 60 million sesterces.
- Emperor's Household and imperial gifts = 50–100 million sesterces.

Han state spending (per annum)
- Salaries to officials (120,285 officials): 2,000 million cash (= 400 million sesterces).[8]
- Northern Army including 25,000 career soldiers: 180 million cash (= 36 million sesterces).
- During periods of war an army including 200,000 conscripts: 1,440 million cash (= 288 million sesterces).

- Annual cost of war with the Qiang (Tibet-Burma): 2,000 million cash (= 400 million sesterces).[9]
- Payments to foreign powers: 800+ million cash (= 160+ million sesterces).[10]

Silk prices (Chinese Empire)

- Silk fragment from Dunhuang bearing the official stamp: 'A roll of silk from Kangfu in the Kingdom of Rencheng; width 2 *chi* and 2 *cun* (20 inches); length 40 *chi* (12 feet); weight 25 ancient *liang* (12.2 ounces); value 618 *qian* (coins)' = 20 square feet.[11]
- A bolt of plain silk (12 ounces) = 600 cash (one month's standard wage).

Silk prices (Roman Empire)

- Plain silk fabric baught from Persian suppliers (undervalued price) = 500 sesterces.[12]
- A pound of white silk in Roman markets (high price) = 1,000–2,000 sesterces.[13]
- State-assessed value for gold-embroidered silk chitons = 2,600 sesterces.[14]
- A pound of imperial silk = 4,500 sesterces.[15]
- Expensive silk dresses in Rome = 10,000 sesterces.[16]
- A pound of purple-dyed silk fabric = 24,000 sesterces.[17]

APPENDIX B

Economic Comparisons

Ancient Empires

- Han Empire: 36 Commanderies (202 BC).
- Roman Empire (Early Imperial): 40 provinces and 6 client kingdoms (landmass: 2 million square miles).
- Kushan Empire: Bactria, Arachosia, Indus Kingdoms and Northern India. (landmass 1.5 million square miles).
- Parthian Empire: 18 kingdoms (landmass: 1 million square miles).[1]

Chinese Donghai Commandery (one fortieth of the Han population)

- Tax in cash: 266.6 million cash (= 53 million sesterces with 29 million spent in region and 24 million sent to capital).
- Tax in produce: 43,000 tons of grain (35,000 tons used in region and 8,000 sent to Central Government).

Roman Provinces

- Annual revenues from the Kingdom of Commagene in Anatolia (AD 18–38): 5 million sesterces.[2]
- Annual tribute from Chersonesos Kingdom in Crimea (first century BC): 4.8 million sesterces.[3]
- The 'tribute-money from three provinces' = 10 million sesterces.[4]

Roman Mediterranean shipments

- Size of grain dole delivered to Rome: 88,000 tons.[5]
- Contribution of Egypt: 29,000 tons.[6]

Crimean shipments

- Crimea-Greece: 16,000 tons of cargo carried aboard 213 ships (75-ton capacity).[7]
- Tribute from Chersonesos Kingdom in Crimea (first century BC): 7,800 tons of grain.[8]

Roman Bullion Exports: 100 million sesterces

- Roman bullion exports to Southern Arabia, India and China (AD 75): 100 million sesterces.[9]
- Bullion exports to India including Hindu Kush Silk Routes: 50 million sesterces (gold and silver).[10]

APPENDIX C

The Han Economy

Han Empire

- Population (2 BC): 59.6 million people in 12.4 million households and 827 million *mou* (147,105 square miles) under cultivation.[1]
- Han military stores: 23 million items of military equipment, including 500,000 crossbows and over 11 million crossbow bolts.[2]

Han revenues (per annum): 12,300 million cash[3]

- Tax income valued as currency by Government Treasury: 4,000 million cash.
- Revenue received by Emperor's Treasury: 8,300 million cash.
- (Tax in produce: value = 6,000 million cash.)[4]

Revenues from Donghai Commandery (Shandong) (15 BC)[5]

- 1.4 million people in 266,000 households (one fortieth of Han population).
- 31 million *mou* (5,521 square miles) under cultivation.
- Tax income in coin: 266.6 million cash.
- Tax in produce: 506,600 *shi* of grain.
- Tax expended in region = 145.8 million cash and 412,600 *shi*.

Payments to foreign powers (AD 50–100): 800+ million cash

- Tarim regions: 75 million cash.
- Xianbei (Mongolian Steppe): 270 million cash.
- Southern Xiongnu (steppe frontiers): 101 million cash.[6]
- Wuhuan (Inner Mongolia): 101 million cash (?).[7]
- Qiang (Tibet-Burma): 270 million cash (?).[8]

Chinese silk payments to the Xiongnu

- 51 BC: 6,000 catties of silk floss and 8,000 silk rolls.
- 49 BC: 8,000 catties and 9,000 silk rolls.[9]
- 33 BC: 16,000 catties and 18,000 silk rolls.
- By 25 BC: 20,000 catties and 20,000 silk rolls.[10]
- By 1 BC: 30,000 catties (15 tons) and 30,000 silk rolls (12 tons) and 370 suits.[11]

APPENDIX D

Roman Revenues

Revenues of the Roman Empire: 1,150 million sesterces

Revenues (per annum): 640 million sesterces

- Revenues of the Roman Republic (61 BC): 300 million sesterces (340 million with silver production).[1]
- Tribute from Greater Gaul (newly conquered in 50 BC): 40 million sesterces.[2]
- Revenues of Roman Egypt: 300 million sesterces.[3]

Bullion Revenues: 120+ million sesterces (during periods of high-level production)

- Spanish silver mines: less than 39 tons of silver, worth 36 million sesterces.[4]
- Iberian gold mines (AD 73): more than 7 tons of gold, worth 80 million sesterces.
- Gold mine in Dalmatia (Croatia) (discovered in AD 55): 70 million sesterces worth of gold.[5]

Trade Revenues: 390+ million sesterces

- Value of imports India-Egypt: 1,104 million sesterces subject to quarter-rate customs tax (the *tetarte*) = 276 million sesterces.[6]
- Value of imports Persia-Syria (via Palmyra): 360 million sesterces subject to quarter-rate customs tax = 90 million sesterces.[7]
- Roman exports = at least 100 million sesterces subject to quarter-rate customs tax = 25 million sesterces.[8]

APPENDIX E

Military Capacities

Early Han Empire (206 BC–AD 9)

- Han army: up to 400,000 trained conscript soldiers.[1]
- 300,000 soldiers mobilized and deployed in one region to ambush a Xiongnu raiding force (133 BC).[2]
- 85,000 Han cavalry mobilized to expel the Xiongnu from border regions (177 BC).[3]
- Two large Han armies campaigned on the steppe each comprising 100,000 infantry and 50,000 cavalry (119 BC). Total: 200,000 infantry and 100,000 cavalry.

Han Expansion

- Han expedition across the Tarim territories to Ferghana: 60,000 soldiers, 100,000 oxen and 30,000 horses (104–101 BC).[4]
- Allied Tarim kingdoms attack on the Chanyu steppe fortress: 40,000 troops (36 BC).[5]

Later Han Empire (AD 25–220)

- Military units at capital Louyang: 3,536 soldiers.[6]
- Northern frontier (3,100 miles): perhaps 20,000 soldiers including the military strongholds established to monitor subject steppe nations.[7]
- 30,000 Southern Xiongnu serving in the Chinese army (campaign AD 89).[8]

Early Roman Empire (30 legions)

- 300,000 professional soldiers in permanent service.
- Roman Legion: 5,000 legionaries and 120 cavalry.[9]
- Each Legion supported by 5,000 auxiliaries.[10]
- Each Legion supported by auxiliary Ala units comprising 500 cavalry.

Scale of Roman Military Activities (Early Imperial)

- Roman army on the Rhine Frontier: 80,000 soldiers (8 legions). Comprising up to 40,000 legionaries, 40,000 auxiliaries and perhaps 5,000 cavalry.
- Danube army (8 legions).
- Roman army in Syria and Asia Minor: 40,000 soldiers (4 legions). Comprising up to 20,000 legionaries, 20,000 auxiliaries and perhaps 2,500 cavalry. Supported by troops raised by client kingdoms.
- Roman Black Sea: 3,000 soldiers and 40 war-galleys. Over 1,000 soldiers (several cohorts) stationed in the Chersonesos client kingdom (Crimea).[11]

Parthian Empire (Iran-Iraq)

- Mounted army: 40,000 archers and 4,000 heavily-armoured lancers.[12]

Roman-Parthian Wars (Republican Era)

- **Roman invasion of Mesopotamia (Crassus, 53 BC)**: 35,000 Roman infantry (7 legions) with 5,000 auxiliary cavalry.[13]
- Parthian army: 9,000 mounted archers and 1,000 heavily-armoured cataphract riders.[14]
- Casualties: 20,000 Romans killed, 10,000 captured and transferred to Merv in Central Asia.[15]
- **Roman invasion of Media (Mark Antony, 36 BC):** 60,000 Roman infantry (from 16 legions) with 10,000 cavalry.[16]
- Parthian army: 36,000 mounted archers and 4,000 cataphracts.
- Parthian casualties at the Battle of Phraaspa (a Roman victory): 80 dead and 30 prisoners.[17]
- Roman casualties on campaign: 40,000 legionaries and 4,000 cavalry killed or captured.[18]

Western Asia

- Armenian army: 10,000 armoured cavalry, 6,000 horsemen, and 30,000 infantry.[19]
- Caucasian-Iberia: 19,000 infantry.[20]
- Roman client kingdom Commagene (Asia Minor): 2,000 cavalry, 3,000 infantry, 3,000 archers.[21]

Hellenic Armies in Central Asia (250–140 BC)

- Greco-Bactrian Kingdom: 20,000 phalanx infantry and 10,000 cavalry.[22]
- Indo-Greek army (Hindu Kush and Indus): 60,000 mainly Indian troops raised by levies.[23]

Kushan Empire (Afghanistan and Northern India)

- Defensive – Yuezhi nation: 100,000 mounted warriors.[24]
- Offensive – Kushan army: 70,000 including mounted archers and armoured cataphract cavalry.[25]
- From military levies in India: 60,000 combatants, 200 elephants.[26]

Xiongnu (East Asian Steppe)

- Xiongnu Nation: 24 commanders leading up to 240,000 mounted warriors.[27]
- Xiongnu Empire including steppe allies: 320,000 mounted warriors mobilized to defend their territory (200 BC).[28]
- Offensive – 100,000 Xiongnu warriors assembled to invade Chinese territory and seize a main city (133 BC).[29]
- Occupation – Xiongnu occupations of Han territory: 30,000 in Shang Commandery and 30,000 in Yun-chung Commandery (158 BC).[30]

Steppe Nations (Asian Steppe)

- Wuhuan – Inner Mongolia: Subject to Han Empire and distributed across northern Chinese frontiers. Groups of 3,000 mounted warriors in Han service.[31]
- Xianbei – Mongolian Steppe: 100,000 mounted warriors.[32]
- Xiongnu – East Asian Steppe: 240,000 mounted warriors.

- Wusun – Ili Valley and Lake Balkhash (Central Steppe): 188,000 mounted warriors. Offensive army: 80,000 warriors.[33]
- Kangju – Sogdia-Ferghana: 90,000 mounted warriors.[34]
- Sakas – Ili Valley displaced to Sogdia-Bactria and moving south to conquer the Indus Kingdoms: 20,000 mounted warriors.[35]
- Scythian army (Pontic Steppe): 30,000 mounted warriors fighting 20,000 Siraces (Sarmatians).[36]

Sarmatians (Western Steppe)
- Alani-Aorsi (Yancai) Caspian Steppe: 100,000 mounted warriors.[37]
- Siraces (East Pontic Steppe): 20,000 mounted warriors.[38]
- Roxolani (Pontic Steppe – Danube): 50,000 mounted warriors.[39] Raiding force 9,000 warriors.[40]
- Iazyges (Hungary): possibly 20,000 mounted warriors. Foreign service: 8,000 mounted warriors transferred to the Roman army after conflict with the Empire.[41]

Late Antiquity:

Roman Empire – Army divided between Eastern and Western states
- 389,704 soldiers with 45,562 in fleet (fourth century AD).[42]
- 500,000 soldiers if at full unit strength (AD 395–420).[43]

Steppe Invasions (fourth–fifth century AD)
- 'Han Zhao' from the Southern Xiongnu – 'Hun-nu' (Hexi Corridor and Northern China): five clans providing 50,000 mounted warriors. Sacked Chinese capitals Louyang and Chang'an and captured two Jin Emperors (AD 311–316).[44]
- Huns (Pontic-Caspian Steppe and Hungarian grasslands). Offensive army: 60,000 warriors (AD 425).[45]

Hunnic Empire of Attila (manpower potential)
- Hungarian Plain: 20,000 mounted warriors.[46]
- Pontic Steppe: 70,000 mounted warriors (Goths, Scythians, Alani, Huns).[47]
- Further Germanic subjects fighting as infantry. A single Germanic faction could field 10,000 fighting men with Amal Goths, Rugians, Scirii, Thuringians, Franks, Gepids, Burgundians and Heruli fighting in Hunnic armies. Perhaps 80,000 Germanic fighters available for military campaigns.[48]
- Allied Huns/Alani from the Caspian steppe: possible 100,000 mounted warriors.[49]

Germanic/Alani populations fleeing Hunnic advance
- Single Germanic faction: 10,000 fighting men.
- Goths: Tervingi (10,000 fighters) and Greuthungi (possibly equivalent numbers) invade the Balkans (AD 376–378).[50]
- Goths led by Radagaisus invade Italy (AD 405–6) with 12,000 freemen fighters surrendering to the Roman army.[51]
- Vandals/Alani occupy Spain and invade North Africa (409–429) with a total population of 80,000 including women and children.[52]

Notes

Introduction: The Ancient World Economy

1. *Weilue*, 5–6; 9; 23; 25.
2. *Periplus*, 64.
3. Cosmus, *Christian Topography*, 1.137.
4. Strabo, 2.3.4.
5. *Hou Hanshu*, 88.12.
6. Dio, 51.21. Augustus, *Res Gestae*, 15.
7. Strabo, 2.5.12.
8. *Muziris Papyrus* records the value of an Indian cargo worth over 9 million sesterces removed from a Roman merchant ship the *Hermapollon* (*P. Vindob. G.* 40822). Merchant fleet of 120 ships (Strabo, 2.5.12). McLaughlin, *The Roman Empire and the Indian Ocean* (2014).
9. Aramaic inscription in Funerary Tower number 70 on the Umm Belqis. The same total given in three monetary units: denarii, *staters* and *myriads* (equal to 90 million sesterces). McLaughlin, *The Roman Empire and the Oasis Kingdoms: The Ancient World Economy and the caravan routes through Egypt, Syria, Arabia, Petra, Palmyra and Persia* (forthcoming).
10. See Appendix A.
11. McLaughlin, *Rome and the Distant East* (2010).
12. See Appendix A.
13. Pliny, 12.41.

Chapter 1: Steel and Silk

1. Frier, 'Population' in *Cambridge Ancient History, volume 11, The High Empire* (1996), 812–14.
2. Augustus, *Res Gestae*, 15 (recording male citizen numbers).
3. Tacitus, *Annals*, 3.55; Pliny, 9.59.
4. *Hou Hanshu*, 12.
5. Appian, *Civil Wars*, 5.9.
6. Pliny, 34.41.
7. Vegetius, *Epitoma Rei Militaris*, 4.8.
8. Vitruvius, *On Architecture*, 6.2.
9. Ovid, *Metamorphisis*, 14.712.
10. Horace, *Odes*, 1.16.9.
11. Horace, *Epodes*, 17.70–71.
12. Galen, *Material, Execution and Ornamentation*, 2.682.
13. OR/22 and OR/21.
14. Mayer, *The Ancient Middle Classes* (2012), 68–70.
15. Alfoldy, *Noricum* (1974), 73–4.
16. Martial, 4.55.
17. *Hou Hanshu*, 120.5b.
18. *Hanshu*, 70.7b. Yu, *Trade and Expansion in Han China* (1967), 68.
19. Plutarch, *Crassus*, 18; 24–5; 27.
20. Pliny, 34.41.
21. *Hou Hanshu*, 88.12.
22. *Periplus*, 49; 56; 64.
23. Ctesias, 2.9.

24. Curtius Rufus, 9.8.1.
25. Pliny, 34.43.
26. Apuleius, *Florida*, 6.
27. Justinian, *Digest*, 39.4.16.7.
28. Clement, *The Instructor*, 2.3.
29. Florus, 46.3.11.
30. Aristotle, *History of Animals*, 5.19.
31. Pliny, 11.26–7.
32. Propertius, 1.2. Tibullus, 2.3.
33. Propertius, 2.3.
34. Raschke, 'New Studies in Roman Commerce with the East' (1978), 625.
35. Procopius, *Secret History*, 25.14.
36. *Diocletian Price Edict*, 23–4.
37. Pliny, 9.60–4.
38. Pliny, 9.65; 21.22.
39. *C.I.L.* 14.3711–12.
40. *C.I.L.* 14.2793, 2812.
41. *C.I.L.* 6.9892. Gleba, *Making Textiles in Pre-Roman and Roman Times* (2013) 114–15.
42. *C.I.L.* 4.1507.
43. *Diocletian Price Edict*, 7; 2.
44. *Edict*, 20.
45. Oxyrhynchus Papyri, 5758.
46. *Historia Augusta, Aurelian*, 45.
47. *Diocletian Price Edict*, 19.
48. *Ibid.*, 23–4.
49. One day's labour: One silver denarius (*New Testament, Mathew*, 20.2).
50. Lady Leizu, wife of the Yellow Emperor. Barber, *Prehistoric Textiles* (1991), 31.
51. Kuhn and Needham, *Science and Civilisation in China: volume 5* (2004), 283–90.
52. Wood, *The Silk Road* (2002), 52.
53. *Yan Tie Lun* (*Discourses on Salt and Iron*), 2.14.
54. *Hanshu*, 19A.4b, 72.5b (Former Han); *Hou Hanshu*, 36.5a (Later Han).
55. Wang, *Money on the Silk Road* (2004), 256.
56. *Hou Hanshu*, 103.1b. *Yan Tie Lun*, 2.14.
57. Pausanias, 6.26.7.
58. Xuanzang, *Da Tang Xiyu Ji* (*Great Tang Records on the Western Regions*).

Chapter 2: Silk in Roman Society

1. Pliny, 19.6.
2. Dio, 43.24.
3. Dio, 59.12.
4. Pliny, 19.6.
5. Seneca, *Phaedra*, 352.
6. *Periplus*, 49, 56, 64.
7. Pliny, 19.6. Tacitus, *Annals*, 13.31.
8. Dio, 63.6.2.
9. Statham, *A History of Architecture* (1950), 94.
10. Lucretius, *On the Nature of Things*, 4.75–83
11. *Roman Inscriptions of Britain*, 1171.
12. Pliny, 21.8.
13. Arnobius, *Adversus Gentes*, 3.21 (AD 306).
14. Apuleius, *Golden Ass*, 11.47.
15. *Ibid.*, 8.36.
16. Rufus Festus Avienus, 1.1008.
17. Prudentius, *Psychomachia*, 1011–50.

18. Apuleius, *Golden Ass*, 2.9.
19. Propertius, 4.2.1–64
20. Dio, 59.17.
21. Suetonius, *Caligula*, 52.
22. Josephus, *Jewish War*, 7.4–5.
23. *Historia Augusta, Commodus*, 13.
24. *Historia Augusta, Pertinax*, 8.
25. *Historia Augusta, Elagabalus*, 26.
26. *Ibid.*, 5.
27. *Ibid.*, 29.
28. *Ibid.*, 32.
29. *Historia Augusta, Marcus Aurelius*, 17.
30. *Historia Augusta, Alexander Severus*, 4.
31. *Ibid.*, 40.
32. *Ibid.*, 33.
33. *Historia Augusta, Aurelian*, 45.
34. *Historia Augusta, Tacitus*, 10.
35. Martial, 8.33.
36. Plutarch, *De Pythiae Oracula*, 4.
37. Suetonius, *Augustus*, 40.
38. *Historia Augusta, Hadrian*, 22.
39. Cicero, *Against Vatinius*, 30–2.
40. Isidorus, *Origins*, 19.24.6.
41. Adkins, *Handbook to Life in Ancient Rome* (1994), 383.
42. Livy, 5.41.2.
43. Cleland, Davies and Llewellyn-Jones, *Greek and Roman Dress from A to Z* (2007).
44. Cicero, *On Duties* 1.150–2; Paulus, *Opinions*, 5.28a3.
45. Tacitus, *Annals*, 2.33.
46. Dio, 57.15.
47. Suetonius, *Caligula*, 52.
48. Pliny, 8.54.
49. Quintilian, *Institutes of Oratory*, 12.10.47.
50. Seneca, *Epistulae morales ad Lucilium*, 90.
51. Claudian, *Panegyric on the Consuls Probinus and Olybrius*, 1.
52. Augustus, *Res Gestae*, 15.
53. *Ibid.*, 8.
54. Martial, 3.82.
55. Apuleius, *Golden Ass*, 2.11.
56. Pliny, 11.27.
57. Philo, *On Dreams*, 2.53.
58. Ausonius, *Epigrams*, 26.
59. Apollinaris Sidonius, 2.2.
60. *Historia Augusta, Aurelian*, 15.
61. Sidonius Apollinaris, *Carmen*, 23.
62. *Diocletian's Price Edict*, 22.
63. *Ibid.*, 7.
64. Pliny, 11.27.
65. Pliny, 11.26.
66. Horace, *Satires*, 1.2.86–110.
67. Lucan, *Pharsalia*, 10.169–71.
68. Properties, 4.5:1–78.
69. Horace, *Satires*, 1.2.86–110.
70. Alciphron, 4.14.4.
71. Tibullus, 2.3.

72. Propertius, 2.2.3–4.
73. Apuleius, *Golden Ass*, 2.6–10.
74. Juvenal, 6.259
75. Propertius, 1.14.
76. Propertius, 2.1.
77. Seneca, *On Benefits*, 7.9.
78. Seneca, *Tragedies*, 1.387–91.
79. Seneca, *On Benefits*, 7.9.
80. Martial, 11.8.
81. Martial, 8.68.
82. Propertius, 4.5.2.
83. Horace, *Odes* 4.13.
84. Horace, *Epodes*, 8.15.
85. Martial, 9.59.
86. Ovid, *Amores*, 1.14.
87. Appendix A.
88. Procopius, 4.5.1–78.
89. Tibullus, 2.4.
90. Ovid, *Ars Amatoria*, 2.8.
91. Martial, 14.24.
92. Apuleius, *Golden Ass*, 4.31.
93. Juvenal, 9.50; Martial 14.28.
94. Propertius, 4.8.23.
95. Martial, 11.27.
96. Apuleius, *Golden Ass*, 3.46.
97. Claudian, *Epithalamium of Honorius and Maria*, 10 (AD 398).
98. Sebesta and Bonfante, *The World of Roman Costume* (2001), 55.
99. Petronius, *Satryricon*, 8.104.
100. Plutarch, *Moralia: Advice to Bride and Groom, 48.*
101. Heliodorus, *Aethiopia*, 10.309 (AD 390).
102. Pliny, *Letters*, 5.16
103. Statius, 5.1.
104. Clement, *The Instructor*, 2.11.
105. *Ibid.*, 2.11.
106. *Ibid.*, 2.11.
107. Jerome, *Letters*, 117.6 (AD 405).
108. Gerontius, *Melania*, 4, 6.
109. Apuleius, *Golden Ass*, 2.9.
110. Ammianus Marcellinus, 23.6.
111. Galen, *Methods of Medicine*, 13.22.
112. *Revelations*, 18:12.
113. Zosimus, 5.41.4.
114. McLaughlin, *The Roman Empire and the Oasis Kingdoms: The Ancient World Economy and the caravan routes through Egypt, Syria, Arabia, Petra, Palmyra and Persia* (forthcoming).
115. *Hou Hanshu*, 88.13 (49 days Parthian frontier to Balkh).
116. Ptolemy, *Geography*, 1.12 (seven months Stone Tower to Sera).
117. Sima Qian, *Shiji*, 123.6a.
118. *Zhou shu*, 50.2340c.
119. Silk: 370 suits, 30,000 rolls, 30,000 catties of silk floss (33,000 lbs). *Hanshu*, 94b.8a.
120. *Chin Shu*, 26.5.
121. Strabo, 15.1.20; Virgil, *Georgics*, 2.120.
122. Pliny, 6.20.
123. Pausanias, 6.26.6–7.
124. Mela, 1.11.

125. Silius Italicus, *Punic Wars*, 17.595–6.
126. Heliodorus, *Aethiopica*, 10.25.
127. Ausonius, *Technopaegnion*, 11.6.

Chapter 3: The Chinese Empire and the Xiongnu

1. Graf, 'The Roman East from the Chinese Perspective' (1996).
2. *Hou Hanshu*: Hill, *Through the Jade Gate to Rome* (2009).
3. Hill, *Weilue: The Peoples of the West* (forthcoming).
4. *Hou Hanshu*, 88.11.
5. Sima Qian, *Shiji*, 43.1808.
6. Sima Qian, *Shiji*, 6; 110.
7. *Ibid.*, 88.
8. *Ibid.*
9. Sima Qian, *Shiji*, 110. Translated: Watson, *Records of the Grand Historian: Volume 2* (1961), 183.
10. Dawson, *The First Emperor: Selections from the Historical Records* (1994), xxii.
11. *The Cambridge History of China* (1996), 103–28.
12. Population increase: 57.7 million by AD 2. Loewe, *The Government of the Qin and Han Empires* (2002), 142.
13. Chi I, *Hsin Shu*, 4.41; Sima Qian, *Shiji*, 110.8a.
14. Appendix E.
15. *Hanshu*, 94A.12a–b (early occurrence 2,000 Xiongnu). Yu, *Trade and Expansion in Han China* (1967), 14.
16. Peers, *Imperial Chinese Armies* (1995), 16.
17. Boulnois, *Silk Road* (2012), 295.
18. Loewe, *The Men who Governed Han China* (2004), 77–8.
19. Sima Qian, *Shiji*, 6.
20. Porta, *The First Emperor* (2007), 204.
21. Nickel, 'The Terracotta Army' (2007), 158–79.
22. Zhang, *The Qin Terracotta Army* (1996), 72.
23. Tanner, 'Figuring out Death' (2013), 75.
24. Lin, 'Armour for the Afterlife' (2007), 180–91.
25. Man, *The Terracotta Army* (2010), 92.
26. Luo, *China's Imperial Tombs and Mausoleums* (1993), 216.
27. Lindesay and Baofa, *The Terracotta Army of the First Emperor of China* (2009).
28. Sima Qian, *Shiji*, 6.
29. Grave-sites southwest of Tomb Mound near Zhaobeihu Village; east of Wusha Factory; east of Lintong.
30. Howard, *Chinese Sculpture* (2006), 74.
31. Nunn, *Climate, Environment, and Society in the Pacific during the Last Millennium* (2007), 9.
32. *Hanshu*, 94a.3743.
33. *Yan Tie Lun (Discourses on Salt and Iron)*, 14.70; Yu, *Trade and Expansion in Han China* (1967), 40.
34. *Hanshu*, 94a.3743.
35. Luttwak, *Grand Strategy of the Byzantine Empire* (2011), 23–4.
36. Sima Qian, *Shiji*, 110.
37. Sima Qian, *Shiji*, 110.2890–2.
38. *Hanshu*, 94b.3752; 3766.
39. Sima Qian, *Shiji*, 8.16a; 93.1b–2a; *Hanshu*, 1b.5a; 33.3b–4a; Sinor, *The Cambridge History of Early Inner Asia, Volume 1* (1990), 121–2.
40. Sima Qian, *Shiji*, 110.6b; *Hanshu*, 94a.4b; Yu, *Trade and Expansion in Han China* (1967), 41.
41. *Hanshu*, 94a.12b; Yu, *Trade and Expansion in Han China* (1967), 49.
42. Sima Qian, *Shiji*, 110.2896; *Hanshu*, 94a.3756–7.
43. Sima Qian, *Shiji*, 123.3162.
44. Justin, 42.1–2.
45. Chinese Historical Atlas: *Chung-kuo li-shih ti-t'u chi*, 2.17–18.

46. *Ch'ao Ts'o Chi Chu-yi*, 8. Quoted: Di Cosmo, *Ancient China and Its Enemies* (2002), 203.
47. *Hanshu*, 49.2281; *Ch'ao Ts'o chi chu-yi*, 8.
48. *Chung-kuo li-shih ti-t'u chi*, 2:17–18.
49. Sima Qian, *Shiji*, 110.2892.
50. Sima Qian, *Shiji*, 110. Translated: Watson, *Records of the Grand Historian: Volume 2* (1961), 177–8.
51. Sima Qian, *Shiji*, 102.4a; *Hanshu*, 50.3a.
52. Yu, *Trade and Expansion in Han China* (1967), 99–100.
53. Chi I, *Hsin Shu*, 4.41.
54. *Yan Tie Lun*, 4 (81 BC).
55. Sima Qian, *Shiji*, 110.10a.
56. *Yan Tie Lun*, 4.
57. Sima Qian, *Shiji*, 110. Translated: Watson, *Records of the Grand Historian: Volume 2* (1961), 177–8.
58. *Hanshu*, 94a.12b.
59. *Hou Hanshu*, 120.2b. Yun-chung Province (Northern Suiyuan).
60. Sima Qian, *Shiji*, 110.8a.

Chapter 4: Roman Routes to China

1. Sima Qian, *Shiji*, 123.
2. Sima Qian, *Shiji*, 108.2b–3a; 110.10a–b. *Hanshu*, 52.8b–9a; 94a.7b–8a.
3. Loewe, 'The Campaigns of Han Wu-ti' (1974).
4. Sima Qian, *Shiji*, 30.11; *Hanshu*, 24b.18a.
5. Sima Qian, *Shiji*, 109.
6. Cosmo, *Ancient China and its Enemies* (2002), 241–86.
7. Sima Qian, *Shiji*, 109; *Hanshu*, 54.
8. Justin, 41.6.
9. Sima Qian, *Shiji*, 123.
10. *Ibid.*, 123.3166.
11. *Hanshu*, 96a.3895.
12. Sima Qian, *Shiji*, 30.1032.
13. *Ibid.*, 30.1037–40.
14. Hansen, *The Silk Road* (2012), 9–10.
15. Wood, *The Silk Road* (2002), 75.
16. Murrin, *Trade and Romance* (2014), 15–16.
17. Sima Qian, *Shiji*, 123.3168.
18. *Ibid.*, 123.7b; Hanshu, 96a.8b.
19. Sima Qian, *Shiji*, 123.3.h8; Translated: Watson, *Records of the Grand Historian: Volume 2* (1961), 272.
20. Holt, *Alexander the Great and Bactria* (1989), 23.
21. Sima Qian, *Shiji*, 123.3174–77; *Hanshu*, 96.
22. Boulnois, *Silk Road* (2012), Chapter 4.
23. *Hanshu*, 28b.2a (cadastral registure); *Hou Hanshu*, 33.4b.

Chapter 5: Securing the Silk Routes

1. *Hou Hanshu*, 118.9b; Sima Qian, *Shiji*, 123.9b; *Hanshu*, 96a; 1b.
2. Sima Qian, *Shiji*, 123.3172–3.
3. *Hanshu*, 96b.8b.
4. *Hanshu*, 70.2b.
5. *Hanshu*, 96b.4b–6a.
6. *Hou Hanshu*, 118.9b.
7. *Hanshu*, 96b.10b.
8. *Yan Tie Lun*, 1.
9. Sima Qian, *Shiji*, 123.6a.
10. *Ibid.*, 123.3168.
11. *Hou Hanshu*, 77.4b.

12. *Ch'uan Hou-Han wen*, 25.4a. Yu, *Trade and Expansion in Han China* (1967), 194–5.
13. Appendix E.
14. *Hanshu*, 70.3b.
15. Dubs, *A Roman City in Ancient China* (1957); Refuted: Sampson, *The Defeat of Rome* (2008), 182–5.
16. Matthew, 'Greek Hoplites in an Ancient Chinese Siege' (2011).
17. *Hanshu*, 70.3b.
18. Yu, *Trade and Expansion in Han China* (1967), 89–91.
19. *Hanshu*, 94b.1b–2a.
20. *Hanshu*, 94b.2a–b.
21. *Hanshu*, 94b.3b (49 BC).
22. *Hanshu*, 94b.8a.
23. Yu, *Trade and Expansion in Han China* (1967), 45–7.
24. *Hou Hanshu*, 119.6b.
25. *Ibid.*, 75.2b.
26. *Ibid.*, 119.6a.
27. Sima Qian, *Shiji*, 123.3172.3.
28. 'The Parthians first attained prominence under a certain Arsaces, from whom their succeeding rulers received the title of Arsacidae.' Dio Cassius, 40.14.
29. Isidore, *Parthian Stations*.
30. *Hou Hanshu*, 88.12.
31. *Periplus*, 64.
32. *Periplus*, 49, 56.
33. *Hou Hanshu*, 88.11.
34. *Ibid.*, 88.12.
35. *Hou Hanshu*, 88.12.
36. Propertius, 4.8.1–88.
37. Hill, *Through the Jade Gate to Rome* (2009), Appendix B.
38. *Hou Hanshu*, 88.12.
39. *Ibid.*
40. Dio, 68.3–4.
41. *Hou Hanshu*, 88.12.
42. *Ibid.*, 88.10.
43. Strabo, *Geography*, 11.11.1.
44. Mela, 1.11.
45. Mela, 3.59–60.
46. Pliny, 6.20; 24.
47. Ptolemy, *Geography*, 6.16.
48. Ammianus Marcellinus, 23.6.64.
49. *Ibid.*, 23.6.66.
50. *Periplus*, 38.
51. Pausanias, 6.26.9.
52. Pliny, 6.24.
53. Pliny, 34.41.
54. Mallory and Mair, *The Tarim Mummies* (2000).
55. Strabo, 15.1.34.
56. Barber, *The Mummies of Urumchi* (2000) 47–70.
57. Pranidhi: Scene 5, Temple 9.
58. Pliny, 6.24.
59. Mela, 3.60.
60. Origen, *Contra Celsum*, 7.62–4.
61. *Periplus*, 64.
62. *Tung-kuan Han-chi*, 143.
63. *Hou Hanshu*, 72.3a.

Chapter 6: The Kushan Empire

1. *Hou Hanshu*, 88.13.
2. Justin, 42.1–2.
3. Strabo, 11.11.4.
4. Aristotle, 1265a15.
5. Diodorus, 18.7.
6. Menander, 627–9 (Greek dramatist 320–310 BC).
7. Appian, 11.57.
8. Curtius Rufus, 7.3.23; Diodorus, 17.83 (7,000 Bactrians, 3,000 Greek).
9. Sima Qian, *Shiji*, 123.
10. Strabo, 11.11.2.
11. Arrian, *Alexander*, 3.28.
12. Cohen, *The Hellenistic Settlements in the East from Armenia and Mesopotamia to Bactria and India* (2013), 225–44.
13. Polybius, 11.34.
14. Polybius, 10.49.
15. Strabo, 11.11.1.
16. Strabo 15.1.3.
17. Justin, 41.6.4.
18. Strabo, 11.11.2.
19. *Amphipolis (Bactria)* 1.
20. Ctesias, *Fragment*, 1.7.
21. *Hanshu*, 96b.1b.
22. Strabo, 11.8.2; 4.
23. Mielczarek, *Cataphracti and Clibanarii* (1993), 71.
24. Nikonorov, *The Armies of Bactria* (1997), 75.
25. *Hanshu*, 96a.10b.
26. *Ibid.*, 63.
27. *Ibid.*, 56.
28. Sima Qian, *Shiji*, 123.3162 (Tang Dynasty annotation).
29. *Hanshu*, 96a.14b.
30. *Hou Hanshu*, 88.13.
31. *Periplus*, 47.
32. *Hou Hanshu*, 88.14.
33. *Ibid.*, 88.13.
34. Sima Qian, *Shiji*, 123.
35. Nikonorov, *The Armies of Bactria* (1997), 63.
36. Faulkner, *Rome* (2013) 218.
37. *Hou Hanshu*, 88.13.
38. Josephus, *Antiquities*, 20.4.
39. *Hou Hanshu*, 77.4a–7a.
40. *Hou Hanshu*, 88.13; Yan Gaozhen (Vima Takto).
41. *Hou Hanshu*, 88.15.
42. *Weilue*, 7.
43. *Hou Hanshu*, 88.15.
44. *Hou Hanshu*, 118.13b.
45. Naweed, *Art through the Ages in Afghanistan* (2013), 134–6.
46. *Fu fa-tsang yin yuan chuan*, 316.2.16 (transcribed AD 470).
47. *Tripitaka* (*Sampradaya-nidana*).
48. Dani, *History of Civilizations of Central Asia* (1996), 279–84.
49. *Ibid.*, 261.
50. *Ibid.*, 356.
51. *Ibid.*, 352–3.
52. Mukherjee, *The Rise and Fall of the Kushana Empire* (1988), 315.

53. Nikonorov, *The Armies of Bactria* (1997), 70.
54. *Ibid.*, 72.
55. Dani, *History of Civilizations of Central Asia* (1996), 424–7.
56. Text: Naweed, *Art through the ages in Afghanistan* (2013), 136.
57. Dio Chrysostom, 53.6; Aelian, *Various Histories*, 12.48.
58. Ladislav, *Greek Gods in the East* (2012), 212.
59. Tarn, *The Greeks in Bactria and India* (1938), 179; Cohen, *The Hellenistic Settlements in the East from Armenia and Mesopotamia to Bactria and India* (2013), 325–7.
60. Philostratus, *Apollonius*, 2.20.
61. Erdosy, *The Archaeology of Early Historic South Asia* (1995), 290–1.
62. Pugachenkova, 'Kushan Art' (1999), 367.
63. Liu, *The Silk Road in World History* (2010), 50.
64. Chandra, *Trade and Trade Routes in Ancient India* (1977), 10.
65. Drummond and Nelson, *The Western Frontiers of Imperial Rome* (1994), 30.
66. Dio, 68.15.
67. Rosenfield, *The Dynastic Arts of the Kushans* (1967), 58.
68. Dio Chrysostom, 32.43.
69. Dio Chrysostom, 72.3.
70. *Hou Hanshu*, 77.4a–7a.
71. Tacitus, *Annals*, 14.25.
72. *Hou Hanshu*, 77.4a–7a.
73. Plutarch, *Pompey*, 70.
74. *Historia Augusta, Hadrian*, 21.
75. Tacitus, *Annals*, 14.25.
76. Aurelius Victor, *Roman History*, 15.4.
77. Whitehouse, 'The Glass from Begram' (2012), 54–64.
78. Strabo, 2.5.12.
79. *Taiping Yulan*, 359.1650.
80. *Periplus*, 39.
81. *Periplus*, 49.
82. Pliny, 6.26; 12.41.
83. *Arthashastra*, 2.22.
84. Gold: 360 Babylonian talents-weight.
85. Silver: 468 Attic talents-weight. Herodotus, 3.90–6.
86. Strabo, 15.1.69.
87. Dionysios Periegetes, 1143–6.
88. Apuleius, *Florida*, 6.
89. Xuanzang, 1.134.
90. Columella, 3.3 (15 sesterces); *C.I.L.* 4.1679 (Pompeii: 12 sesterces).
91. John Lydus, *On the Magistracies*, 2.28.
92. Bennett, *Trajan* (2003), 103, 175.
93. *Papyrus Baden*, 37. Frank, *An Economic History of Rome* (1959) 425–6, 443–4.
94. Harl, *Coinage in the Roman Economy* (1996), 302.
95. Pausanias, 3.12.4.
96. *Digha Nikaya*, 31.26.
97. Samad, *The Grandeur of Gandhara* (2011), 108.
98. Faxian (AD 399–412); Sung Yun (AD 518), Xuanzang (AD 630).
99. Phuoc, *Buddhist Architecture* (2010), 179–80.
100. Fazio, Moffett and Wodehouse, *A World History of Architecture* (2003), 125–6.
101. Alikuzai, *A Concise History of Afghanistan: Volume 1* (2013), 849.
102. *Acts of Thomas*, 3.
103. Ball, *Rome in the East* (2000) 141.
104. *Hou Hanshu*, 88.15.
105. *Ibid.*, 72.3a.

106. *Ibid.*, 88.15.
107. *Ibid.*, 118.6a.
108. *Taisho Shinshu Daizokyo*, 224. Nadeau, *The Wiley-Blackwell Companion to Chinese Religions* (2012), 69.
109. Sengyou, *Chu Sanzang Jiji*; Hansen, *The Silk Road* (2012), 32.
110. Warmington, *The Commerce between the Roman Empire and India* (1928), 299.
111. Suetonius, *Tiberius*, 66.
112. Porphyry, *De Abstinentia ab esu Animalium*, 4.17; Stobaeus, *Eclogues*, 3.56.141 ('Antoninus from Emesa' = Elagabalus).

Chapter 7: The Sogdian Intermediaries

1. *Hou Hanshu*, 88.17.
2. Herodotus, 7.66.
3. *Charters of Susa*.
4. Herodotus, 3.89–97 (300 Babylonian talents = 455 Attic talents).
5. Bug, *The Cambridge Companion to the Hellenistic World* (2006), 17.
6. Holt, *Into the Land of Bones* (2012), 126–8
7. Sima Qian, *Shiji*, 123.
8. *Hanshu*, 70.3b.
9. Pliny, 6.18.
10. *Hanshu*, 96a.7b.
11. Xuanzang, *Record of the Western Regions*, 1.
12. *Xintangshu*, 221.6243–4.
13. Pliny, 6.18.
14. Dio, 54.8.
15. Pliny, 6.5, 18, 31.
16. *Hanshu*, 96b.1b.
17. *Hanshu*, 96a.
18. Vaissière, *Sogdian traders* (2005), 79–81.
19. *Ibid.*, 81, fn. 43.
20. Shatial, no. 254.
21. Hansen, *The Silk Road* (2012), 30–2.
22. *Kharosthi Documents*, 35.
23. *Kharosthi Documents*, 140.
24. *Kharosthi Documents*, 149.
25. *Kharosthi Documents*, 225.
26. Liu, *Silk and Religion* (1996), 13.
27. Faxian, *A record of Buddhist Kingdoms*, 3 (AD 399–412).
28. *Saddharma Pundarika Sutra* (*Lotus Sutra*). Avalokiteshvara, 'Lord who Gazes Down' or Lokanatha, 'Lord of the World'.
29. Huntington and Bangdel, *The Circle of Bliss* (2003), 180.
30. Whitfield, *The Silk Road* (2004), 143.
31. Liu, *Connections across Eurasia* (2007), 86–7.
32. *Ibid.*, 87–8.
33. *Niya Documents*, 706 (AD 269). Hansen, *The Silk Road* (2012), 51–2.
34. *Niya*, 693.
35. *Niya*, 701.
36. *Niya*, 673.
37. *Niya*, 697.
38. *Niya*, 684.
39. *Niya*, 680, 702.
40. Hansen, *The Silk Road* (2012), 54.
41. *Ibid.*, 44.
42. *Loulan Document*, 886.

43. *Loulan Document*, 46.
44. Vaissière, *Sogdian Traders* (2005), 57, fn. 38.
45. *Ibid.*, 57.
46. *Ibid.*, 58.
47. *Shule Document*, 509.
48. *Tun-huang*, 15.a.1.3 (Tun-huang = Dunhuang).
49. *Hou Hanshu*, 72.2a (AD 107–114).
50. Hansen, *The Silk Road* (2012), 237.
51. *Shule*, 170.
52. Hansen, *The Silk Road* (2012), 15.
53. *Ibid.*, 17.
54. Faxian, *A Record of Buddhist Kingdoms* (AD 399–412).
55. *Sui Shu*, 35.1098.
56. Liu, *The Silk Road in World History* (2010), 64.
57. *Sogdian Letter III* (5 caravans leaving China in 3 year period).
58. Boulnois, *Silk Road* (2012), 217.
59. *Sanguo Zhi*, 4.895.
60. *Zhou Shu*, 50.2340c.
61. *Sogdian Letter*, 5.
62. *Hou Hanshu*, 93.5a.
63. *Periplus*, 39; 49; 56; *Hou Hanshu*, 88.12.
64. *Sogdian Letter*, 2. Roman goods: *Hou Hanshu*, 88.12; *Weilue*, 12.
65. Sima Qian, *Shiji*, 123.
66. Marshak, 'Central Asian Metalwork in China' (2004), 47–55.
67. *Sogdian Letter*, 2.
68. Vaissière, *Sogdian Traders* (2005), 271.
69. *Al-Tabari*, 2.1188–9.
70. *Sogdian Letter*, 2.
71. Jerome, *To Principia*, 3.
72. Jerome, *To Demetrius*, 19.
73. Hansen, *The Silk Road* (2012), 265, fn. 58.
74. Stewart, *The Everlasting Flame* (2013), 24–7.
75. Zürcher, *The Buddhist Conquest of China* (1959), 51–5.
76. *Liang Shu*, 464–520.
77. 'Tocharian donors', Kizil Caves (seventh century); 'Sogdian donors', Bezeklik, Thousand Buddha Caves (ninth century).
78. Hansen, *The Silk Road* (2012), 116–17.
79. *Sogdian Letter*, 2.
80. Vaissière, *Sogdian Traders* (2005), 53.
81. *Sogdian Letter*, 2.
82. *Sogdian Letter*, 2.
83. *Sogdian Letter*, 2.
84. *Sogdian Letter*, 5.
85. 1 *Liu* (125 grams) of silver = 1,000 cash (AD 9) (*Hanshu*, 24b.20b); Gold values: bamboo strips found near the Chinese frontier, 1 *Liang* (15.25 grams) of gold = 1,327 cash (12 BC) (*Juyan Hanjian Shiwen Hexiao*, 506.27); Further examples: 504.13; 505.20; 506.11.
86. *Sogdian Letter*, 5.
87. *Sogdian Letter*, 3.
88. *Sogdian Letter*, 1.

Chapter 8: Caspian Routes and the Crimea

1. *Hou Hanshu*, 88.12.
2. Strabo, 2.1.15.
3. Arrian, *Alexander*, 3.29.

4. Pliny, 6.21.
5. Ammianus Marcellinus, 23.6.59.
6. Strabo, 11.11.5.
7. Strabo, 11.5.8.
8. Josephus, *Jewish Wars*, 7.8.4.
9. Ammianus Marcellinus, 23.6.59.
10. Sima Qian, *Shiji*, 123.
11. *Hou Hanshu*, 88.18–19.
12. *Weilue*, 25.
13. Herodotus, 1.203.
14. Pliny, 6.15.
15. Tacitus, *Annals*, 6.34.
16. Strabo, 2.1.15.
17. Diocletian, *Price Edict*, 17; 35; Greene, *Archaeology of the Roman Economy* (1983), 40.
18. Herodotus, 1.203.
19. Pliny, 2.67.
20. Strabo, 11.6.1.
21. Strabo, 11.11.6.
22. Pliny, 6.15.
23. Apollonius Rhodius, *Argonautica*, 2.316.
24. *Ibid.*, 2.549.
25. Strabo, 1.2.10.
26. Pliny, 4.12.
27. Herodotus, 4.86.
28. Pliny, 4.12.
29. Mela, 1.108.
30. Aeschylus, *Prometheus Unbound*.
31. Green, *The Argonautika* (1997).
32. Trofimova, *Greeks on the Black Sea* (2007).
33. Strabo, 7.5.
34. Strabo, 7.6.
35. Cernenko, *The Scythians 700–300 BC* (2012).
36. Diocletian, *Price Edict*, 17; 35; Greene, *Archaeology of the Roman Economy* (1983), 40.
37. Strabo, 7.6.
38. Diodorus, 12.31.
39. Demosthenes, 20.29–31 (Leucon, 390–350 BC)
40. Demosthenes, 18.87.
41. Demosthenes, 20.31–2.
42. Demosthenes, 35.20.
43. Strabo, 7.6.
44. Didymus, 10.34–11.5.
45. Theopompus, fragment 115; Philochorus, fragment 328.162.
46. Strabo, 7.4.6.
47. Demosthenes, 20.32–3.
48. Strabo, 7.4.4.
49. Strabo, 7.4.6.
50. Strabo, 7.8.11.
51. Plutarch, *Pompey*, 32–8.
52. Appian, *Mithridatic Wars*, 103.
53. Pliny, 6.19.
54. Pseudo-Scymnus (probably Pausanias of Damascus), *Periodos to Nicomedes*, 934 (fragment 20).
55. Pliny, 2.67.
56. Strabo, 11.2.17.
57. Plutarch, *Pompey*, 36–8.

58. Plutarch, *Pompey*, 41–2.
59. Plutarch, *Caesar*, 50; Suetonius, *Julius Caesar*, 37.
60. Strabo, 7.6.
61. Strabo, 7.7.
62. Dio, 54.24.4–6.
63. Josephus, *Antiquities*, 16.2.1–2.
64. Eutropius, 7.9.
65. Tacitus, *Annals*, 12.15.
66. Josephus, *Jewish War*, 2.16.3.
67. *I.L.S.* 2824
68. Strabo, 12.3.11.
69. Tacitus, *Annals*, 13.39.
70. *I.L.S.* 8795. Gamqrelize, *Researches in Iberia-colchology* (2012), 155–6.
71. Strabo, 11.2.1.
72. Pliny, 6.26.
73. Strabo, 11.2.1.
74. Strabo, 11.1.5.
75. Suetonius, *Augustus*, 48.
76. Pliny, 6.15.
77. Pliny, 6.12.
78. Suetonius, *Nero*, 19.
79. Pliny, 6.15.
80. Tacitus, *Histories*, 1.6.
81. Tacitus, *Annals*, 3.47–8.
82. Strabo, 11.2.1.

Chapter 9: Black Sea Voyages

1. *Cambridge Ancient History, Volume 11: The High Empire* (2000), 139, 605.
2. Isaac, *The Invention of Racism in Classical Antiquity* (2004), 371.
3. *Historia Augusta, Hadrian*, 13.
4. Arrian, *Periplus*, 12.
5. *Historia Augusta, Hadrian*, 1.
6. *Ibid.*, 17.
7. Arrian, *Periplus*, 1; Xenophon, *Anabasis*, 4. 7.24.
8. Pitassi, *Roman Warships* (2011), 119–23 (Triremes); 123–6 (Liburnians).
9. Arrian, *Periplus*, 1.
10. Arrian, *Periplus*, 3.
11. Liddle, *Arrian: Periplus Ponti Euxini* (2003), 93.
12. *Historia Augusta, Hadrian*, 10.
13. Arrian, *Periplus*, 3.
14. *Ibid.*, 4.
15. *Ibid.*, 6.
16. *C.I.L.* 10.1202 = *I.L.S.* 2660.
17. Pliny, 6.4.
18. Liddle, *Arrian: Periplus Ponti Euxini* (2003), 95–6.
19. *Ibid.*, 96.
20. Arrian, *Periplus*, 6.
21. Apollonius Rhodius, *Argonautica*, 4.452–76.
22. Cicero, *De Lege Manilia*, 22.
23. Arrian, *Periplus*, 7.
24. Strabo, 11.2.17.
25. Liddle, *Arrian: Periplus Ponti Euxini* (2003), 8.
26. Pliny, 6.4.
27. Strabo, 11.3.4.

28. Strabo, 11.2.17.
29. Strabo, 11.3.4.
30. Pliny, 6.12.
31. Strabo, 11.3.4.
32. Strabo, 11.2.16; 18.
33. Apollonius Rhodius, *Argonautica*, 2.1262.
34. Appian, *Mithridatic Wars*, 103.
35. Virgil, *Georgics*, 4.367.
36. Arrian, *Periplus*, 9.
37. Apollonius Rhodius, *Argonautica*, 1.936.
38. Strabo, 11.2.17.
39. Arrian, *Periplus*, 9.
40. Strabo, 11.2.3 (Pontic Steppe slaves).
41. Pliny, 21.17.
42. Strabo, 11.2.17.
43. Arrian, *Periplus*, 11.
44. *Ibid.*
45. *Ibid.*
46. Apollonius Rhodius, *Argonautica*, 2.1242.
47. Strabo, 11.2.16.
48. Pliny, 6.5.
49. Arrian, *Periplus*, 10.
50. Liddle, *Arrian: Periplus Ponti Euxini* (2003), 103–4.
51. Arrian, *Periplus*, 17.
52. Pliny, *Letters*, 63.
53. Lucian, *Alexander the False Prophet*, 57. King Eupator: AD 153–174.
54. *Historia Augusta*, *Antoninus Pius*, 9.
55. Arrian, *Periplus*, 17.
56. *Ibid.*, 18.
57. Strabo, 7.4.4.
58. Pliny, 4.12.
59. Strabo, 7.3.18.
60. Strabo, 11.2.3; Pliny, 4.12.
61. Arrian, *Periplus*, 19.
62. Pliny, 6.7.
63. Strabo, 11.2.3.
64. Strabo, 11.2.2.
65. *Weilue*, 25.
66. Strabo, 11.2.3.
67. Pliny, 4.12.
68. Strabo, 7.4.4.
69. Strabo, 7.4.3.
70. Arrian, *Periplus*, 19.
71. *I.L.S.* 986.
72. Ptolemy, 3.6.2.
73. Rostovtzeff, 'Romische Besatzungen in der *Krim* und das Kastell *Charax*' (1902), 80–95.
74. National Preserve of Tauric Chersonesos (Sevastopol).
75. Pliny, 4.12.
76. Strabo, 7.3.17.
77. Pliny, 37.11.
78. Dio Chrysostom, 36.3.
79. *Ibid.*, 36.4.
80. Dio Chrysostom, 36.6.
81. Herodotus, 4.20; 107.

82. Dio Chrysostom, 36.7.
83. Arrian, *Periplus*, 21.
84. Pliny, 10.78; Pausanias, 3.19.11.
85. Arrian, *Periplus*, 23.
86. Pliny, 4.12.
87. Arrian, *Periplus*, 24.
88. *I.S.M.* (Inscriptiones Scythiae Minor) 2.186.
89. *I.S.M.* 2.60; 2.132; 2.320; 2.403.
90. *I.S.M.* 2.153.
91. *I.S.M.* 2.463.
92. *I.S.M.* 1.82.
93. Ptolemy, *Geography*, 5.1.

Chapter 10: The Sarmatians

1. Strabo, 11.2.1.
2. Strabo, 7.3.17
3. Herodotus, 4.46.
4. Strabo, 7.3.1.
5. Strabo 7.3.18.
6. Dio Chrysostom, 36.4.
7. Pliny, 22.2.
8. Strabo, 7.3.1.
9. Ammianus, 31.2.20.
10. Strabo, 7.4.8.
11. Ammianus, 17.12.2.
12. Strabo, 7.3.17.
13. Strabo, 11.5.8; Alani allied/subject to Kangju (*Hou Hanshu*, 19; *Weilue*, 25).
14. Lucian, *Toxaris*, 39.
15. Sima Qian, *Shiji*, 123. Ptolemy, *Geography*, 6.9 (Alan-Aorsi = 'Alanorsi').
16. Tacitus, *Annals*, 12.15.
17. *Ibid.*, 12.16–17.
18. Pausanias, 6.26.5–8.
19. Ammianus, 17.12.1.
20. Tacitus, *Histories*, 1.79.
21. Valerius Flaccus, *Argonautica*, 6.219.
22. Brzezinski and Mielczarek, *The Sarmatians* (2003), 33–4.
23. Tacitus, *Histories*, 1.79.
24. Valerius Flaccus, *Argonautica*, 6.233.
25. Arrian, *Ars Tactica*, 4.
26. Tacitus, *Histories*, 1.79.
27. Pausanias, 1.21.5.
28. Brzezinski and Mielczarek, *The Sarmatians* (2003), 39.
29. Ammianus, 16.10.7.
30. Ammianus, 16.12.39.
31. Ammianus, 17.12.2.
32. Tacitus, *Histories*, 4.51; Suetonius, *Vespsian*, 6.
33. Tacitus, *Annals*, 6.33.
34. *Ibid.*, 6.34–5.
35. Tacitus, *Annals*, 6.33.
36. Josephus, *Wars*, 7.4.3.
37. Suetonius, *Domitian*, 38.
38. *Cambridge Ancient History, Volume 11: The High Empire* (2000), 309.
39. Dio, 68.7.
40. *L'Année épigraphique* (1951) 263.

41. Cowan, *Roman Battle Tactics* (2007), 9.
42. Arrian, *Array against the Alani*, 30; Campbell, *The Roman Army* (1994), 93; 97–100.
43. *ILS*, 986. Elton, *Frontiers of the Roman Empire* (1996), 107–9.
44. Tacitus, *Histories*, 1.79.
45. *Ibid.*, 3.5.
46. Josephus, *Wars*, 7.4.3.
47. Suetonius, *Domitian*, 6.1.
48. Ala I Ulpia Contariorum (Roman Cataphracts); *The Cambridge Ancient History: Volume 12, The Crisis of Empire* (2005), 111.
49. *C.I.L.* 3.1457; *C.I.L.* 6.41142 (Marcus Claudius Fronto).
50. Dio, 72.13, 16.
51. Dio, 72.7.
52. Dio, 72.15–16.
53. Dio, 72.17.

Chapter 11: The Parthian Empire

1. Herodotus, 3.89–97.
2. Pliny, 6.29.
3. Grainger, *Rome, Parthia and India* (2013).
4. Polybius, 10.49; 11.34.
5. Livy, 35.43–50.
6. Livy, 36.16–19. Appian, *Syrian Wars*, 16–20.
7. Livy, 37.39–40; 44.
8. Polybius, 21.42.
9. *New Testament, Matthew*, 20.2.
10. Justin, 38.10.
11. *Ibid.*
12. Justin, 42.1.
13. Pliny, 6.30.
14. Strabo, 11.33.1.
15. Sima Qian, *Shiji*, 123.
16. Plutarch, *Sulla*, 5; Livy, 70.7; Festus, 15.2.
17. Plutarch, *Sulla*, 5.
18. Plutarch, *Pompey*, 33; Orosius, 6.13.2; Florus, 1.46.4.
19. Plutarch, *Pompey*, 33.
20. *Ibid.*, 45.
21. Dio 39.55.3; Cicero, *Against Piso* 48, 49; Plutarch, *Antony* 3.2; Cicero, *Pro Rabirio Postumo*, 21, 30 (payment).
22. Sampson, *The Defeat of Rome* (2008).
23. Plutarch, *Crassus*, 16.
24. Livy, 9.17.
25. Plutarch *Lucullus*, 28.
26. Plutarch, *Crassus*, 18.
27. *Ibid.*, 16.
28. *Ibid.*, 17.
29. *Ibid.*, 19.
30. Dio, 40.20. Appian, *Civil War*, 2.18.
31. Diodorus Siculus, 17.17.3–4.
32. Plutarch, *Crassus*, 20.
33. *Ibid.*, 17.
34. *Ibid.*, 18.
35. Orosius, *History*, 6.13.
36. Plutarch, *Crassus*, 22.

37. *Ibid.*, 21, 'Margianian steel glittering keen and bright', 24; 'the spear which the Parthians thrust into the horses was heavy with steel', 27.
38. *Ibid.*, 21, 'horses clad in plates of bronze and steel', 24; 'breastplates of raw hide and steel', 25.
39. *Ibid.*, 21–2.
40. *Ibid.*, 23.
41. *Ibid.*, 23.
42. Florus, 46.3.11.
43. Plutarch, *Crassus*, 24.
44. *Ibid.*, 24: 'the velocity and force of the arrows fractured armour and tore through every covering, hard or soft.'
45. *Ibid.*
46. *Ibid.*, 25.
47. Sima Qian, *Shiji*, 109.
48. Plutarch, *Crassus*, 25.
49. *Ibid.*
50. *Ibid.*
51. *Ibid.*, 26.
52. *Ibid.*, 25.
53. *Ibid.*, 26–7.
54. Sima Qian, *Shiji*, 109; *Hanshu*, 54.
55. Plutarch, *Crassus*, 27–30.
56. Dio, 40.27.
57. Plutarch, *Crassus*, 31.
58. *Ibid.*, 32.
59. Pliny, 6.18.
60. Sima Qian, *Shiji*, 123.3172–3.
61. Pliny, 6.18.
62. Isidore, *Parthian Stations*.
63. Dio Cassius, 54.8.
64. *Hanshu*, 70.
65. Dubs, *A Roman City in Ancient China* (1957).

Chapter 12: Parthia and Rome

1. Plutarch, *Caesar*, 58.
2. Florus, 2.20 (16 legions).
3. Plutarch, *Antony*, 37–8.
4. Dio, 49.26.
5. Plutarch, *Antony*, 39.
6. *Ibid.*
7. *Ibid.*, Dio 49.26–7.
8. Plutarch, *Antony*, 40.
9. Dio, 49.28.
10. Plutarch, *Antony*, 46.
11. Florus, 2.20 (former Roman); Plutarch, *Antony*, 46–7 (Iranian).
12. Plutarch, *Antony*, 47.
13. *Ibid.*, 48.
14. *Ibid.*, 49.
15. *Ibid.*, 50.
16. Florus, 2.20 (one third).
17. Sheldon, *Rome's Wars in Parthia* (2010), 66–73.
18. Appian, *Civil Wars*, 2.110.
19. Horace, 3.12.
20. Horace, 3.2.3–6.
21. Horace, 2.13 (23 BC).

22. Horace, 3.3.43–4.
23. Horace, 3.5.
24. *Arthashastra*, 2.11.
25. Statius, *Silvae*, 3.3.101–2.
26. Pliny, 37.10.
27. Pliny, 37.7.
28. Plutarch, *Antony*, 58.
29. Pliny, 37.10.
30. Athenaeus, 11.72.
31. Pliny, 37.10.
32. Achilles Tatius, *Clitophon and Leucippe*, 2.3.
33. Philostratus, *Lives of the Sophists*, 21.603 (city house: 40,000 sesterces).
34. Pliny, 37.11.
35. Martial, 3.82.
36. Propertius, 4.5.
37. Propertius, 3.5.
38. Philostratus, *Apollonius*, 3.27.
39. Pliny, 37.10.
40. Pliny, 37.10.
41. Pliny, 37.7.
42. *Ibid.*
43. *Historia Augusta*, *Verus*, 10.
44. *Ibid.*, 5.
45. Pliny, 37.10.
46. Seneca, *On Anger*, 3.40.
47. Pliny, 37.7.
48. Pliny, 37.10.
49. Tacitus, *Histories*, 1.20.
50. Appendix D.

Chapter 13: Roman Invasion Plans for Parthia

1. Propertius, 4.3.
2. Suetonius, *Augustus*, 21.
3. Propertius, 2.9.
4. Propertius, 4.3.
5. Pliny, 6.31.
6. Pliny, 6.31.
7. Propertius, 4.3.
8. Millar, 'Caravan Cities' (1998), 120.
9. Isidore, *Journey around Parthia* (fragment: Athenæs, 3.46); Statius, *Silvae*, 3.3.101–2 (Roman treasury pearls).
10. Herodotus, 5.52–3.
11. Isidore, *Parthian Stations*, 1.
12. *Ibid.*
13. Plutarch, Crassus, 17.
14. Isidore, *Parthian Stations*, 6.
15. *Ibid.*, 3.
16. *Ibid.*, 6.
17. *Ibid.*, 7. Justin, 41.5.
18. Pliny, 6.17 (Hamadan = Ecbatana).
19. Strabo, 11.7.1.
20. Pliny, 6.17.
21. *Ibid.*
22. Engels, *Alexander the Great and the Logistics of the Macedonian Army* (1978), 157.

23. Isidore, *Parthian Stations*, 8–10.
24. *Ibid.*, 11.
25. *Ibid.*, 12.
26. Diakonoff and Livshits, *Parthian Economic Documents from Nisa* (1976).
27. Brosius, *The Persians* (2006), 118–19.
28. Isidore, *Parthian Stations*, 13–14.
29. Pliny, 6.18.
30. Curtius Rufus, 7.10.15.
31. Strabo, 11.10.1–2.
32. Pliny, 6.18.
33. Du Huan, *Jingxingji*.
34. Bader and Gaibov, 'Walls of Margiana' (1995), 40.
35. Pliny, 6.18.
36. Strabo, 11.10.1.
37. *Nisa Document*, 280.
38. Horace, 3.5.5–9
39. Pliny, 6.19.
40. Strabo 11.10.2
41. Isidore, *Parthian Stations*,16–17.
42. *Ibid.*, 18–19.
43. Strabo, 11.11.1.
44. Isidore, *Parthian Stations*,19.
45. Suetonius, *Augustus*, 21.
46. Ctesias, *Fragment*, 1.7 (530 BC).
47. Paulus Orosius, 6.21.19.
48. Strabo, 15.1.73.
49. *Res Gestae*, 31.
50. Dio, 54.9.
51. Livy, 30.15.
52. Livy, 30.17.
53. Marshall, *Taxila Minor Antiquities* (1975), 544.
54. Revealed by coin issues.
55. Dio Cassius, 54.8.
56. Augustus, *Res Gestae*, 29.
57. Josephus, *Jewish War*, 18.40.
58. Dio, 54.8.3; Augustus, *Res Gestae*, 29.
59. Ovid, *Fasti*, 5.580–594.
60. Horace, 2.1.270.
61. Velleius Paterculus, 2.94; Suetonius, *Octavian*, 21; Orosius, 6.21.
62. Strabo, 6.4.2.
63. Orosius, 6.21.
64. Strabo, 16.1.28.
65. Horace, 1.12.26–8.
66. Suetonius, *Augustus*, 29.
67. Dio, 55.10. Ovid, *Ars Amatoria*, 1.6.
68. *Ibid.*
69. Dio, 51.21.
70. Ovid, *Ars Amatoria*, 1.6.
71. *Ibid.*
72. Josphus, *Antiquities*, 18.2.4.
73. Dio, 55.10.20.
74. Velleius Paterculus, 2.101–2.
75. Velleius Paterculus, 2.102; Dio, 55.10; Florus, 2.32.
76. Josephus, *Antiquities*, 18.2.4.

77. Strabo, 6.4.2.
78. Josephus, *Antiquities*, 18.2.4; Tacitus, *Annals*, 2.2–3.
79. Tacitus, *Annals*, 2.3

Chapter 14: Roman Routes to China

1. Strabo, 17.1.45.
2. *Periplus*, 64.
3. Pliny, 6.26.
4. Ptolemy, *Geography*, 1.14.
5. *Ibid.*, 7.3; 7.5; 7.7; 8.1; Berggren and Jones, *Ptolemy's Geography* (2000), 22.
6. *Hou Hanshu*, 88.10.
7. Procopius, *Secret History*, 25.
8. Ptolemy, *Geography*, 1.
9. *Ibid.*, 1.11.
10. Cary, 'Maes, qui et Titianus' (1956).
11. Velleius Paterculus, 2.94; Suetonius, *Octavian*, 21; Orosius, 6.21.
12. Strabo, 16.1.28.
13. Strabo, 11.33.1.
14. Ptolemy, *Geography*, 1.11.
15. *Hou Hanshu*, 4.14 (November, AD 100).
16. Ptolemy, *Geography*, 1.11.
17. Leslie and Gardiner, *The Roman Empire in Chinese Sources* (1996), 148.
18. *Hou Hanshu*, 4.14; 88.1.
19. *Ibid.*, 4.14.
20. Juvenal, 6.400–3.
21. *Hou Hanshu*, 88.12.
22. Equator: 24,901 miles.
23. Sheldon, *Rome's Wars in Parthia* (2010), 155–7.
24. Tacitus, *Annals*, 14.25.
25. *Hou Hanshu*, 88.15.
26. Leslie and Gardiner, *The Roman Empire in Chinese Sources* (1996), 137; 153.
27. Needham, *Science and Civilisation in China, Volume 4* (1971), 3–38.
28. Buddhist Parthian prince An Shigao: biographies in *Chu Sanzang Jiji* and *Gaoseng Zhuan*.
29. *Hou Hanshu*, 88.12.
30. Hirth, *China and the Roman Orient* (1885), 173–8.
31. Dio, 71.2.
32. *Historia Augusta, Lucius Verus*, 8.1–4.
33. Galen, *Opera Omnia*, 19.17–18.
34. *Historia Augusta, Lucius Verus*, 11.
35. *Sammelbuch*, 16.12816.
36. *C.I.L.* 3.5567.
37. *Hou Hanshu*, 65/55.2133 (4a–b).
38. Leslie and Gardiner, *The Roman Empire in Chinese Sources* (1996), 100–1.
39. Yao Silian, *Liang-shu*, 48.
40. Li, *China at War* (2012), 454–5.
41. Yao Silian, *Liang-shu*, 48.

Conclusion: The Silk Routes and the Economies of China and Rome

1. Muziris Papyrus: *P. Vindob. G.* 40822 (*Papyri Vindobonensis Graecus*); Merchant fleet 120 ships (Strabo, 2.5.12); McLaughlin, *The Roman Empire and the Indian Ocean* (2014).
2. Funerary Tower number 70 on the Umm Belqis. McLaughlin, *The Roman Empire and the Oasis Kingdoms: The Ancient World Economy and the caravan routes through Egypt, Syria, Arabia, Petra, Palmyra and Persia* (forthcoming).
3. *New Testament, Luke*, 2:1.

4. Pliny, 3.3.
5. Frier, 'Population' in Cambridge Ancient History, volume 11, The High Empire (1996), 812–14.
6. *Hanshu*, 28b.1640. *Cambridge History of China: Volume I: the Ch'in and Han Empires* (1986), 596.
7. Loewe, *The Men who Governed Han China* (2004), 60.
8. Scheidel, 'State Revenue and Expenditure in the Han and Roman Empires' (2012) 3.
9. Xu and Dull, *Han Agriculture* (1980), 76–7.
10. Scheidel, 'State Revenue and Expenditure in the Han and Roman Empires' (2012), 5.
11. Chang, *The Rise of the Chinese Empire* (2007), 78.
12. Loewe, *The Men who Governed Han China* (2004), 284–6.
13. *Yan Tie Lun (Discourse on Salt and Iron)*.
14. Chang, *The Rise of the Chinese Empire* (2007), 82–5.
15. Loewe, *The Men who Governed Han China* (2004), 60.
16. *Ch'uan Hou-Han Wen*, 14.2b; Yu, *Trade and Expansion in Han China* (1967), 62.
17. *New Testament, Luke*, 2:1.
18. *Shule Document*, 509.
19. Appendix D.
20. Loewe, *The Men who Governed Han China* (2004), 60.
21. Seneca, *De Consolatione ad Helviam Matrem*, 10.4. McLaughlin, *The Roman Empire and the Indian Ocean* (2014).
22. Suetonius, *Julius Caesar*, 25 ('Three Gauls' formed five provinces).
23. Suetonius, *Caligula*, 16.
24. *Cambridge Ancient History*, volume 11 (2000), 738.
25. *New Testament, Luke*, 2:1.
26. Appian, *Syrian War*, 50.
27. Tacitus, *Agricola*, 19; Josephus, *Life*, 13.
28. *Digest Roman Law*, 50.15.3; 50.8.7.
29. Demosthenes, 20.32–3.
30. *The Cambridge Ancient History, Volume 11: The High Empire* (2000), 813.
31. Augustus, *Res Gestae*, 15; Aldrete and Mattingly, 'Feeding the City' (1999), 178.
32. Hopkins, 'Models, Ships and Staples' (1983), 86.
33. Josephus, *Jewish War*, 2.16.4.
34. Tacitus, *Annals*, 12.43.
35. *The Cambridge Ancient History, Volume 12: The Crisis of Empire* (2005), 37–55.
36. Wolfram, *History of the Goths* (1979), 59–63.
37. Plutarch, *Pompey*, 45.
38. Suetonius, *Julius Caesar*, 25.
39. Philostratus, *Lives of the Sophists*, 548.
40. *Herodotus*, 3.90.
41. Strabo, 17.1.13.
42. Josephus, *Jewish War*, 2.16.4; *Antiquities*, 19.8.2.
43. Pliny, 33.21.
44. Strabo, 3.2.10.
45. Appendix D.
46. McLaughlin, *The Roman Empire and the Silk Routes II: The Ancient Economy and the Realms of Egypt, Petra and Palmyra* (forthcoming).
47. Hardy, *The Establishment of the Han Empire and Imperial China* (2005), 43.
48. *Ch'uan Hou-Han wen*, 14.2b (2 billion cash).
49. Dio, 56.41; Augustus, *Res Gestae*, 8.
50. Hopkins, *Death and Renewal* (1985), 186.
51. Duncan-Jones, *Money and Government* (1994), 33–45.
52. Appendix A.
53. Loewe, *The Government of the Qin and Han Empires* (2006), 63.
54. Yu, *Trade and Expansion in Han China* (1967), 83–4.

55. Standard cohort: 480 soldiers. *The Cambridge Ancient History, Volume 10: The Augustan Empire* (1996), 385. Alternative figures: Scheidel, 'State Revenue and Expenditure in the Han and Roman Empires' (2012), 23.
56. Loewe, *Records of Han Administration* (1967), 90–1.
57. For instance: *Hou Hanshu*, 1.110–11.
58. *Shule Document*, 509.
59. Appendix C.
60. Yu, *Trade and Expansion in Han China* (1967), 61.
61. *Hou Hanshu*, 117.9a; 11b.
62. John Lydus, *De Mensibus*, 1.27.
63. *The Cambridge History of Greek and Roman Warfare, Volume 2* (2007), 271.
64. Lewis, *The Early Chinese Empires* (2007), 132.
65. *Hou Hanshu*, 119.
66. *Zizhi Tongjian Xinzhu*, 47.1636; *Hou Hanshu*, 89.
67. Wu, 'Debates and Decision Making: Battle of the Altai Mountains' (2013), 63–71.
68. *Ch'uan Hou-Han Wen*, 73.1b; *Hou Hanshu*, 120.5b.
69. *Hou Hanshu*, 103.1a; *San-kuo Chih, Wei Chih*, 30.5a; Yu, *Trade and expansion in Han China* (1967), 83–4.
70. Yu, *op.cit.*, 61.
71. *Sogdian Letter*, 2.
72. *Zizhi Tongjian*, 96.
73. *Weishu*, 103.2290.
74. Sima Qian, *Shiji*, 2.138. Keightley, *The Origins of Chinese Civilization* (1983), 447 fn. 2.
75. Ammianus, 16.9, 17.5, 18.6, 19.1.
76. *History of Civilizations of Central Asia: Volume 3* (1999), 169.
77. Faustus, 5.7, 5.37.
78. Procopius, 1.3.2–7; *The Cambridge Companion to the Age of Attila* (2014), 173–92.
79. Zosimus, 4.34.
80. Claudian, *In Rufinum*, 1.325.
81. Ammianus, 31.3.7.
82. Ammianus, 31.2.10.
83. Zosimus, 4.34.
84. Jordanes, 24.127–8; 49.255.
85. Procopius, *Secret History*, 7.
86. Jordanes, 24.127–8.
87. Ammianus, 31.2.2.
88. Sidonius, *Panegyric on Anthemius*, 262–6.
89. Ammianus, 31.2.3.
90. Vegetius, *Mulomedicina*, 3.6.2; 3.6.5; 3.7.1.
91. Jordanes, 24.126.
92. Zosimus, 4.34.
93. Claudian, *In Rufinum*, 1.325.
94. Ammianus, 31.2.8–9.
95. Ammianus, 31.3.1.
96. Procopius, *Wars*, 5.27–9.
97. Procopius, *Wars*, 6.2.22–3.
98. Sidonius Apollinaris, *Panegyric on Avitus*, 289–92.
99. Sozomen, 7.6.8.
100. MacDowell, *Catalaunian Fields AD 451* (2015), 6.
101. Sidonius Apollinaris, *Panegyric on Avitus*, 253–5.
102. Strabo, 11.5.8.
103. Asterius of Amasia, *Phocas*, 40.313.
104. Ammianus, 31.3.7.
105. Zosimus, 4.34.

106. MacDowell, *Adrianople AD 378* (2001).
107. Ammianus, 31.6.3 (AD 376).
108. Claudian, *Gothic War*, 536.
109. Jerome, *Letter*, 77.8.
110. *Ibid.*, 60.17.
111. Procopius, *Wars*, 3.5.18–19.
112. Zosimus, 5.45.6; 5.11.4.
113. Zosimus, 5.50.1.
114. Philostorgius, 12.14.
115. Jordanes, *Getica*, 50.259.
116. *Ibid.*, 35.180–2.
117. Blockly, *Fragmentary Classicizing Historians of the Later Roman Empire: Volume 2* (1983), 315.
118. Priscus, *Fragment*, 23.
119. *Ibid.*, 1b.
120. *Chronicle of 452*: entry for 447.
121. Priscus, *Fragment*, 5.
122. *Ibid.*, 1.
123. *Ibid.*, 5.
124. *Ibid.*, 9.3.
125. John Lydus, 3.43.
126. Priscus, *Fragment*, 8.
127. Jordanes, *Getica*, 35.183.
128. Priscus, *Fragment*, 8.
129. *Ibid.*, 11.2.
130. *Ibid.*, 15.
131. Gregory of Tours, *History of the Franks*, 2.7.
132. MacDowell, *Catalaunian Fields AD 451* (2015).
133. Jordanes, 42. 219–22.
134. Jordanes, 42.223.
135. Jordanes, 43.225–6.
136. Priscus, *Fragment*, 24.
137. Eckardt, *Roman Diasporas* (2010), 10.

Appendix A: Economic Figures

1. Tacitus, *Annals*, 1.17. Suetonius, *Domitian*, 7 (12 aurei = 1,200 sesterces).
2. Tacitus, *Annals*, 4.5.
3. Herz, 'Finances and Costs of the Roman Army' (2010), 308–11.
4. Tacitus, *Annals*, 1.17 (land-grants in place of cash bonuses). *I.L.S.* 2302; *C.I.L.* 3.6580 (discharge numbers).
5. Wang, *Money on the Silk Road* (2004), 38; *Shule Document*, 509.
6. *Xinlun*, 14:2b.
7. Cambridge academics: Duncan-Jones, *Money and Government* (1994), 33–45; Hopkins, 'Rome, Taxes, Rents and Trade' (2002), 200.
8. *Hanshu*, 19 (officials); *Xinlun*, 14.2b (cost).
9. War: 24,000 million cash in twelve years (AD 107–118). *Hou Hanshu*, 117.9a, 11b.
10. Yu, *Trade and Expansion in Han China* (1967), 61–4.
11. Wang, *Money on the Silk Road* (2004), 38.
12. Procopius, *Secret History*, 25. Price 8 gold *solidi* (36 grams of gold) per pound = 5 aurei (first century prices).
13. *Diocletian Price Edict*, 22 (AD 301). Price: 12,000 debased denarii (25–50 debased denarii for 1 day's labour = 4 sesterces at first century rates).
14. *Oxyrhynchus Papyrus*, 5758 (AD 325). Price: 65,000 debased denarii.
15. *Historia Augusta, Aurelian*, 45 (third century). Price: 1 pound of silk = weight in gold (45 aurei at first century prices).

16. Martial, 11.27. Price: 100 gold coins.
17. *Diocletian Price Edict*, 22. Price: 150,000 debased denarii.

Appendix B: Economic Comparisons

1. Pliny, 6.29.
2. Suetonius, *Caligula*, 16 (100 million sesterces over twenty years).
3. Strabo, 7.4.6 (Mithridates VI).
4. Seneca, *De Consolatione ad Helviam Matrem*, 10.4.
5. Hopkins, 'Models, Ships and Staples' (1983), 86.
6. Josephus, *Jewish War*, 2.16.4.
7. Didymus, 10.34–11.5 (230 ships); Demothenes, 20.31–2 (16,000 tons).
8. Strabo, 7.4.6.
9. Pliny, 12.41.
10. Pliny, 6.26.

Appendix C: The Han Economy

1. Pliny, 6.26.
2. Loewe, *The Men who Governed Han China* (2004), 77–8.
3. *Xinlun*, 14.2b.
4. *Hou Hanshu*, 64.8a. Yu, *Trade and Expansion in Han China* (1967), 63.
5. Loewe, *The Men who Governed Han China* (2004), 60.
6. Yu, *op. cit.*, 61.
7. If Wuhuan payments similar to Southern Xiongnu.
8. If Qiang payments similar to Xianbei.
9. *Hanshu*, 94b.3b.
10. *Hanshu*, 94b.5b.
11. *Hanshu*, 94b.8a. Yu, *Trade and Expansion in Han China* (1967), 47.

Appendix D: Roman Revenues

1. Plutarch, *Pompey*, 45.
2. Suetonius, *Julius Caesar*, 25.
3. Josephus, *Jewish War*, 2.16.4; *Antiquities*, 19.8.2.
4. Strabo, 3.2.10.
5. Pliny, 33.21. Roman pound (*libra*) = about 329 grams.
6. Tax from single Indian cargo = 2.3 million sesterces (*Muziris Papyrus*) × 120 Roman ships sailing to India (Strabo, 2.5.12). Value of imports: 1,104 million sesterces based on cargo value of 9.2 million in *Muziris Papyrus*.
7. Funerary Tower number 70 on the Umm Belqis.
8. Pliny, 12.41.

Appendix E: Military Capacities

1. Chu-Han Contention (206–202 BC).
2. Sima Qian, *Shiji*, 108.2b–3a; 110.10a–b. *Hanshu*, 52.8b–9a; 94a.7b–8a.
3. Chinese Historical Atlas: *Chung-kuo li-shih ti-t'u chi*, 2.17–18.
4. Sima Qian, *Shiji*, 123.3174–77; *Hanshu*, 96.
5. *Hanshu*, 70.3b.
6. Scheidel, 'State Revenue and Expenditure in the Han and Roman Empires' (2012), 23.
7. Dunhuang-Shuofang frontier (620 miles): 3,250 soldiers (Loewe, *The Men who Governed Han China* (2004), 63).
8. Chu-Han Contention (206–202 BC).
9. Josephus, *Jewish War*, 3.6.2 (cavalry).
10. Tacitus, *Annals*, 4.5.
11. Josephus, *Jewish War*, 2.16.3; Tacitus, *Annals*, 12.15.
12. Plutarch, *Antony*, 44 (40,000 Parthians); *Crassus*, 21. (ratio cataphracts to archers).

13. Plutarch, *Crassus*, 20.
14. *Ibid.*, 21.
15. *Ibid.*, 31.
16. Plutarch, *Antony*, 37–8.
17. *Ibid.*, 39.
18. *Ibid.*, 50–51.
19. Plutarch, *Crassus*, 19.
20. Plutarch, *Pompey*, 34.
21. Josephus, *Jewish War*, 2.18.9 (AD 66).
22. Diodorus, 18.7; Polybius, 10.49.
23. Justin, 41.6.4.
24. *Hou Hanshu*, 88.13.
25. *Ibid.*, 77.4a–7a.
26. Arrian, *Alexander*, 6.2.2.
27. Sima Qian, *Shiji*, 110:9b–10b (Title: 'Chief of Ten Thousand Horsemen' with some commanding smaller forces).
28. Sima Qian, *Shiji*, 110.6b; *Hanshu*, 94a.4b.
29. Sima Qian, *Shiji*, 108.2b–3a; 110.10a–b; *Hanshu*, 52.8b–9a; 94a.7b–8a.
30. *Chung-kuo li-shih ti-t'u chi*, 2:17–18.
31. *Hou Hanshu*, 103:1a.
32. *Ch'uan Hou-Han Wen*, 73.1b; *Hou Hanshu*, 120.5b.
33. *Hanshu*, 61; 96.
34. Sima Qian, *Shiji*, 123.3b.
35. Ctesias, *Fragment*, 1.7 (Sakas fighting for Persian King Cyrus in 530 BC).
36. Lucian, *Toxaris*, 39.
37. Sima Qian, *Shiji*, 123.
38. Strabo, 11.5.8.
39. Strabo, 7.3.17.
40. Tacitus, *Histories*, 1.79.
41. Dio, 72.15–16.
42. John Lydus, *De Mensibus*, 1.27.
43. *Notitia Dignitatum* (*The List of Offices*).
44. *Zizhi Tongjian*, 96. Grousset, *The Empire of the Steppes* (1970), 56.
45. Philostorgius, 12.14.
46. Dio, 72.15–16 (Iazyges); Linder, 'Nomadism, Horses and Huns' in *Past and Present*, 92.1 (1981) 3–19 (estimates 15,000 mounted warriors based on grassland capacity and ten mounts per rider).
47. Figures suggested by Siraces and Roxolani fielding 20,000 and 50,000 mounted warriors.
48. Battle of the Catalaunian Plains (AD 451).
49. Sima Qian, *Shiji*, 123 (military potential); Ammianus, 31.3.1(Alani merged with Huns); Priscus, *Fragment*, 11.2 (Attila planned to invade Persia through Caucasus).
50. Ammianus, 31.12.
51. Olympiodorus, *Fragment*, 9
52. Victor Vitensis, *History of the Persecution*, 1.2.

Bibliography

Adkins, L. and Adkins, R. *Handbook to Life in Ancient Rome* (Oxford University Press, 1994).
Aldrete, G. and Mattingly, D. 'Feeding the City' in Potter, D. (ed.) *Life, Death, and Entertainment in the Roman Empire* (University of Michigan Press, 1999) 171–204.
Alfoldy, G. *Noricum* (Routledge & Kegan Paul, 1974).
Alikuzai, H. *A Concise History of Afghanistan: Volume 1* (Trafford Publishing, 2013).
Allchin, F. *The Archaeology of Early Historic South Asia* (Cambridge University Press, 1995).
Bader, A. and Gaibov, V. 'Walls of Margiana' in Invernizzi, A. (ed.) *In the land of Gryphons* (Le Lettere, 1995) 39–50.
Ball, W. *Rome in the East* (Routledge, 2001).
Barber, E. *Prehistoric Textiles* (Princeton University Press, 1991).
Barber, E. *The Mummies of Urumchi* (Norton & Company, 2000).
Bennett, J. *Trajan* (Routledge, 2003).
Berggren, L. and Jones, A. *Ptolemy's Geography* (2000).
Blockly, R. *Fragmentary Classicizing Historians of the Later Roman Empire: Volume 2* (1983).
Boulnois, L. *Silk Road* (Odyssey Publications, 2012),
Bowman, A. (ed.) *Cambridge Ancient History, Volume 11: The High Empire* (Cambridge University Press, 2000).
Bowman, A. (ed.) *The Cambridge Ancient History, Volume 10: The Augustan Empire* (1996).
Bowman, A. (ed.) *The Cambridge Ancient History, Volume 11: The High Empire* (2000).
Bowman, A. (ed.) *The Cambridge Ancient History: Volume 12, The Crisis of Empire* (2005).
Brosius, M. *The Persians* (Routledge, 2006).
Brzezinski, R. and Mielczarek, M. *The Sarmatians* (Osprey, 2003).
Bugh, G. *The Cambridge Companion to the Hellenistic World* (Cambridge University Press, 2006).
Campbell, B. *The Roman Army* (Routledge, 1994).
Cary, M. 'Maes, qui et Titianus' in *The Classical Quarterly* 6.3 (1956), 130–4.
Cernenko, E. *The Scythians* (Osprey, 2012).
Chandra, M. *Trade and Trade Routes in Ancient India* (Abhinav Publications, 1977).
Chang, C. *The Rise of the Chinese Empire* (University of Michigan Press, 2007).
Cleland, L. *Greek and Roman Dress from A to Z* (Routledge, 2007).
Cohen, G. *The Hellenistic Settlements in the East from Armenia and Mesopotamia to Bactria and India* (University of California Press, 2013).
Cowan, R. *Roman Battle Tactics* (Osprey, 2007).
Dani, A. *History of Civilizations of Central Asia* (UNESCO, 1996).
Dawson, R. *The First Emperor: Selections from the Historical Records* (Oxford University Press, 1994).
Di Cosmo, N. *Ancient China and its Enemies* (Cambridge University Press, 2002).
Diakonoff, I. and Livshits, V. *Parthian Economic Documents from Nisa* (Lund Humphries, 1976).
Drummond, S. and Nelson, L. *The Western Frontiers of Imperial Rome* (Routledge, 1994).
Dubs, H. *A Roman City in Ancient China* (China Society, 1957).
Duncan-Jones, R. *Money and Government in the Roman Empire* (Cambridge University Press, 1994).
Eckardt, H. 'Roman Diasporas' (*Journal of Roman Archaeology*, 2010).
Elton, H. *Frontiers of the Roman Empire* (Routledge, 1996).
Engels, D. *Alexander the Great and the Logistics of the Macedonian Army* (University of California Press, 1978).
Faulkner, N. *Rome: Empire of the Eagles* (Routledge, 2013).

Fazio, M. and Moffett, M. *A World History of Architecture* (Laurence King, 2003).
Frank, T. *An Economic History of Rome* (Johns Hopkins, 1959).
Frier, B. 'Population' in *Cambridge Ancient History, Volume 11, The High Empire* (Cambridge University Press, 1996), 811–16.
Gamkrelidze, G. *Researches in Iberia-Colchology* (Gela Gamkrelidze, 2012).
Gleba, *Making Textiles in Pre-Roman and Roman Times* (2013).
Graf, D. 'The Roman East from the Chinese Perspective' in *Annales Archeologiques Arabes Syriennes* 42 (1996), 199–216.
Grainger, J. *Rome, Parthia and India* (Pen & Sword, 2013).
Green, P. *The Argonautika* (University of California Press, 1997).
Greene, K. *Archaeology of the Roman Economy* (University of California Press, 1983).
Grousset, R. *The Empire of the Steppes* (Rutgers University Press, 1970).
Hansen, V. *The Silk Road* (Oxford University Press, 2012).
Hardy, G. and Kinney, A. *The Establishment of the Han Empire and Imperial China* (Greenwood, 2005).
Harl, K. *Coinage in the Roman Economy* (Johns Hopkins University Press, 1996).
Herz, P. 'Finances and Costs of the Roman Army' in Erdkamp, P. *A Companion to the Roman Army* (Wiley-Blackwell, 2010), 306–22.
Hill, J. *Through the Jade Gate to Rome* (Create Space Independent Publishing Platform, 2009).
Hill, J. *Weilue: The Peoples of the West* (forthcoming).
Hirth, F. *China and the Roman Orient* (Kessinger Publishing, 1885).
History of Civilizations of Central Asia: Volume 3 (Unesco, 1999).
Holt, F. *Alexander the Great and Bactria* (Brill, 1989).
Holt, F. *Into the Land of Bones* (University of California Press, 2012).
Hopkins, K. 'Models, Ships and Staples' in Garnsey, P. (ed.) *Trade and Famine in Classical Antiquity* (Cambridge Philological Society, 1983), 84–109.
Hopkins, K. 'Rome, Taxes, Rents and Trade' in Scheidel, W. (ed.) *The Ancient Economy* (Edinburgh University Press, 2002), 190–232.
Hopkins, K. *Death and Renewal* (Cambridge University Press, 1985).
Hopkins, 'Models, Ships and Staples' in Garnsey, P. *Trade and Famine in Classical Antiquity* (Cambridge University Press, 1983).
Howard, A. *Chinese Sculpture* (Yale University Press, 2006).
Hulsewe, A. *China in Central Asia* (E.J. Brill, 1979).
Huntington, J. and Bangdel, D. *Circle of Bliss: Buddhist Meditational Art* (Serindia Publications, 2003).
Isaac, B. *The Invention of Racism in Classical Antiquity* (Princeton University Press, 2004).
Keightley, A. *The Origins of Chinese Civilization* (University of California Press, 1983).
Leslie, D. and Gardiner, K. *The Roman Empire in Chinese Sources* (Bardi Editore, 1996).
Lewis, M. *The Early Chinese Empires* (Harvard University Press, 2007).
Liddle, A. *Arrian: Periplus Ponti Euxini* (Bristol Classical Press, 2003).
Lin, J. 'Armour for the Afterlife' in Portal, J. (ed.) *The First Emperor* (British Museum Press, 2007).
Linder, R. 'Nomadism, Horses and Huns' in *Past and Present*, 92.1 (1981) 3–19.
Lindesay, W. and Baofa, G. *The Terracotta Army of the First Emperor of China* (Odyssey Books, 2009).
Liu, X. *Connections across Eurasia* (McGraw-Hill Higher Education, 2007).
Liu, X. *Silk and Religion* (Oxford University Press, 1996).
Liu, X. *The Silk Road in World History* (Oxford University Press, 2010).
Loewe, 'The Campaigns of Han Wu-ti' in Kierman, F. (ed.) *Chinese Ways in Warfare* (Harvard University Press, 1974).
Loewe, M. *The Government of the Qin and Han Empires* (Hackett Publishing, 2002).
Loewe, M. *The Men who Governed Han China* (Brill, 2004).
Loewe, M. *Records of Han Administration* (Routledge, 1967).
Luttwak, *Grand Strategy of the Byzantine Empire* (Belknap Press, 2011).
Maas, M. (ed.) *The Cambridge Companion to the Age of Attila* (2014).
MacDowell, S. *Adrianople AD 378: The Goth's Crush Rome's Legions* (Osprey, 2001).
MacDowell, S. *Catalaunian Fields AD 451: Rome's Last Great Battle* (Osprey, 2015).
Mallory, J. and Mair, H. *The Tarim Mummies* (Thames and Hudson, 2000).

Man, J. *The Terracotta Army* (Bantam, 2010).
Marshak, 'Central Asian metalwork in China' in Watt, J. *China: Dawn of a Golden Age* (Yale University Press, 2004), 47–55.
Marshall, *Taxila Minor Antiquities* (Bhartiya Publishing House, 1975).
Matthew, C. 'Greek Hoplites in an Ancient Chinese Siege' in *Journal of Asian History* 45.1 (2011), 17–37.
Mayer, E. *The Ancient Middle Classes* (Harvard University Press, 2012).
McLaughlin, R. *Rome and the Distant East: Trade Routes to the Ancient Lands of Arabia, India and China* (Bloomsbury, 2010).
McLaughlin, R. *The Roman Empire and the Indian Ocean: The Ancient Economy and the Kingdoms of Africa, Arabia and India* (Pen & Sword, 2014)
McLaughlin, R. *The Roman Empire and the Oasis Kingdoms: The Ancient World Economy and the caravan routes through Egypt, Syria, Arabia, Petra, Palmyra and Persia* (forthcoming).
Mielczarek, M. *Cataphracti and Clibanarii* (Oficyna Naukowa, 1993).
Mukherjee, B. *The Rise and Fall of the Kushana Empire* (Firma KLM, 1988).
Murrin, M. *Trade and Romance* (University of Chicago Press, 2014).
Nadeau, R. *The Wiley-Blackwell Companion to Chinese Religions* (Wiley-Blackwell, 2012).
Naweed, H. *Art through the Ages in Afghanistan* (AuthorHouse, 2013).
Needham, J. and Yates, R. *Science and Civilisation in China: Volume 5* (Cambridge University Press, 2004).
Needham, J. *Science and Civilisation in China, Volume 4* (Cambridge University Press, 1971).
Nickel, 'The Terracotta Army' in Portal, J. *The First Emperor* (British Museum, 2007).
Nikonorov, V. *The Armies of Bactria* (Montvert Publications, 1997).
Nunn, P. *Climate, Environment, and Society in the Pacific during the Last Millennium* (Elsevier BV, 2007)
Peers, C. *Imperial Chinese Armies* (Osprey, 1995).
Phuoc, L. *Buddhist Architecture* (Grafikol, 2010).
Pitassi, M. *Roman Warships* (Boydell Press, 2011).
Portal, J. (ed.) *The First Emperor* (British Museum Press, 2007).
Pugachenkova, G. 'Kushan Art' in Dani, A. *History of Civilizations of Central Asia* (UNESCO, 1996), 323–85.
Raschke, M. 'New Studies in Roman Commerce with the East' in *Aufstieg und Niedergang der Römischen Welt*, 9.2 (1978), 604–1378.
Rosenfield, J. *The Dynastic Arts of the Kushans* (University of California Press, 1967).
Rostovtzeff, M. 'Romische Besatzungen in der *Krim* und das Kastell Charax' in *Klio* 2 (1902), 80–95.
Sabin, P. (ed.) *The Cambridge History of Greek and Roman Warfare, Volume 2* (2007).
Samad, R. *The Grandeur of Gandhara* (Algora Publishing, 2011).
Sampson, *The Defeat of Rome* (Algora Publishing, 2008).
Scheidel, 'State Revenue and Expenditure in the Han and Roman Empires' (2012).
Sebesta and Bonfante, *The World of Roman Costume* (University of Wisconsin Press, 2001).
Sheldon, *Rome's Wars in Parthia* (Valentine Mitchell & Co Ltd, 2010).
Sheldon, J. *Commentary on George Coedes' Texts of Greek and Latin Authors on the Far East* (Studia Antiqua Australiensia, 2012).
Sinor, D. (ed.) *The Cambridge History of Early Inner Asia, Volume 1* (1990).
Stanco, L. *Greek Gods in the East* (Karolinum Press, 2012).
Statham, H. *A History of Architecture* (B.T. Batsford, 1950).
Stewart, S. *The Everlasting Flame: Zoroastrianism in History and Imagination* (I.B. Tauris, 2013).
Tanner, J. 'Figuring out Death' in Chua, L. *Distributed Objects* (Berghahn Books, 2013), 58–87.
Tarn, W. *The Greeks in Bactria and India* (Cambridge University Press, 1938).
Trofimova, A. *Greeks on the Black Sea* (J. Paul Getty Museum, 2007).
Turnbull, S. *The Great Wall of China* (Osprey, 2012).
Twitchett, D. (ed.) *Cambridge History of China: Volume I: the Ch'in and Han Empires* (Cambridge University Press, 1986).
Twitchett, D. (ed.) *The Cambridge History of China: The Ch'in and Han Empires* (1996).
Vaissière, E. *Sogdian Traders* (Brill, 2005).

Wang, H. *Money on the Silk Road* (British Museum Press, 2004).
Warmington, E. *The Commerce between the Roman Empire and India* (Cambridge University Press, 1928).
Watson, B. *Records of the Grand Historian: Volume 2* (Columbia University Press, 1961).
Wenli, Z. *The Qin Terracotta Army* (Scala Books, 1996).
Whitehouse, D. 'The Glass from Begram' in Aruz, J. (ed.), *Afghanistan: Forging Civilizations Along the Silk Road* (Metropolitan Museum of Art, 2012), 54–64.
Whitfield, S. *The Silk Road* (University of California Press, 2004).
Wolfram, H. *History of the Goths* (University of California Press, 1979).
Wood, F. *The Silk Road* (University of California Press, 2002).
Wu, S. 'Debates and Decision Making: Battle of the Altai Mountains' in Lorge, P. *Debating War in Chinese History* (2013), 41–78.
Xu, Z. and Dull, L. *Han Agriculture* (University of Washington Press, 1980).
Yu, Y. *Trade and Expansion in Han China* (University of California, 1967).
Zhewen, L. *China's Imperial Tombs and Mausoleums* (Foreign Languages Press, 1993).
Zürcher, E. *The Buddhist Conquest of China* (Brill, 1959).

Index